Luminos is the Open Access monograph publishing program from UC Press. Luminos provides a framework for preserving and reinvigorating monograph publishing for the future and increases the reach and visibility of important scholarly work. Titles published in the UC Press Luminos model are published with the same high standards for selection, peer review, production, and marketing as those in our traditional program. www.luminosoa.org

A

[signature]

BOOK

The Philip E. Lilienthal imprint
honors special books
in commemoration of a man whose work
at University of California Press from 1954 to 1979
was marked by dedication to young authors
and to high standards in the field of Asian Studies.
Friends, family, authors, and foundations have together
endowed the Lilienthal Fund, which enables UC Press
to publish under this imprint selected books
in a way that reflects the taste and judgment
of a great and beloved editor.

The publisher and the University of California Press Foundation
gratefully acknowledge the generous support of the
Philip E. Lilienthal Imprint in Asian Studies,
established by a major gift from Sally Lilienthal.

Bibliotactics

ASIA PACIFIC MODERN

Takashi Fujitani, Series Editor

1. *Erotic Grotesque Nonsense: The Mass Culture of Japanese Modern Times*, by Miriam Silverberg
2. *Visuality and Identity: Sinophone Articulations across the Pacific*, by Shu-mei Shih
3. *The Politics of Gender in Colonial Korea: Education, Labor, and Health, 1910–1945*, by Theodore Jun Yoo
4. *Frontier Constitutions: Christianity and Colonial Empire in the Nineteenth-Century Philippines*, by John D. Blanco
5. *Tropics of Savagery: The Culture of Japanese Empire in Comparative Frame*, by Robert Thomas Tierney
6. *Colonial Project, National Game: A History of Baseball in Taiwan*, by Andrew D. Morris
7. *Race for Empire: Koreans as Japanese and Japanese as Americans during World War II*, by T. Fujitani
8. *The Gender of Memory: Rural Women and China's Collective Past*, by Gail Hershatter
9. *A Passion for Facts: Social Surveys and the Construction of the Chinese Nation-State, 1900–1949*, by Tong Lam
11. *Redacted: The Archives of Censorship in Transwar Japan*, by Jonathan E. Abel
12. *Assimilating Seoul: Japanese Rule and the Politics of Public Space in Colonial Korea, 1910–1945*, by Todd A. Henry
13. *Working Skin: Making Leather, Making a Multicultural Japan*, by Joseph D. Hankins
14. *Imperial Genus: The Formation and Limits of the Human in Modern Korea and Japan*, by Travis Workman
15. *Sanitized Sex: Regulating Prostitution, Venereal Disease, and Intimacy in Occupied Japan, 1945–1952*, by Robert Kramm
16. *Outcasts of Empire: Japan's Rule on Taiwan's "Savage Border," 1874–1945*, by Paul D. Barclay
17. *In Search of Our Frontier: Japanese America and Settler Colonialism in the Construction of Japan's Borderless Empire*, by Eiichiro Azuma
18. *Provincializing Empire: Omi Merchants in the Japanese Transpacific Diaspora*, by Jun Uchida
19. *North Korea's Mundane Revolution: Socialist Living and the Rise of Kim Il Sung, 1953–1965*, by Andre Schmid
20. *The State's Sexuality: Prostitution and Postcolonial Nation Building in South Korea*, by Park Jeong-Mi
21. *In the Global Vanguard: Agrarian Development and the Making of Modern Taiwan*, by James Lin
22. *Bibliotactics: Libraries and the Colonial Public in Vietnam*, by Cindy Anh Nguyen
23. *The Narrowing Sea: Fukuoka, Pusan, and the Rise and Fall of an Imperial Region*, by Hannah Shepherd

Bibliotactics

Libraries and the Colonial Public in Vietnam

Cindy Anh Nguyen

UNIVERSITY OF CALIFORNIA PRESS

University of California Press
Oakland, California

Suggested citation: Nguyen, C. A. *Bibliotactics: Libraries and the Colonial Public in Vietnam*. Oakland: University of California Press, 2026.
DOI: https://doi.org/10.1525/luminos.259

Library of Congress Cataloging-in-Publication Data

Names: Nguyen, Cindy Anh, author.
Title: Bibliotactics : libraries and the colonial public in Vietnam / Cindy Anh Nguyen.
Other titles: Asia Pacific modern ; 22.
Description: Oakland, California : University of California Press, [2026] | Series: Asia Pacific Modern ; 22 | Includes bibliographical references and index.
Identifiers: LCCN 2025013807 (print) | LCCN 2025013808 (ebook) | ISBN 9780520423602 (cloth) | ISBN 9780520416222 (paperback) | ISBN 9780520416239 (ebook)
Subjects: LCSH: Libraries—Vietnam—Hanoi—History. | Libraries—Vietnam—Ho Chi Minh City—History.
Classification: LCC Z845.V5 N45 2026 (print) | LCC Z845.V5 (ebook) | DDC 027.09597/3—dc23/eng/20250616

LC record available at https://lccn.loc.gov/2025013807
LC ebook record available at https://lccn.loc.gov/2025013808

GPSR Authorized Representative: Easy Access System Europe, Mustamäe tee 50, 10621 Tallinn, Estonia, gpsr.requests@easproject.com

34 33 32 31 30 29 28 27 26 25
10 9 8 7 6 5 4 3 2 1

For Eric and Thiên Anh

CONTENTS

ILLUSTRATIONS

FIGURES

TABLE

ACKNOWLEDGMENTS

I dreamt of writing this part of the book for years as a celebration of a collective journey marked by laughter, learning, and kinship. Countless individuals and communities transformed my intellectual thinking in ways that transcend traditional citations and disciplinary standards. At the University of California, Berkeley, this project found its earliest and sustained support through my advisor, Peter Zinoman, who grounded my research in historical context and Vietnamese studies. My appreciation extends to Cathryn Carson, who invited me into histories of science and data, and to my intellectual mentors who generously cultivated my scholarly journey: Penny Edwards, Jeffrey Hadler, David Bamman, Paul Duguid, Janaki Bakhle, and Nguyễn Nguyệt Cầm. I found my way to a humanistic inquiry of print culture and circuits of knowledge production through engagements with librarians, digital humanists, and the Society of Fellows in Critical Bibliography. To all those who joined in experimental feminist writing sprints, thank you for building community with me in profound ways. Thank you to my former students turned cothinkers who contributed to my reworking of this project, specifically students in my Print and Power in Southeast Asia and Global Libraries and Decolonial Futures courses. I find myself experiencing an intellectual homecoming returning to UCLA and the scholarly community of my wonderful colleagues in information studies, Southeast Asian studies, and digital humanities. Among my UCLA community, I am particularly grateful for the intellectual camaraderie of Evyn Lê Espiritu Gandhi, Kelly Nguyen, Thuy Vo Dang, Noopur Raval, Nguyễn-Võ Thu-hương, George Dutton, Oona Paredes, and Jasmine Nadua Trice. My developmental editor, Rachel Kantrowitz, shepherded this intellectual work and me as a scholar-human, sustaining me as I birthed Thiên Anh Seneca and this book. I am grateful for my intellectual community around the world that nurtured this book throughout various stages, bringing it to its final shape: Charles Keith, Cynthia Brokaw, Cécile Capot, Yen Vu, Rebecca Nedostup, Nguyễn Thị Minh, Cao Vy, Nu-Anh Tran, Tara Tran, Nicole Yow Wei, Sonya Bui, Katherine Drorbaugh, Lauren Yapp, Weishin Gui, Paulina Hartono, and Christopher Goscha (who first proposed this creative title). I am immensely grateful for the close reading of the full book manuscript and profound insights from Claire Edington, Martina Nguyen, Jody Blanco, and my two peer reviewers.

Postdoctoral support at Brown University (from the Cogut Institute for the Humanities and the Department of History) and the University of California, San Diego (the Departments of Literature and History) provided the structures and community to make the writing and dreaming of this book possible. The manuscript revision and fieldwork in Phnom Penh were funded by the Center for Khmer Studies Senior Fellowship and the Society for the History of Authorship, Reading, and Publishing Research Development Grants. My initial fieldwork in Vietnam and France, completed during my history doctorate, was generously funded by the Fulbright Program, the Social Science Research Council, the École française d'Extrême-Orient, the D. Kim Foundation for the History of Science and Technology in East Asia, and the National Academy of Education / Spencer Foundation. Thank you for the conversations and feedback from the many scholarly engagements with this work, specifically at the Yale Council on Southeast Asia Studies, the Library History Roundtable at the American Libraries Association, the Vietnam National University–University of Social Sciences & Humanities in Ho Chi Minh City, Global Asias at Penn State University, the Asia Research Institute at the National University of Singapore, the European Association for Southeast Asian Studies, and the Association for Asian Studies.

A heartfelt appreciation especially to the librarians and archivists who have inspired my thinking through their generosity of time, wisdom, and labor: Virginia Shih, Judith Henchy, Bùi Thu Hằng, Hà Tố Tâm, Trường Minh Hoà, Nguyễn Thị Minh Trung, Larry Ashmun, the staff at Trung tâm lưu trữ quốc gia 1, 2, and 3, Thư viện quốc gia Việt Nam, Thư viện khoa học tổng hợp Thành phố Hồ Chí Minh, Thư viện khoa học xã hội, Bibliothèque nationale de France, the Archives nationale d'Outre-Mer, and the Kyoto University Southeast Asia Library. Sections of chapter 2 have been published as "Reading Rules: The Symbolic and Social Spaces of Reading in the Hà Nội Central Library, 1919–1941" in the *Journal of Vietnamese Studies* 15, no. 3, and parts of chapter 5 appeared as "Creating the National Library in Saigon: Colonial Legacies, Fragmented Collections, and Reading Publics, 1946–1958," in *Building a Republican Nation in Vietnam, 1920–1963*, edited by Nu-Anh Tran and Tuong Vu (Honolulu: University of Hawai'i Press, 2023). I thank both University of California Press and University of Hawai'i Press for their permissions to reprint revised editions and excerpts in this book. Working with the University of California Press as part of the pilot First Gen Scholars program has been a wonderful experience as this book evolved into its final form through the helpful peer reviews, editorial review, copy edits and the conversations with my editor Enrique Ochoa-Kaup and series editor Takashi Fujitani. I am grateful that folks at UC Press supported my transdisciplinary work of libraries and print media infrastructure within the cultural and historical series Asia Pacific Modern.

This book had its true beginnings with my parents and ancestors, who proudly come from at least two generations without formal lettered training. Their education came from survival, creative entrepreneurship, and commitments to community and spiritual practice throughout times of hardship, war, and displacement. In splendid fashion, my *mẹ* consistently introduces me as the one whose education she never had to pay for. The sacrifices and everyday forms of love, labor, and nourishment from my *ông ngoại, bà ngoại, ba*, and *mẹ* bring me back to the present embrace of a whole life. Their humanity inspired this book to ultimately be about people and practices. And finally, this book would have only been a fantasy and a haunting if not for the constant love and playful embrace of Eric and Thiên Anh. In the simplicity of everyday life, you give language and home to my dreams.

Introduction

Civilized people are people who love to read. . . . In the central library reading room in Hanoi, one rarely finds an empty seat. Unfortunately, it is because many have come to the library . . . to do nothing; some come to the library because they are bored at home, others come because they want to find in the library not books but fans in the summer, and in winter a place a little less cold than their house. Lovers also rendezvous in the library.

—"AT THE CENTRAL LIBRARY," *L'ANNAM NOUVEAU*, NOVEMBER 28, 1935[1]

From 1932 to 1936 an anonymously authored series titled "At the Central Library" was published in the pages of the popular Vietnamese French-language journal *L'Annam Nouveau*. The series chronicled the current state of affairs at the Hanoi Central Library, expressing concern over the misuse of library space for idle behavior, comfortable retreat, and socializing. The author's critiques rested upon a vision of the library as a space for civilizing norms of public behavior by serious readers. In contrast, the everyday reality points to how the library was a popular urban space reinscribed with various social meanings by a diverse colonial public. This book uncovers the emergence of a colonial public sphere within the library in Vietnam.[2] The colonial public sphere comprised builders and users of the library—French and Vietnamese government bureaucrats, library personnel, journalists, intellectuals, and everyday library readers—committed to defining the political role and everyday meaning of the public library. I challenge the assumption of the library as a neutral space, a storehouse of accumulated knowledge scientifically assembled by anonymous librarians and quietly perused by modern readers. Instead the library was a debated institution informed by contradictory politics of intellectual liberation and colonial dominance, and reimagined through social practice and public critique.

This book traces the history of the Central Library in Hanoi and Cochinchina Library in Saigon from colonial to postcolonial Vietnam. Libraries reinforced colonial power as visible infrastructures of a colonial information order, serving as functional repositories and propagators of colonial knowledge. The physical buildings of libraries embodied Enlightenment intellectual emancipation from ignorance, standing as symbolic castles of Western knowledge methodically organized by French concepts of library and information science. The library collections of a Western canon and exclusionary policies of access and public behavior rationalized a French civilizing mission, colonial knowledge, and colonial rule. Libraries functioned as crucial instruments of preserving and propagating French colonial documentation during the early French conquest of the Southeast Asian region, beginning with the creation of the first government joint archives and library in Saigon in 1865. In 1917 the Directorate of Archives and Libraries (Direction des Archives et des Bibliothèques, henceforth referred to as the Directorate) was founded in Hanoi with the mandate to centralize all documentation throughout French Indochina, which by then extended across the peninsular region to include five *pays* (countries): Cochinchina, Tonkin, Annam (three regions that today comprise the nation-state of Vietnam), Cambodge (Cambodia), and Laos. The Directorate sought to standardize archival procedures of official government documents and to build central libraries in Saigon, Hanoi, Phnom Penh, Hue, and Vientiane. Throughout the French colonial period, government resources and operations were concentrated in the Vietnamese regions, as seen in the development of the central archives and libraries in Hanoi and Saigon. The small French expatriate population of government officials, rotating military, and commercial workers was also concentrated in the cities of Saigon, Hanoi, Haiphong, and Phnom Penh. The formation of the Directorate in 1917 and the opening of the Hanoi Central Library in 1919 aligned with a political shift in French colonial policy from assimilationist colonial hegemony to associationist civilizing projects built on a French and Vietnamese collaboration to carry out the labor of the colonial administration across colonial Indochina. Under the Directorate and the colonial policy of Franco-Vietnamese collaboration, the central libraries in Hanoi and Saigon henceforth operated with hybrid duties to train primarily Vietnamese government officials in documentation methods and to implement aspirational French models of modern information and education in colonial Vietnam.

With an increase of urban populations in Saigon and Hanoi and an expansion of the colonial education system in the 1920s to 1940s, the central libraries became vibrant public spaces and reading centers for the growing population of Vietnamese who moved between the city and provinces. As a wider demographic of Vietnamese readers joined the existing population of colonial bureaucrats and French expatriate readers, the library became the fundamental institution to debate questions of the "public." What types of public behaviors were permissible in the library, and which members of colonial society—French and Vietnamese, male and female, government officials, students, professionals, and intellectuals—were included in the library public? The library was an important political battleground for Vietnamese journalists and French colonial reformists to debate the limitations of Franco-Vietnamese collaboration and the promise of modern institutions such as schools and libraries for the Vietnamese masses.

In addition to public debate, the library infrastructure facilitated "public reading culture," the social practices of urban life, self-directed erudition, and interactions with state bureaucracy by a colonial public of emerging elites. The Hanoi and Saigon libraries offered a wide range of reading matter for serendipitous discovery and self-interested pleasure, providing a modicum of leisure, rest, and playful encounter for an eclectic community of readers. The library reading room and lending section provided a valuable resource for broad self-directed learning and free access to global literature, reference works, and news periodicals in French and *quốc ngữ* (romanized script of vernacular Vietnamese language). The colonial library represented a different type of knowledge grounded in a Francophone Western canon and different practices of scholarly, literary, and social engagement. Rather than the Confucian classics in *chữ hán* (Literary Sinitic) and Vietnamese works in *chữ nôm* (character–based script of vernacular Vietnamese), readers were introduced to a Western canon of works ranging from eighteenth- to twentieth-century French classical literature and reference works such as Diderot and d'Alembert's multivolume *Encyclopédie* project, popular genres such as historical fiction and adventure by Alexandre Dumas and Victor Hugo, and sentimental novels by Delly to translated global literature by Rudyard Kipling, Pearl S. Buck, and Mark Twain. Readers were also enmeshed within a colonial-era body of orientalist knowledge about the Far East and French Indochina, including histories, ethnographies, maps, dictionaries, and contemporary periodicals. The colonial library facilitated self-directed reading and learning distinct from the precolonial Confucian practices of memorization-based studying for civil service examinations.[3] The library also differed from Franco-Vietnamese schools that focused on language acquisition and basic general education. Instead, library readers self-selected reading matter to supplement classroom learning, expand literacy in French and Vietnamese *quốc ngữ*, or access reference texts for research. The library represented a widening of Vietnamese reading cultures beyond a handful of men aspiring to scholar-administrative positions under Confucian training to an urban multilingual burgeoning elite engaged in experimental forms of reading: reading in public, multilingual reading (French, Vietnamese, Literary Sinitic), reading across wide-ranging genres and formats, and leisure reading.

These new reading practices were part of larger twentieth-century transformations in print culture beyond the library, spearheaded by the vibrant publishing industry of overlapping French- and Vietnamese-language and private and state-subsidized presses, printers, and publishing houses. This colonial print industry produced at mass quantities more cheaply available reading matter, ranging from local and global newspapers and magazines, serialized novels and translated fiction, nonfiction reference works, language primers, educational texts, and histories to religious tracts.[4] The vibrant print sphere was led by networks of Vietnamese, French, and Chinese publishers, intellectuals, translators, commercial venturers, religious leaders, political organizers, and those who worked within or alongside the colonial administration as interpreters, secretaries, bureaucrats, and librarians. The Indochina publishing sphere and book market centered in commercial hubs, such as Hanoi, Haiphong, Saigon, and Cholon, expanded across the Mekong Delta and Hue and connected to other print networks in Phnom Penh, Siam, and southern China.[5] Alongside its vast collections of Francophone reference materials, literature, and orientalist knowledge, the Hanoi and Saigon libraries incorporated reading matter from this burgeoning Indochina print sphere.

The Hanoi Central Library and Saigon Cochinchina Library were the largest and most widely used public libraries during the French colonial period (1858–1945) and functioned as the national libraries for northern and southern Vietnam in the postcolonial period (1945–75).[6] These important institutions have long histories with changing missions. During the colonial period they were the only "public" library institutions in Vietnam, paid through colonial state funds (through taxation, monopolies, and custom duties) and in principle accessible to anyone over the age of eighteen (later sixteen) who could provide proof that they were residents of the cities of Hanoi and Saigon.[7] The Hanoi and Saigon libraries served as a research reference library, educational textbook resource, lending section for popular novels, and central urban space to freely consult periodicals, news, and reference works from Indochina, France, and around the world. In 1931, the Hanoi Central Library reading room recorded over 51,000 annual book consultations and the lending section recorded over 60,000 loans, even more than many libraries in France during the same time.[8] In 1939, the Hanoi reading room welcomed over 91,000 total visits by Vietnamese readers, compared to only 28,000 visits by French expatriates in the colony. By 1954, the Hanoi Central Library was regarded as one of the most developed and largest libraries in all of Southeast Asia, with over 150,000 volumes and 2,000 periodicals.[9] Across the wider French empire, the Directorate of Archives and Libraries in Indochina produced one of the most extensive documentation records and library collections and served as a model for other French colonies, such as those in French West Africa.[10] The symbolic meaning, public space, literary collections, and modern bureaucracy of the colonial Hanoi and Saigon libraries shaped Vietnamese debates on nationhood throughout the colonial and into the postcolonial period. As the first comprehensive history of the colonial turned national library in Asia, this book engages with three fields of scholarship: Vietnamese history, colonial and postcolonial studies, and histories of libraries, reading, and information.

COLONIAL PUBLICS IN VIETNAM: UNEQUAL, CONTENDING, PLURAL

I examine the history of the Hanoi and Saigon libraries as public infrastructure and social practices, expanding scholarship on publicity and reading culture currently dominated by European and American contexts.[11] This book builds on work from information, technology, and urban studies that consider infrastructure as a community of practice and socio-technical negotiation, what Susan Leigh Star and Geoffrey C. Bowker describe as "infrastructural inversion" and "boundary infrastructure."[12] Following what Deborah Cowen describes as "infrastructure of empire," I show how the Directorate operated as the top-down documentation regime and literary repository of the French imperial nation-state.[13] Within the colonial urban landscape of Hanoi and Saigon, the libraries served as an incomparable resource of public space and reading matter, bringing together a diverse public of French and Vietnamese government officials, journalists, and students to participate in an emerging civic discourse on the cultural mission of the library and the responsibility of the state to provide fair access.[14] Public critiques of the library and demands for reform brought to light the contradictory shape of the French imperial nation-state, informed by emancipatory and oppressive visions of the colonial civilizing mission, discourse of French republican liberties, and bureaucratic authoritarianism.[15]

This book demonstrates that rather than acting as a singular egalitarian public sphere, the colonial library in Vietnam was home to plural and unequal colonial publics. The library stood as a contradiction. On one hand it was a symbolic opening of a world of ideas through universal education, access to modern knowledge, and shared public spaces. On the other hand, the claim of intellectual emancipation was predicated on a French colonial paternalistic relationship of essentialized difference between colonizer and colonized. The library purported to be freely accessible to those who met the age and residency requirements, yet readers were subject to different borrowing privileges and experiences in the library space based on their race, gender, profession, and age. Official internal library records further bifurcated readers, documenting daily library use by readers according to categories of race. The social stratification of readers reflected shifting legal and racial categories as Indochinese "subject-citizens." According to these everyday use statistics, the majority of library readers were male, reflecting the stark gender imbalance among French expatriates, educational inequities in colonial society, and a spatial politics of the library as a masculine space. Of the male readers, most were young Vietnamese exhibiting an emergent bourgeois class identity of socioeconomic privileges through educational opportunities, familiarity with operating in Francophone and urbanizing environments, employment within the government administration, or time for leisure and erudition. This bourgeois class identity was tied to historical transformations of Hanoi and Saigon as urban centers of public infrastructure, economic activity, and government bureaucracy, drawing in large populations moving between the provinces and cities.[16] French women formed another sizable group of readers who regularly used the lending section to read books outside of the library space, suggesting a gendered and racialized spatial politics with the majority Vietnamese male readers who occupied the reading rooms. Besides statistical accounts of library use, library personnel and the popular press reported on misbehaviors and constructed caricatures of library reading publics. For example, the leisurely, loud, and potentially politically subversive "Vietnamese male youth" emerged as a distinct reading public, mirroring the colonial administration's anxieties and state repression of ongoing waves of anticolonial Vietnamese political organizing, particularly in the 1920s to 1940s. Defiant young students were relationally defined against a "serious reader public" of rule-abiding French and Vietnamese researchers and government officials. The colonial public sphere was constituted by two levels of exclusionary techniques in the library, firstly by separating those who were permitted to enter the library walls and secondly by reinforcing demographic stratification in reader statistics and governing norms of public behavior. I examine the history of the colonial public sphere in Vietnam, a plurality of publics that coexisted, overlapped, and were relationally constituted in the library institutions—the bourgeois elites, colonial bureaucrats, Francophone and Vietnamese-language readers, Vietnamese male youth, French female expatriates and their children, intellectuals and journalists, and serious and leisure readers.

My analysis of a colonial public sphere in Vietnam pushes against the public-private divide within Western scholarship, which fails to capture the relational and gendered complexity of civic discourse and public space and conflates publicity with democratic freedom of expression.[17] This work contributes to provincialized framings of public spheres beyond a one-directional export of metropolitan institutions and examines how unequal contexts and authoritarian states shape public life, particularly in cases such as Vietnam, where the commercial press was never wholly outside state control.[18] Existing scholarship on Vietnam examines public spheres as an oppositional space of nationalistic anticolonial organizing. These histories of the Vietnamese public sphere focus on the development of vernacular Vietnamese-language newspapers and publishing houses in the 1920s and 1930s, culminating in nationalist political identity. Hue-Tam Ho Tai and David Marr laid the groundwork for the intellectual history of Vietnamese radicalism, focused on generational Vietnamese political organizing and print communities in the late colonial period.[19] Surveying the printed materials collected through the colonial-era legal deposit in the French National Library in Paris, Shawn McHale's pioneering work addressed the rise of Buddhist, Confucian, and communist print-based spheres of discourse that "staked out zones of autonomy from the colonial state."[20] McHale describes the Vietnamese public sphere as a "relatively vibrant but hierarchical public realm of debate" built on Confucian and Buddhist concepts of an enlightened elite guiding others.[21] Philippe Peycam examined Saigon's 1920s "oppositional journalism" public sphere as expressions of early nationalistic identity.[22] Yet this literature does not address the coexistence and exchange between the Francophone public sphere and a vernacular Vietnamese-language public sphere, locating the rise of nationalism as only outside and diametrically opposed to colonialism and its institutions. Recent literature by Martina Thucnhi Nguyen, Duy Lap Nguyen, Van Nguyen-Marshall, and Kevin Pham expands the realm of political identity beyond a procolonial or anticolonial binary, considering more nuanced political projects of cosmopolitan nationalism, cultural criticism, civil society, and national dignity.[23] Ultimately the scholarship on publicity in Vietnamese studies and beyond remains dominated by a focus on discursive spheres of political debate and imagined communities, constrained by a teleology toward anticolonial nationalist and nation-state ends. Furthermore, abstracted forms of nationalist-driven collective belonging are removed from social spaces and material culture that fundamentally shape the history of public life.

This book uncovers the evolution of a colonial public sphere produced through both political discourse and the experienced infrastructure of the library. The colonial library brought together multiple overlapping publics and counterpublics "formed under conditions of dominance and subordination."[24] This book builds upon Nancy Fraser's critiques of a Habermasian framing of an elite bourgeois masculinist public sphere idealizing a "discourse of publicity touting accessibility, rationality, and the suspension of status hierarchies."[25] The colonial publics of the library in Vietnam found educational meaning, collective experiences, and contradictions of self-direction and sociopolitical control within the library walls, collections, and hierarchical bureaucracy. The fundamental mission of the library was to build literary collections and to circulate them to the public, and these intertwined roles were debated and deployed by diverse actors, from French colonial officials to Vietnamese intellectuals, from librarians to readers. Vietnamese intellectuals debating the library represented a wide-ranging political spectrum, from colonial reformists and modernist cultural critics to socialists and anticolonial nationalists whose interactions within the Hanoi and Saigon colonial libraries shaped their political visions of alternative libraries outside French colonial control. The builders and users of the library grappled with the meaning of the public on the political and everyday level, raising questions of Vietnamese civilization and modern citizenship within the confines of a French colonial political system discursively informed by republican values and modernization. This internal contradiction within the library fomented a political consciousness and cultural mentality of collective belonging grounded in public space, language politics, and literary heritage. This cultural and political vision of publicity shaped twentieth-century debates of Vietnamese nationalism and nationhood, modernity and modernization.[26] In the postcolonial period, the two competing Vietnamese states in the north and south carried out nation-making projects of language nationalism and literary heritage grafted upon the colonial-turned-national library. In this way I revise scholarship on Vietnamese publicity by centering the colonial library as a nexus for bureaucratic state making, public life, modern subjectivity, and collective imagining.

BIBLIOTACTICS AS THEORY AND METHOD

I propose the concept of "bibliotactics" to reveal the everyday politics of the public sphere within the library, where individual agency operated within an institution of colonial power. The "colonial library" has been theorized and contested within postcolonial studies as a body of texts that constitute epistemologies of subjectivity and alterity of colonized societies, a discursive construction of the "Orient" and the "invention of Africa," and described as a "colonization of the mind."[27] Gaurav Desai expands beyond V. Y. Mudimbe's characterization of the African colonial library and instead calls for a relational examination of texts where African subjects refashion and reimagine meanings. My concept of bibliotactics reframes the colonial library as an everyday politics of infrastructural negotiation rather than centered on top-down epistemologies and discourse. Readers were active individuals cultivating their own erudition and inscribing new meaning to library space, creatively envisioning a "third space" of public community and access to global knowledge. This "third space of enunciation" acts as an interstitial space of reimagining, ambivalence, and a hybridity of culture rather than a duality of oppression and resistance or exclusion and inclusion.[28] Drawing from histories of the book and communication, the library exists as a complex space of social gathering and material culture, a fundamental part of what Robert Darnton calls a "communication circuit" of news, media, and rumor bringing together publishers, printers, shippers, sellers, readers, and authors.[29] Libraries are distinctive spaces to understand actual reading practices as part of what Thomas Adams and Nicolas Barker describe as a "whole socio-economic conjuncture," the multistage book circuit of publication, manufacture, distribution, reception, and survival.[30] I bring together the expansive scholarship on cultural practice and histories of reading to move beyond what Michel de Certeau calls "practiced space" and Roger Chartier describes as the "actualization of texts."[31] Instead, bibliotactics calls for an examination of everyday library practices as expressions of publicity and power. In the colonial library in Vietnam, readers defined publicity through library reading in public space and interactions, negotiations, and confrontations with colonial bureaucracy. Readers also participated in plural and nuanced forms of dissent such as socializing in public space and violating library decorum, a "tactics" of individualized operations of the marginalized within an official system of power.[32]

The tactics of library users included not only individualized subversions, but also collective expressions of dissent and refusal such as Vietnamese outcries in the public press to boycott the state library or to form alternative Vietnamese-language community libraries. Existing studies of Vietnamese colonial power and resistance overemphasize generational politics and overt forms of anticolonial nationalism. This framing of anticolonial or procolonial shrouds the everyday practices within the library such as subtle spatial subversions of authority, encounters with bureaucracy and public citizenship, educational empowerment, and leisurely socialization.

Rather than simply a top-down or bottom-up structure of power confined within a library space, my concept of bibliotactics advances a relational and multidirectional theory of power that blurs the arbitrary divide between rule makers and the rule breakers, or the library personnel and the patrons. For the Vietnamese male librarian staff who regularly arrived late to work, stole books, and read during work hours, how did his everyday actions reflect a resistance to or negotiation within an institution of colonial dominance? Bibliotactics takes an intersectional revision of power relations to consider the racial, class, gender, and rural-urban backgrounds of the majority Vietnamese male laborers of the library—librarian-archivists, secretaries, orderlies, groundskeepers, guards—and their interactions with their managers and patrons.[33] Professional interactions such as Vietnamese male librarians enforcing library regulations upon French women readers, or French library directors rejecting petitions from young Vietnamese readers, produced norms of bureaucratic surveillance and governing effects on everyday conduct, or what David Scott calls a "colonial governmentality."[34] Professional and patron social interactions in the library can also be understood as political economies of "intimacies," drawing from the foundational work of Ann Stoler and Lisa Lowe, to examine subjects operating relationally within unequal spaces of colonial dominance.[35] Furthermore, the library can be conceptualized as what Hannah Arendt describes as a "space of appearance," a public political stage and "web of relations" of agency, action, and interaction.[36] My approach of bibliotactics examines the individual embedded within a system of colonial governance, sociocultural practices of public reading contextualized within material architectures of the colonial information order.

My methodology of bibliotactics critically unfolds the documentation record produced by the colonial information order, including internal letters, hand-tabulated statistics, and published annual reports produced by the Directorate of Archives and Libraries of Indochina, Hanoi Central Library, and Saigon Cochinchina Library now housed in the national archives in Vietnam and France. During the colonial period, librarian-archivists collected data on readers: their demographic background, checkouts, library visits, and library card applications. Extensive records exist on the physical library collections: catalogs, genres, lists of books donated, destroyed, lost, stolen, requiring repair, and most popular among readers. Libraries differed in their method and consistency of data collection. The statistics and detail of collections and reader consultations for the Hanoi Central Archives and Library were always more extensive than those for the archives and libraries in Saigon, Phnom Penh, and Hue. Detailed reports and statistics on collections, library use, and legal deposit were summarized in yearly bibliographies, legal deposit records, and reports from 1923 to 1943 published by the Directorate. Why the statistics were recorded is just as significant as what they convey. First, these statistics provided valuable information to guide internal library needs and priorities. The documentary monitoring of the library and its users were fundamental to the evolving field of library sciences (*bibliothéconomie*) as technical labor and scientific knowledge. Second, high library usage numbers and publication of library and archives development justified continual government financial investment in the Directorate as an instrument for cultural propaganda and state documentation.[37] Developing in conjunction, French colonial libraries and archives controlled the preservation, curation, and circulation of print matter and supported the bureaucratic operations of the colonial state. Colonial archives have been theorized extensively as "epistemological experiments" and "technologies of rule," promoting Western discourses of racialized difference and universalized concepts of modern subjectivity, humanity, and liberalism.[38] Yet libraries, while interrelated as state projects with archives, have not received equivalent levels of critical attention. This book expands scholarship on colonial knowledge by shedding light on libraries as public-facing institutions of colonial moralization and modernization, providing access to urban public space for self-directed education yet within the racialized structures of the colonial information order.

The data on readers is strikingly uneven—at times extremely detailed for specific readers and at other times only a tick mark in the total number of reader visits. Readers and library personnel were surveilled and documented, and their behaviors often emerge when in violation of library decorum. Piles of paperwork record troublesome readers who lost books, disrupted the reading room, or demanded exceptions for reading rules. Library administrators closely reported on their inferiors, thus Vietnamese library clerks, groundskeepers, and reading room overseers regularly appear in the archival record as failing to log checked-out books, coming in to work late, reading during working hours, or having a temperament "unfit" for library work. Yet often these misbehaviors that emerge in archival documents and newspaper reports were the exception to the norm; the vast majority of library use and operations continued on with more subtle dramas and everyday negotiations that were not as directly reported in archival documentation. I thus "read along the grain" of the library documentation to conceptualize everyday social relations and technical labor, paying attention to the seemingly mundane bureaucratic procedures such as library regulations and statistical reporting of circulations, acquisitions, and card registrations.[39] I approach these documentary traces as historical evidence of everyday social life within an aspirational surveillance regime of books, bodies, and behaviors. With attention to library users, experienced architectures, and public discourse, I also analyzed colonial and metropolitan newspapers in Vietnamese and French, examined historic photographs, and conducted site visits to the present-day Hanoi and Saigon library buildings. Qualitative narrative accounts such as reader complaints, applications, and letters balance the quantitative statistical top-down knowledge produced by the library documentation regime. Through this interwoven analysis of official archives, public discourse, visual and material culture, and critical analysis of statistics, I contribute valuable insight into the historical patterns of Vietnamese reader behavior, demographics, library collections, and book circulation.

THE BIBLIOTACTICS OF COLONIAL PUBLICS

This book approaches the history of the library as institution and practice. Libraries are material repositories reflecting collecting regimes of librarians, contemporary definitions of "books of value," and state visions of national heritage, as well as the global and local book market at certain historical and political moments. Everyday library operations reflect changing technical, cultural, and social practices around book preservation, public reading, and demands for certain types of reading matter for educational, leisure, and professional purposes. Libraries are part of a complex ecosystem of intentional and unintentional book circulation shaped by politics, culture, economics, technology, and logistical randomness. Distinct from publishing houses and bookshops, libraries play an important role in secondary distribution, reflecting the movement of text to unintended audiences not anticipated by author or publisher.[40] Libraries carry deep cultural meanings. As an assemblage of book objects of knowledge and narrative, libraries connect individuals to imagined communities of reading and ideas. Libraries perform prestige and scholastic identity, and as spaces for intellectual inquiry and the pursuit of curiosities. Libraries are gathering spaces of humans and knowledge, architectural feats of state infrastructure. Libraries carry tremendous social and cultural capital as battlegrounds for the definition of the public. The value of libraries was a centerpiece of critique by intellectuals, statesmen, readers, librarians, activists, and revolutionaries throughout the colonial and postcolonial periods. Builders and users debated whom should the library serve, the immediate public with specific language, literary, and intellectual needs or the imagined public of the future?

Experiences within and critiques of the library cultivated the cultural, political, and bureaucratic practices that defined the colonial public sphere. The chapters follow a chronological and thematic structure following five bibliotactics of the colonial public: to document, to be in public, to circulate, to read, and to reassemble. Each chapter considers the relationship between the builders and users of libraries, enacting individual and collective meanings of publicity within a colonial institution. Chapter 1, "To Document," traces the interwoven development of the French colonial state and a colonial information order, an elaborate infrastructure for the production, preservation, and circulation of print matter. This chapter establishes the histories, visions, and key personnel of the two institutions examined in the book, the Saigon Cochinchina Library and the Hanoi Central Library. With the centralized formation of the Directorate of Archives and Libraries of Indochina in 1917, the French colonial government attempted to standardize administrative documentation practices geographically throughout Indochina and integrated with the metropole.[41] The Directorate was instrumental to the bureaucratic maintenance of the colonial state and implementation of Franco-Vietnamese collaborationist colonial policy, a liberal form of colonial rule based on administrative partnership of French and Vietnamese elites from 1917 to the 1940.[42] French colonialism transformed concepts of encyclopedic libraries and public access through curation of a Western canon and orientalist knowledge for circulation to an envisioned public.[43] The colonial information order competed with an existing world of letters grounded in Confucian bureaucracy and Literary Sinitic reading cultures.[44] The training of Vietnamese library and archives staff in the functional tools of colonial bureaucracy and documentation contributed to important technical knowledge that carried over to the formation of Vietnamese nation-states in the postcolonial period.

As a counternarrative to the first chapter on builders, chapter 2, "To Be in Public," focuses on the library users and their experience of public infrastructure in the Hanoi Central Library and Saigon Cochinchina Library. I highlight the ways in which library readers' bodies were made "modern" within public space—legible, individualized, ordered, and monitored. Specifically, I examine race-based restrictions to library access and regulations on proper public behavior to demonstrate the construction of colonial hierarchies of Frenchness and Vietnameseness as evolving debates of racialization, cultural practice, language, and legal rights within library institutions and social life. By the 1920s and 1930s, Vietnamese male students had become the majority library users and subverted the colonial vision of the library as an exclusive space for French readers, government officials, and scholarly researchers. I argue that Vietnamese library users redefined the meaning of public space and public citizenship by contesting library rules, demanding reform and increased access, and reinscribing the actual and symbolic infrastructure of the library through everyday behavior. I reveal how the central library reading rooms transformed into a space of urban social life, self-directed reading of library collections, and civic engagement with colonial bureaucracy, a phenomenon I call "public reading culture." This chapter contributes new insight into the Vietnamese literary reception and print culture landscapes, centering library reading practices as embedded within a larger network of Vietnamese "provincial cosmopolitan" engagements with contemporary, local, and global literature.[45]

Chapter 3, "To Circulate," examines the interwoven political and technical instrumentalization of libraries for cultural propaganda in the late colonial period. Colonial officials envisioned circulating libraries as loose surveillance vehicles to propagate politically "safe" and morally "good" reading, facilitate healthy leisure activities, and distract provincial Vietnamese readers from consuming tendentious anticolonial and communist texts in the 1920s to 1940s. In an attempt to extend state control into the countryside, French colonial officials proposed a comprehensive Indochina-wide regime of cultural propaganda through state-sponsored circulating libraries and publishing modeled on the Dutch East Indies Balai Pustaka network. At the same time, the Directorate experimented with a bibliobus project, where book vehicles circulated library books from the urban Hanoi and Saigon central libraries into the provinces. Inspired by the turn-of-the-twentieth-century international library sciences and public library movements in the United States, England, and France, the Indochina bibliobus project was presented as benevolent modernization and public moralization.[46] This chapter also sheds light on the public reception and popular use of the bibliobus circulating libraries by provincial French and Vietnamese readers. I uncover how the bibliobus functioned as an important instrument of book distribution, survival, and reception, ultimately transforming late colonial reading cultures and literacy in French and *quốc ngữ*.

The first three chapters focus on the evolution of a colonial public sphere within the library walls, where builders and users debated the meaning of "public" through the functions of colonial state libraries to serve its readers and preserve literary heritage. In comparison, chapter 4, "To Read," moves beyond the walls of state libraries and uncovers a movement to create *bình dân thư viện* (public libraries, or libraries for the people) responding to the limitations of the Hanoi Central Library and Saigon Cochinchina Library as Francophone-dominated, urban elite institutions built upon a colonial system of exclusion and racial hierarchy. Throughout the popular press, Vietnamese intellectuals debated the significance of reading and building personal and shared *quốc ngữ*–language library collections as political projects of Vietnamese language nationalism, where vernacular reading practices could cultivate an enlightened society of cultured readers and inquisitive cosmopolitan thinkers. Throughout the 1920s to the 1940s, Vietnamese intellectuals and community leaders experimented in creating *bình dân thư viện*, collections of reading resources in membership associations and donation-based reading rooms to provide mass education and expand literacy in Vietnamese. Through building shared community spaces of *quốc ngữ* reading matter, *bình dân thư viện* functioned as experiments in vernacular public spheres, envisioning Vietnamese nationhood tied to *quốc ngữ* language, self-erudition, and literary heritage. This chapter contributes a cultural history of Vietnamese collective identity through tracing the intertwined debates on language, libraries, and community within the vernacular press and associational life.[47]

Chapter 5, "To Reassemble," examines the unraveling of the colonial information order through the decolonization of the Hanoi and Saigon libraries into the national libraries of the Democratic Republic of Vietnam (DRV) in Hanoi and Republic of Vietnam (RVN) in Saigon. I demonstrate how the struggle for political sovereignty over Indochina during the First Indochina War manifested in the Hanoi and Saigon libraries, institutions that navigated a semicolonial administrative structure of changing Vietnamese autonomy. Challenging an abrupt rupture from colonial to postcolonial, this chapter centers the library institution within French recolonization, the semicolonial French-Vietnamese "associated state," and postcolonial nation building. I reveal how decolonization was a fragmented process of reassemblage—a process of reexamining the colonial infrastructures of information and its legacies, and translating and making sense of them for a postcolonial future. By tracing the struggle over the library mission and patrimony of collections from 1945 to 1955, this chapter expands the understanding of Vietnamese decolonization and postcolonial nationhood.

This book moves between Hanoi and Saigon and is bookended by two moments of library development: the formation of the Directorate of Archives and Libraries of Indochina in Hanoi in 1917 and the reopening of the Republic of Vietnam National Library in Saigon in 1958 after the reorganization of its inherited colonial-era collections and transferred materials from the Democratic Republic of Vietnam National Library in Hanoi. The temporal framing of the book across colonial-postcolonial divides intervenes in orthodox studies of Vietnam that do not explicitly examine decolonization and postcolonial nation building and instead conflate decolonization with an external framing of anticolonialism, the Cold War, and American militarism. The teleology toward a unified communist Vietnam in 1975 reifies a rigid division between colonialism and postcolonialism and ultimately elides the complex 1950s history of competing Vietnamese visions of nationhood and postcolonial institutions. This book seeks to join critical studies of empire by drawing attention to historical processes of decolonization of the libraries as a debated process of infrastructural transformation, cultural patrimony, and collective identity.[48] Besides rethinking temporal divisions, scholarship that undertakes a framework inclusive of both Hanoi and Saigon offers new insight into the particularities of Vietnamese regions and how the two urban centers and national capitals evolved in relationship.[49] By studying the material, ideological, and cultural meanings of the former colonial and reimagined national Vietnamese library in both Hanoi and Saigon, I offer alternative *longue durée* framings of decolonization and collective identity tied to shifting meanings of publicity and cultural practice.

This book closes with an epilogue on the transformation and legacies of the colonial information order and public reading culture. I consider how the two national libraries diverged in the RVN and DRV in the early years of postcolonial nation-building from 1954 to 1958. In the case of Saigon, public reading culture

FIGURE 1. Cochinchina Library reading room, Saigon, ca. 1920s–1930s. *Source*: Archives Privées Papiers Boudet 86, Archives nationales d'outre-mer, Aix-en-Provence, France, folder 52.

cultivated through the French colonial era Cochinchina Library was fundamental to shaping the political culture of Vietnamese republicanism. In the case of Hanoi, public reading culture of the colonial era Hanoi Central Library was repressed as part of official state policy, replaced by an internationalist communist model of libraries as part of cultural transformation. Both institutions confronted the technobureaucratic and Francophone legacies of the colonial information order in the library collections, buildings, and operations and considered alternative information models for postcolonial Vietnamese library organization and popular education. This epilogue revisits the fundamental ways in which libraries continued to be spaces of political vision and everyday critique, a social practice and collective imagining of the public.

1

To Document

Building Libraries and a Colonial Information Order

You [Paul Boudet] arrived with this ardor that protects the neophytes. You reached the Asiatic waters and its mysteries as a man of letters possessed by a curiosity that is like the execution of a science. In a domain unexplored by a "chartist" you embarked on a task, and, my, what a task! French Indochina, its history, its past, its "actions" by the first conquerors, the imprint of its first government officials! You were going to be the secular Benedictine who would save, conserve this heritage of the past. Indochina? What a destination! Its founders? What a subject [of study]. Protect and pass down its treasures? What a mandate!

—PIERRE PASQUIER, FOREWORD TO *LES ARCHIVES ET LES BIBLIOTHÈQUES DE L'INDOCHINE*, 1919[1]

In June 1917, twenty-eight-year-old Paul Boudet arrived in Hanoi tasked by the École française d'Extrême-Orient (EFEO), or French School of the Far East, with a scientific mission to report on the state of the archives in Indochina.[2] In his extensive report Boudet described conditions of government documentation as an abandoned mess in urgent need of centralization and conservation under the direction of specialists. He also called for the organization of encyclopedic libraries that assembled "all levels of knowledge" in stable collections and the development of public lending libraries distributing "valuable" reading matter.[3] By November the governor general of Indochina, Albert Sarraut, formally expanded Boudet's scientific mission into a sweeping project to direct an integrated system of colonial documentation through the newly established Directorate of Archives and Libraries of Indochina (Direction des archives et des bibliothèques de l'Indochine, henceforth referred to as the Directorate).[4] From 1917 to 1945, the Directorate functioned as an elaborate top-down (general government to local level) network of a central archives, library, legal deposit, and "national bibliography" based in Hanoi, and regional archives and library branches in Saigon, Hue, Phnom Penh, and Vientiane.[5] Boudet was trained as an archivist-paleographer at the renowned

Chartes national archives and libraries school in Paris, and had served as an archivist and curator in the Vosges and Rouen prior to his arrival in Indochina. In his description of Paul Boudet, Pierre Pasquier (who would later serve as governor general of Indochina from 1928 to 1934) presented Boudet's task as a heroic mandate and glorious duty to preserve the treasures of French colonial history.[6] Pasquier described Boudet's work of document preservation as a romantic hero's journey, a scientific quest to protect the papers from the environment and pests that threaten not just destruction of the material documents, but also the wisdom and history the documents contained.[7] To protect the documents signified the preservation of colonial history and colonial power.

From 1917 to 1945 Boudet would be the administrative director and principal visionary for the Directorate of Archives and Libraries of Indochina, the governmental body that defined documentation procedures, literary curation, and the preservation of print matter in Indochina. Within the Directorate system, the Hanoi Central Library, founded in 1919, stood as the most important monument of the French colonial cultural propaganda project of spreading "civilization" and carrying out a benevolent colonial collaboration of French and Vietnamese. The Hanoi Central Library was afforded a relatively large annual budget, similar to those of large libraries in France.[8] No other French colonial territory had ever undertaken such a multilayered documentation project, and no other region in Southeast Asia would have a collection that would compare to the extensive and popular library collections of the Hanoi Central Library. As the second largest and most popular library, the Cochinchina Library, founded in 1865, functioned as an ambitious administrative reference library from the beginning of French colonial conquest; it later transformed into an extensive lending library and public urban space for Saigon readers.

I argue that the Directorate of Archives and Libraries system was central to the production of a "colonial information order"—a technically sophisticated infrastructure of libraries, archives, and documentation procedures that legitimized French colonial knowledge and bureaucratic governance over the Indochina region. In other words, libraries and archives of Indochina carried out the essential information order tasks of production, preservation, and circulation of print matter, which included governmental reports, maps, statistics, historic and contemporary books, and serials. Organized according to French library scientific standards and a discourse of colonial modernity, the Hanoi Central Library and the Saigon Cochinchina Library formally institutionalized a Western literary canon through its collecting regime as well as shaped the contours of colonial knowledge on "Indochina" and the "Far East" as a political, historical, and academic construct. The French colonial state instrumentalized the libraries to displace competing forms of documentary authority and literary culture grounded in precolonial Vietnamese mandarin governance and a Sinitic Confucian-based literary canon. Far from an objective disinterested scientific project, the Hanoi and

Saigon libraries functioned as a cultural propaganda tool of the French *mission civilisatrice* (civilizing mission) and as a symbol of *collaboration Franco-Annamite* (Franco-Vietnamese collaboration), a reformist policy of benevolent modernization and social progress that dominated the late colonial period. While the first half of this chapter focuses on the political visions of the colonial information order, the second half moves into the bottom-up operational reality and everyday work of libraries characterized by documentation torpor, uneven implementation, and financial challenges in labor and materials. I dedicate attention to the development of librarianship as a colonial profession and the ways in which library personnel navigated a bibliotactics of power hierarchies stratified by race, gender, and educational backgrounds through their everyday labor of library operations.

THE COMPETING WORLD OF LETTERS: BOOK COLLECTIONS AND CONFUCIAN EDUCATION IN PRECOLONIAL VIETNAM

In November 1920 the governor general of Indochina, Maurice Long, his wife, Madame Long, the general inspector of public instruction, Monsieur Cognacq, and the military diplomat Captain Bernard toured the newly opened Hanoi Central Library. The newspaper *Courrier d'Haiphong* reported their highly publicized visit: "Guided by the young and learned archivist Paul Boudet, the group visited the various library departments, marveling in the simplicity, good taste, and ingenuity of the classified, arranged, and well-integrated collections—all of human genius unified with religious care by Boudet."[9] Described as a model of modern public libraries in Indochina, the central library had "great reading rooms with comfortable chairs, large tables, good lighting, and quiet fans to help the studious readers overcome the tropical temperatures." Written a year after the opening of the library in 1919, this commentary envisioned the library as an intellectual center and storehouse of knowledge, particularly for French expatriates:

> The colonialist who seeks to join the study of European intellectual movements but could not find it here [in Indochina] . . . will be grateful to this young, audacious, and artistic young man [Paul Boudet] for building in the heart of Tonkin a small temple consecrated for the cerebral efforts. The library serves as a storage of the historical treasures of the colony and thus permits the French in exile to connect with the spirit of universal knowledge.

The newspaper article praised the newly opened French colonial library as an embodiment of "universal" knowledge, which was grounded in European intellectual movements, a Western literary canon, and French colonial history.

What the newspaper did not publicize was the tumultuous history of French colonial conquest and the gradual displacement of cultural and governmental

FIGURE 2. Hanoi Central Library, front exterior view with surrounding gardens, ca. 1920s. *Source*: Archives Privées Papiers Boudet 86, Archives nationales d'outre-mer, Aix-en-Provence, France, folder 52.

authority on the precise grounds on which the Hanoi Central Library was built. Before the grounds became home to the French beaux arts–style library building surrounded by manicured gardens, the space served as an important regional Confucian examination camp, a *trường thi* or *camp de lettres*.[10] Vietnamese candidates and their accompanying servant entourages would reside on the campsite and engage in Confucian examinations for placement in civil service positions.[11] The Vietnamese civil service examination system had existed in dispersed yet important ways in Vietnam since 1463, with some sources pointing to the first examinations being held since 1075.[12] Literacy in the precolonial period was developed primarily within the framework of educational training for the Vietnamese mandarin administrative civil service modeled after the Chinese Confucian mandarin system. Through studying the Confucian Four Books and Five Classics in Literary Sinitic (*chữ hán*, also referred to as classical Chinese), Vietnamese students participated in a series of examinations for placement in the mandarin administrative civil service. These literati officials played an important role in carrying out the work of documentation legibility, or what John Whitmore describes as maintaining "paperwork" (census documents, reports, and land and village registers) in the Đại Việt early modern state.[13] With a capital in Thăng Long (Hanoi), the Đại Việt kingdom was based in the Red River Delta in what is now the northern region of Vietnam, roughly between the eleventh and sixteenth centuries, a period that includes ethnic Việt southern colonization into Cham and Khmer lands.[14] Those candidates who did not gain high marks or failed often returned to their villages to become teachers. Alexander Woodside describes the mandarinate system as part of a shared political and religious world of Mahayana Buddhism, Confucianism, the experience of the Chinese Han-Tang empire (for Korea and northern Vietnam), and the influence of Literary Sinitic upon historical records, law, and the organization of specialized administrative ministries.[15] With the official written language of the administration as *chữ hán*, precolonial Vietnamese literature was highly immersed in the cosmopolitan Sinitic literary sphere.[16] Vietnamese literati perceived themselves as part of and in conversation with the cultural-linguistic realm of manifest civility defined by the Northern Kingdom.[17] Furthermore, the sinographic script held a culturally prestigious value of sagely wisdom and civilized governance. Besides literacy in Literary Sinitic, a small number of Vietnamese also wrote vernacular literature in *chữ nôm*, the sinographic script for the Vietnamese spoken language developed since the twelfth century. In the seventeenth century, Portuguese and Italian Catholic missionaries developed *chữ quốc ngữ*, the romanized Vietnamese alphabet, initially as a vehicle of religious proselytizing. Yet throughout the early modern period, *chữ hán* and *chữ nôm* remained the preferred script for Vietnamese administrative and literary writing. Recent scholarship by John Phan sheds light on a bilingual speaking society of "Annamese Middle Chinese" and "Northern Vietic" in the Red River plain and their language shifts across the tenth to fourteenth centuries, complicating understandings of regional vernaculars and written scripts.[18]

Book culture in Đại Việt was immersed in the Sinitic world of letters that circulated around Eastern Asia, and an extensive book trade of manuscripts and books printed in southern China such as the Thirteen Classics body of Confucian literature used in the imperial examinations, pronunciation guides, and medical texts, made their way to Đại Việt. Kathleen Baldanza characterizes the literary world of the turn of twentieth century Vietnam as "composed of the local and the imported, the vernacular and the classical."[19] Nguyễn Tuấn Cường describes the multiple roles of libraries in early modern Vietnam: They were a place to store books, to make woodblock printings, and for religious worship, and they also functioned as academies for teaching, cultural exchange, and syncretism of the Three Teachings (Confucianism, Buddhism, and Daoism).[20] The practice of copying and recopying texts was a key part of Confucian learning, preserving literary heritage, and disseminating knowledge to future generations. Through the task of copying, students studied the work, memorized it, and in turn created a copy for their own private book collection. Private book collections also conveyed sociocultural prestige, where books functioned as cultural objects to be observed, admired, and cared for by a closely tied and often exclusive community of literati.

This early modern period was followed by a period (the sixteenth to eighteenth centuries) of competing fragmented authorities between the northern region

(Đàng Ngoài) based around the Red River Delta and newly colonized provincial southern lands (Đàng Trong) based around the Mekong Delta, central coast, and south-central highlands. This period culminated in the Tây Sơn Rebellion (1771–1802), which scholars such as George Dutton and Alexander Woodside argue mark the modern period of Vietnam.[21] The periodization of the modern period sheds light on the important role of early Vietnamese statemaking rather than defining modernity and modern states as tied exclusively to Western intervention. This period of warring political and military contestation ended when Emperor Gia Long (Nguyễn Phúc Ánh, r. 1802–20) unified the northern and southern regions of the country, moved the capital from Thăng Long (Hanoi) to Hue, and established the Nguyễn dynasty, which officially continued through the French colonial period until 1945. Book collecting played an important role in imperial state-building projects of the Nguyễn court (who came from the central and southern regions) in exerting legitimacy over the historical record written by previous rival Vietnamese dynasties (Lê and Trịnh) based in the northern regions. George Dutton examines how the Nguyễn emperors attempted to build the state book collections through imperial edicts requesting the general public submit volumes, official book purchases, and direct requests from specific scholars to donate books ranging from historical chronicles to literary texts.[22] Particularly under Emperor Ming Mạng (1820–41), the Nguyễn dynasty ushered in neo-Confucian forms of large-scale administrative centralization and the production of "documentary authority" through "the creation and dissemination of evidentiary texts."[23] Books were perceived as worldly prestige items. Alexander Woodside, for example, describes how Emperor Ming Mạng gifted "Western eyeglasses and bottles of perfume upon his assembled officials and urged them to borrow and read the 'strange books from the four corners of the world' that he kept in his library."[24] Book requests and book giving cultivated a symbolic relationship between the emperor and the scholar.

At the time of French encroachment in the southern Mekong region of the peninsula in the 1860s, Vietnam had a long documentation history shaped by vernacular Vietnamese *chữ nôm*- and Literary Sinitic–based literary culture and the Confucian bureaucratic mandarinate system. Under the unified geopolitical administration of the Nguyễn dynasty (1802–1945), imperial state libraries contributed to legitimizing the ruling authority. Yet French colonialism and its bureaucratic institutions of centralized archives and libraries marked a shift in modern state making distinct from Vietnamese imperial states. Alexander Woodside describes this shift as a "lost modernity" under which Asian mandarinate political systems in Vietnam, China, and Korea were displaced by a Western political rationality and scientific management theory. The colonial library was the principal institution to carry out the introduction of a different colonial information order based on French documentation sciences and a Western literary canon in Indochina. French library administrator André Masson characterized the colonial Hanoi library as the inheritor of the Vietnamese Confucian "glorious literary past"; he ruminated on how the student readers of the French colonial library were "heirs to the literati of yesteryear . . . who [now] come to the same place to draw the elemental waters of Western knowledge."[25] Yet the process of reorienting Vietnamese literati culture around Francophone literature and colonial history was more of a gradual competing world of letters between East and West, vernacular and classical, local and imported. From the period of initial French encroachment to the formal creation of the Directorate in 1917 and the opening of the Hanoi Central Library in 1919, a world of letters in *chữ hán* and *chữ nôm* persisted in fragmented forms through Vietnamese academies, private libraries, and collections in Buddhist temples.

A PIECEMEAL FRENCH COLONIAL ADMINISTRATION AND BUILDING THE SAIGON COCHINCHINA LIBRARY

From the beginning of French encroachment into the Vietnamese southern regions in 1858, colonial authorities established joint libraries and archive services that served as central documentation institutions. French colonial encroachment began in southern Vietnam with a military invasion in 1858 and expanded into the peninsula through diplomats, missionaries, and naval officers in piecemeal contestation with Việt, Khmer, and Lao monarchs and ambassadors over the course of a tumultuous forty years. In 1862 the Nguyễn court in Hue ceded three provinces to France (Gia Định, Biên Hoà, Mỹ Tho), yet France continued to expand through the region, creating a French colony of Cochinchina (direct rule) and Cambodge (Cambodia) as a protectorate in 1863. The interdependent institutions of libraries and archives preserved the paper trail of the expanding French colonial administration through reports, legal decrees, correspondence, and statistics. Archives and libraries also curated research materials (maps, histories, dictionaries, ethnographies, periodicals, scientific manuals) for colonial government officials and orientalist scholars, developing in parallel with research organizations such as the École française d'Extrême-Orient, which originated in 1898.[26] The task of documentation went hand in hand with military and economic operations to exert control and exploit resources in a new colony. The colonial secretary Trần Văn Kỳ summarized justifications for archival preservation and organization for the French colonial administration: "These documents—which are great in number and are of a priceless value for the history of the colony—are currently so disorderly that they render all research impossible; for that matter, over time, little by little, bundles of documents are destroyed because they are abandoned without precautions taken for the humid climate of Cochinchina. If we are not careful, nothing will remain of the information they hold."[27] The Colonial Council of Cochinchina reasserted the importance of the organization of documents with the statement, "It is completely impossible to make a legitimate administration in the colony without a perfectly organized archive service."[28]

Officially organized in 1865, the Cochinchina Library in Saigon existed as one of the earliest institutions of the French colonial information order, functioning as a documentation center and popular reference library for government officials.[29] Government officials understood that building the library was an essential part of building colonial infrastructure: "Among so many other urgent preoccupations, like the construction of lighthouses, hospitals, and a telegraphic service, [the administration] recognized it necessary to create a library. Certainly, it intended the library not to be an institution largely for the public but rather a reference library."[30] In the early years of its existence, the Saigon Library carried a range of French-language materials varying from administrative tracts to literature, science textbooks, travelogues, and Paris literary magazines. "Next to the administrative and juridical works, there was a spot dedicated for less austere works to help the colonialists to stay abreast of the current intellectual movements of the metropole. For example, one finds the *Revue des deux mondes*, parts of [the magazines] *Archéologie* . . . and *Illustration* (such as the valuable reportages of the expedition and woodcut illustrations of Cochinchina)."[31] Initial collections of the library included subscriptions to periodicals from France, the Dutch East Indies, and other French colonies as well as local Cochinchina publications. Most of the periodicals and reading material in the library covered the following topics: comparative colonialism, maps, and early research on Vietnamese customs, governance, and society. On October 26, 1866, the governor of Cochinchina, Admiral Pierre-Paul de la Grandière, wrote to the minister of colonies in Paris and requested a list of French books to be sent to Saigon, paid for by the local budget. He wrote, "It is of great interest to the colony to create a collection of the principal works of our [France's] literature."[32] In the following letter on May 9, 1867, Admiral de la Grandière reiterated to the minister of colonies the importance of building a library collection in order to "provide an element of occupation for our military officers whose idleness is often a cause of bad behavior."[33] Books functioned as sources of entertainment and healthy leisure, and they extended a sense of productive order over the European community of military officials, civil servants, merchants, soldiers, and missionaries in the 1860s and 1870s.[34] Furthermore, the library served the growing population of colonial-trained Vietnamese civil servants and interpreters. In 1868 Admiral de la Grandière also began to develop an official Cochinchina archive and ordered that government dossiers be preserved and classified.

In 1884 the French colonial government expanded northward from its colony of Cochinchina and designated Tonkin (northern Vietnam) and Annam (central Vietnam) as French protectorates. In 1887 the French government officially created the Indochinese Union, known more commonly as French Indochina, which included the five *pays* (countries): the direct colony Cochinchine and the protectorates Annam and Tonkin (three regions that today comprise the nation-state of Vietnam) as well as Cambodge and Laos (added to the union in 1893). The French colonial government system created a top-down structure of power and control, with a governor general at the top who was appointed from Paris and followed orders from the Ministry of Colonies. In everyday practice the colonial administration carried on with relative autonomy from the French Ministry of Colonies and relied upon preexisting local Vietnamese, Cambodian, and Laotian governance for district and village administration, particularly throughout the protectorate territories. The building of the administrative apparatus of French colonial Indochina drew upon the labor of lower-level Vietnamese officials, interpreters, and soldiers who carried out an "internal colonization" of Laos and Cambodge.[35] At the turn of the twentieth century, parallel forms governance and decentralized education existed particularly throughout Tonkin and Annam, where the Hue court under the Nguyễn monarch symbolically maintained local governance through the Confucian mandarin-style civil service administration. At the same time, professional schools such as the Hanoi-based Collège des interprètes (College of Interpreters) were founded to train Vietnamese civil servants, and technical education, vocational, and apprentice arts schools were established to promote local industries.[36] The official language of the administration was French, and the promotion of the French language and Vietnamese *quốc ngữ* was part of a political effort to distance the new French colonial administration from China and the long-standing cultural-linguistic influence of Literary Sinitic in Vietnam. In addition, the colonial administration was threatened by the role of Vietnamese scholar-gentry teachers and mandarins who mobilized anticolonial resistance in the late nineteenth and early twentieth centuries.[37] This cultural propaganda project of language rupture was executed through the education system and the library collections policy in which French-language materials dominated.

This gradual and piecemeal process of colonial conquest was reflected in the fragmented Indochina institutions such as the libraries and archives. During the early years of French colonial conquest in Indochina, each of the five territorial regions managed their own government library and archive through the local administration. The archives and libraries documented government functions, provided reference reading matter for officials, and over time extended access to its collections beyond governmental officials. During this period of colonial expansion into the Indochinese Union, the Cochinchina Library also underwent parallel processes of transformation. In 1882 the Saigon Library was designated as a public library and considered an essential responsibility within the tasks of maintaining internal affairs through the Directorate of the Interior.[38] In 1902, Governor General Paul Beau, who served from 1902 to 1908, placed the library under the supervision of the government of Cochinchina, formalizing the role of the joint institution to serve both the government and the larger public. Together the Cochinchina library and archives were placed on the second floor of a compound on 27 rue de La Grandière, recently built in 1888 to house the new government of the Cochinchina secretariat, the administrative department that included the former Directorate of the Interior. According to the 1903–6 dossier of borrowers, nearly a thousand request slips were submitted to the Cochinchina Library requesting permission to borrow books to read at home.[39] Although the library was not yet an official lending library, both French and Vietnamese governmental officials and nonofficials requested permission to borrow books and take them out of the library. As evident in the borrowing logs from 1907, the Cochinchina Library expanded beyond serving French government officials to serve the larger Saigon colonial public, including French businessmen, women, teachers, and a growing community of Vietnamese government officials, journalists, merchants, and students.[40] According to the newly created Cochinchina Library catalog, the collections held the following wide-ranging materials: general works (almanacs, dictionaries, manuals), law (political economy, codes, jurisprudence), science (philosophy, morality, religion, medicine, technology), culture (colonialism), history and biography (French, army, modern), geography-ethnography-travel (Europe, Asia, Indochina, Africa), literature (literary criticism, children's books, novels, poetry, plays), and art (music, albums).[41] By 1909 the library collection featured over ten thousand books and periodicals on science, history, literature, and law.

AN ORDERLY COLONIAL STATE: PAUL BOUDET AND THE DIRECTORATE OF ARCHIVES AND LIBRARIES OF INDOCHINA

In an attempt to rationalize and centralize the bureaucracy, on November 29, 1917, Governor General Albert Sarraut (who served 1911–14 and 1917–19) issued decrees to centralize at scale Indochina libraries, archives management, and public records into a unified Directorate, integrating Indochina procedures with French documentation across metropole and colonies.[42] The Directorate outlined a standardized classification structure for an expandable, infinitely divisible letter and decimal system according to thematic categories, allowing for a replicable system of documentation throughout the administrative offices in Indochina. Furthermore, the Directorate would guide the development of public libraries with collections of "indispensable, useful, and interesting" materials and hold "permanent technical control" of uniform structure and order.[43] Lara Jennifer Moore described "order" as characteristic of the nineteenth-century French Republic's bureaucratic pursuit to enact national control over French cultural heritage and public knowledge through the creation of national library collections, archives, universal French national bibliographies, and standardized methods of *bibliothéconomie* (library sciences).[44] By the French Third Republic (1870–1940), the intertwined building of the French Republic national libraries and archives informed the French colonial government in Indochina, which considered the task of documentation a fundamental imperative for the building of an orderly and functional colonial state.

A centralized archives and libraries system would preserve publications and government documentation for everyday operations as well as record colonial history for posterity. Furthermore, the French colonial Directorate efforts in Indochina in the first decades of the twentieth century intersected with international documentation movements and modernist efforts to reimagine public libraries, bibliography, and information organization.[45]

On November 30, 1917, Sarraut appointed Paul Boudet (1888–1948) as director of the newly centralized Directorate of Archives and Libraries in Indochina. French libraries administrator André Masson described Boudet as an ambitious, "extraordinary twenty-eight-year-old-leader" who "tirelessly pursued a policy of construction and development according to the most modern standards of library science and archival work."[46] As the only colonial-era director, Paul Boudet built his entire career in Indochina leading the development and standardization of technical practices on libraries, archives, and documentation. Paul Boudet approached the work of libraries in Indochina as a scholar and bureaucrat. As director of the Hanoi Central Library and the Directorate, Boudet envisioned his work to be a scholarly research mission to curate the colonial history of Indochina and to define universal knowledge through the library collections. As a graduate of the hybrid archives-libraries Chartes school (1909–14), Boudet was trained in textual curation of a national record and the work of paleography, or the study of writing systems and the dating of historic documents. Boudet spearheaded the institutionalization of colonial knowledge through managing the Directorate, publishing comprehensive Indochina bibliographies and organizing exhibitions on colonial history from the library and archives collections. For example, for the Paris Colonial Exhibition in 1931, Boudet and Masson also compiled and published a collection of valuable iconography related to the long history of French involvement in Indochina, from Catholic missionaries in the seventeenth century to official intervention in the nineteenth century.[47] Along with his administrative duties, Boudet was actively involved in academic life in the colonies. His personnel files in the Archives Nationales d'outre mer, the colonial archives in Aix-en-Provence, France, reveal a wealth of unpublished research manuscripts on topics such as Vietnamese history from the tenth to eighteenth centuries, Vietnamese intellectual figures, the precolonial Vietnamese and Cambodian administrative systems, and studies of architecture, book history, and archives in Europe, as well as the relations between Indochina and Japan, Cambodia, China, Laos, and Siam. Boudet taught history and geography at the École de droit et de pédagogie de Hanoi (1918–22) and Vietnamese history at the Faculté de droit de l'Indochine (1939–45). A member of the Council of Scientific and Historical Research, the EFEO, and the Society of Geography in Hanoi, Boudet also published in the *Extrême-Asie* and *Revue indochinoise* (and served as its director from 1925 to 1930).

Over the course of his career, Boudet was also informed by the French popular library movement and the American and English public libraries movement,

FIGURE 3. Paul Boudet in his office at the Hanoi Central Library, 1920s. *Source*: Archives Privées Papiers Boudet 86, Archives nationales d'outre-mer, Aix-en-Provence, France, folder 52.

which raised questions of public access and the moralization of the masses. The French popular library movement gained momentum in the late nineteenth century, spearheaded by booksellers, industrialists, and artisans who created associations and reading lists of "good books." This movement intersected with a rise in French education and literacy and a growing demand to revitalize public (state-funded municipal) libraries to serve a greater population of readers beyond erudite scholars.[48] Boudet drew from metropole library models, library science approaches, and global public library movements, experimenting with and elaborating his vision of libraries in the colonial context of Indochina. Throughout his career, colonial libraries in Indochina took on overlapping and at times contradictory characteristics in attempts to be encyclopedic, centralized, state sponsored, scholarly, and public.

HANOI CENTRAL LIBRARY AS ENCYCLOPEDIC REPOSITORY OF COLONIAL KNOWLEDGE

On September 1, 1919, the Hanoi Central Library, also called the Central Public Library of Indochina, opened on 31 rue Borgnis-Desbordes in the French administrative quarter of Hanoi. The library was regulated by the inspector general of public instruction, the director of higher education, and the governor general of Indochina, and it was managed by the director of archives and libraries, Paul Boudet.

FIGURE 4. Building complex and gardens of the Central Library (background left) and Central Archives building (foreground right), ca. 1935. *Source*: Archives Privées Papiers Boudet 86, Archives nationales d'outre-mer, Aix-en-Provence, France, folder 52.

At the end of a grand entryway lined with ornate vases and hedges, the library was situated within a landscaped gated complex of buildings that included the Central Archives of Indochina. These French colonial beaux arts–style buildings stood on the former space of Confucian literary examination campgrounds and Nguyễn bureaucratic authority.[49] The Central Archives occupied the former palace of the Kinh Lược (viceroy), the representative of the Vietnamese Hue court authority in Tonkin, which was created in 1886, when the French colonial administration began to separate the northern Vietnamese region from the complete authority of the Nguyễn Hue court. The viceroy position was abolished on July 26, 1897, and the French colonial resident superior (*résident supérieur du Tonkin*) assumed the duties as a representative of the Nguyễn court. This dissolution in 1897 formally stripped the Nguyễn court of its authority, removing the ability to appoint a mandarin administrative class in the northern region. The archives of the Kinh Lược Sự were integrated into the Central Archives and included documents from 1837 onward, reflecting materials of a transitional and overlapping government authority: from archival materials on the triennial examinations and imperial patents, to documents on colonial soldiers and pirates.[50] The construction of the library, archives, and colonial governmental buildings was a continuation of the architectural transformation of Hanoi under Governor General Paul Doumer (who served 1897–1902) into a grandiose colonial administrative capital of the French colonial union beginning in 1902.

From its beginnings, the expansive Central Library building included a reading hall, lending section, a newspaper and magazine room, working offices for the administration, book binding, copyright, and bibliography, and an extensive book storage depot. In 1919 Paul Boudet also proposed the reorganization of existing libraries and the establishment of new lending libraries following the

Hanoi Central Library in the cities of Haiphong, Saigon, Hue, Phnom Penh, and Vientiane. Each of the five territories of Indochina would continue to maintain its regional library and archive with a deputy director, who reported back to the director in Hanoi. Boudet explained the organization of the Indochina archives as a "favorable decentralization . . . with a unity of technical methods."[51] The Directorate of Archives and Libraries in Hanoi outlined technical protocols for documentation and the classification of archives and libraries throughout Indochina, yet in reality the surveillance system of paperwork, records, and publications varied widely based on specific personnel and the local needs of each regional archive and library.

Paul Boudet envisioned the new Central Library to be a model library marked by modern functionality, comprehensiveness, links to the metropole, and wide public access, functioning as an essential institution of public knowledge within the landscape of public education.[52] These evolving missions and the everyday use of the central libraries in Hanoi and Saigon by the widening colonial public distinguished them from their sister organization, the EFEO, whose mission was to focus on specialist knowledge on Indochina. Cécile Capot also notes the distinguishing characteristic of the EFEO and Directorate as a division of private scientific research and public documentation.[53] In a newspaper article published prior to the opening of the Central Library, the author praised Paul Boudet's organizational efforts and the potential for the new Central Library to provide an important resource to Hanoi, described as "the capital, intellectual, and university center of Indochina."[54] The author anticipated the future of the library with optimism: "One will find at the library all the documentation presented by the service in an economical way: reports, notices, statistics, etc. This will be of great use. University students will replace the library staff in the evening, and thus be introduced to the science of classification and preservation of books." The author argued the importance of the library as a methodologically organized "set of tools built according to the newest progressive [methods], bringing together the shelves, files, card catalogs."[55] As characterized by this newspaper article on the Central Hanoi Library, libraries were idealized as "modern," technically advanced, and centralized institutions of documentation.

Throughout the colonial period, the Hanoi Central Library carried out two priorities in its collections policy: First, it pursued encyclopedic comprehensiveness, shaped by epistemological notions of order and literary value grounded in a Western canon. Second, as the premier library in the capital of the Indochina union, the Hanoi Library operated like a "national" repository of all materials produced in French Indochina as well as a reference collection of materials on the Extrême-Orient (Far East). In a 1927–28 report Boudet listed the addition of notable works of value into the Hanoi Central Library general collection: the "best editions of Greek and Latin authors," such as *Bibliotheca classica latina* by Lemaire and the Guillaume Budé collection; texts from the Middle Ages such as *Société des anciens textes français*; the "great French classics" in the collection *Les grands écrivains de la France*; histories of art in antiquity by Georges Perrot and Charles Chipiez; and several works by Eugène Emmanuel Viollet-le-Duc on French architecture such as *Le Dictionnaire de l'architecture*; and several volumes on French art history by Paul Gauthier such as *Villes d'art, Petites monographies de grands édifices*, and *Les grands artistes*.[56] The subsequent annual Directorate report listed notable works that included Western classics and reference collections on art history, archaeology, classics, science, and technology that covered an expansive time period, from classical antiquity through the nineteenth century. These annual reports on notable additions of valuable books points to how the Hanoi Central Library functioned to canonize a body of Francophone literary classics and reference works within its library collections.

Besides serving as an encyclopedic library, the Hanoi Central Library also functioned like a "national" library of Indochina to organize regional and public libraries, to preserve all the works published in Indochina through legal deposit, and to broadcast its collections through bibliographies. In this way the Hanoi Central Library functioned like a representative colonial extension from the metropolitan Bibliothèque nationale de France in Paris. Paul Boudet argued that the Indochina legal deposit, the requirement that copies of new publications be sent to Hanoi and Paris, was essential to building the collections of the Hanoi Central Library and the French National Library. Prior to the formation of the Directorate, the colonial administration loosely applied a French law requiring legal deposit from 1881 to new publications in Indochina. During these years only a limited number of Indochinese materials, primarily from Cochinchina, made their way to France.[57] In 1919 Boudet proposed the following regime for legal deposit: Four copies of all publications (including all print media such as books, pamphlets, newspapers, images, maps, and records) published in Indochina must be filed to the legal deposit by the publisher. Two of those legal deposit copies were then transferred to the French National Library, one to the Central Library in Hanoi, and one to respective regional branches of the five Indochina *pays*.[58] For example, a publication from Cochinchina must submit one copy to the Saigon Library, one to the Hanoi Central Library, and two to the National Library of France. Boudet concluded that with this application of legal deposit, "the Central Library would become both an encyclopedic library—indispensable in an intellectual center like Hanoi—and a deposit of all that is printed in Indochina."[59] In a 1927 report to the Ministry of Colonies in Paris, Maurice Monguillot, the secretary to the governor general of Indochina, summarized the successes of the legal deposit: "Effective control has been exercised over the literary production of the five *pays* of the union. Shipments are made regularly every month to the National Library of France. Every semester, the Directorate of Archives and Libraries publishes in the *Journal officiel de l'Indochine française* a list of works deposited during the six preceding months."[60] The National Bibliography of France included some of these

Indochinese publications in its yearly bibliography. Monguillot remarked that the legal deposit and bibliography publications brought international attention to Indochinese literary culture and cited how the New York Public Library, the John Crerar Library of Chicago, the American Geographical Society, the Library of the National Assembly of Czechoslovakia, the Library of Brussels, and the Library of the Colonial Institute of Rome requested published lists of the legal deposits from Indochina. Central to the new colonial information order, the legal deposit and bibliography created a surveillance system to understand, record, and preserve the publication record in French colonial Indochina.

In the Central Hanoi Library, the special Indochinese Far East Collection, separate from the general collection, developed from the Indochina legal deposit and through purchases of orientalist scholarship published in France. Boudet noted the procurement of "rare principal books" into the Far East collection, including the following: *Relation du voyage de monseigneur l'évêque de Béryte, vicaire apostolique du royaume de la cochinchine*, by M. de Bourges (1668); the *Lettres édifiantes et curieuses sur la visite apostolique de M. de la Baume évêque d'Halicarnasse à la Cochinchine en l'année 1749*, by M. Faure (1753); and the *Dictionarium annamitico-latinum*, by Pigneau de Béhaine, the bishop of Adran, edited in 1838 by Monseigneur Taberd. "The most precious of our ancient books is the *Catechismus pro iis qui volunt suscipere baptismum* by father Alexandre de Rhodes (1651), the first work printed in *quốc ngữ*, that was freely given to the library by M. Salles, inspector of the colonies."[61] Many of the works noted in the reports were first-edition works of early European explorers and missionaries in the Indochina region from the seventeenth to eighteenth centuries. Over the course of the colonial period, the Hanoi Central Library reading room collection reflected two acquisitions priorities: first, the general collection, which was dominated by European and French classics in a pursuit of "encyclopedic" comprehensiveness; and second, a Far East collection reflecting orientalist scholarship acquisitions and the Indochina legal deposit repository of literary production in colonial Indochina. The collections of the Hanoi Central Library also incorporated the collections from previous nineteenth- and early twentieth-century Hanoi libraries, including the Superior Residence, Tonkin Popular, and Franco-Vietnamese Libraries. The majority of the works in the Hanoi collection were in French, yet through the legal deposit, vernacular languages such as Vietnamese *quốc ngữ*, Literary Sinitic, and Khmer were also represented in the Indochina collections, coinciding with the rise of vernacular print industries from the 1930s onward. As elaborated in the following chapter, the lending section collection reflected a different collecting regime from the reading room General and Far East collections and served a diverse reading public with expansive literary interests, demands for contemporary bestsellers, and language needs in both French and Vietnamese.

The organization of the Hanoi Central Library reflected Enlightenment ideas of classification of knowledge and curation by experts. During his tenure, Boudet developed important classification schemes for the archives and libraries and produced the first abridged annual bibliography of books published in Indochina, *Bibliographie de l'Indochine*, published in 1922. The bibliography was prefaced by the essay "Pour mieux connaître l'Indochine: Essai d'une bibliographie" (To Better Know Indochina: Essay on Bibliography), in which Paul Boudet justified the importance of a "useful" bibliography of works published on Indochina.[62] Boudet criticized existing bibliographies for being "too complete," motivated by "vain curiosity" and an intellectual impulse to create totalizing, overly scholarly knowledge; these bibliographies did not efficiently and systematically curate the "imposing mass of colonial literature."[63] Boudet perceived his project as a synthesis of knowledge on Indochina with a functional use for a wider public of scholars, government officials, students, teachers, and businessmen alike. Besides the *Bibliographie de l'Indochine* project, Boudet also proposed a more concise, efficient reference bibliography only for colonial officials. The booklet would be brief but would contain all the "necessary" information and allow French officials to "become familiar with the colony."[64] Drawing a connection between empire and knowledge, Boudet argued that Frenchmen, scholars, and writers were "dangerously" uninformed about even elementary aspects regarding Indochina:

> One is amazed to find in every instance ignorance where colonial questions arise, even with the cultured Frenchman: The most elementary geographic concepts, situation of countries, nomenclature of major cities and rivers are the occasion of resounding blunders still frequent in our time. One easily confuses Laos and Cambodia, Tonkin and Cochinchina. This ignorance is not without danger. It breeds disinterest in the French with regard to programs emphasizing the commercial, industrial, or social development of our colonies. It estranges the scholars and writers from colonial concerns and problems. It allows for the most perfidious campaigns against our administration. It discredits the colonial profession and turns people away from taking these already unpopular jobs.[65]

Boudet explained that this ignorance produced a sense of estrangement from colonial concerns and undermined the colonial administration. Drawing parallels to analogous "French indifference" in French West Africa, Boudet explained that Georges Hardy, former director of education of French West Africa, had suggested that a remedy to indifference was the organization of colonial history and documentation. Boudet concluded his essay with the mission of the bibliography: to help "better understand and love the beautiful country of Indochina." Both Paul Boudet and the governor general of Indochina, Pierre Pasquier, emphasized the important symbolic and logistical significance of documents for government officials; they embodied the colonial administrative past, its leaders, and its philosophies.[66]

MONUMENTS OF CIVILIZATION AND THE FRANCO-VIETNAMESE COLLABORATION

The founding of a new French colonial system of archives and libraries between 1917 and 1919 coincided with several administrative and symbolic ruptures characterized as a "modernization" of Vietnamese culture and society under French tutelage and colonial modernity. Under the auspices of the governor general of Indochina, Albert Sarraut, the Direction de l'enseignement supérieur de l'Indochine (Directorate of Higher Education of Indochina) was founded in 1917, the Vietnamese mandarin examination system was dissolved in 1918, and a new cultural and political era of Franco-Vietnamese collaboration (*collaboration Franco-Annamite, Pháp-Việt đề huề* or *hợp tác Pháp quốc Annam*) was initiated in 1919.[67] On April 27, 1919, in the heart of Hanoi at the Temple of Literature (Văn Miếu), an important Confucian examinations site that also held the stone stelae bearing the names and birthplaces of successful exam candidates, Albert Sarraut announced the beginning of a Franco-Vietnamese collaboration. The famous speech declared the transformation of the educational system and cultural orientations of Vietnamese intellectuals away from an "outmoded" Confucian education toward an aspirational French model of modern education and Western knowledge. Ben Tran describes this intellectual and political break from a Confucian literati world toward a colonial modernity of bureaucracy and intellectual tradition as "post-mandarin."[68] Sarraut envisaged a liberal republican form of colonial rule based on a collaborative association between Vietnamese and French political and economic elites. Given the relatively small number of French settlers to Indochina, the expanded training of Vietnamese colonial bureaucrats was essential to carry out the colonial operations throughout the five *pays* of Indochina. Franco-Vietnamese collaboration was marked by the rhetoric of republican reform, social welfare, and civic representation, which ultimately justified a stronger and sustained French colonial state authority.[69] The push toward a stronger top-down colonial authority reflected repeated political crises between 1907 and 1908 and 1930 and 1931 sparked by anticolonial uprising, student movements, and communist activity.[70] Furthermore, many of the cultural and political policies were interwoven with economic motivations of *mise en valeur* (economic development, exploitation, and modernization) to develop Indochina into a financially viable economic resource for France and to retain global power in the aftermath of the First World War.[71] During his two terms in office (1912–14 and 1917–19), Sarraut implemented his policy of Franco-Vietnamese collaboration through the transformation of the following institutions: the creation of an indigenous affairs bureau, the expansion of local councils, an increase in the size of the Cochinchinese Colonial Council to include more Vietnamese, the reopening of the Indochinese University in Hanoi (which was opened in 1906 and closed in 1908), and the development of Franco-indigenous education elaborated in the next chapter.[72]

The Central Library was indispensable to this new Franco-Vietnamese stage in colonialism that moved away from hegemonic assimilation to collaborative "association" characterized as modernizing projects of development of the local economy, education system, urban landscape, and government institutions. Shortly after the opening of the Hanoi Central Library, Vietnamese librarian Nguyễn Khắc Nguyên wrote a press release calling for his Vietnamese compatriots to visit the library.[73] The announcement was published in the pages of the magazine *Trung Bắc Tân Văn* on September 24, 1919. Emphasizing the public good of the library, he declared, "This library is like a higher education establishment for all, from the farmer to the official, to come and learn and improve their professional skills and develop their intelligence." With glowing and earnest praise for the colonial state and libraries, Nguyên declared,

> How fortunate we are to have Governor General Albert Sarraut, who always thinks to improve the future of our country. He established many great public works in Indochina, such as the library where you can find all kinds of books. And possibly due to the grace and politics of this good Chief of Colonies, our Annam [Vietnam] stands among the powerful nations of the world. Oh! My dear compatriots, come, let us come in crowds to learn in this library, not to betray the hope of our country and that of the Governor General Sarraut![74]

Along with the large-scale French colonial public infrastructure projects such as schools, roads, train stations, and opera houses, libraries were an important part of transforming the urban landscape of Hanoi. The Hanoi Central Library was located in the heart of the administrative French quarter, an expansive grid-patterned construction of French colonial administrative buildings surrounding the east and south of Hoàn Kiếm Lake in Hanoi, including city hall, the chamber of commerce and agriculture, the governor's palace, and villa residences for colonial officials. Addressing Vietnamese readers, Nguyên exclaimed that the library served as a public extension of education, contributing to the advancement of the Vietnamese civilization and "the future of our country." Emphasizing the importance of education for empowerment, he stated, "Today we are ignorant, we do what we can. But when we gain sufficient education, we can better our conditions of existence." Calling the Vietnamese "powerless" and "poor," Nguyên bid his readers to look to their neighbors, Japan and China, as models of civilizational empowerment through study abroad in the West. "See our neighbors: Japan and China. Why have they sent their children to Europe or America? It is not to spread [their own civilization to other countries] but to collect the seeds of great civilizations from two worlds." Nguyên concluded with a reminder that the library was truly open for all Indochinese—both Vietnamese and Europeans. Vietnamese library administrators such as Nguyễn Khắc Nguyên along with Vietnamese journalists and elites reproduced the language of the civilizing mission and the reformist political discourse of the Franco-Vietnamese collaboration.[75]

French library administrators envisioned libraries such as the Central Library as an institution of global French cultural propaganda for the colonial public of French expatriates as well as local readers. Henri Lemaître (1881–1946), the French librarian, researcher, and director of the metropolitan-based publications *Revue des bibliothèques* and *Archives et bibliothèques*, commented extensively on the extraordinary operations of the Hanoi Central Library in comparison to other French colonial libraries and foreign libraries. In the Parisian-based colonial newspaper *Dépêche coloniale*, Lemaître reported that each month the Hanoi Central Library had 2,300 reader visits (800 French and 1,500 Vietnamese), and readers consulted a total of 1,800 volumes and 900 periodicals.[76] By the end of 1925, the reading room of the library collection had nearly forty thousand volumes of carefully selected books. The most demanded works were those on literature, science, philosophy, mathematics, history, art, current affairs, and the Far East. According to Lemaître's records, the lending section had about ten thousand volumes and five thousand readers registered with borrowing cards.[77] Each year approximately sixty thousand book-lending requests were submitted, averaging out to twelve volumes borrowed by each reader a year.[78] Lemaître compared these numbers to the great libraries in France, many of which had far fewer reader visits. Lemaître described the diverse groups of readers in the Central Library reading room and lending section: professors and scientists researching a specific technical question or relaxing with a novel, or a Vietnamese person wishing to understand Western knowledge. Lemaître claimed that reading in the library offered a cultural and civilizing potential, teaching Vietnamese readers French language through French literature. Lemaître observed that in the Hanoi Central Library there was a comparatively high "taste for serious reading" among readers, who read philosophy and science, and the number of Hanoi readers of literature exceeded the number commonly seen in other libraries. Lemaître concluded that Indochina stood as the first of the French colonies that had developed an extensive library system and approach, and he encouraged continued government investment to develop the existing libraries and create new ones. He concluded that there was an overt double interest to continue this work of library development in Indochina: "social first, then national."[79] Gesturing toward social progress through libraries in Indochina, Lemaître's primary interests in colonial libraries were to serve as an extension of French national culture overseas. Committed to the development of French libraries and the librarianship profession in the metropole, Lemaître served from 1924 to 1934 as editor in chief of the *Revue des bibliothèques*, the important publication of the Association des bibliothécaires français (ABF, or Association of French Librarians).[80] A month later Lemaître published another article comparing libraries in the colonies, classifying the libraries by regional French colonial projects.[81] In Asia, he noted the comprehensive Indochina system of libraries and lists libraries in Pondicherry (French India), Saint-Denis (Réunion), Nouméa (New Caledonia), and Tahiti (French Polynesia); for Africa, he critiqued the limited library developments, which were limited to a library in Saint Louis (Senegal) and Conakry (French Guinea); and for the Caribbean and Latin America, he briefly listed the Schoelcher Library in Fort-de-France (French Antilles), the Pointe-à-Pitre and Basse-Terre libraries (Guadeloupe), and the Franconie Library in Cayenne (French Guiana). Lemaître was concerned primarily with the communication of French books and French culture overseas and concluded his analysis by focusing on the importance of libraries for the French colonial expatriates who lived in cultural isolation from France.[82]

In comparison to Lemaître, Paul Boudet envisioned the Central Library as serving the wide demographics of the changing colonial public in Hanoi—from French colonial expatriates and state officials to Vietnamese intellectual elites and the youth of the Indochinese University in Hanoi.[83] Boudet emphasized that with the extensive Indochina legal deposit and collections, the library was vital for academics and the general everyday user. Surrounded by gardens and equipped with adequate lighting, the library reading room offered "workers and simple readers a pleasant and quiet retreat."[84] Boudet also situated the library and archives as central to the "liberal and emancipatory politics" of Sarraut's educational- and republican-inspired social reform.[85] The Hanoi Central Library stood as a monument to Franco-Vietnamese collaboration, and as a crowning achievement of an enlightened republican form of collaboration between East and West, Vietnamese and French.

In 1935 the Hanoi Central Library was renamed the Bibliothèque de Pierre Pasquier in a highly publicized series of events and exhibitions commemorating the governor general of Indochina, Pierre Pasquier, who served from 1928 and 1934 and died suddenly in an airplane crash.[86] Under the presence of Governor General René Robin (who served as acting governor general in 1928, 1930, and 1934), the inauguration of the newly renamed Pierre Pasquier Library was attended by a large number of French officials, librarians, and scholars, such as the secretary general Y. C. Chatel, the director of public instruction Captain Bernard, the director of the EFEO Georges Cœdès, the resident superior official Émile Vayrac, officials from the departments of radiotelegraph, finances, and customs, and university faculty. Also present were representatives of Vietnamese associations, president of the Society of Mutual Education in Tonkin, and the minister of education (court of Hue) Phạm Quỳnh.[87] During the renaming ceremony two stone tablets commemorating Pasquier were constructed on the sides of the main library entryway.

Embossed with gold lettering, one in Latin, one in *chữ hán* and *chữ nôm*, the memorials declared the following:

> The Central Library of Indochina was established from 1917. The former governor general of Indochina, Pierre Pasquier, was a devotee and lover of literature and fine arts. On January 15, 1934, he died in an accident while returning to France. His name was chosen to be given to this library. On February 28, 1935, the governor general of Indochina René Robin came to erect the stone tablets in the presence of the resident superior of Tonkin, Auguste Tholance, the resident mayor of Hanoi, Henri Virgitti, the director of the Archives and Libraries of Indochina, Paul Boudet, and young students of Hanoi.

The decision to engrave the memorials in Latin and Sinitic characters reinforced the symbolic importance of the Central Library as a public monument of "Thái-Tây và Á-đông" (West and East), where the Franco-Vietnamese Hanoi library stood as the legitimate inheritor of two classical worlds of letters.[88] Boudet's speech at the public inaugural event was widely publicized in the French and Vietnamese press. A Vietnamese-language newspaper summarized Boudet's public speech, which described the sanctity of the library space that continued to bear the scholarly aura from the previous generations of Confucian examination candidates.[89] Boudet spoke of the tremendous cultural transformations of Vietnamese culture and its orientations toward the West, where "modern attire has almost completely replaced the austere dress and turbans. Where [there are] no more Chinese-style brushes and inkwells, no more papers with silky reflections. Traditional culture has given way to European letters and sciences."[90] Notably, Boudet emphasized the important position of the Directorate as conservator of "traditional culture" (displaced by Western knowledge) through the public mounting of the two inscriptions written in "an antiquated script," Latin and Sinitic. A close friend of Pierre Pasquier during his time in Indochina, Paul Boudet affirmed that these symbolic inscriptions honored Pasquier as a "protector of letters and arts" and reflected Pasquier's fondness for classical antiquity and tradition. Besides declaring the Pierre Pasquier Library as a public monument of West and East, antiquity and modernity, the inauguration ceremony reaffirmed the role of the Directorate as a repository of colonial heritage and history. The ceremony included a tour of the grounds for the honorary government officials as well as an extensive exhibition of colonial books and images featuring archival materials from the navy admiral rule in Indochina and Pierre Pasquier's research.

From the 1920s to 1940s, internal and public reports of the Central Library would reiterate the rhetoric of a mutually beneficial Franco-Vietnamese collaboration, where the French colonial relationship was necessary to guide and develop civilizing projects such as libraries, schools, and cultural conservation. Yet the Franco-Vietnamese collaboration existed with its inherent contradiction

FIGURE 5. Commemorative stone tablet engraved in Latin, 1935. *Source*: Direction des archives et des bibliothèques, Trung tâm lưu trữ quốc gia 1, Hanoi, Vietnam, folder 598.

FIGURE 6. Commemorative stone tablet engraved in *chữ hán* and *chữ nôm*, 1935. The top line reads “Pierre Pasquier,” phonetically written in *chữ nôm*, 悲吣 Pierre 博稽 Pastier, followed by “library” (thư viện 書院), 1935. *Source*: Direction des archives et des bibliothèques, Trung tâm lưu trữ quốc gia 1, Hanoi, Vietnam, folder 598.

FIGURE 7. Façade of Hanoi Central Library, renamed the Pierre Pasquier Library at an inauguration event on February 28, 1935. *Source*: Direction des archives et des bibliothèques, Trung tâm lưu trữ quốc gia 1, Hanoi, Vietnam, folder 598.

of liberation within hegemony: The promise of cultural, political, and economic development of Indochina into a modern "civilization" and eventual independence from France was left ambiguous and unfulfilled.[91]

EVERYDAY TACTICS: LIBRARY LABOR AND SOCIAL HIERARCHIES

"To document" encapsulated a set of technical practices and philosophical assumptions grounded in the evolving field of *bibliothéconomie* (library sciences) that brought together Enlightenment notions of classification, French documentation sciences, and Anglo-American library professionalization.[92] These international currents in library training and technical procedures were discussed in sections of Vietnamese periodicals and became topics of debate through the technical operations of the Directorate of Archives and Libraries of Indochina.[93] Within the context of colonial Indochina, the profession of archivist-librarian emerged as a distinct labor system of technical training, social mobility, and government operations. A cohort of French "Chartists" (trained at the École des Chartes in Paris for archives and libraries) served high general management positions as *conservateurs* (curators or head librarians of the regional library branch) or *archivistes-bibliothécaires* (archivist-librarians from ranks one through four) and established the majority of their documentation careers rotating around posts in Indochina. For much of the nineteenth and early twentieth centuries, the division between archives and libraries was not disciplinarily rigid, and the École des Chartes trained archivists-librarians as scholars of documentation and curation.[94] Notably, the Chartists Paul Boudet, André Masson, Rémi Bourgeois, Simone de Saint-Exupéry, and Ngô Đình Nhu and the non-Chartist Léon Saint-Marty contributed to building collections, developing operations manuals, organizing exhibitions of historic documents, and training indigenous secretaries and archivist-librarians throughout Indochina. This cohort of Chartists drew from their metropole training in French documentation and attempted to carry out "control work," the replicable management of print matter through accounting for its material conditions, bibliographic information, and its circulation or "communication" to readers in the colony. However, throughout the colonial period French techniques of documentation and preservation had to be adapted to a very different and often challenging environment of untrained laborers, lack of personnel, and a tropical climate of humidity and pests. Besides the higher-level Chartists who held managerial positions, most of the librarian personnel in Indochina were Vietnamese men who held lower-level positions such as secretaries, reading room overseers, orderlies, night guards, and groundskeepers. In the Saigon Library, many of the lower-level library-archivist and secretarial positions were also held by French women who were not formally trained at Chartes.

Librarian staff tactically moved through the internal dynamics of library operations and interactions with the broader reading public. Everyday conflicts between workers and readers, French and Vietnamese, are scattered throughout internal library documentation. Chartes-trained André Masson (1900–1986) worked as a curator alongside Boudet in the Directorate of Archives and Libraries in Hanoi from 1926 to 1934. Masson recounted some of the violent library dramas he encountered at the library and archives service in Hanoi.[95] In one account he discovered an archive clerk had committed suicide hanging from the rafters, his feet floating above a stack of archival folders—the same folders that were the reason for a verbal reprimand by Masson the day prior. In another instance Masson witnessed a French nun throw their journey fare to the ground to avoid touching the hand of a Vietnamese chauffeur.[96] According to an internal letter between the Cochinchina reading room secretary and the library curator, readers on entering the library found the groundskeeper Ngô Văn Tố shirtless, lying on one of the tables in the reading room, apparently making the library space his "home" and the downstairs steps his "bathroom" during closing hours.[97] While these accounts fall on the extreme spectrum of altercations and dramas in the library, they point to an underlying everyday tension among library personnel, managers, lower-level staff, and library patrons.

The majority of Vietnamese lower-level library personnel were acutely managed by Chartist-trained directors on the basis of "conduct, morality, professionalism, duties, and manner of service."[98] On June 14, 1925, the curator of the Saigon Cochinchina Library, Léon Saint-Marty, reported to the Office of Personnel the many misbehaviors and constant tardiness of library assistant Lê Thế Vĩnh: "He reads constantly during hours of the Lending Service. Distracted, he made many errors, forgetting to record certain works borrowed by readers and on the other hand also wrongly recorded works already returned, which he had neglected to erase."[99] Over time, Lê Thế Vĩnh became the central object of Saint-Marty's criticisms of Vietnamese personnel. Saint-Marty described Vĩnh's neglect of his duties as being so numerous that they "profoundly affected the proper functioning of the [library] service . . . which requires impeccable attention and goodwill."[100] Vietnamese personnel of the Cochinchina Library were often the most avid readers, borrowing up to four books each time. For example, in 1925 Lê Thế Vĩnh borrowed works of French poetry, French grammar books, and a book on physics.[101] At times, Vietnamese librarians' reading behavior interfered with their work, much to the chagrin of French library administrators. Administrators submitted regular monthly reports on the state of the libraries—from the collections and statistics of reader use and finances to the performance of library personnel. In the March 1925 report, Saint-Marty wrote, "M. Huê has just returned from leave. He seems a little too preoccupied with his personal affairs. Monsieurs Tuất and Thông provide satisfactory service. The work of Monsieur Lê Thế Vĩnh in his new job in the lending section has a lot to be desired. Bad spirited and lazy. Never at his post. Monsieurs Nhung and Võ Thành Vĩnh of the archives work well but too slowly."[102]

By June 1925 Saint-Marty had grown weary of Lê Thế Vĩnh and fired him from his post. In his letter to the Office of Personnel, Saint-Marty accused Vĩnh of stealing works from the library:

> Finally, to conclude, I think I can no longer show him confidence by committing him to the custody of our collections. The number of works that disappeared during this year is greater than that of any other year. Separate from the transgressions already mentioned, Monsieur Lê Thế Vĩnh has been surprised by the several instances where newspapers, magazines, and books were found at his home that he in fact had not recorded into the loan registry. During the closure of the library [for repair], magazines arrived by courier have disappeared, yet a guard has always closed the doors behind the painters and masons and made sure that their hands and pockets were empty. I am morally convinced that the magazines have been taken by someone in the service. The suspicions are naturally directed to the one who has already been at fault for the same issues.[103]

This case demonstrates how Vietnamese librarian personnel such as Vĩnh were avid readers of the library material, reading during work and possibly taking books home without officially recording them as library loans. Saint-Marty's extensive reporting and criticisms of Lê Thế Vĩnh reveal the hierarchy of French library administrators and their attempts to control the majority Vietnamese staff. The internal policing of lower-level librarian staff also points to the emergence of occupational expectations around the labor of library work. Saint-Marty described the necessity of the "impeccable attention" required of librarian personnel in order to keep an accurate account of library materials. Other commentary on performance such as regarding punctuality, speed, and accountability suggests the professional expectations of a French colonial library and government employee. Yet these critiques of staff misbehaviors perpetuate a racialization of labor norms between French and Vietnamese, with French directors defining idealized professional behavior and Vietnamese being the objects of chastisement. Paul Boudet in Hanoi and Saint-Marty in Saigon were expected to manage their staff in the operational tasks of protecting and conserving the documents for posterity.[104] Following French library and archives law from 1855, the Indochina Directorate of Archives and Libraries also established living quarters within or nearby the buildings for library and archives staff to "protect the works of value," described as the "right of lodging."[105] The director was required to reside within the library and archives compound to conduct "unceasing surveillance" of the materials.

Vietnamese library staff navigated internal hierarchies with their higher-level French Chartist-trained supervisors as well as with French library readers. Vietnamese library clerk T. Phúc reported to Boudet a verbal and physical altercation between him and a French library patron, Monsieur Guy Maurice.[106] Phúc detailed the event and its witnesses, and he begged Boudet to stand up for his rights and reprimand Maurice. The incident was reported as follows: On November 16, 1922, at 7:15 p.m., Phúc was working alone in the lending section of the Central Library. A reader named Guy Maurice brought to the lending desk four books to return tied together in a bundle. Maurice demanded that Phúc untie the bundle of books, record the return, and process four new books to read at home. However, since Phúc was working alone and busy recording the books, he could not untie the bundle of books. Maurice grew angry at Phúc, took his books that had not yet been borrowed, and stormed out of the lending section. Maurice returned with someone named Vinh from the reading room to serve as interpreter; Maurice then proceeded to verbally and publicly insult Phúc, calling him an imbecile, an idiot, a country bumpkin (*nhà quê*). Afterward, Maurice slapped Phúc twice, threw the bundle of books, forced Phúc to record the books, and demanded an orderly to tie up the books. This report is significant because it shows the underlying racial tensions in the library between French patrons and lower-level Vietnamese personnel. Phúc sought justice for this public insult and physical altercation through legal and bureaucratic methods. Phúc cited as witnesses four Vietnamese readers—a diverse group of Vietnamese men, governmental secretaries, and teachers. Phúc also wrote directly to Boudet, calling upon him to stand up for Phúc's legal rights. However, there are no archival documents that show any legal action against or reprimand of Maurice for his behavior.

During the colonial period, most positions in the libraries and archives as well as those in the overall colonial administration were held by men. French women often held lower-level positions in the Directorate, such as secretarial roles, and others held interim positions, such as Madame Catherine Ruffier, who temporarily replaced Saint-Marty as director from February 1922 to August 1923.[107] In 1924 Boudet contested the nomination of Madame Laugier to take up Ruffier's position at the Saigon Library and critiqued the hiring of women, which he considered uneconomical. Boudet criticized the female labor force for being unskilled, unreliable, and expensive, comparing the capacity of Ruffier to even "worse than an indigenous employee or clerk." Boudet declared, "I firmly resolve to give an unfavorable opinion to all female candidates of this kind, who are often hired based on their likeability rather than capability."[108] Boudet proposed instead hiring Monsieur Jean Bouchot in a contracted short-term position as an archivist-librarian in training to support the work of Saint-Marty. Jean Bouchot (1886–1932) was knowledgeable about archives and libraries from his previous work at the French National Library and had completed two years at École des Chartes (though he was not able to complete his degree), and he had worked in China as a journalist and teacher.[109] After hiring Bouchot on March 19, 1926, for the archives and library in Cochinchina, both Boudet and Saint-Marty glowingly praised Bouchot's classification of the archives and methodical work in Saigon.

Throughout the colonial period, only one woman, Simone de Saint-Exupéry, and one Vietnamese person, Ngô Đình Nhu, held permanent administrative management positions in the Directorate of Archives and Libraries and made notable contributions to the Indochina archives and libraries. Simone de Saint-Exupéry (1898–1978), born in Lyon, was the older sister of the famous writer Antoine de Saint-Exupéry. Her personnel dossier noted language skills in Vietnamese, German, English, and Italian. She studied to be an archivist-paleographer at the École des Chartes from 1922 to 1928 and was one of the earliest female graduates of the renowned school. Saint-Exupéry first worked in the archives in Lyon and began to work in the Indochina Directorate in 1931. Noting Saint-Exupéry's formal training at Chartes, Paul Boudet in 1932 recommended that Saint-Exupéry hold a more permanent position as archivist-librarian and replace Bouchot, who had departed due to health reasons in 1930.[110] Saint-Exupéry spent over twenty-five years shaping libraries, archives, and documentation procedures in Indochina and played an important role in the decolonization of the Directorate in the 1950s.[111] In addition to Saint-Exupéry, two other women held notable positions in the Directorate: Paulette Téchiné, Paul Boudet's second wife, worked at the Directorate from 1921 until she passed away in 1934, and Marie-Victoire Duval (who studied at the École des Chartes from 1937 to 1939) worked in Indochina beginning in 1940.[112]

While best known for his political role in the southern postcolonial Vietnamese state, Ngô Đình Nhu also had an extensive and important career as the first Vietnamese Chartes-trained archivist-librarian during the colonial period. Ngô Đình Nhu (1910–63) was born into a scholarly mandarin family in Phước Qua, near Hue. He completed his *baccalauréat* (French high school diploma) in Saigon in Latin, languages, and philosophy.[113] Continuing to expand his interests in languages, Nhu journeyed to Paris in 1931, expanded his study of English, Italian, and Latin, and studied Chinese at the language and cultural institute École nationale des langues orientales vivantes. In 1933 Nhu completed formal studies of history at the elite university in Paris, the Sorbonne. During Nhu's time in France he embedded himself within academic life at the Sorbonne and the École normale supérieure. Nhu also immersed himself in the vibrant political life and helped to organize L'action sociale indochinoise (Indochinese Social Action), a group of Vietnamese emigrés in France who debated a wide range of political and social issues regarding patriotism, nationalism, internationalism, and Bolshevism through the lens of Catholic social thought.[114] Nhu was deeply shaped by philosopher and Sorbonne scholar Emmanuel Mounier, the leading figure of the French personalist movement, which advocated for a balance between the individual and the community.[115] Nhu's early cosmopolitan education, language training, and embeddedness in French political life imprinted a comparative political outlook that might have informed his later political philosophies of Vietnamese personalism and anticommunist nationalism.

In 1934 Nhu began his formal four-year training at Chartes in paleography, Latin translation, philology, theoretical and practical bibliography, French history, and archives, and he completed his internship at a municipal library in Rouen in 1936.[116] In his last year of study he was the first student at Chartes to complete a thesis on Indochina, examining a documentary history of Vietnamese culture through missionary records such as the writings of Father Alexandre de Rhodes. The thesis, titled "Moeurs et coutumes des Tonkinois aux XVIIe et XVIIIe siècles d'après les voyageurs et missionaires" (Culture and customs of Tonkinese in the seventeenth and eighteenth centuries according to travelers and missionaries), received an honorary prize from the French Ministry of National Education. Nhu was officially given the title archivist-paleographer on February 18, 1938, at age twenty-seven, and he was the first Vietnamese person to complete a diploma in archives and libraries from the competitive École des Chartes. In 1938 Nhu was appointed to work in the Central Library in Hanoi alongside Boudet as the deputy curator following André Masson's resignation and departure from Indochina in 1934. During Nhu's time in Hanoi he led the compilation of the extensive three-volume *Recueil général de la législation et de la réglementation de l'Indochine* (General compendium on legislation and regulations of Indochina). Nhu's extensive archival work, organizations of historical exhibitions, and organization of precolonial Vietnamese documents reflect an intertwined technical approach to archival work and historical research.[117] Nhu's extensive French technical training as a Chartist and longtime bureaucratic career within the colonial Indochina government institutions as an archivist-paleographer possibly shaped his approaches to government documentation and national heritage in his later political roles in the postcolonial Republic of Vietnam.[118]

With a limited budget allotted annually from the central colonial government and local administration, the Directorate balanced the considerable costs of personnel, building maintenance, and the expansion and preservation of library collections. In the 1930s, the Great Depression caused a cash flow crisis in the French colonial economy and an overall tightening of administrative budgets.[119] As a consequence, the Directorate shifted its personnel structure to alleviate the fiscal burden of higher-salaried European staff: It reduced its number of European staff at the upper managerial levels to four in Hanoi, two in Saigon, and one in Phnom Penh, and it relied on a cadre of lower-level indigenous personnel to maintain operations.[120] Reforms in personnel included the consolidation of positions so that secretaries now carried out the duties of a librarian assistant and orderlies retrieved books and managed the reading and lending rooms. On October 25, 1930, the colonial administration began to formally train a cadre of lower-level indigenous archivists, librarians, and secretaries.[121] From 1930 to 1945, the Directorate graduated a total of 216 students after successful completion of a six-month internship course, four exit examinations on theory (archives, libraries, book history, and administration), and two tests on archives and libraries practices.[122] Held at the Hanoi Central Library and Central Archives, these courses trained indigenous secretaries, archivists,

FIGURE 8. Participants in a training course for secretaries and archivist-librarians, 1939–1940. In the front row, pictured from left to right, are Directorate archivist-librarians administrators Phạm Đình Giệm, Rémi Bourgeois, Paul Boudet, Ngô Đình Nhu, and Trần Văn Kha. The back row comprises administrators based in Laos, Annam, Hải Dương, and Saigon completing the course. *Source*: Archives Privées Papiers Boudet 86, Archives nationales d'outre-mer, Aix-en-Provence, France, Folder 88.

FIGURE 9. Participants in a training course for secretaries and archivist-librarians, 1942–1943. Seated left to right are Rémi Bourgeois, Paul Boudet, and Simone de Saint-Exupéry. Standing left of Bourgeois is Marie-Victoire Duval. *Source*: Iconothèque 115, Archives nationales d'outre-mer, Aix-en-Provence, France.

and librarians in the following wide range of theoretical and practical skills: protecting the materials from insects and humidity; understanding the Indochinese colonial administration; communicating the collections to government officials and the public; classifying materials, methodic organization and cataloging; library history (the history of libraries in France, America, and Britain) and the history of the book and bibliography in Indochina; types of libraries and library organization (practical knowledge of the reading room and increasing the library collection through purchases, gifts, and legal deposit); and the function of the legal deposit in France and Indochina.[123] By 1932, sixteen out of nineteen of all the Indochinese administrative bodies were staffed with a secretary trained through the six-month Directorate training course.[124] Government officials hoped that these trained personnel would continue to share their organization skills with other government departments, and thus propagate a uniform classification structure for documentation throughout the colonial Indochina administration and provinces. In 1939 the Saigon Cochinchina Library replicated Hanoi's formal training of indigenous archivist-librarians to remedy operations burdened by a "ceaseless coming and going of staff," who were often transferred to other government offices in Saigon.[125] These library scientific training courses offered a socioeconomic pathway of mobility through a wide range of bureaucratic technical training for placement in colonial government positions.

ORDER IN THE LAND OF DISORDER: THE SAIGON COCHINCHINA LIBRARY

Compared to the Hanoi Central Library, the Saigon Cochinchina Library operated in a slapdash, disorderly manner, reflecting the limitations in reliable personnel and a constrained building that housed both the archives and libraries service. The Cochinchina Library had a longer operational history under the management of the local Saigon administration, predating the top-down centralization efforts of the Directorate of Archives and Libraries of Indochina and efforts to build out Hanoi as the administrative capital of Indochina.[126] An unpublished report dated September 1934 illuminates the dismal material conditions of the Cochinchina Library and archives facilities, organization, and collections. The report described the library and archives building as poorly maintained and overrun with pests:

> The building is old and dirty. One enters through a vestibule still cluttered with bicycles; the readers do not know where to go, the reading room is on the first floor intended in the past for only the archives, [the reading room] has walls with holes held together by wire netting to assure the ventilation of the documents. These wire nets retain dust and spider webs. The lending section is one day next to the stairs, on another day in the gallery crowded by furniture over two meters tall, which obstructs

FIGURE 10. Cochinchina Library exterior after its move across the street to 34 rue de Lagrandière, ca. 1930s. Above the front doorway reads "Bibliothèque," and the main reading rooms are located on the floor above. During the colonial period the library continued to share the space with the archives. *Source*: Archives Privées Papiers Boudet 86, Archives nationales d'outre-mer, Aix-en-Provence, France, folder 52.

> the airflow and the daylight. This state of ventilation favors the presence of enormous mosquitos and bats, which bother and discomfort the readers. [The bats] even go so far as to nest on the shelves. Ants crawl all over the walls.[127]

Since 1902 the entire Saigon Library service had functioned in a shared space with the archives on 27 rue de La Grandière in the government secretariat complex. In 1920, the library and archives were moved from the former building across the street to 34 rue de La Grandière (now 34 Lý Tự Trọng), located next to the police station on the corner of Catinat and La Grandière. In 1925, the annual report noted how a quarter of the shelving designated for the archives materials was used for library storage.[128] After thirty years of operation the Saigon archives and library still shared a cramped building, resulting in a haphazard state of conservation and maintenance. On December 16, 1926, the lending section was moved to its own building at 160 rue Catinat, freeing up room for the Saigon Library to have a designated space for the reading room and another room for consulting periodicals.[129]

The 1934 report continued to describe the disorderly state of the library and archive offices:

> Small shelves are scattered around; these hold the old newspapers, incomplete magazines, and pamphlets not yet cataloged. . . . The management office room is cluttered with messy books. The secretariat [administrative] office is next to the reading room. Besides the fact that it is not aesthetically pleasing to see this place in disorder, the constant noise of the typewriters discourages the readers and is already the subject of complaints.[130]

The report did not refrain from targeting the administration's negligence in "maintaining order" in the library collections and in keeping up sanitation on the building grounds. "In the storage room, next to the cataloged books, are shelves littered with uncataloged books and pamphlets and a dusty, motley group of objects: rat traps, rat feces, pieces of wood, old boxes, etc."

Furthermore, library and archives managers were concerned about the budget necessary to sustain the living quarters and proper sanitation for personnel who resided near or within the building complex.[131] The 1934 Cochinchina report criticized the lack of separation between the unhygienic staff living space and the public library and archives services.

> The courtyard and two small storage facilities are the domain of the staff, who have transformed the space into a *village negrè*. Overflowing onto the ground floor of the archives are old clothes, shoes, dirty towels, and toiletries, including several portable washrooms. They cook under the awning, facing the storage building. The wall that separates the courtyard from the registration building is covered in mold and on the verge of ruin. The *boys'* lodging quarters, kitchens, and toilets are attached to this wall next to the registration space, and all the smells uncomfortably mix together. The toilet set up for the library is also in very bad condition and very dirty.[132]

The use of the pejorative "*boys*" (for male domestic servants) and the description of the staff living quarters as a "*village negrè*" reveal the racial condescension toward library and archives staff, who were majority Vietnamese.[133] According to this report, the smells and sight of the Vietnamese living quarters seeped into the space designated for registration of library cards and thus interfered with readers' experiences. This report carried not only an air of racial condescension toward Vietnamese personnel, but also a critical judgment of the overall state of libraries management in Indochina.

By June 1935 several library improvements had been implemented: the building of a garage for bicycles, a new washroom with a modern toilet, new furniture and painting for the reading rooms and offices, and the reorganization of collections for improved reader access. Furthermore, the library restructured its catalog, adopting the methods from the French National Library, and integrated all the collections into a single catalog—described as "flexible and organized in the manner of a dictionary."[134] In addition to these limited improvements, the author of the report emphasized the tremendous need to continue to improve building facilities, classification methods, conservation and bookbinding of materials, and collections size.

DOCUMENTATION TORPOR: LIMITATIONS IN INDOCHINA-WIDE LIBRARY STANDARDIZATION

From the formation of the Directorate in 1917 through the period of late French colonial rule to 1945, the implementation of a comprehensive colonial information order that centralized documentation in Indochina and connected the colonies to the metropole was characterized by documentation torpor and uneven development. From the perspective of the larger French empire, the colonial information order of archives and libraries in Indochina operated with shifting autonomies and was fragmented from the French national documentation regime.[135] The Directorate of Archives and Libraries of Indochina dedicated immense efforts to the task of bibliographic control, the interwoven work of description and classification of archives and publications to organize, preserve, and retrieve materials. This bibliographic control work was a laborious top-down effort to exert documentary comprehensiveness and standardization throughout the five regions of Indochina. Throughout the colonial period, the Directorate repeatedly demanded publishers and printers to follow through with legal deposit. Furthermore, local administrative offices were expected to compile monthly lists of new publications, of which the Directorate in Hanoi would generate its yearly bibliography of new works, the *Bibliographie de l'Indochine*. Attempts to update and produce a yearly bibliography were inconsistent. In 1929 Paul Boudet and Rémi Bourgeois published a retrospective bibliography, *Bibliographie de l'Indochine française 1913–1926*. Rémi Bourgeois (1897–1947) worked alongside Boudet as the chief archives curator during the colonial period and served as interim director from 1938 to 1939.[136] Later volumes of *Bibliographie de l'Indochine française* were published sporadically: Volume 2 was published in 1931 covering the years 1927–29; volume 3, published in 1933, focused on just one year, 1930; and volume 4 covered the years 1930–35 and was not published until 1943.

Ever since the formation of the Directorate in 1919, Paul Boudet had outlined an elaborate legal deposit policy for new publications across the five Indochina regions. On January 31, 1922, the legal deposit law changed the responsibilities from the publisher to the printer and added a timeline for submissions. The new law required the local government offices (of the resident superior or mayor) to transfer the legal deposit copies to the Directorate of Archives and Libraries in Hanoi before the end of each month. Each month the central legal deposit in Hanoi submitted two copies of legal deposits to the Ministry of the Interior in France, which was responsible for distributing one copy to the National Library of France and another copy to a major French library. Yet in implementation, Indochina publishers, authors, and printers found the legal deposit to be a "huge inconvenience" and did not always submit materials to the Indochina legal deposit in Hanoi.[137] By 1925 new legislation required both printers and publishers to legal deposit copies. Although the legal deposit produced an uneven and incomplete record of published materials in Indochina, it provides an important glimpse of the publishing landscape of Indochina and the publishing boom of vernacular publishing in the 1930s.[138] For example, the 1937 legal deposit recorded 938 new works, of which 63.9 percent were in Vietnamese, 25.9 percent were in French, 10.24 percent were in other languages.[139] Furthermore a close analysis of the legal deposit sheds light on the geographic expansiveness of Indochina publishing. For example, Vy Cao's analysis of the legal deposit record uncovers 102 printing and publishing houses in Cochinchina, where local publishing extended beyond the central publishing hub in Saigon to also include Chợ Lớn, Đa Kao, Tân Định, Thủ Dầu Một, and Thủ Đức, as well as other provinces of the Mekong Delta.[140]

The development of libraries in the five regions of Indochina was starkly imbalanced, reflecting the concentration of the colonial administration in the urban centers of Hanoi in Tonkin and Saigon in Cochinchina. The uneven efforts of documentation and colonial development across Indochina can be seen in the imbalanced publishing industry through the recorded number of legal deposits, ranking highest from Tonkin and Cochinchina, followed by materials from Cambodia and Annam, with Laos having the lowest number of recorded deposits.[141] From July to August 1923, Paul Boudet and Nguyễn Khắc Nguyên from the Hanoi Central Library traveled throughout Indochina to inspect and advise the implementation of the information technical standards for libraries and archives in Indochina.[142] A round-trip 4,032-kilometer journey by automobile, rivers, and sea, the pair traveled from Hanoi to Vinh, Hue, Saigon, Phnom Penh, and back to Hanoi. Boudet explained that the focus of this trip was to advise measures for a Hue library, to guide the construction of a new building and improve the personnel working for the Saigon library, and to develop a new library and archives facility in Phnom Penh. The demands for libraries were often not met quickly enough through the top-down official building project of the Directorate of Archives and Libraries, especially in the case of Annam (central Vietnam). Instead, associations such as the Association of Friends of Old Hue and the Society of Mutual Education played a large role in providing reading material to the intellectual and reading communities of Hue as elaborated in chapter 4. A joint archives-library building maintained archival and reference material for the administration through the Superior Residence of Annam in Hue. In 1929, the administrative library called the Bibliothèque de Hue reported having only a small collection of 1,507 volumes and official colonial publications. In the same year, Boudet reflected on the unfortunate absence of a general library freely accessible to the French and Vietnamese public, which could serve as "an indispensable instrument of progress" in the capital of Annam.[143] The Annam resident superior administrative library continued to grow slowly through purchases and donations. In 1939, the administrative library

FIGURE 11. Exterior of the Central Library of Cambodge (foreground), with the archives building in the back, ca. 1930s. The building features a European museum-like structure that combines neoclassical architecture, a portico entrance, and an Italian-style wall design of Cambodian motifs. *Source*: Archives Privées Papiers Boudet 86, Archives nationales d'outre-mer, Aix-en-Provence, France, folder 52.

annexed the library of the École des hautes études (1,514 works), bringing the total number of works to 2,269. After decades of attempts by scholarly associations and the local administration to develop a centralized and dedicated building for a public library and archives in Hue, the Annam central archives and library was opened in 1942, with Ngô Đình Nhu appointed as its director.[144]

The development of libraries in Cambodia and Laos underwent a different path than that of the libraries in Hanoi and Saigon due to their distinctive administrative designation as protectorates and the continued important role of the royal monarchy and Buddhist institutions. After many delays regarding budget and the collections, the Bibliothèque de Phnom Penh (Library of Phnom Penh, also called the Central Library of Cambodge) was opened to the public on December 24, 1924.[145] Placed under the Directorate of Archives and Libraries of Indochina, the Central Library of Cambodge absorbed the Bibliothèque du Protectorat (Library of the Resident Superior of Cambodge), which had functioned from 1897 to 1914. Throughout the colonial period, the Central Library of Cambodge developed a sizable collection of administrative, historical, and periodical reference matter to serve its primary patrons, French and Vietnamese colonial officials. The library also developed a popular lending section that became heavily used by a variety of patrons, including French women and their children, Vietnamese commercial workers, government officials, teachers, Cambodian high school students and royal officials.[146]

The administrative Library of Cambodge was part of the landscape of other important cultural and religious institutions founded during the French colonial period, including the scholarly Royal Library in Phnom Penh, the Institute indigène des études du bouddhisme du petite véhicule (Indigenous Institute for the Study of Buddhism of the Little Vehicle) or the Institut bouddhique (Buddhist Institute), the École Supérieure de Pali, and the Musée du Cambodge (Musée Albert Sarraut). These institutions played important roles in the shaping of twentieth-century Cambodian print culture, national identity, and Buddhism.[147] With its headquarters in Phnom Penh, the Buddhist Institute focused on Pali education and Buddhist publications and promoted a centralized notion of a revived "Indochinese Buddhism" in Cambodia, Laos, and Cochinchina.[148] Colonial development of libraries, archives, and publishing in Laos was significantly limited in scope, budget, and administrative support compared to those in Tonkin, Cochinchina, and Cambodge. Efforts to develop a central and public library as part of the Directorate did not materialize, and instead it appears that only an administrative archive and library existed in the offices of the resident superior during the French colonial period.[149] In 1918 the commissar of government and King Sisavong Vong (1904–59) created the Royal Library of Luang Prabang, which collected manuscripts from the area. The Royal Library was located in the Département des Cultes, managed by the Lao curator Chao Citammarat and organized within the EFEO. According to reports, the Royal Library was used by monks, civil servants, and inhabitants of the Luang Prabang area.[150] In the case of Cambodge and Laos, state archives and libraries focused primarily on administrative tasks and worked closely with royal libraries and the Buddhist Institute.

CONCLUSION

This chapter examined the establishment of a French colonial information order through the creation of the Directorate of Archives and Libraries of Indochina. The colonial information order of libraries, archives, bibliographies, and the legal deposit challenged previous forms of documentary authority grounded in a Vietnamese Confucian-style bureaucracy and Sinitic literary canon. The Directorate and its institutions were driven by the political, cultural, and technical discourses of the civilizing mission, Franco-Vietnamese collaboration, French library sciences, and Western concepts of encyclopedic knowledge. The Hanoi Central Library became the cornerstone of this colonial information order, serving as a repository of the Francophone Western canon and colonial knowledge about Indochina and the Far East. An Indochina-wide network of central libraries and archives in Hanoi, Saigon, Hue, Phnom Penh, and Vientiane sought to consolidate governmental documents, create reference collections for government officials, and record new publications through the legal deposit. State libraries developed unevenly throughout the five regions of Indochina, with the most resources allotted to Hanoi and Saigon. Overall, Indochina libraries often lacked funds and trained personnel who could extensively implement French library science principles of organization, recordkeeping, and the implementation of legal deposit rules. This chapter traced the emergence of librarianship as a socio-technical occupation among Vietnamese staff, who gained bureaucratic training for social mobility and on an everyday level tactically navigated bureaucratic operations as avid readers. Phạm Đình Giệm, Ngô Đình Nhu, and Trần Văn Kha worked for multiple decades as higher-level archivist-librarians throughout the colonial period; their technical knowledge and leadership would carry over into building the postcolonial Vietnamese states examined later in this book.

The process of creating libraries in Indochina was an aspirational political standardization and a decentralized social reality. The failure to realize the proposed projects for Indochina libraries was rooted in a conflicting mission of the library: Whom should the library serve? From 1858 to 1919, colonial documentation primarily served the French colonial state. Archives and libraries recorded colonial history and provided resources such as maps, statistics, and news for a small number of colonial officials and French expatriates. With the opening of the Hanoi Central Library in 1919, the institution symbolized the promises of Franco-Vietnamese collaboration through public education and modern institutions. Over the course of the 1920s and 1930s, the colonial public of the library widened to include Vietnamese students, scholars, journalists, urban professionals, and teachers actively using the Hanoi and Saigon libraries for study, research, work, and socializing. The next chapter will explore how the Hanoi and Saigon libraries transformed into a public space of modern urban practices such as social reading, collective citizenship, and self-directed learning. While this chapter focused on the builders, the next chapter focuses on library users and the contested use of the library as urban public space.

2

To Be in Public

Infrastructures of Public Reading Culture

In the summer one is bound to see a heart-wrenching sight: at one table, a man slumped over a book, sleeping. At another table, a man with his cheek leaning on a book is also sleeping! There was even a man snoring so loudly that the librarians had to say something. . . . There are two types of readers. One who comes to learn more. The other comes to sit under the refreshing fans and all of a sudden, the sleepy spirit comes and glues together their eyelids, forcing them to sleep. The readers regularly come here to socialize with the sages but only in their dreams. . . . [Asleep,] a man even washed the library table with a puddle of his drool!

—THÁI PHỈ, MARCH 16, 1932[1]

In the article "Mấy cái tệ lưu hành ở thư viện" (Bad things circulating at the library), prominently featured on the front page of the daily *quốc ngữ* publication *Hà Thành Ngọ Báo* in 1932, Thái Phỉ presented the Hanoi Central Library as a practiced space of publicity based on a notion of collective commons and public image. The author reported on how readers leave the library and simply take others' bikes and hats, not thinking twice that their behavior was harmful. He reported that this type of greedy behavior akin to "kleptomania" occurred widely, even in an institution of learned intellectuals.[2] While discussing the issue of stolen personal items, the author alluded to the responsibility of each individual to take care of their own things instead of relying on signs or security guards. Besides the issue of stolen bikes and hats, Thái Phỉ notes in comedic detail the common occurrence of readers "relying on the fans of the government to have a nice long sleep" instead of sleeping at home. He remarked that sleeping in public, although bad for the library's public image, did not necessarily harm the common good and public benefit of the library. In contrast, he declared that the regular practice of readers ripping out pages from books was a cause for concern. He caricatured this type of reader as someone too lazy to copy the information, leading them to rip out the pages for themselves, their self-centered behavior taking away from future generations. The author warned against this type of behavior as a "crime against literature and history."[3] Thái Phỉ argued that if men like this just came and took things for themselves, then a future national institute of letters (*quốc học đồ thư quán*) would be impossible. In the description of both practices, the author evaluated the damages to public image and public good as measures of bad behavior. In other words, the author defined "the public" through individual interactions within a collective body, or self-interested behaviors and potential harm upon others.

This account is significant because it sheds light on two important historical developments in colonial Vietnam: First, the library was a highly sought-out urban space not only for reading but also for idle play and comfortable retreat; and, second, public behavior and public space were issues of important cultural and political debate among Vietnamese readers, librarians, and the popular press.[4] Who comprises the public of the library and how should one behave in its public space? This chapter examines the social practices and public mentalities cultivated in the distinctive infrastructure of the Hanoi and Saigon state libraries, a phenomenon that I term *public reading culture*. Public reading culture comprised of three interwoven practices within library infrastructure: the social and political use of urban public space, self-directed reading of library collections, and civic encounters with the colonial bureaucracy. With the urbanization of Hanoi and Saigon and the expansion of Franco-indigenous education in the 1920s and 1930s, a new generation of bilingual Vietnamese urbanites defined public reading culture through their extensive use of the library space and intellectual debates on public modern life. The library space was a microcosm of urbanizing life in Hanoi and Saigon, reflecting an expanded colonial public, from primarily French officials, French women, and Vietnamese government workers in the early decades of the twentieth century to a wider range of Vietnamese urban readers, including university and high school students, journalists, commercial workers, and teachers in the late colonial period. The physical infrastructure of the library offered a unique central, urban space, free and open to readers and with extensive operating hours throughout the day and night. The sheer scale of diverse and valuable reading matter in the library was incomparable to that available in any other space, and many works were expensive and impossible for an individual to obtain outside the Hanoi and Saigon libraries. Compared to other spaces of reading available to Vietnamese readers, such as schools, private libraries, and associations with more targeted curricula and communities, the colonial library cultivated an individualized, anonymized, voluntarist experience of reading. This type of reading broke away from Confucian-style scholarly libraries built on a connected network of readers and private collections. Readers of the colonial libraries freely selected their reading matter based on their intellectual curiosities and political interests, pursuing research inquiries in Indochina history or immersing themselves in contemporary periodicals from around the world. Exposure to French and global literature, new genres of fiction (detective, fantasy, adventure, and science fiction), and new media forms opened to readers a cosmopolitan and comparative worldview. In this dynamic space of public urbanism and boundless literary matter, readers were not simply passive consumers but were self-directed scholars of their own erudition.

I examine the historical emergence of public reading culture in late colonial Vietnam fomented within the infrastructures of the Hanoi and Saigon libraries. I employ an expansive definition of infrastructure, including not only the physical structures and urban dimensions of the Hanoi and Saigon libraries, but also the urban community, bureaucratic rules regime, and diverse collections of reading matter of Francophone literature, Indochina reference materials, and contemporary Vietnamese *quốc ngữ* publications. Through a socially embedded analysis of rules, books, and buildings, I show how the library infrastructure contributed to the organization of urban social behavior and modern public life. Furthermore, the experience of reading in a state institution brought Vietnamese readers into direct contact with the colonial state and its bureaucrats. Through applications for reader cards and agreement to codes of library behavior and use, Vietnamese readers confronted top-down state regimes of rules and surveillance. Library privileges operated as public citizenship for Vietnamese readers: They submitted themselves to a social contract binding individual responsibility in exchange for the right to access the library space and collections. Privileges were granted on conditional terms of public behavior, and violations could be met with revocation of privileges, fines, or legal repercussions based on the colonial penal code. The Hanoi and Saigon library infrastructures perpetuated an internal contradiction of equality and hierarchy, where readers were subjected to different rules, experiences, and consequences based on race, profession, and age.

This chapter first examines the infrastructure of rules that defined reader access and colonial norms around idealized library reader behavior and the civic use of public goods. I then focus on Hanoi and Saigon sequentially, examining the bibliotactics of Vietnamese readers—how readers navigated the infrastructure of buildings, public urban space, and reading matter to reinscribe the library space with a distinctive public reading culture beyond the top-down visions of the colonial information order. This chapter uncovers how the colonial library space was rearticulated and contested on the individual and collective levels–from individual rule breaking to public debates demanding that the state be responsible for providing fair public access and educational services. "To be in public" was a performance of the self within a public space, an everyday negotiation and political debate on library use and access.

LANGUAGE LANDSCAPES AND LIBRARY ACCESS FOR FRENCH AND VIETNAMESE READERS

The Hanoi and Saigon library collections functioned as an important supplement to formal education, providing access to an extensive collection of reading matter for self-directed learning. The libraries were particularly valuable and important given the extremely uneven and fragmented colonial educational system and the limited number of opportunities for higher education or technical and vocational training in Hanoi and Saigon.[5] In the first decades of the twentieth century, colonial education across Indochina experimented with different models, such as teaching in indigenous languages, communal education, and building on existing local education systems, such as pagoda schools in Cambodia and Laos. As part of the Franco-Vietnamese collaboration policy, Governor General Albert Sarraut initiated a series of colonial school reforms to develop a Franco-indigenous school system for colonial Indochina, beginning with the Règlement général de l'instruction publique en Indochine, issued on December 21, 1917. The Franco-indigenous system consisted of three years of elementary schooling, two years of primary schooling (after 1927, three years), four years of upper-level primary schooling, three years of secondary education (which concluded with the colonial *baccalauréat*, the French high school diploma), and the University of Indochina, which had recently reopened in 1917. In the case of Vietnam, Franco-indigenous schools were part of a political dismantling of the teaching and cultural influence of *chữ hán* through the introduction of *quốc ngữ* and French as the languages of instruction. According to Pierre Brocheux and Daniel Hémery, the Franco-indigenous colonial school system outlined in 1917 had three goals: "1) To inspire and control the content and the transmission of written knowledge within the villages; 2) To transmit to some extent a minimal modern mass education, on which the colonial system depended for its basic functioning; 3) To adapt the colonized elite to the functions assigned to them by the colonial system."[6] The colonial state's limited investment in a Franco-indigenous education system produced a class of bilingual government officials and other types of professionals (lower-level clerks, teachers, translators) and served as a vehicle for French cultural propaganda through schooling and language. In the late 1920s and 1930s, more Franco-indigenous schools opened up for Vietnamese students, with instruction in *quốc ngữ* at the elementary level and basic French at the primary and secondary levels.[7]

In practice, however, Franco-indigenous schools varied widely in terms of curricula and language instruction, and poor rural areas had a limited number of teachers and access to curricula. The majority of Vietnamese students did not advance past elementary school. For the small number of Vietnamese students who continued on to the primary and secondary levels, many were urban based and were exposed to more French-language reading material and instruction in the higher education levels. In addition to the Franco-indigenous schools, there existed in Hanoi and Saigon a small number of elite French schools, which were designed primarily for expatriate Europeans. These schools, such as the Lycée Chasseloup-Laubat in Saigon, also admitted a small number of non-Europeans. While the majority of Vietnamese students were male, there was an increasing number of female students who pursued post-baccalaureate degrees in Hanoi and Saigon, such as a premedical education in physics, chemistry, and biology (P.C.B.).[8]

Vietnamese inhabitants of Hanoi and Saigon navigated a plural language landscape depending on their profession, class, education, and type of reading matter: The everyday spoken language was vernacular Vietnamese, a subset of the population spoke varying levels of French, and the written scripts included French, *chữ quốc ngữ* (romanized vernacular Vietnamese), *chữ hán* (Literary Sinitic), and *chữ nôm* (sinographic demotic Vietnamese).[9] Scholar Giang-Huong Nguyen argues that French never became a language of daily communication for the Vietnamese population and was pervasive only among the upper echelon, such as economic elites and civil servants.[10] Sabine Huynh explains how only 5 percent of Vietnamese spoke French fluently during the colonial period, and the remaining population either did not understand French or used *tây bồi*, an informal pidgin French, particularly when speaking with French superiors and government officials.[11]

To access the library, one had to pass a certain threshold of knowledge of functional everyday French, the official language of library operations and the language of the vast majority of the Hanoi and Saigon library collections. Thus, most Vietnamese users of the colonial library were urban, trained with some level of French or Franco-indigenous education, or worked in the colonial administration. In most cases, to apply for a library card, readers had to be over the age of eighteen (sixteen for French readers), reside in the city of the library, and submit an application with their name, profession, address, and proof of residence in the city or province of the library. This entry card granted access for on-site reading in the *salle de lecture* (reading room), and an additional application was required to access the *section de prêt* (lending section) for borrowing works to read at home.

From 1902 to 1920, the Cochinchina Library operated in a shared space with the archives in the secretariat compound at 27 rue de La Grandière and primarily functioned as a lending library, serving a dynamic range of Saigon's early colonial population of government officials, military, merchants, voyagers, missionaries, entrepreneurs, ambassadors, students, and translators of different ethno-racial and class backgrounds from across Europe and Asia.[12] The port city of Saigon could be spatially understood as twin urbanizing centers of Saigon and Cholon, an ethnic Chinese enclave that was six kilometers from central Saigon. Beginning in 1931, the two hubs—the most populous urban center in colonial Indochina, with a population of 324,000—were administratively referred to as Saigon-Cholon.[13] Permission to borrow materials was granted only to readers with proof of residency in Saigon, Cholon, and the Gia Định province, but privileges differed depending on employment and ethno-racial categorization. Internal library communications documented regular challenges with certain demographics of the reading public: "poor European military officials who had a habit of returning books damaged and did not have the resources to pay for a replacement, young people, temporary employees of government services, travelers, Indians, and mixed-race populations who were unemployed or worked at a place without a specific address."[14] These concerns focused on the documentary illegibility of specific populations who defied racial-legal categorizations in colonial Saigon, such as poor white Europeans and traveling merchants of Indian, Chinese, and mixed-race backgrounds who had borrowed materials without providing a permanent address.[15] As a result of these ongoing issues, library policies evolved to restrict certain populations and types of behaviors and outlined consequences for violations. In the revised May 7, 1902, Cochinchina Library official rules, members of the military were banned from accessing the library during regular operating hours, when the government secretariat offices were operating.[16] Instead, they were now permitted to access the library space only in the evenings Monday through Friday from 8:30 to 10:30, a concession that was offered to promote beneficial leisure activities among the troublesome military population.

Vietnamese, military, and nongovernment employees were considered a risk to the library and were subjected to different requirements to borrow materials. According to the 1902 Cochinchina Library regulations, all readers were required to leave a deposit to borrow books to read outside the library, yet professional merchants, government functionaries, and employees of colonial services were exempt from the deposit requirement with a letter from their employer. French readers were permitted to borrow three books at once with a required deposit of ten piastres (or one book for four piastres) for a period of fifteen days. Vietnamese readers were only allowed to borrow one book at a time and had to leave a deposit of four piastres to borrow a book for a maximum of eight days. The restriction on the number and duration of book loans prevented Vietnamese readers and nongovernment workers from actively using the Cochinchina Library lending section. Furthermore, considering that the average wage for Vietnamese was less than one piastre a day, the requirement to leave a deposit of four piastres was a financial obstacle for much of the Vietnamese population.[17] These new library rules included the revocation of borrowing permissions from military, who had "returned books several times in a deplorable state, necessitating replacement of the works."[18] By 1905 another requirement was placed on nongovernmental employees in order to check out books to read at home: They were now required to provide a guarantor who was an existing library patron or government official to vouch for them, just in case borrowed materials were overdue, stolen, or lost.[19]

With the formation of the Directorate in 1917 and the opening of the Hanoi Central Library in 1919, top-down policies for standardized library access and borrowing privileges across Indochina were implemented. These differing library privileges based on race, age, profession, and residence shed light on the evolving colonial constructs of racialization, citizenship, indigeneity, and migration as carried out through bureaucracy. The official library regulations of the Hanoi Central Library in 1922 permitted the following types of readers: "1) Europeans over the age of sixteen, 2) Vietnamese teachers, 3) higher education students, and 4) Vietnamese and Asians (*Annamites et Asiatiques*) over the age of eighteen who, after investigation, have proven that they are sufficiently educated or are employees of various Indochinese administrative departments."[20] In colonial Indochina intersecting constructs of race, toponymic identity from the five *pays* ("nations" or regions), cultural practices, and colonial citizenship shaped demographic classification.[21] The categories of *français* (French), *européen* (European), *indigène* (indigenous), *protégé* (subject), *annamite* (Vietnamese, but the term could also refer to inhabitants of the protectorate of Annam), *métis* (mixed race), *asiatique étrangers* (Asian foreigners), *khmer* (Khmer, as ethnicity), *cambodgien* (Cambodian, as nationality), and *lao* (Lao, both ethnicity and nationality) were fluid, depending on the context of legal rights, social practice, and political debate. Beginning in 1889, colonial law outlined the possibility of colonial subjects applying for French citizenship through completing military service as well as identification with French cultural values in public life (and later, beginning in 1913, in private life as well). Through an extensive and arbitrary investigation, indigenous applicants answered questions of cultural values pertaining to language, property, finances, and religion, as well as more intimate practices of eating customs, furnishing, clothing, and social practices.[22] In practice, a very small number of Vietnamese obtained formal rights of French citizenship. Yet questions of legal rights and political representation were highly debated issues of the Franco-Vietnamese collaboration, particularly among the French expatriates and Vietnamese elites in Saigon.

Within the colonial institutions of the Hanoi and Saigon libraries, two general categories existed to demographically stratify personnel and readers: European-French and indigenous-Vietnamese. The flattened category of European was often used interchangeably with French and implied the white French expatriate population of library personnel and readers. The category of indigenous was used inclusively to characterize Vietnamese and Asian, and the majority of library documentation used indigenous and Vietnamese interchangeably given the majority Vietnamese readers. The category *asiatique étrangers* or at times just *asiatique* appeared in a handful of documents in the Hanoi Central Library and Saigon Cochinchina Library to characterize the ethnic Chinese populations.[23] The Saigon and Phnom Penh central libraries mirrored the library regulations issued from the Hanoi Central Library, with region-specific adjustments on the use of the terms *indigène* and *asiatique*.[24]

Requirements for bureaucratic documentation also differed between French and Vietnamese, formalizing a hierarchy of access to the library. For applications to use the Hanoi lending section to borrow books to take home, French readers needed only to submit a simple form with their name, profession, and address, demonstrating residence in the city or neighboring provinces. Vietnamese applicants had to submit an application and in addition include two photographs (one for the card, one for the application) and documentary proof of both their home address and employment. If the reader was a university student, the application required a letter from the school's director confirming their student status. Exceptions to the age requirement were made through an extensive case-by-case evaluation by the director of the library. For example, in 1922, the director of the Lycée de Hanoi directly requested of Director Paul Boudet that the school's Vietnamese and French high school students have access to the Central Library reading room.[25] Boudet approved the exception for Vietnamese high school students under the age of eighteen, with the requirement that Vietnamese applicants must carry a recommendation letter from their teacher or government official. In comparison, the exception for French students under the age of sixteen required only a recommendation letter from their parents.

Differences in the privileges and regulations based on race and profession were keenly recognized as discrimination in the popular press. On May 24, 1933, the Tonkinese Fraternity Lodge complained to the Hanoi Central Library that high school and university students did not have access to all the materials in the Central Library reading room.[26] Furthermore, Vietnamese commercial employees did not have the same privileges as government officials and students. The letter exclaimed, "Would it not be possible to make the reading room and all its books absolutely and equally accessible to any eighteen-year-old regardless of profession, as long as he holds a reading card issued by the library?" In a more publicized case of racism, the author of a 1935 article in *L'Annam Nouveau* complained that libraries in other countries were more accessible to the public than the Hanoi Central Library.[27] The author claimed that the Central Library discriminated against Vietnamese readers because the front desk clerk demanded an identification card from Vietnamese readers but never from French readers when they entered the library. Most likely the front desk clerk was a Vietnamese worker, suggesting how French citizens were excluded from rules and institutional expectations. These incidents characterize the underlying racial tensions in the colonial library and discrimination against readers based on race, age, profession, and residence. Additionally, these cases reveal how readers vocalized public demands for fair access to the Hanoi Central Library.

I PLEDGE TO FOLLOW THESE RULES: INDIVIDUAL BEHAVIOR AND PUBLIC GOODS

Library card registration included a list of requirements and rules that applicants were required to pledge to obey to access the library. The general rubric included demographic requirements for library cards, how many books a reader could consult or borrow at any one time and for how long, and fines for damages and lost books. Library rules contributed to a regime of proper reader behavior in "modern" and "public" spaces: The reader must be respectful, trustworthy, courteous, orderly, and quiet. Readers were required to comply with a kind of social contract of proper behavior defined by a code of shared and mutually beneficial resources, transparency in reporting faults, and a protocol of consequences and recompense. To access the Cochinchina Library in 1905, readers were required to recognize that the library was a "public good" and acknowledge that when a book was checked out, it would deny someone else the public good of reading that book.[28] In other words, library rules emphasized the interconnected relationship between individual reader decisions and the greater public good of the library. The curbing of individual and selfish desires was also implicit within the detailed rules regarding overdue fees, damages, and the loss of library books. If there were any damages to the binding or tears to the pages of borrowed books, the reader was responsible for immediately reporting the issue to the administration and then proceeding to make amends. The reader was required to replace the book or pay an expensive replacement fee: twice the cost of the book or the cost of the series, if the work was part of a multivolume set.

To consult materials in the reading room of the Central Library in Hanoi, readers referenced the card catalogs and submitted a request form for each work. Readers could peruse an alphabetical card catalog organized by author (*catalogue d'auteurs*) or a catalog compiled by topic (*catalogue analytique de matières*).[29] The topic catalog organized the library materials by alphabetized categories and nested subcategories on general topics, and each title was given a card filed by publication date within this catalog system. Readers then completed a request form with their name, library card number, title, and the book's call number and then submitted the form to the reading room overseer at the desk. After approximately half an hour, the reader received the work to read in the reading room. A limited number of reference works, such as periodicals, dictionaries, and encyclopedias on art, law, geography, history, language, philosophy, religion, and science, were available on the open shelves along the two sides of the reading room for readers to consult freely. The library overseer's desk was located in the center of the room and faced the tables where readers consulted their books. The overseer monitored the

FIGURE 12. Hanoi Central Library reading room, ca. 1919–1934. Note the card catalogs in the back left and right of the room and the reading room overseer's desk in the center. Records of the original layout of the Central Library reading room describe it as having three long tables and sixty chairs with arms. *Source*: Archives Privées Papiers Boudet 86, Archives nationales d'outre-mer, Aix-en-Provence, France, folder 52.

reading room, enforced silence, and was also responsible for "responding politely to reader questions and guiding readers in their search for materials from the library catalog."[30] The Central Library reading room was equipped with three long wooden tables and a total of sixty wooden chairs with arms for readers to consult materials on site.

Upon successful registration for a library entry card, a reader was allowed to consult books on site in the reading room and could submit an additional application to the lending section to borrow works to take home. In 1933, the Hanoi Central Library was open every day from nine in the morning to ten in the evening, except for Sunday afternoons, Monday mornings, and holidays.[31] By this year the Central Library in Hanoi boasted an extensive collection of over sixty thousand volumes, four hundred current periodicals, and nine hundred discontinued periodicals for free perusal without a formal submission of a request slip to the reading room overseer.[32] Readers were constantly reminded of library rules and the consequences for violations, contributing to bureaucratic norms of reader behavior. On April 13, 1921, Paul Boudet issued a public notice addressed to all readers of the Hanoi Central Library reading room in an attempt to surveil reader use and curb certain types of reader behavior. Boudet now required all readers to fill out a form with their name, profession, address, and the titles of books or periodicals they consulted on their visit to the reading room. Boudet also reminded readers that "any damage, mutilation, or theft of library materials makes the perpetrator subject to Articles 254, 255, and 257 of the penal code and exposes them to legal proceedings, with possible fines and imprisonment." Directly addressing high school and university students, and generally all young Vietnamese, Boudet publicly reminded the young readers that usage of the reading room solely for reading newspapers was not permitted, and that library entry cards would be revoked for those who disregarded this rule.[33]

Vietnamese readers highly valued their library cards and reading privileges. For example, in 1923 reader Phạm Thế Ban, a former student at the protectorate secondary school, wrote to Boudet requesting access to the Hanoi Central Library.[34] He described his passion for reading and the importance of reading for his education:

> I am one of those who love reading. Having acquired some notions of complementary studies, I have come to understand that which is called reading, the advantage it offers, and the pleasures one experiences while reading. I want to expand my understanding with new knowledge, which is why I devote myself to reading. However, interesting books are not at my disposal. . . . I ask you, then, to allow me to visit the Central Library and to borrow the books by making me an entry card and a lending card. This is how I could obtain from you the greatest benefit.

Ban attached his birth certificate and certificate of profession to the letter and was later granted reading room and lending section cards.

If library borrowing privileges were revoked due to a violation of library rules, readers begged library personnel to reinstate their library cards. Reader Đoàn Thanh Chước noted that reading at the Central Library was his only educational option given his limited access to formal classroom learning.[35] Over the course of two years, Chước submitted at least three pleas to the Hanoi Central Library staff to forgive him and reinstate his library card. In his letter directed to Boudet, Chước described himself as the "best reader" in the library, frequently consulting works in a respectful manner. Not providing any details about the actions that led to this consequence, he mentioned that his "small mistake" caused the severe consequence of the revocation of library privileges, described as a swift and brutal "cut to his path of self-study." Chước also wrote directly to two Vietnamese library staff, Nguyễn Khắc Nguyên and Tham Liễn [*sic*], with the hope that they would petition their administrative superiors on his behalf. On October 23, 1923, the library administration responded to Chước's request with a brief rejection, stating that exceptions to rules were impossible.

Đoàn Thanh Chước's case was not exceptional but part of a larger pattern of petitions: Vietnamese readers begged library administrators to have sympathy for their situation, but they often received a cold systematic rejection that cited

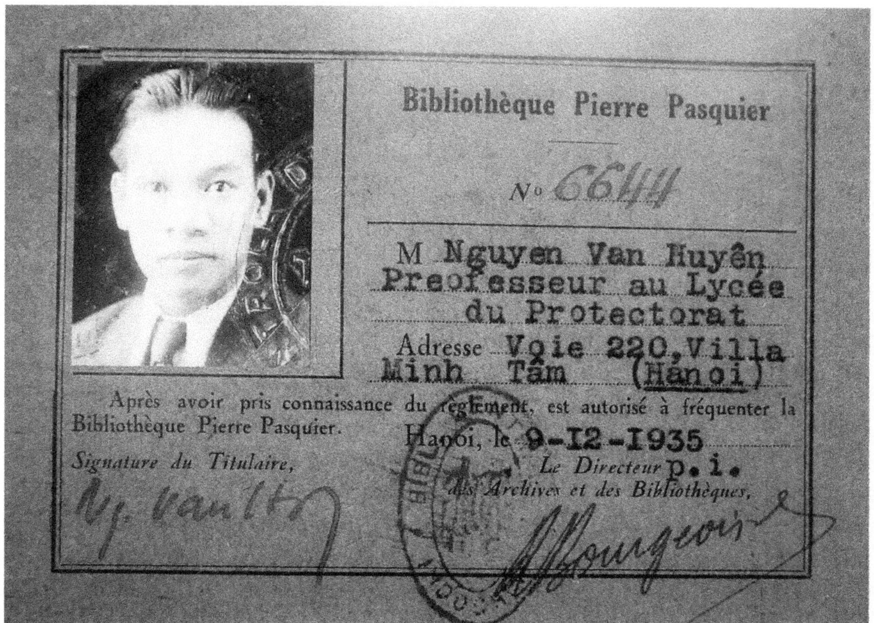

Bibliothèque Pierre Pasquier

No 6644

M Nguyen Van Huyên
Preofesseur au Lycée
du Protectorat
Adresse Voie 220, Villa
Minh Tâm (Hanoi)

Après avoir pris connaissance du règlement, est autorisé à fréquenter la Bibliothèque Pierre Pasquier.

Hanoi, le 9-12-1935

Signature du Titulaire,

Le Directeur p. i.
des Archives et des Bibliothèques,

FIGURE 13. Example of a reader entry card to use the reading room at the Hanoi Central Library, issued to Nguyễn Văn Huyên, 1935. Nguyễn Văn Huyên (1905–1975) was a prominent Vietnamese scholar and professor, and he later became the first minister of national education of the Democratic Republic of Vietnam from 1946 to 1975. *Source*: Nguyễn Văn Huyên Museum, Lai Xá, Hoài Đức, Hanoi, Vietnam. Photograph by author, 2018.

library policy. The contrast between emotion and logic, between individuals and a bureaucratic system, is striking in the style and tone of the letter exchanges. The appeals to reconsider library regulations express the importance of the library for the individual reader. Readers implore in detail and with emotional tenacity their reasons for violating library policy. Detailed explanations include the story of Nguyễn Xuân Tạo, accounting secretary at Maison Chanson & Thibault, who was unable to return overdue books because he was hospitalized; the misuse of the library card of Nguyễn Đồng Thăng, secretary of the judicial service, by Thăng's younger brother; and the accusation that Nguyễn Văn Điền, secretary of the Forestry Department, wrote in borrowed library books.[36] These passionate appeals from Vietnamese readers to reinstate their borrowing privileges were often met promptly with a concise rejection by librarian personnel. For example, the bureaucratic response to Nguyễn Xuân Tạo's explanation of his overdue books on account of his hospitalization read, "Sir, I politely respond to your letter on the twenty-third of this current month to inform you that the facts that have motivated the decision to revoke your library privileges were determined as serious; this does not permit me to favor your request to return." As illustrated in the Hanoi Central Library, Vietnamese readers often violated and contested these rules, at times intentionally and at other times accidentally. A tension existed between builders and users of the library. Builders curated collections and established regulations based on a vision of library behavior as a shared public good. Yet on an everyday level, administrators noted with frustration the excessive chaos and constant violations by library readers in the public space.

CONTROL WORK: MONITORING READER USE AND BOOK CIRCULATION

Librarians actively engaged in control work—the implementation of standardized bibliographic control as examined in the previous chapter, as well as documenting details about reader use and the condition of circulated library materials. Administrators struggled to carry out the library's two essential missions: to conserve or to circulate? Library budgets had to cover the expenses of salaries, building maintenance, and furniture, as well as the high costs of purchasing print media to build the library collections. Books, newspaper subscriptions, and maps were expensive to purchase, transport, and store. Library materials circulated to the public, which subjected the materials to additional costs related to damage, theft, and lost works. Books were valuable, and library administrators had to balance their commitment to circulate books with preserving their condition for future users. Libraries posted extensive rules that required patrons to treat books with care: "For the benefit of the public good, do not write on or fold back pages, damage the binding by opening up the book too widely, or throw books around."[37] Prior to checking out a book, patrons were responsible for noting the material state of the book. Patrons were required to report all damage, such as missing or folded pages, handwriting, or a damaged binding, and to have the damages confirmed by the library staff. Bookbinding extended the shelf life of a book or periodical by protecting its pages from damages due to overuse and climate. Library bookbinders sewed together the pages, reinforced the spine, and added a soft or hard cover board to protect the internal pages from fraying. This method was also used to bind together periodicals or series to make it easier to access complete collections. Bookbinding was expensive, requiring staff and equipment that the libraries in Indochina often did not have. In 1907, Monsieur Exiga from the joint bookbinding department in the Cochinchina Library and the Colonial Printer (L'imprimerie colonial) presented to the lieutenant-governor of the Second Bureau the greatest challenge of a library: how to circulate books while conserving them for posterity.[38] In 1907 there were a total of 24,304 visitors to the Saigon Library. During that year, 12,381 library visitors borrowed a total of 28,519 books to read at home. The more a book was checked out, the more a book became worn and damaged.

Bookbinding was not only a technology of conservation, but it also reflected library priorities and reader consumption. Library administrators prioritized binding of the most "valuable" works, which was determined by their price or limited availability, for long-term conservation; they also selected the most popular and worn works in need of repair and reinforcement through binding. On August 12, 1925, the Saigon Library submitted the budget and priorities for binding newspapers, administrative works, books with illustrations, and luxury limited editions.[39] Some of the books sent to the bindery included world literature that was translated into French, such as Ferdinand Ossendowski's *L'homme et le mystère en Asie* (*Man and Mystery in Asia*, published by a Polish writer in 1923 about Lenin and the Russian Civil War), Walter Scott's *L'abbé* (*The Abbot*, a Scottish historical novel originally published in 1820); French classics such as Alexandre Dumas' *Le trois mousquetaires* and *Le Vicomte de Bragelonne*, French novelist Léon Frapié's *Le aîné précieux* and *La figurante*, and Émile Nolly's *La barque annamite* (a novel about Tonkinese customs first published in 1910).

Since library collections were highly valued, librarians carefully monitored book loans, returns, and whether the materials were overdue, lost, damaged, or stolen. An archive folder extensively recorded cases of books lost or stolen from the Saigon Library between 1907 and 1919.[40] These cases document readers who moved from Saigon or returned to France and did not return borrowed library materials. The cases show the extensive and prolonged control work of monitoring materials and readers: "Monsieur Chazot had embarked for France without returning the volumes he had kept. We have written to the General Le Recureau praying to send our letter of complaint to Chazot. This official had replied that he had sent these volumes to Monsieur de Glostka, who, after receiving our letter, returned the volumes in question by parcel post." Some of the books were returned, while other cases spanned several years and were left unresolved. For example, the lost books of the "Crozel case" were never returned, nor did Monsieur Crozel compensate the library with double the value of the lost books. In another case, reader M. Paul Ricard used another reader's name unbeknownst to that reader (Louis Goron) to borrow books. The majority of these cases concern French readers, pointing to how more French readers evaded library protocol in comparison to Vietnamese readers, who immediately had their borrowing privileges revoked for small violations.

Each year the Hanoi Central Library and the Saigon Cochinchina Library closed their services to patrons for one month during the summer to assess their collections. During this inventory month, the library updated its catalogs with new materials, compiled its monthly statistics of readers and consultations, and evaluated the material state of its collections, documenting damages, overdue materials, and lost and stolen works. The library generated many of its annual reports and statistics during this month. For example, in 1923 the Hanoi Central Library created a detailed inventory and statistics of its lost materials from the lending section.[41] From August 1922 to July 1923 (eleven months of operations), there were approximately 29,499 French reader visits and 6,274 Vietnamese reader visits to the lending section, and a surprisingly large number of volumes (5,832) were missing.

Library administrators attempted to control the movement of books and bodies through extensive documentary procedures. They recorded every book's use and misuse in an uneven manner, compiling statistical information on readers' book checkouts, race, gender, age, employment, and residence that accumulated into glimpses of the reader as a subject navigating the library infrastructure. Through a documentary regime of rules, readers' bodies were made "modern"—legible, restricted, quieted, and ordered. Readers were expected to maintain "order" in the library—a notion that extended to keeping orderly the reading matter and public space and following proper library rules and bodily decorum or else accept the consequences of losing library privileges. The performance of order was predicated on the definition of disorder. Racialized constructs of Western modernity, the civilizing mission, and scientific order shaped this policing of bad behavior, with Vietnamese personnel and patrons the common target of disciplinary action. The infrastructure of rules attempted to organize reader behavior around the notion that the library space and collections were a public good, yet the constant violation of these rules points to conflicting ways that builders and users envisioned the space of the library. This discursive and politically fluid definition of improper library behavior was also a concerned response to the changing demographics of library readers; by the late 1920s, the number of Vietnamese students and leisure social readers in the Hanoi and Saigon libraries increased significantly, transforming the public space and the meaning of the library.

HANOI LIBRARY AS A SPACE OF URBAN PUBLIC MODERNITY

Throughout the colonial period, the reading room and lending section of the Hanoi Central Library were crowded and heavily used, even compared to many French libraries in France. For example, in 1931 the Hanoi reading room recorded 51,932 book consultations in one year (both French and Vietnamese readers) out of a collection of seventy thousand works. Book consultations in the Hanoi reading room (51,932) were astonishingly high, especially when compared to the number of consultations in large French cities such as Lyon (63,362), Rouen (30,545), and Marseille (25,000). Excluding Paris, the Hanoi Central Library ranked second in budget and second in book consultations after the Lyon library.[42] The 1931 report continued to commend the Central Library lending section's popularity in comparison to French libraries:

> The Hanoi Central Library records sixty thousand annual loans, with a circulating collection of ten thousand volumes; each volume is checked out on average six times each year. This brilliant result and enthusiasm of the public, especially the indigenous of the library, is due to the existence of the great facilities provided for the readers. The reading room is open each day from nine in the morning to ten in the evening. The lending section is open every day from nine in the morning to eight in the evening without interruption, except for its closure Sunday morning. Furthermore, there has been a great effort to improve the catalogs in the Central Library [reading room] and the methodic classification on the shelves of the lending section.[43]

Over the course of the colonial period, the total number of French settlers in Indochina was relatively small. According to Marie Paule-Ha, the total number of Europeans in Indochina never surpassed forty-five thousand at any one time, accounting for less than 0.2 percent of the total population, and most lived in the Vietnamese cities of Saigon, Hanoi, and Haiphong.[44] Despite their small number, French expatriate readers of around six thousand accounted for most Hanoi Central Library users in the early years of its operation, with fourteen thousand French reader visits and nine thousand Vietnamese reader visits over the course of 1920.[45] By the late 1920s, the demographics of Hanoi Central Library users had significantly shifted from majority French to Vietnamese. By 1928 the total number of Vietnamese readers entering the library had surpassed that of French readers. From 1929 to 1941, the number of Vietnamese reader visits increased from 35,815 to 102,704. In the same period, the total number of French reader visits remained stagnant at around forty thousand visits per year, paralleling the stagnation of the overall population of French in Tonkin at around ten thousand.[46] The changing reading public of the Hanoi Central Library in the 1930s reflected the rise in overall urban population as well as an increased number of educated Vietnamese who were literate in French and Vietnamese *quốc ngữ*.

The library administration acutely observed the disparity between French and Vietnamese in the Hanoi reading room. From 1920 to 1941, the library administration collected detailed statistics on the racial breakdown of visitors to the reading room, noting the gradual decline of French readers and the rapid increase of Vietnamese readers.[47] In 1929, French patrons of the reading room started to decline each year while the number of Vietnamese patrons increased rapidly, approximately doubling in number every five years. In 1929, 25,815 Vietnamese users visited the reading room, increasing to 87,397 in 1941. In comparison, in 1929 French visits to the reading room numbered 10,549, decreasing to 3,860 in 1941. The numbers of French and Vietnamese readers who used the reading room were in indirect relationship to one another, pointing to how potential readers competed for the sixty seats available to consult materials on site. The overwhelming majority of reading room patrons were Vietnamese. For example, in 1936 the

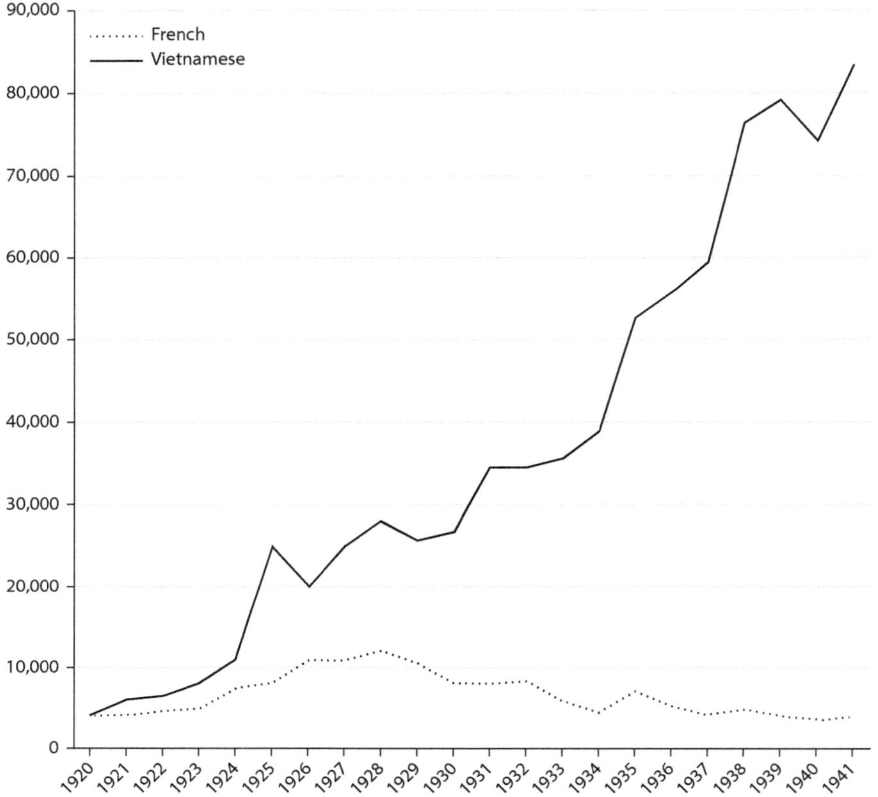

FIGURE 14. French and Vietnamese reader entries to the Hanoi Central Library reading room from 1920 to 1941. This chart shows the total number of readers who entered the library, not the absolute number of readers registered for the year. *Data Source*: Direction des archives et des bibliothèques, Trung tâm lưu trữ quốc gia 1, Hanoi, Vietnam, folder 1627.

daily average of Vietnamese visits to the reading room was 278 compared to only 17 French.[48]

One possible reason for the decreasing number of French readers to the reading room could be the limited number of seats, which were often taken up by Vietnamese readers who staked out space and used the library for socializing. From 1935 to 1936, a series titled "At the Central Library" chronicled and critiqued the state of everyday library affairs and the pervasiveness of improper public library use:

> A number of people deplore this common practice at the Central Library; someone puts a book open on the table to reserve their place while they leave the library for a meal or take a walk. There is nothing more shocking than seeing a great number of unoccupied chairs while readers are forced to stand in front of the windows or lockers due to lack of space. Moreover, it is not only library cardholders who come

> here. Many people are not in possession of a card yet nevertheless occupy chairs in the morning to ten in the evening. . . . Why come to the library, you will say, these men who have no card? Well! If they cannot borrow books they bring their own. The library is a very comfortable room, warm in the winter, refreshing in the summer, is it not?[49]

The author of the series publicly requested the library director take measures to curb this disruptive behavior, which harmed the interests of "serious readers." As seen in this commentary, the public space of the Hanoi reading room had been transformed into a popular space for informal retreat, socializing, and leisure reading. Undermining the rules regime of the library, some entered the public space without a library card, bringing their own reading matter to use in the comfortable central space of the library.

This bifurcation of seriousness and leisure, rule abiding and rule breaking, contributed to wider debates about proper "civilized" behavior in a public space. Articles such as the ones in *L'Annam Nouveau* raised questions about the meaning and practice of "being civilized," drawing from examples in Japan as well as the West.[50] In the preface to the series "At the Central Library," another author associated proper library etiquette with "civilized peoples." The author brings up Japan as a benchmark and writes, ""A civilized people are a people who love reading . . . for example, we know from the example of Japan, where the number of readers is considerable and increases rapidly." Drawing a direct connection between civilization and reading, the author compared the handful of public libraries in Vietnam to the spectacular number of libraries and readers in "civilized" Japan. According to this report, in 1912 fifty-four libraries with nearly four million readers existed in Japan, and by 1925 the numbers increased to an unbelievable 4,725 libraries with over twenty-eight million readers.

The library was a contested space to debate urban public modernity and civilized collective practices throughout the French- and Vietnamese-language presses. As shown at the beginning of this chapter, Thái Phỉ chronicled how individual actions in the library—the theft of bikes and hats, ripping out pages of books—impacted the public benefit of the library and the collective reputation of Vietnamese. The author declared, "For the sake of collective honor, for the sake of self-respect, I had to force myself to do the job of exposing these issues."[51] While Thái Phỉ took some creative license and possibly exaggerated the behaviors of sleeping and stealing, this article points to the broader intellectual movement of self-critical reflection on public behavior that permeated the popular press, literature, and arts in late colonial Vietnam. Thái Phỉ, was the pen name of Nguyễn Đức Phong (1903–45), a journalist and public intellectual who was committed to the educational reform of Vietnamese youth as a channel for wider social and civilizational reform. Throughout the 1930s, he wrote educational guides, published several newspaper articles on literature and social commentary, and created his own newspaper, Vietnam's first youth periodical,

Cậu Ấm.[52] His concern for public behavior at the Central Library coincided with his broader commitment to cultivating a sense of Vietnamese collective ethics and public civic duty.

Other Vietnamese intellectuals commented more broadly on the importance of urban public modernity as an extended commentary on the rapid social and economic transformations wrought by colonialism and urbanization. In Vũ Trọng Phụng's sidewalk novel *Số Đỏ* (*Dumb Luck*), the author caricatured the practices of urban public modernity in 1930s Hanoi, which included the "thirty-six streets" of the old quarter, as well as tennis courts, shops, cafes, hotels, and government offices in the French quarter.[53] In Nhất Linh's *Tây Du* (*Going to France*), a serialized semi-autobiographical and satirical short story based on his own visit to France, the narrator comments on urban hygiene and public leisurely life: "In France people have almost abandoned private family entertainment and are all happy to go out in society. Only sick people stay at home."[54] The travel story *Tây Du* is an extended set of observations about the differences between France and Vietnam; the narrator highlights French civil society and public life associated with urban sites such as restaurants, cafes, and dance halls, as well as their separation from a home space. Phạm Quỳnh (1892–1945), the intellectual and editor in chief of the popular *quốc ngữ* periodical *Nam Phong* and minister of education at the court of Hue, also wrote on public life based on his journey to France. In his account, he admires the joyful lightheartedness of Marseille public life and "*công trường*" (public squares or public sites, a new word in Vietnamese), where the streets are full of people leisurely walking, speaking, laughing, gathering in crowds, and good-humoredly teasing, cursing, and fighting with one another.[55] Comparing French streets to Vietnamese streets, Phạm Quỳnh critiqued the current state of Vietnamese streets, describing them as unhygienic from sewer water and uninviting to the humanistic practice of walking for pleasure.[56] By questioning what it meant to "be in public," Vietnamese intellectuals debated the nuances of an urban public modernity ranging from public consciousness to public social life.

WHOM SHOULD THE LIBRARY SERVE? SERIOUS, LEISURE, AND STUDENT READING PRACTICES

In 1928 the library director Paul Boudet reported on the alarming crowdedness of the Central Library space: "The working room of the Central Library is day by day more frequented and has become insufficient. The development of schools brings to us a mass number of indigenous, who have now become difficult to accommodate. It is necessary to envision for the future the creation of one to several study libraries that can be designated for the indigenous."[57] This commentary suggests Boudet's concern about the domination of the library by Vietnamese students and the necessity of separating them from other readers. Boudet reported the following year, "The overseer of the reading room has seen on various occasions indigenous and French readers forced to leave without using the resources of the library because they could not find a place to sit due to the crowdedness. There is no better argument for demonstrating the necessity and extreme urgency for expansion."[58] Library administrators expressed concern about the changing demographic of library users, particularly of Vietnamese students gathering in the limited space in the reading room and displacing other readers, such as French and Vietnamese government officials, teachers, and commercial workers. The June 1935 to May 1936 statistics recorded a daily average of 229 readers visiting the reading room.[59] On one day, the reading room reached a peak of 403 readers. Library administrators noted that out of 403 readers, 390 were Vietnamese and 13 were French, reflecting a significant racial imbalance. In a year spanning 1935 and 1936, 531 reader cards were issued, bringing the total number of registered readers to 7,073. By 1936, the reading room collection held 78,073 volumes.

On January 15, 1936, a newly reorganized lending section and reading room were inaugurated, moving the lending section into the former building of the General Inspection of Agriculture, which would "offer to readers conditions of greater convenience and comfort."[60] Furthermore, the number of chairs in the reading room was increased from fifty-four to ninety-six, and the library initiated a new system of reserved seating, designating certain seats in the reading room for "workers who were not students."[61] This separate category points to the logistical management of students, who were taking up space that the library had intended for a wider variety of readers. Two weeks after this new system was installed, a library reader publicly questioned the application of this policy in the article "For Whom Are These Places Reserved in the Central Library?"[62] The article, signed "Tân Dân" (Modern Man), recounted the author's own experience: He had entered the library to consult some reference works available on the shelves, sat down in the section labeled "reserved seats" (most of which were vacant), and then was immediately told by the library personnel to take a different seat in the unreserved section. On inquiring for whom the places were reserved, the worker did not know and only asked the reader to please comply with the instructions from the director of the library. This article highlights the vagueness of library policy even among personnel, and the public critiques of unfair library policies.

Among library administrators and internal reports, readers were categorized into demographic groups based on race, age, and profession. Each category had associated regulations and were described with moralistic undertones as "serious" or "leisure" readers where serious readers were considered more deserving of access to the limited library space. According to internal 1937 statistics, of 6,076 Vietnamese readers with an entry card, the vast majority were students, 71 percent of them students of higher education, high school, or upper-level primary school. This large number of young students might be due to the growing number of students by the late colonial period as well as the recent permission granted to Vietnamese students ages sixteen and up to apply for a reader card. In comparison, 17 percent of Vietnamese readers were government officials (specifically listed as nonstudents in the internal document). The remaining groups recorded were commercial workers, journalists, teachers, and the unemployed (with a high school or higher education degree).[63]

The increasing congregation of Vietnamese young men in the urban central space of the Hanoi reading room became an important subject of debate among library administrators and in the popular press. Vietnamese- and French-language newspapers exclaimed that Vietnamese students were taking over the library. Described as rambunctious leisure readers, male Vietnamese students formed the majority of reading room readers, consuming textbooks, youth literature, and novels. On December 11, 1932, Hy Tống published an article titled "The Crisis of the Reading Room in Hanoi" in *L'Annam Nouveau* in which he criticized the Vietnamese students for crowding the Central Library and reading "useless" books.[64] Hy Tống complained,

> Certainly the reading room cannot serve as a rendezvous for all the intellectuals who tend to find there the best refuge to pleasantly pass their days [and also serve as a space for] careless youth in the company of action and adventure novels and illustrated reviews. A reading room is not made so that schoolchildren of all kinds can play truant in the reading room and disturb the calm and meditation of the serious readers.

Contrasting young leisure readers with serious researchers, Hy Tống claimed that if the library could not satisfy its intellectual readers, it would fail its mission as an encyclopedic resource for scholarly learning. Directing his remarks to the members of the High Council of the Hanoi Central Library, Hy Tống also warned of the political dangers of neglecting the direction of the youth in the reading room. He described Vietnamese youth as vulnerable to secret societies, unhealthy ideas, and "incendiary and fallacious revolutionary doctrines" and called for the Directorate to "distribute books carefully chosen for this army of readers eager to learn." The author drew attention to the political dangers of young Vietnamese men congregating unbridled without moral direction in public spaces. Hy Tống described the group as socially displaced and the library as an open oasis, referring to "all the panic and anguish of young people in need of education and work, refused at all the doors except perhaps at the public reading room at boulevard Borgnis Desbordes." The author emphasized that the library did not have enough space to receive this large group of neglected students, pointing to the growing demographic of urban male youth as an issue of public concern.

Furthermore, the criticisms of leisure readers conveyed a vision of the library as an important institution of modern states and societies. Hy Tống continued to argue for the expansion of reading rooms and circulating libraries following the model of "industrialized countries like England, whose circulating libraries

FIGURE 15. In January 1936 the Hanoi Central Library reading room was reorganized with smaller tables (that seated twelve) and some longer tables (that seated twenty-four) and with the use of narrower chairs without arms as seen in this photograph, ca. 1936–1940. According to records, this type of rearrangement allowed for more seating (eighty-four seats), yet it also possibly cultivated a different type of social organization for groups of readers to commingle at the tables. As shown here, young Vietnamese men occupied many of the seats. *Source*: Tổng Thư viện, Trung tâm lưu trữ quốc gia 2, Ho Chi Minh City, Vietnam, folder 1.

play such an important role such that they currently number over seven hundred branches."[65] Recognizing the costs of expanding the reading room, the article also emphasized the critical importance of the library as a public service and state responsibility: "How does one evaluate a country? Not based on superficial institutions to justify heavy taxes. Nor does one evaluate an administration based on the number of public services. Instead, one praises a government founded on a few institutions thoughtfully organized rather than many superficial and ineffective institutions." In this statement, Hy Tống alluded to the hypocrisy of exorbitant colonial state taxes, levied under the guise of providing public services and institutions. Addressing the members of the High Council of the Central Library, the author called for an additional loan to the general budget for the next financial year. This loan would provide the Directorate of Archives and Libraries an increased budget for 1933 from 77,560 piastres to at least that of 1932 (96,110 piastres). This budget would enable the library to expand its reading room and pay for personnel and materials costs.

Other readers also requested that the administration improve the facilities in the Central Library. In the July 19, 1931, issue of the newspaper *France Indochine*, a Hanoi library reader demanded improved electric lights in the reading room.[66] The reader complained that the current lamps were hung so high on the ceilings that they tortured readers wanting to read in the later hours of the day. Proposing that the library lower the hanging electric lights or provide desk lamps, the reader claimed that this small reform would be appreciated by many readers of the library. In the January 2, 1936, issue of *L'Annam Nouveau*, author "Thế Chương" noted that the project to expand the reading room was "a task that brings joy to the young studious Vietnamese more so than the French." The author also eagerly awaited for the construction of a garage for readers to leave their bicycles, since currently readers were "forced to leave bicycles *pêle-mêle* on the stoop outside of the entrance door or leaned against the walls, which interfere with the beautiful image of this great public monument."[67] These articles show the significance and popularity of library reading to the larger community, as well as the importance of lighting in the library, since the opening hours extended late into the evening.

RACE AND READING: LENDING NOVELS, *QUỐC NGỮ*, AND YOUNG ADULT BOOKS TO READ AT HOME

The Hanoi Central Library maintained extensive statistics on reader behavior in the reading room and lending section, paying particular attention to race and genre. Reading along the grain of this colonial documentation unearths the everyday literary consumption and cosmopolitan engagements of French and Vietnamese Hanoi readers. In an internal accounting of Vietnamese consultations in the reading room, the statistics reflect how colonial librarians categorized genres and the vast popularity of literature among Vietnamese readers. Over the course of one year, Vietnamese readers consulted 7,862 periodicals and 89,035 books on site: literature (46.7 percent), periodicals (8.2 percent), philosophy (6.8 percent), mathematics (6.3 percent), sciences (6.3 percent), and law (6 percent). The grouped category of "pedagogy, travel, religion, agriculture, and hygiene" was 4.3 percent, and the remaining categories were between 1 and 2 percent: philology, sports, geography, biography, news, the Far East, history, and art.[68]

In comparison to the popular reading room, where readers consulted materials on site, the lending section reflected a different set of cosmopolitan and leisure reading practices. Readers with a lending card could borrow works to read outside of the library space and engage with separate collections of reading matter—the general collection, novels, young adult books, and *quốc ngữ* literature. The lending section of the Hanoi Central Library first operated from the reading room. On August 1, 1921, the lending section was moved to a separate space and then, in January 1936, it was transported to a new room, twenty-five by ten meters, located on the first floor of the former building of the General

FIGURE 16. Hanoi lending section prior to moving to larger space, ca. 1921–1935. The overseer desk is located to the right. *Source*: Archives Privées Papiers Boudet 86, Archives nationales d'outre-mer, Aix-en-Provence, France, folder 52.

Inspection of Agriculture.[69] The lending section was open from nine in the morning to eight in the evening without a midday break, and it was closed Sunday afternoons. In 1935 the collection included approximately 11,500 works, primarily novels, as well as textbooks on science, arts, and letters. In contrast to the reading room, the lending section was designed for readers with a lending card to freely browse the books on the shelves (*principe du libre access aux rayons*), read books on site at the two designated tables, or borrow books to read at home by submitting a request and leaving a monetary deposit. The library operations manual emphasized the importance of the layout of the lending section: "Works on the shelves must be carefully classified, and the librarian desk must be positioned to monitor the shelves and the exit. The layout must also not disturb the readers of the lending section."[70]

According to lending section statistics from 1920 to 1941, French readers borrowed more books from the lending section, often double the number borrowed by Vietnamese readers. For example, in 1931 there were 26,965 loans to French readers compared to 8,955 loans to Vietnamese readers; in 1941, 38,332 loans to French readers compared to 19,167 loans to Vietnamese readers.[71] The extensive use of the lending section by French readers is significant given the relatively small population of French inhabitants in Hanoi (approximately six thousand). It is important to recognize that this data only accounts for readers who borrowed materials from the lending section, not readers who consulted materials on site at the designated

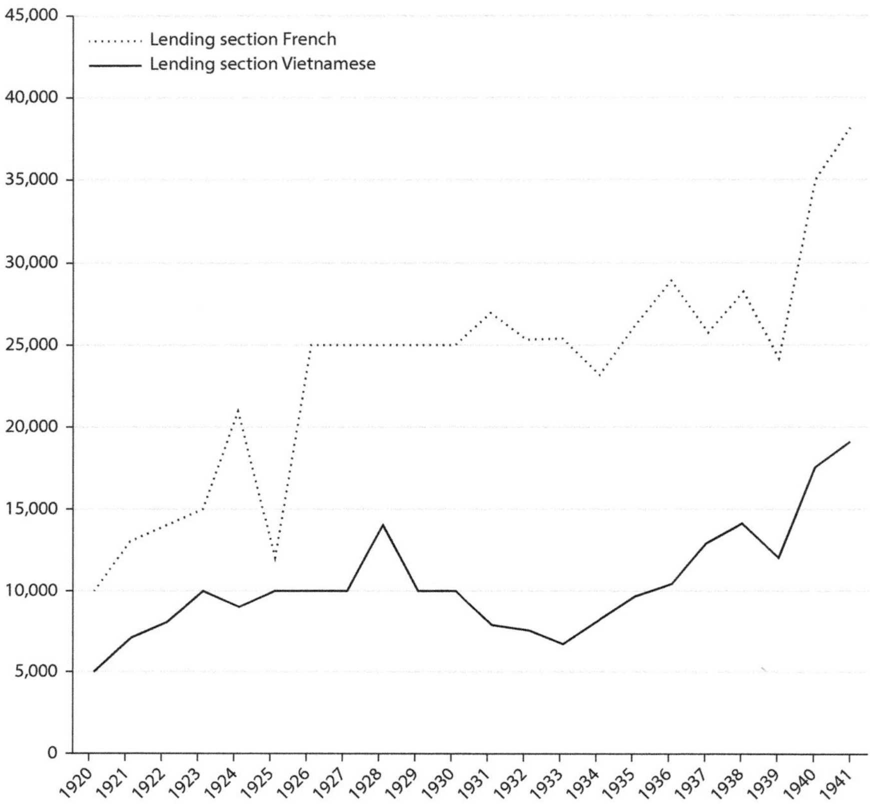

FIGURE 17. Approximate number of readers from the lending section of the Hanoi Central Library from 1920–1941. French readers appear to have used the lending section much more frequently than Vietnamese readers based on these numbers. Note that the Central Library statistics only recorded instances in which readers requested to borrow books to take home. These numbers do not account for users who consulted books from the lending section on site. *Data Source*: Direction des archives et des bibliothèques, Trung tâm lưu trữ quốc gia 1, Hanoi, Vietnam, folder 1627.

tables. Vietnamese readers possibly used the lending section to consult materials and read on site rather than borrowing the materials to read at home.

Furthermore, the comparatively lower number of Vietnamese loans from the lending section could be related to differing notions of spatial and social reading, as well as the popularization of leisure self-directed reading practices in the colonial period. As discussed in the previous chapter, Vietnamese reading practices were grounded in smaller communities of scholarly networks, Confucian academies, and religious practices. The Hanoi Central Library provided a common, scholarly, well-lit, and furnished area for readers to consult materials within the confines of the library institution. For Vietnamese readers, using state library materials—a public shared good—in the common area made more logistical sense. Library books were public objects, and the heavy fines for damaged and lost works could have deterred Vietnamese readers from actively borrowing materials from the lending section. Furthermore, as described in newspaper articles and reader statistics, the reading room was a popular social space for Vietnamese readers to congregate and access valuable library materials such as journals, literature, maps, reference works, and science manuals. In May 1936, the lending section recorded a total of 39,397 reader visits (73.5 percent French, 26.5 percent Vietnamese).[72] In comparison, the reading room counted 63,133 reader visits (7.6 percent French, 92.4 percent Vietnamese). According to the 1935–36 yearly report of popular books checked out from the lending section of the Hanoi Central Library, Vietnamese read literature, French youth read young adult books, and women voraciously read the adventure and sentimental romance novels by Delly. Delly, the pen name of the brother and sister authors Jeanne-Marie and Frédéric Petitjean de La Rosière, are best known for their popular romance novels and easily read train station literature (*littérature de gare*), such as *L'héritier des ducs de Sailles, Un amour de prince,* and *L'infidèle.* Most reports did not distinctly categorize gender; however, this report noted the popularity of Delly among women and exclaimed that "rarely do these books remain on the shelves!"[73] The mention of women in the Hanoi lending section is notable given the stark library gender imbalance and the comparatively small population of French women in Hanoi compared to the population of French women in Saigon.[74]

More readers visited the reading room than the lending section each year, but readers of the lending section individually checked out a higher number of books. In May 1939 there were approximately 2,561 registered cards (1,158 French, 1,403 Vietnamese) for the lending section.[75] Over the course of the same period, the readers made 92,508 loans in total, which averages to approximately thirty-six loans per reader per year. Thirty-six book loans per user per year is an impressive number when compared to an average of only twenty-one book loans per year by an American library user in 1937.[76] Additionally, this number excludes the times readers consulted and freely read materials in the lending section room but did not submit a request to borrow and take materials out of the library. Taking into consideration the relatively small size of the lending section collection (11,500 works in 1935), 92,508 book checkouts and thirty-six loans per reader in a year suggests an actively used lending section.

A close analysis of the 1938–39 lending section use statistics sheds light on borrowing patterns by race, genre, and collection.[77] The Lending Section reported a monthly average of 458 instances of French and 389 instances of Vietnamese on-site consultation of materials from the general collection. Figure 18 shows the monthly average of loans by genre from the lending section general collection according to race. According to this monthly average of loans from the general collection, the genres of books loaned most frequently were as follows: French

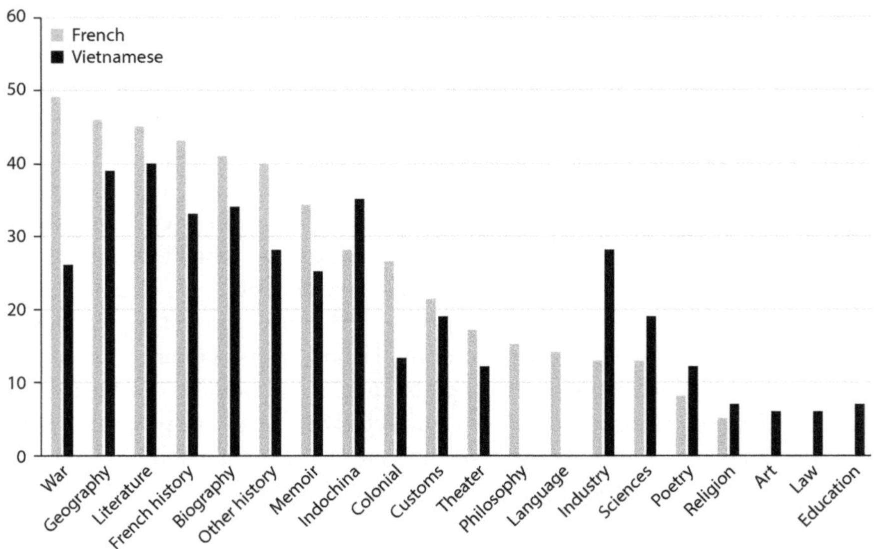

FIGURE 18. Monthly average of books loaned from the general collection in the Hanoi lending section by topic and race from May 1938 to May 1939. *Data Source*: Direction des archives et des bibliothèques, Trung tâm lưu trữ quốc gia 1, Hanoi, Vietnam, folder 2211.

readers preferred to read works on war (on average forty-nine loans a month), geography (forty-six), literature (forty-five), French history (forty-three), and biography (forty-one). In comparison, Vietnamese readers preferred materials on literature (forty), geography (thirty-nine), Indochina (thirty-five), biography (thirty-four), and French history (thirty-three). Reader tastes diverge the most for French readers who preferred war, philosophy, and language genres while Vietnamese preferred professional topics such as industry, Indochina, law, education, sciences, and art. This suggests that Vietnamese used the lending section to supplement their education or professional vocation, a common pattern that occurred also in the reading room of the Hanoi Central Library. Overall, reader preferences spanned newly popularized genres in Indochina such as biography (19 percent), literature (20 percent), geography (20 percent), and history (32 percent). Since many of the library readers were government officials and students, nonfiction works on Indochina, geography, language, sciences, and war were also popular.

In addition to the general collection, the lending library of the Hanoi Central Library created three separate collections of materials: Vietnamese *quốc ngữ* books, literary novels, and young adult books. The majority of the works in both the reading room and lending section were in the French language, and the development of a separate *quốc ngữ* collection reflected the increased legal deposits of new works published in vernacular Vietnamese and the increased literacy in Vietnamese in the 1930s. Created in 1939, the *quốc ngữ* collection became the most popular collection among Vietnamese readers in the lending section: From January 1939 to May 1939 there were 1,360 loans from this collection, averaging 272 loans a month.[78] In comparison, French readers checked out books from the young adult collection the most (on average 201 loans a month); the young adult collection was also popular among Vietnamese (150 loans a month). During 1939 we also see the number of Vietnamese readers visiting the lending section exceeding that of the French.[79]

The 1938–39 lending section also recorded the most popular authors loaned from the novels collection. A close reading of consumption trends sheds light on how French (669 monthly average) and Vietnamese readers (650 monthly average) engaged with the specific lending section collections. In previous years, the library reported that Alexandre Dumas was the most-read author among French readers. However, in 1938–39 French readers in the lending section began to read Delly (129) significantly more than Dumas (69). Dumas was followed by Rudyard Kipling (55), Rosny Aîné (41), and Pierre Benoit (35). In comparison, the most popular authors read by Vietnamese readers were Dumas (135), Delly (86), Anatole France (64), Maurice Dekobra (53), and Henry Bordeaux (40). The tremendous popularity of middlebrow and classic authors in the lending section of the Central Hanoi Library points to the availability and consumption of a wide gamut of light, classic, and escapist reading among Hanoi library readers. Reader consumption in the library paralleled larger literary trends in late colonial book market preferring popular sentimental romance, classic realist novels, and journalistic, historic, and adventure novels. Demands for adventure novels are reflected in the soaring popularity of Alexandre Dumas's *The Count of Monte Cristo* and *The Three Musketeers* among Vietnamese readers who enjoyed themes of justice, morality, and camaraderie.[80] According to Peter Zinoman, narratives of imprisonment and perseverance were popular among Vietnamese intellectuals and shaped the development of Vietnamese revolutionary writing throughout the twentieth century.[81] Popular French authors among Vietnamese library readers such as Nobel Prize–winning Anatole France (1844–1924) and father of the modern short story Guy de Maupassant (1850–93) also circulated across Vietnamese reading culture more broadly as *quốc ngữ* translations, serialized editions, and adaptations.[82]

Library reader consumption was dependent on both reader tastes and the library collections, which were determined by networks of book donations and print markets, limited library budgets, and the availability of cheaper editions and mass print runs. Thus, most of the lending section consisted of French popular authors, while the remaining works were best-selling authors translated into French, such as British authors Rudyard Kipling, John Galsworthy, and Joseph Conrad. These authors followed literary consumption trends for translated global literature and bestsellers throughout Asia in the first decades of the twentieth century. For example, in the Dutch East Indies (today Indonesia), translations of

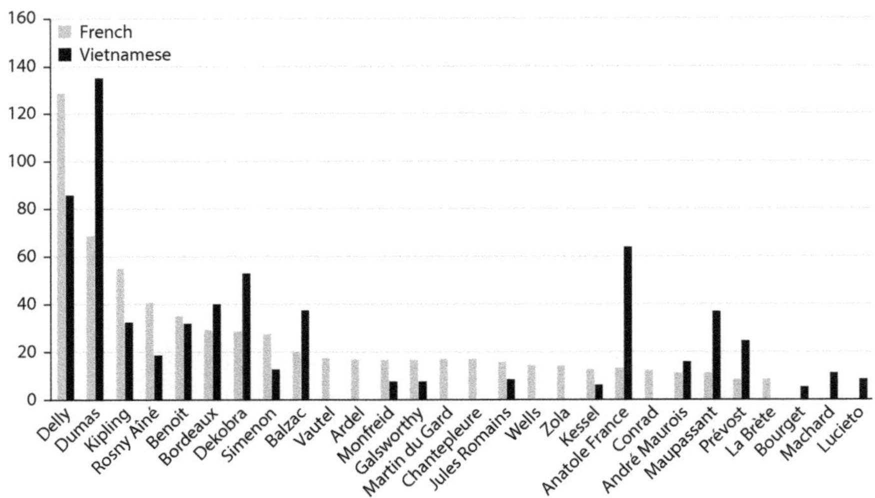

FIGURE 19. Monthly average of books loaned from the novels collection in the Hanoi lending section by author and race from May 1938 to May 1939. *Data Source*: Direction des archives et des bibliothèques, Trung tâm lưu trữ quốc gia 1, Hanoi, Vietnam, folder 2211.

Alexandre Dumas's *The Three Musketeers* and *The Count of Monte Cristo*, Mark Twain's *The Prince and the Pauper*, and Rudyard Kipling's *The Jungle Book* were among the most popular books circulated through the state publisher and library Balai Pustaka.[83] During the turn of the twentieth century in China, Chinese-language translations of English detective stories and French authors Maupassant, Dumas, Hugo, and Verne gained popularity among Chinese readers.[84]

SAIGON, A WORK OF FANTASY OR PUBLIC BENEFIT

On October 29, 1917, an article in *La Tribune Indigène* raised the question of whether the Saigon Cochinchina Library was in fact a "work of fantasy or a public benefit." The author explained that building a library is undeniably important, but it only has meaning if readers can easily access the library. During this time, the library was located at the secretariat administrative compound at 27 rue de La Grandière and had recently reduced its opening hours to ten in the morning to five-thirty in the evening in accordance with the hours of other surrounding administrative offices. The author remarked that another newspaper had publicly protested this measure to the local administration in vain. According to the article, the limited hours created unfair access: Only those who had the luxury of time could come to the library, yet these individuals already had "the means to procure newspapers and books to read at home." He claimed that most of the dedicated readers of the library, who were low-level government officials and commercial employees, could no longer access the library.

In comparison to the debates about civilizational comportment in public spaces in the Hanoi Central Library, the question of public access was at the center of operational critiques and public discourse on the Saigon Library. Library administrators and the Saigon popular press constantly questioned the limited hours, uninviting building, documentation torpor, and lack of reading room space. Documentation torpor included administrative delays, the logistical hassles of reader cards, and unevenly and unfairly applied rules such as restrictions on the number of books one was permitted to borrow from the lending section. With the opening of the Hanoi Library in 1919, readers often compared the Saigon Library to the model Hanoi Library, demanding more funds for expanding library space, collections, and services. The question of public access was tied directly to the challenges with Saigon Library infrastructure, from buildings and books to labor and rules. Complaints from readers show how the various roles of the library were debated; the Saigon Library functioned as a symbol of colonial urbanism and technical modernity as well as a public resource for the expanding reading community in Saigon.

On February 15, 1920, the library curator Léon Saint-Marty wrote a scathing internal report chronicling the inhospitable layout and disorderly functions of the Saigon Cochinchina Library.[85] He called on Governor Georges Maspero to immediately revise the budget for necessary improvements to the library and archives of Cochinchina. Designated by Paul Boudet to improve the organization and functions of the Saigon Library, Saint-Marty did not hold back from his criticisms of the library operations that made the library inaccessible and challenging for readers.

> Due to the limited opening hours, the library is only open to idlers because it is open during hours when potential readers are at work. This is illogical and, dare I say, immoral. The building is nondescript and gives off a rather gloomy impression. The entrance staircase is adorned with unwelcoming forbidding placards: "It is forbidden to bring in dogs." "We do not store bicycles." "The library closes Saturday night." This makes potential visitors grumpy as soon they enter. Unfortunately, nothing inside the library cheers them up; quite the contrary.

Saint-Marty continued to highlight other challenges for readers, such as the disruptive reading room, confusing catalog system, and inadequate retrieval process for the lending section:

> What if the reader tries to read on site [in the reading room]? Well, the incessant coming and going of readers in the room where he thought he could read distracts him and diverts his attention. The reader arrived full of good intentions, but now he is unable to maintain a distracted eye on his newspaper. . . . As soon as the reader enters the room where the lending section books are contained, he is met with the obsessive prohibitive notices: "It is absolutely forbidden to touch the books on the shelves. Instead address the clerk . . ." The statement is very declarative, and any true

> friend of books who loves books and knows how to handle them can only be offended by such a notice. Indignant or resigned, our reader consults a work titled "Catalog." He diligently chooses the authors who will delight him in his leisure hours, and he carefully notes the call number on a form that was given to him at the entrance [to the lending section]; he hands over the slip of paper to the important official whom he trusts as a competent government official but is only just a clerk. After a long wait, the clerk comes back empty-handed about three times out of five. At times the bibliophile might open the book and stop on the front page with a stamp that says, "This work must not leave the library." Nothing from the catalog notified him in advance of this restriction. Determined, the reader picks up the catalog and request slip, playing this "true lottery" of submitting requests to borrow books. I have seen readers make five or more attempts without success (which means five times three volumes each time, fifteen volumes sought).

This report details how a potential reader navigated the documentation torpor and unwelcoming rules of the Saigon Library infrastructure. Saint-Marty emphasized how the uninviting placards and disorderly technical procedures undermined the essential functions of the library. Following Saint-Marty's critique of the library as well as a series of critiques from the press by library users, the Saigon Library closed for the month of March 1920 for a complete reorganization.

The library reopened on April 1, 1920, with the implementation of several changes following the model of the Hanoi Library and Boudet's classification systems. It extended its operating hours until eight in the evening, created a separate room for young readers, and used a more efficient method of classification of works. In an article published in *La Tribune Indigène*, the author celebrated the reopening of the library and remarked how the loyal readers of the library came running to its steps after a month of being denied access to "this temple of science and literature."[86] For a month, readers were abandoned "without communing with French thought, without immersing oneself in the invigorating source of sciences and the arts whose treasures our colonial library holds." With exuberant praise for the colonial institution, the author, most likely a French expatriate residing in Saigon, elaborately narrated the intentional spatial and technical layout of the newly reorganized library under the efforts of the librarian-curator Saint-Marty:

> [In the lending section] novels or books of science and letters are placed at your fingertips. The reader, without having to resort to a clerk or secretary, can see the books and leaf through them. If it is a book to borrow from the lending section the reader submits a certain simple and quick formality by submitting their identity and address and can register and check out a book. . . . Next door, in the adjoining room devoted to on-site reading, are sturdy shelves with textbooks, dictionaries, books on sciences, law, modern languages, and French, and foreign journals are also close at hand. The regulations, in the interest of the public, prohibit the lending of [the on-site reading] books at home, but researchers will be able to come there easily

> for study of the precious documents after working in industries such as commerce or public administration. The library remains open long after the closure of the administration offices and the large buildings in the same square. But the presence of young schoolchildren, who frequently visit the library and who like to move around and talk, must not disturb the grown-ups working in the large reading room.[87]

The article raises two important roles of the Saigon Library. First, the article points to the diverse community of readers that the Saigon Library served, from government officials and commercial workers to young student readers. Secondly, the article alludes to the symbolic value of the Saigon Library and the French presence in Asia. The article concludes with praise for Saigon as a colonial city "having three thousand European inhabitants, twenty thousand indigenous, and a location for tourist lines to Cambodia and Annam, a stopover point for the great airlines of the Far East, and the capital of the most beautiful French colony."[88] This celebration of the library as a colonial monument also appears in Saint-Marty's 1921 report, in which he argued that developing the facilities and services of the Saigon Library was "imperative for the important capital city of Cochinchina, the center of our influence in the Far East."[89] In another article describing the services of the Saigon Library, the author argues that "any city worthy of a name should have a library of at least fifty thousand books, such as in the United States."[90] Calling newspaper readers to donate their books to the library, the author notes that the Saigon Library reading room had only eight thousand works and needed much more development of its collection.

After the library reopened in 1920, the director of the library, Saint-Marty, reported a steadily increasing number of visitors consulting the collection of works on topics such as law, administration, literature, art, history, and geography as well as dictionaries.[91] In order to access the reading room materials for on-site consultation, readers with a library card consulted the newly organized alphabetical and topic catalog and submitted a request form to the front desk. A separate periodicals section provided readers access to local, metropolitan, and regional newspapers from Japan, China, the Indies, the Philippines, and Siam. The periodicals section was open from eight in the morning to noon and from three in the afternoon to eight in the evening.

According to Saint-Marty's calculations for 1920, 2,071 request slips were submitted in the reading room, and the following categories of works were the most popular: magazines (583), official bulletins (378), scientific works (237), literature (217), reference works (208), and history-geography-travel (161). Saint-Marty noted that this number of request slips would average only seventeen readers a day—an inaccurate accounting of the actual use of the library because it excluded readers consulting the newspapers, periodicals, and reference works available freely on the shelves. Saint-Marty commented on readers' hesitancy to submit request slips:

> Indeed, readers of newspapers, periodicals, and reference works do not fill out a form because they find the works they desire, while the other works beyond their reach must be requested to the staff by a form. Some readers feel a mistrust toward the request slip and believe it brings an incursion to the librarian. . . . From the current number of readers, there is an absence almost totally of the schoolboy who could use the library as a resource for his studies. . . . Nevertheless, from a general observation and to my great satisfaction, the [library] institution is most popular around the hours of 7 p.m., when the readers are forced to sit closely together in order to make room for the many readers.[92]

Saint-Marty's observations shed light on the emerging social life and reading tastes in the Cochinchina reading room: Readers most often consulted periodicals and reference works in the evenings and hesitated to engage with the librarian with a bureaucratic request form. Like the reading room, the lending section confronted many challenges with its organization, facilities, and limited collections. Many of the policies and the organizational structure of the Saigon Library were legacies from its operations as an administrative library since 1865. By July 1920, Saint-Marty reported that a new system of organization for the lending section had been implemented to reduce friction for readers who were requesting works. "The method permits people to move between the shelves and choose their work, where previously they had to request a clerk to search for the work, which cost time and prolonged the congestion of services for a small number of readers."[93]

In 1920 the lending section included approximately five thousand literary and popular works, and Saint-Marty sought to develop a children's section "to satisfy the young, passionate, and assiduous Saigonese's craving for reading."[94] According to Saint-Marty, the existing collection "was barely enough to satisfy our seven hundred borrowers; the return and exchange of books seems to accelerate, and it is not uncommon to see readers exchange their books several times a week." In his July 1921 report, Saint-Marty closely analyzed the 766 monthly readers and how frequently they visited the lending section:

> 20 visit every day
> About 30 visit every three days
> About 80 visit every seven days
> About 120 visit every ten days
> About 280 visit every fifteen days
> About 90 visit every twenty days
> 146 visit rarely

Based on the frequency of reader visits and the number and types of works loaned, Saint-Marty concluded that "250 of these readers are very diligent readers, 280 average around three works, and 236 are intermittent readers."[95] Through these fine-grained statistics, Saint-Marty observed the emergence of a public reading culture divided between committed readers and those preoccupied with Saigon's urban commercial life.

By May 1924 the reading room had expanded and contained 8,963 works in its collections. Librarian Jacques Quesnel reported, "The expansion of the buildings has given the public a spacious room for frequent readers of books or newspapers and for working. On [monthly] average, 728 educated persons spend their days there, with a daily average of 28, and 1,508 request slips. The improvements only temporarily alleviate the many issues of the Saigon Library: The collection of the library overflows into another room, and the incoming books must be stored in the archives along with two thousand other books that should belong in the library collections."[96] Quesnel observed that the library served mainly government officials rather than teachers, students, and specialists. In 1924, the Saigon Library attempted to set up a library exchange with other libraries, such as the New York Public Library, in hopes of expanding the Saigon collection. By 1927, the yearly report noted that more students had begun to visit the reading room of the Saigon Library.[97]

PUBLIC READING CULTURE TASTES AND THE POPULARITY OF THE LENDING SECTION

A rare borrowing registry provides insight into the diversity of reader tastes for users of the Saigon Library lending section from 1920 to 1925.[98] The registry recorded the following: date, name and address of borrower, library catalog code, type of work, date of return, and borrower signature. From this registry, most of the readers from 1920 to 1925 were colonial administration workers who borrowed a range of books, including those on the question of French colonialism, Cicero, histories of imperialism around the world, books on Indochinese spirituality and magic, and language primers in Vietnamese, French, and Chinese. A close analysis of the borrowing registry showcases the social life and literary tastes of the lending section readers. For example, on December 22, 1924, Monsieur Thịnh, the treasurer of Cholon, borrowed the popular escapist narratives *Claudine s'en va* (by Collette and Willy, first published in 1903) and *Histoire complète de la Révolution Russe* (*The Complete History of the Russian Revolution* by Aimé Masson and published in 1918). Besides borrowing books to read at home from the lending section, Thịnh most likely consulted works on site such as the reference books in the reading room and journals in the periodicals section. During his visits, he might have encountered other readers such as French women, French and Vietnamese male government officials, journalists, and students. This diverse group of readers of the lending section included Madame Tholance, who borrowed *Connaissance de l'est* (*Knowledge of the East* by Paul Claudel, published in 1900), a book of poetry and prose written of his firsthand impressions of China, and Mademoiselle Borel, who borrowed *Cinq leçons sur la psychanalyse* (*Five Lectures in Psycho-Analysis* by

Sigmund Freud, published in 1910 in German as *Über Psychoanalyse* and translated to French in 1920) as well as *Essai sur la metaphysique d'aristote* (*Essay on the Metaphysics of Aristotle* by Felix Ravaisson, published in 1837). It was likely that Thịnh interacted with French male readers such as the customs inspector Monsieur Augommir, who borrowed Julius Caesar's commentaries. Thịnh probably encountered other Vietnamese male readers like himself who worked in the colonial administration or were journalists, like Monsieur Trịnh Hưng Ngẩu, an editor of the Saigon French-language newspaper *L'Écho Annamite*, who on his visit borrowed Charles Maybon's history of modern Annam from the sixteenth to nineteenth centuries.

In both Hanoi and Saigon, library books read on site and borrowed from the lending section spanned three significant categories: French works on history and science and collected volumes on topics like art and literature; French literary novels, leisure reading, and translations of global bestsellers; and Far East and Indochina reference works, such as those on history and religion, and maps. Public reading culture encompassed these extensive cosmopolitan reader tastes, self-directed research practices, and global sensibilities through metropolitan and local periodicals and reference matter. Public reading culture in 1920s Saigon encompassed a diverse reading public of four groups of readers: French and Vietnamese government officials, Vietnamese journalists and teachers, French women, and students. Some of the most frequent borrowers from the lending section were the library personnel themselves, such as Huê, Thông, and Lê Thế Vĩnh, who borrowed materials, often as frequently as on a weekly basis. Huê's borrowing record from 1924 to 1925 ranged from volumes on arithmetic, geometry, and notary work to Anatole France's *Le jardin d'épicure* (essays on metaphysics, religious life, and philosophy, first published in 1894) and a book on automobiles. While the majority of readers who borrowed from the lending section were men, French women also borrowed materials. Several of these French female readers worked as secretaries in the library or were married to French colonial officials, as noted in the registry. The registry records French women who borrowed books on civil law, economic development in French Indochina (*La mise en valeur des colonies françaises*), and Greek philosophy (*L'état ou le république*). In total, the borrowing registry recorded 3,016 loans from April 7, 1920, to June 2, 1925, addressing topics of administration, religion, Indochina, France, dictionaries, science, and world history.[99] In 1923 the Saigon Library collection size was 7,640. The collection increased dramatically by 1929, to 25,934, and by 1941 it had almost doubled, to 45,376.

In comparison to the Hanoi Central Library, the Saigon Cochinchina Library reading room and lending section were smaller in collection size and total readers, but they were still extremely popular among Saigon readers.[100] While Hanoi readers crowded into the reading room, Saigon readers preferred using the lending section. In 1931, the number of loans from the Cochinchina lending section almost equaled that of the Hanoi Central Library lending section. The popularity of the

FIGURE 20. Saigon Cochinchina Library reading room after reorganization and the addition of new tables to allow for more seating, ca. 1930s. The Vietnamese librarian seated on the right table oversees the room operations. Note that figures 20 to 23 appear to be part of a similar collection of staged photographs, possibly advertising the updates to the library in the 1930s. *Source*: Archives Privées Papiers Boudet 86, Archives nationales d'outre-mer, Aix-en-Provence, France, folder 52.

FIGURE 21. Additional tables outside the Saigon Cochinchina Library reading room for consulting reference materials on site, ca. 1930s. *Source*: Archives Privées Papiers Boudet 86, Archives nationales d'outre-mer, Aix-en-Provence, France, folder 52.

FIGURE 22. Saigon Cochinchina Library reading room for newspapers, ca. 1926. *Source*: Archives Privées Papiers Boudet 86, Archives nationales d'outre-mer, Aix-en-Provence, France, folder 52.

Saigon Library lending section could be due to the limited seating in the reading room and the unwelcoming facilities for readers due to its shared space with the archives. On December 16, 1926, the lending section moved to a building on 160 rue Catinat around the corner, which freed up space for a designated newspaper and periodical room for readers consulting materials on site at the Cochinchina Library at 34 rue de La Grandière. The separate location of the lending section offered a more hospitable space for patrons to consult and borrow books compared to the overcrowded and poorly maintained reading room. In 1923 the total reader visits numbered 19,200, and it had more than doubled, to 51,712, by 1926.[101] The total reader visits remained stagnant at fifty thousand from 1926 to 1938, possibly as a result of the colonial economic shock from the Great Depression. In 1935 reading room visits increased dramatically after the building expansion, which brought in additional tables and chairs. This expansion resulted in an increased number of patrons to the reading room, which averaged ninety-four patrons each day.[102] In 1938 to 1939, the total number of readers at the Saigon Library increased to 36,371, compared to 29,523 in the previous year, bringing the average to 133 readers a day. Continuing the previous year's trend, the lending section was comparatively more popular than the reading room, with both the number of borrowers in the lending section (30,919) and the total number of book loans (55,152) increasing

FIGURE 23. Two-story storage depot of the Saigon Cochinchina Library, ca. 1930s. *Source*: Archives Privées Papiers Boudet 86, Archives nationales d'outre-mer, Aix-en-Provence, France, folder 52.

by nearly 30 percent from the previous year. It seems that the increase in the number of readers at the Saigon Library could be due to the extended hours of the library; in 1939 the library was open from 9 to 11:45 in the morning and 3 in the afternoon to 10 in the evening every day except for Sunday afternoon, Monday morning, holidays, and the inventory month in the summer.[103] By 1939, the reading room and lending section of the Saigon Library had continued to increase in popularity, with extended operating hours to ten in the evening and an extensive collection of thirty thousand volumes and periodical collections covering the topics of colonialism, the Far East, law, sociology, and history.

NEGATIVE PERCEPTIONS OF THE SAIGON LIBRARY AND THE QUESTION OF ACCESS

With the growing popularity of the Saigon Library as a resource for public reading culture, the institution also underwent a sharper public critique for its continued limitations in justly serving the Saigon population. On July 27, 1928, the newspaper *La Tribune Indochinoise* published a scathing critique titled "The Bouchot Case" on the Cochinchina librarian Jean Bouchot (1886–1932). According to the article, Bouchot held a privileged and protected position as a civil servant who publicly insulted the Vietnamese through naive scholarship and "incomplete erudition."[104] The newspaper admonished Bouchot's scholarly publications, which claimed that prior to French colonialism, Vietnamese did not legitimately rule lower Cochinchina and in fact the French had helped Vietnamese conquer the Mekong Delta:

> M. Bouchot pretends to be a learned researcher. . . . Nguyễn Phan Long and H.H.T. of the newspaper *L'Écho Annamite* demonstrate the dangers of allowing any rat to enter the doors of the library: It is only necessary that the person have free time and know how to read; Bouchot happens to meet these two conditions. . . . [Bouchot] would like to find in the history of our country irrefutable proof of our indignity, probably with the secret goal of exposing that the Annamese have no legitimate reason to protest the French occupation of Cochinchina, which does not even belong to them.[105]

The article continued to critique Bouchot's public discourse and freedom of expression, declaring that "the freedom to write in newspapers" granted to government officials should not include "the right to insult the readers who pay for the newspapers." This heightened reflexivity over freedom of expression points to the vibrancy of political engagement in Saigon's 1920s Vietnamese-led public sphere, what Philippe Peycam describes as a "newspaper village," a sociopolitical network of journalists, businessmen, and publishers across Cochinchina.[106] Peycam examines this nuanced sphere of political critique within the context of Albert Sarraut's Franco-Vietnamese collaborationist policies as an "oppositional journalism," led by the 1920s Cochinchinese bourgeois elite of *La Tribune Indigène, La*

Tribune Indochinoise, and *L'Écho Annamite*. These French-language publications were able to avoid the more repressive colonial law on Vietnamese- and Chinese-language publications, and in principle Cochinchina publications were governed under the same 1881 metropolitan freedom of the press law.[107] Considered the first Vietnamese independent political newspaper, *La Tribune Indigène* (and the Vietnamese version, *Quốc Dân Diễn Đàn*) was led by two wealthy Vietnamese naturalized French citizens, the publisher Nguyễn Phú Khai and editor in chief Bùi Quang Chiêu (1873–1945), from 1917 to 1925. *La Tribune Indigène* operated as the public forum of the only permissible Vietnamese political party, the Constitutionalists, who advocated for political reforms such as increasing indigenous representation within the Colonial Council of Cochinchina.[108] In 1926 *La Tribune Indigène* was relaunched as *La Tribune Indochinoise*. In 1920 Nguyễn Phan Long (1888–1960) founded the popular liberal newspaper *L'Écho Annamite*, which later operated as a daily from 1924 to 1930.

Public denunciations of Jean Bouchot, his scholarship, and his association with the museum and library permeated Saigon's vibrant public press.[109] These public outcries point to the racial tensions among colonial administrators, Vietnamese intellectuals, and the negative public perception of colonial institutions such as the Saigon Library. The author of the 1928 article in *La Tribune Indochinoise* powerfully called out the French colonial administration and Bouchot as a government agent, who was described as "throwing a cruel insult lacking courage and thought to make us [Vietnamese] feel resigned." The article concluded with a public call to action for Vietnamese to boycott the Saigon Library and Museum Blanchard de la Brosse, where Bouchot worked:

> With regard to M. Bouchot, we ask our Annamese brothers to declare that as long as he remains in office at the library and the museum, the indigenous press will make an energetic campaign with our compatriots to avoid both at once. The Annamites, if they really still want to visit [the library and museum], will refuse to have the slightest contact with this administrator, who is not content to pick up their piastres but has the luxury of insulting them collectively.

The boycott of colonial institutions functioned as strategic resistance to injustice and insult. It is unclear how effective this boycott of the library was in enacting change. In a following article also reflecting on the Bouchot case, the author commented that a public boycott would "deprive Annamites [only] of an excellent library, not of an excellent librarian."[110] Nevertheless, the public denunciation of Bouchot as an insulting colonial official could have conveyed an overall negative perception of the Saigon Library to Vietnamese readers of the popular periodicals such as *La Tribune Indochinoise, L'Écho Annamite*, and *Đông Pháp Thời Báo: Le Courrier Indochinois*, which had condemned Bouchot. From its original founding as a colonial administrative library, the Saigon Library represented colonial knowledge and French administrative authority. Bouchot's association with the library possibly intensified the public perception of the institution as an outwardly pro-colonial institution that reified Vietnamese subjugation. Journalists and readers of *L'Écho Annamite* already had a negative impression of the Saigon Library, insinuating that the library was mirroring the colonial government's fear of political dissent and a free press. A 1926 *L'Écho Annamite* article publicly called attention to the fact that the Saigon Library periodicals collection intentionally did not include *L'Écho Annamite* in its collections.[111] The article recalled that the previous governor, Monsieur Cognacq, brashly perceived *L'Écho Annamite* to be anti-French and revolutionary, and claimed that the Saigon Library must not reflect any political opinion because it functioned as a public institution paid by taxpayer money. The article also defended the newspaper's own freedom of expression to "only tell the truth, nothing but the truth, without hatred or fear." The article emphasized that differences of political opinion should not deny curious library readers who want to consult *L'Écho Annamite*, and described the newspaper as "the most important indigenous French-language newspaper in Cochinchina."

Besides these public critiques of political biases, the dominant public discourse about the Saigon Library centered on the question of public access as a broader debate about the effectiveness of colonial institutions in serving the diverse needs of a colonial public. On September 27, 1928, author "M.N." wrote about how the Saigon Library was still not accessible to all readers.[112] The author critiqued the limited opening hours of nine to eleven in the morning and three to seven-thirty in the evening and demanded that the Saigon Library follow the Hanoi library hours of eight in the morning to ten in the evening. "Many times on my way home from the office—in the evening, of course—I wanted to take the steps up the library stairs to read some magazines. Unfortunately, I realized that the library was about to close, so I stopped halfway and returned home instead." The reader explained that commercial workers and civil servants could never benefit from access to the library. The repeated complaints of the inaccessibility of the Saigon Library in the pages of the popular press point to the demand for the library space and resources and the unrealized potential of the colonial institution to serve its broad reading public.

Articles debated and proposed changes to the library services, collections, and regulations. Other public commentary reflected on everyday happenings, reader tastes, and collections. In 1934, the daily journal *La Dépêche Indochine* published a series of commentaries on the restricted borrowing permissions at the Saigon Library. The article begins by citing a wise adage that teachers used to encourage their students to "read, read. It's better to even read detective novels than not to read at all."[113] The author explained how "reading, just as much as travel, trains youth and entertains the old. Reading also leads to whatever you want to get out of it." The author explained that overall reading is a good thing, but it is not a luxury that everyone can afford. He described how at the Saigon Library, "everyone finds there something to satisfy their tastes according to their temperament." The author then focused his critique on the decreased maximum number of books one could borrow each visit. Previously, each person could borrow two books. However, recently the rules had changed to permit a family, regardless of size, to borrow only two books at a time. He recounted the grievances of one such library reader and his frustration with this new policy: "There are three of us at home with different tastes in reading. My wife loves travel novels, my son loves adventure books, and I love science. As for the three of us, we can no longer carry home more than two volumes, and thus I am forced to abstain from reading." The justification for the new policy was that a handful of individuals were borrowing books and not returning them until more than a month later. The reader proposed three alternative policies in order to ameliorate the issues: first, reinstating the policy of allowing two books to be borrowed per person and implementing a late fee; second, imposing the same type of fine for any book returned in poor condition or with missing pages; and third, having families pay a small deposit if they borrowed more than six books at a time.

This discussion demonstrates how readers valued their library privileges and cultivated specific genre preferences. Five days later another reader responded to this first article in *La Dépêche Indochine* on the critique of the limited borrowing privileges.[114] The author described the restriction of two books per family as "notoriously insufficient, forcing people to commute between home and the library far too often," since it would only take about two days to finish reading the books. The author considered how transportation costs determined library use. The author explained that a journey to the library from their residence in Dakao cost fifteen cents; every two to three days (after finishing the two books checked out), they would need to return to the library to return and borrow new books, costing thirty cents every two to three days. They described this cost as "a ruinous expense." The author proposed that journeying to the library once a week or every fifteen days to check out and return a larger number of books was ideal and more economically feasible.

The author also critiqued the cumbersome registration process at the Saigon Library. He recounted his friend's experience of registering for the lending section of the library, during which an individual first needed to fill out an application form, then "provide documentation of his rent to prove that he did not live under a bridge," and, third, be introduced by a friend already registered at the library to act as a guarantor, followed by a series of interrogations. The applicant complained of the administrative hassle of providing excessive documentation: "I thought they were going to ask me for my certificate of baptism!" The applicant explained that submitting documents for a library registration was reasonable, but the current state of documentary interrogation at the Saigon Library was absurd and insulting. The author signed with the pen name "Vieux Khmer" (Old Khmer). These published newspaper critiques debated the library mission, services, and personnel as political issues of public good. The library existed in the public consciousness of a wide group of interested readers who were invested in the availability of materials in the library and its opening hours for public access.

CONCLUSION

In 1939 a photograph of a new children's reading space in the Saigon Library was published on the inside cover of the annual Directorate report. A sizable portion of the lending section on 160 rue Catinat was dedicated to the new children's corner, opened on November 14, 1938. The annual report explained that the children's corner was equipped with furniture, newspapers, and publications suitable for younger readers; it reported that the children's corner was already very popular, receiving 2,216 requests to borrow books since its opening.[115] In 1942 the lending section and children's corner were advertised to be open regularly from 9 to 11:30 in the morning and from 1:30 to 7:30 in the evening.[116] The creation of the children's corner was a prolonged effort begun in 1920 by librarian-curator Léon Saint-Marty to create a formal designated space for young readers in the Saigon Library.[117] Young readers of the library included Vietnamese students as well as the young children of French women expatriates who were regular library readers.[118] In the 1939 photograph, a group of young readers of various ages—Vietnamese and French, male and female—posed with a book or periodical in hand, surrounded by neat shelves of reading matter. Their body language presents an image of a diverse young reading community immersed in library reading, sitting and standing in close proximity to one another yet still maintaining a semblance of orderly erudition. This photograph advertised the new public space as cultural infrastructure to propagate idealized comportment and bookish civility among the next generation of French and Vietnamese readers.

As shown in this chapter, however, the everyday reality of library use ranged widely from orderly quiet contemplation to crowdedness, socialization, noise, and violations of library procedures such as overdue books, stealing, and entering without a library card. In the popular press, readers complained about the lack of public access, limited operating hours, burdensome procedures, and inadequate facilities. The extensive debates of librarians and readers show how the library was more than just a simple repository of literature or a monument of French civilization. The Hanoi Central Library and Saigon Cochinchina Library were fundamental institutions for the cultivation of a public reading culture characterized by social practices of public space, self-directed reading of cosmopolitan literature, and interactions with a state institution. The library infrastructure was incomparable to other spaces, offering a valuable public urban space of leisurely retreat and a resource for voluntarist learning that supplemented formal education. Readers made use of the valuable library collections to satisfy their own intellectual curiosities, immersing themselves in diverse local reading matter and global literature.

FIGURE 24. Children's corner in the Saigon Cochinchina Library, 1939. This photograph was used in the yearly report of the Directorate of Archives and Libraries and appears to function as an advertisement for the new children's corner in the library. *Source*: Rémi Bourgeois, *Rapport sur la direction des archives et des bibliothèques (1938–1939)* (Hanoi: Imprimerie Le Van Tan, 1939).

Furthermore, the library was central to important political and intellectual debates about civic duties in modern public spaces and fair public access for all, regardless of race, age, profession, and gender. Critiques of the library functioned as experiments in public citizenship, encompassing demands that the colonial administration carry out essential responsibilities to its subjects.

3

To Circulate

Libraries as Vehicles of Cultural Propaganda

Most of these [existing Vietnamese book] productions are mediocre; some of them are dangerous because they are inspired by Bolshevik propaganda pamphlets widely distributed in China, and the censor does not always succeed in stopping them. The best way to combat the harmful influence is to intensify the production of works of intelligent popularization. The automobile library, which permits the distribution of these books not only in the provincial capitals but even in certain prefectures and districts, will be the best agent of distribution.

—PAUL BOUDET, MARCH 6, 1929[1]

In March 1936, the first bibliobus, or book automobile library, in Indochina began its journey through nine provinces in Cochinchina lending books to Vietnamese and French provincial readers. The bibliobus rotated through the provincial capitals twice a month and circulated 832 French and Vietnamese books of popular literature, politics, morality, and science from its headquarters at the Cochinchina Library at 34 rue de La Grandière in Saigon. Vietnamese secretary Lỗ Công Lạc and driver Trần Văn Trà from the Cochinchina Library accompanied the automobile to facilitate book checkouts for a few hours in front of central buildings such as government offices, schools, and hospitals. The bibliobus encountered many delays and logistical challenges during its journey. On September 1, 1937, on the way from Bà Rịa to Biên Hoà, the vehicle struck a tree stump when swerving to avoid hitting a seven-year-old girl who was in the road.[2] This accident damaged the vehicle, and a second bibliobus was sent from Saigon to complete the route while the first vehicle underwent extensive repairs for a month.[3] On November 15, 1937, the newly repaired bibliobus departed from Saigon to complete its forty-fifth rotation throughout the Cochinchina provinces of Gò Công, Mỹ Tho, Bến Tre, Sa Đéc, Trà Vinh, Vĩnh Long, Tân An, Gia Định, Thủ Dầu Một, Bà Rịa, and Biên Hoà.[4]

FIGURE 25. The bibliobus from Saigon Cochinchina Library stationed in front of the central market of Cap Saint-Jacques, December 1937. *Source*: Rémi Bourgeois, *Rapport sur la direction des archives et des bibliothèques (1938–1939)* (Hanoi: Imprimerie Le Van Tan, 1939).

Over the course of a year, the bibliobus served a total of ten thousand provincial readers. After complaints in Vietnamese newspapers that the circulating libraries did not extend into the provinces of the Tranbassac region (western Mekong Delta), a second bibliobus was launched in December 1937 with some operational improvements and a collection of 768 works.[5] The vehicle made tours to eight other provinces of Cochinchina, extending the bibliobus system to provinces farther away from Saigon (Bạc Liêu, Cà Mau, Rạch Giá, Hà Tiên, Châu Đốc, Tây Ninh, Gò Công, and Bà Rịa–Cap Saint-Jacques). To support one another on the exhausting journeys, two librarian secretaries rather than one accompanied the driver on the bibliobus, and they were paid a monthly salary of ten piastres each instead of one piastre for each day the library was stationed. Librarian-archivist of the Cochinchina Library Simone de Saint-Exupéry advocated for better working conditions, such as a higher salary, employment of an additional secretary, and designated resting quarters for the accompanying secretaries of the bibliobus during their provincial tours.[6] This second bibliobus served a total of 21,542 readers over the course of one year.

This chapter uncovers the history of the French colonial bibliobus, a circulating library vehicle system transporting reading matter from the Saigon and

Hanoi urban centers into the provinces. The bibliobus operated as a symbolic and logistical extension of the French colonial state—its ideologies, literature, and reading practices—into the countryside. The circulating libraries physically distributed politically "safe" reading matter to provincial readers in an effort to facilitate healthy leisure activities and public moralization. As seen in the opening statement from Paul Boudet addressed to colonial officials, libraries functioned as cultural propaganda systems to combat the dangerous spread of "mediocre" and Bolshevik-inspired revolutionary texts circulating in cities and the countryside. By the 1920s and 1930s, the French colonial civilizing mission project of intellectual hegemony had evolved into a wide French colonial cultural propaganda project that reinforced colonial rule, economic exploitation (*mise en valeur*), and the Franco-Vietnamese collaboration. Colonial officials proposed circulating libraries as vehicles of cultural propaganda as a concerned response to the spread of politically subversive, anti-French ideas and the rise of mass political organizing and Marixst-Leninist political thought among Vietnamese male urban youth in the 1920s and 1930s. I trace the political debates among colonial officials such as Governor General Pierre Pasquier and director of the Office of Indigenous Publishing Émile Vayrac to create a top-down Indochina-wide regime of cultural propaganda modeled on the Balai Pustaka publishing and distribution network in the Dutch East Indies (today's Indonesia).

In addition to representing a political strategy, the circulating libraries project was driven by evolving techniques of library sciences grounded in bibliographic control, documentation management, and public moralization. The circulating libraries project was deeply influenced by the personal ambitions of Paul Boudet, who wanted to implement a modern library system in Indochina inspired by international library sciences and public library movements in France, America, England, and the Dutch East Indies. Circulating libraries were dynamic experiments in library management that could respond to logistical constraints and readers' literary and language demands. In addition to providing French-language materials, the bibliobus circulating libraries were important distributors of popular Vietnamese *quốc ngữ* literature, shaping provincial literacy and exposure to a booming urban Vietnamese publishing sphere. Through a close study of the bibliobus readers, books, and geographic networks, I uncover the literary circulations and language landscape of Vietnamese reading culture in the late colonial period. This chapter concludes with the transition to more direct methods of censorship and propaganda during the Vichy period in Indochina during World War II (1940–45). Vichy cultural propaganda strategies had roots in the late colonial initiatives of surveillance, distribution, and circulating libraries. Tracing the intertwined political, moral, and scientific strategies of library circulation, I argue that libraries functioned as a technology of statecraft to maintain legitimacy, curb political agitators, and carry out cultural propaganda throughout Indochina.

CULTURAL PROPAGANDA AS STATE PROJECT: VIETNAMESE RADICALISM AND COLONIAL PUBLISHING

Since the early decades of the twentieth century, colonial officials were keenly aware of and threatened by the rise and influence of anticolonial sentiment, political organizing, and the spread of communism in Indochina.[7] Top-down censorship laws and policing surveillance systems attempted to curb the production and circulation of anticolonial publications. One such method of governmental seizure of tendentious materials was to demonstrate its danger to state security or that it violated the legal deposit.[8] Vietnamese publishers, writers, and printers worked within a changing landscape of colonial laws on freedom of the press and different levels of enforcement, and they often worked outside of colonial policy and censors. In principle, Cochinchina newspapers had legal freedoms similar to those of newspapers in the French metropole (according to an 1881 freedom of the press law) and thus developed a wider public sphere of political journalism, especially for Saigon's French-language periodicals. Four general policies curbed Vietnamese-language publishing: (1) *quốc ngữ* and Chinese-language presses were classified as "foreign presses" and thus were subject to more monitoring and prior approval by the governor general, (2) non-French-language newspapers had to submit a copy of their publication to the censor before printing, (3) only French citizens could own and manage newspapers, and (4) non-periodicals such as books did not have to be submitted to censors for prepublication review but could be seized after publication.[9] During the First World War Governor General Albert Sarraut (who served from 1911 to 1913 and 1917 to 1919) created a secret police force (*sûreté*) with the director of political affairs, Louis Marty, as the head in order to systematically monitor Vietnamese communist and anticolonial activity. Colonial officials enlisted the labor of reformist Vietnamese intellectuals to collaborate on a series of state-sponsored or subsidized publications in French and Vietnamese, the most notable of whom were the editors and intellectuals Nguyễn Văn Vĩnh (1882–1936) at the publications *Đông Dương Tạp Chí, Trung Bắc Tân Văn*, and *L'Annam Nouveau*, Phạm Quỳnh (1892–1945) at *Nam Phong*, and Bùi Quang Chiêu (1873–1945) at *La Tribune Indigène*.[10]

The French colonial administration looked to other European colonies as models for cultural propaganda and drew inspiration from the existing Balai Pustaka state-sponsored publishing bureau, distribution office, and library system in the Dutch East Indies.[11] The Balai Pustaka originated in 1908 within the Department of Education, formed its own office in 1917, and over time became the leading

FIGURE 26. A logo of the Balai Pustaka Office of Popular Literature from a pamphlet published in 1925 in the French colonial dossier of research documents. *Source*: "Indes néerlandaises: Notice sur le service pour la littérature populaire" (Batavia: Balai Pustaka, 1925).

state-sponsored publishing and library system in the Dutch East Indies. From the 1920s to 1940s, the Balai Pustaka published and distributed print media to school libraries and built a network of libraries throughout the Dutch East Indies, functioning as instruments of cultural propaganda and socialization. By the 1930s, there were over 2,500 Taman Pustaka (Gardens of Reading) libraries, mainly in Java. Works available in the Taman Pustaka included printed versions of oral legends, Javanese versions of the Mahabharata, and translations into Malay of Western bestsellers.[12] In 1928, the Governor General of Indochina, Pierre Pasquier, commissioned extensive studies on the Dutch East Indies publishing and popular libraries project, seeking to implement a similar project in French Indochina.[13] From April 9 to 20, 1929, Pasquier journeyed to the Dutch East Indies to study colonial infrastructure, information policy, and cultural programs. Serving as governor general from 1926 to 1927 and 1928 to 1934, Pasquier was a conservative, pro-monarchy colonial official who authorized extensive cultural propaganda projects centered on libraries and print distribution in French colonial Indochina.

At the request of Pasquier, the director of the Office of Indigenous Publishing at the office of the resident superior of Tonkin, Émile Vayrac studied the Balai Pustaka, evaluated the publishing industry in Indochina, and generated a widely distributed report, "Notes on the Volkslectuur."[14] The report sheds light on French colonial officials' concerns about the circulation of anticolonial ideologies permeating Vietnamese publishing. Vayrac characterized the dangerous state of Vietnamese literary production as "struggling in anarchy and dragging itself into insignificance. Apart from some re-publications of old poems or ancient moral guides, and a small number of serious works, the majority of Vietnamese print criticizes us and speaks poorly of our civilization."[15] Praising the Dutch East Indies, Vayrac commended the infrastructural extension of the Balai Pustaka to create libraries in schools, police stations, and hospitals and to organize a centralized publishing office for the circulation of procolonial propaganda material. Working in the French colonial administration for decades, Vayrac advanced extensive cultural propaganda projects of *vulgarisation*, the popularization of politically safe and moralistic reading among Vietnamese colonial subjects through state-sponsored publishing, translation, and libraries.[16]

By the 1920s and 1930s, colonial officials spoke of a generational increase in political organizing among the Vietnamese youth. In the 1928–29 essay "Program for the Recovery of the Public Spirit" from his "Notes on the Volkslectuur" report, Vayrac elaborated on the colonial administration's anxieties about Vietnamese radicalism. Vayrac described the existing threat of Bolshevik political ideas, Chinese influence, and anti-French sentiment among a growing generation of dangerous, young, urban Vietnamese radicals eager for change:

> The Bolshevik propaganda and the action of anti-French agitators of all sorts ended up creating among our protégés a detrimental state of spirit. Fortunately, the true people—those of the countryside—are still not yet contaminated. But the population

> of the cities welcome subversive ideas with a complacency that brings dangerous risks to public peace and gradually brings disorder to indigenous society. The workers, the students, and even the schoolchildren especially have received a taste of indiscipline and disorder. All the serious Vietnamese are worried about the insubordination and insolence of the new generation. . . . The evil spirit is even in the primary schools, so that all the sons of those who collaborate with us are insulting us daily. An irresistible desire for change, a thirst for new order, a sort of evil arrogance is quickly spreading throughout all classes of society.[17]

Vayrac called attention to the pervasiveness of Bolshevik-inspired, anti-French agitation among urban Vietnamese, especially workers, students, and youth. This spirit of subversion undermined the Vietnamese family, corrupted the minds of young students, and could potentially permeate into the countryside.

During the first decades of the twentieth century, an earlier generation of Vietnamese thinkers had experimented with political movements (the Đông Du and Duy Tân movements) around study abroad and intellectual modernist networks in China and Japan, as well as the creation of a hybridized Eastern and Western curriculum through the Đông Kinh Nghĩa Thục (Tonkin Free School), which operated from 1907 to 1908 in Hanoi. Spearheaded by the political activism and intellectual thought of Phan Bội Châu (1867–1940) and Phan Châu Trinh (1872–1926), this earlier generation existed between the competing world of letters shaped by Confucian learning, Literary Sinitic language, and Chinese and Japanese debates about social Darwinism, westernization, and civilization. In the 1920s to 1930s, a new generation of urban French- or French colonial–educated Vietnamese radicals and revolutionaries came of age, and they would come to shape the landscape of the next decades of mass political organizing and Vietnamese nationalism. A series of crucial events in 1924–27 sparked the organizing of Vietnamese nationalist and anticolonial associations, mass student-led strikes, and the explosion of underground publishing of political tracts and critiques of the French colonial government. These events included the trial of revolutionary patriot Phan Bội Châu, the death of Phan Châu Trinh, the arrest of prolific radical journalist Nguyễn An Ninh (1900–1943), and the attempted assassination of the governor General of Indochina by Vietnamese activist Phạm Hồng Thái (1896–1924).

Urban and cosmopolitan leaders such as Nguyễn An Ninh and Hồ Chí Minh (1890–1969) shaped the politics of youth organizing, drawing from transnational political and social theories of Marxism-Leninism, Chinese nationalism (inspired by Sun-Yat Sen), French socialism, anarchism, and international communist organizing. Hue-Tam Ho Tai characterizes the late 1920s rise of a Vietnamese radicalism characterized by an "individualist, experimental political mood" and political consciousness.[18] David Marr considers the intellectuals of the late colonial period as a distinct rupture from the previous scholar gentry; this new intelligentsia (*giới trí thức mới*) and mass politics were led by a new generation committed to "thinking, talking, reading, and writing about change."[19] The 1920s to 1930s was a period of variegated political and cultural mentalities, debating various approaches to social and governmental transformation, including constitutionalism, restoration, patriotic reform, republicanism, anarchism, socialism, and cultural conservatism.[20] By the 1930s and 1940s, mass politics and Marxist-Leninist class-based arguments dominated Vietnamese political organizing. Revolutionary organizations formed throughout Vietnam and across spatial networks of Indochina, Hong Kong, Guangzhou, Bangkok, Singapore, Moscow, and Paris.[21] The late colonial period was characterized by the founding of important political groups such as the Jeune Annam, the Secret Society of Nguyễn An Ninh, Tân Việt Cách Mệnh Đảng (the New Vietnam Revolutionary Party), Việt Nam Quốc Dân Đảng (the Vietnamese Nationalist Party), Thanh Niên (the Vietnamese Revolutionary Youth League), founded by Hồ Chí Minh in Guangzhou in 1925, and the Vietnamese Communist Party, founded by Hồ Chí Minh in Hong Kong in 1930 (and which later became the Indochinese Communist Party).[22]

Within this context of increased radicalism and revolutionary organizing, the French colonial administration developed new strategies to control the "spreading evil" and insubordination among the "outspoken Vietnamese." Vayrac believed that carefully crafted and widespread propaganda messages could counter the rising anti-French and revolutionary sentiment of the Vietnamese urban youth. Calling for the "revival of the Vietnamese public spirit," Vayrac proposed a four-part propaganda project: (1) counterpropaganda, (2) indirect, discreet, and unperceivable propaganda, (3) propaganda through actions, and (4) propaganda through public image.

In Vayrac's words, indirect propaganda must be strategic and prudent to be most effective among the Vietnamese:

> It must be avoided at all costs that propaganda resembles advertising. . . . Indirect propaganda alone will be effective. It is indispensable that propaganda is exercised in a very discreet manner and remains unrecognizable. It is not sufficient to only popularize useful knowledge and practical education for the masses. [Instead, indirect propaganda] will take the form of a direction of conscience, of perpetual teaching, of advice to writers, of constant encouragement to progress in all aspects without neglecting the humblest [people]. This enlightened soliciting is for the good of the people and especially for the well-being of the countryside inhabitants.[23]

Vayrac again emphasized the importance of the rural population—the group that he considered not only the humble "true people" of Indochina, but also the population most vulnerable to the political ideologies propagated by urban intellectuals. Vayrac suggested two effective methods of indirect propaganda: propaganda through action (such as *mise en valeur* building projects, improving the agricultural production of rural peasants, and supplying water and fertilizer to the countryside) and propaganda by imagery (through distributing positive representations of colonial projects through indigenous print media).[24] Vayrac provided detailed examples of propaganda by appearance through images, graphs, diagrams, and public display through posters, postcards, and photographs that conveyed French colonial progress and modernity. Vayrac listed the following examples: a comparative image of Haiphong with a small Annamese junk in 1885 compared to a large modern steamer in 1927, with detailed measurements of each; images of irrigation projects; and a comparison of the reinforcement of Tonkin dikes on the eve of French colonialism and in the contemporary period. Vayrac emphasized the power of visual propaganda: "The ignorant people are educated only by the eyes. And everyone, including us, easily retains that which has strikingly impressed us or that which 'leaps to our eyes' [that which is obvious]." Vayrac's report and essay deploy both racialized language and paternalistic visions of executing a project of colonial control. Colonial officials such as Vayrac described Vietnamese as primitive, easily persuaded, and corruptible. In this racist framing Vietnamese are rendered as passive recipients rather than autonomous intellectual actors. At the same time, in these colonial documents Vietnamese are portrayed as outspoken and in need of being skillfully manipulated with a strategic, indirect form of propaganda.

The essay concludes with an attached list of European works to be translated into Vietnamese. Vayrac argued that the best works to translate for Vietnamese readers included "proverbial compilations, French popular medieval literature (such as Charles Perrault's fairy tales, Jean de La Fontaine's fables, the folkloric *Le roman de Renart*), and moral works (such as Dr. Paul Carton's naturalist philosophies and other works on healthy living)." This list focused primarily on instructional, apolitical texts that could civilize and morally uplift Vietnamese readers. The colonial state saw themselves as having a direct political interest in indigenous publishing and libraries in order to produce and promote a procolonial vision of the French colonial Indochina project as benevolent modernization and popular moralization.

Vayrac's study is only one example of the extensive documentation from the colonial administration that shows how control of publishing and libraries was essential as a propaganda tool for the colonial state. Between 1929 and 1931, Governor General Pierre Pasquier requested that the governor of Cochinchina, resident superior in Annam, Cambodge, and Laos, implement an indigenous publishing and libraries project influenced by Pasquier's studies of the Dutch East Indies libraries and Vayrac's project of cultural propaganda.[25] In Cochinchina, the top-down requests from Pasquier launched extensive discussions between the curator of the Cochinchina Library, Léon Saint-Marty, the secretary-general of the Societé des études indochinoises (Society of Indochinese Studies), Jean Bouchot, and the governor of Cochinchina, Jean-Félix Krautheimer.

Saint-Marty wrote to the governor of Cochinchina emphasizing the importance of intellectual nourishment for the Cochinchinese in the context of the rising popularity of the syncretic religion Caodaism: "In the outbreak of religious and philosophical doctrines such as Caodaism in our Cochinchinese colony, the attractiveness of propaganda clearly indicates the necessity of providing to our protégés the elements of intellectual nourishment that counter the metaphorical claims of dangerous utopias."[26] In 1926, the messianic religion Caodaism (Đại Đạo Tam Kỳ Phổ Độ, or Great Way of the Third Time of Redemption) was founded in Tây Ninh and gained tremendous popularity among the ethnic Khmer and Việt populations in eastern Cambodia and southwestern Cochinchina. Colonial officials grew fearful of the rising influence of Caodaism and framed the widespread influence of Caodaism within the 1920s and 1930s rise of mass politics and threats to colonial power. Penny Edwards examines how the colonial protectorate government in Cambodia sponsored Buddhism as a geo-cultural divide to break down the transnational community of Khmer and Việt Caodaists living across the Cambodge-Cochinchine borderlands. The Cambodian protectorate government also feared anticolonial mass movements and subversions to royal authority and shut down the spread of Caodaism, calling it "dangerous propaganda."[27] Back in Cochinchina, the library curator Saint-Marty stressed the important colonial responsibility to "direct the intellectual movement of the people" away from contending spheres of social organizing such as the widely popular Caodaist movement. As a solution, Saint-Marty proposed an Indochina popular libraries project that could control the circulation of indigenous-language books similar to the initiatives in the Dutch East Indies.

Secretary-general Jean Bouchot also responded to Pasquier's circular on behalf of the Society of Indochinese Studies.[28] Bouchot had worked in the Cochinchina Library from 1926 to 1929 and had joined the Society of Indochinese Studies in 1925.[29] In his response to Pasquier, Bouchot expressed concern that a centralized official organization of libraries or publishers "would appear too governmental, controlling, and intervening in the intellectual composition of publications. Official initiatives are effective and invaluable, but in literary matters, [the initiative] would not be as effective if its influence were not discreet and exercised in an indirect and distant manner." Rather, Bouchot proposed the creation of a reading committee drawn from the Petrus Ky Commission, which had been established in 1928 and was composed of select Vietnamese members of the Society of Indochinese Studies who sought to develop "a pure Vietnamese language based on tradition." This committee would be tasked with reading and judging which works should be published, revised, or edited and submitting their recommendations to the Society of Indochinese Studies and the Cochinchina governor. Bouchot described the reading committee as a "semiofficial organ, under administrative control," but also distant enough from the governor general to provide independent recommendations of works for publication.

As for the task of selecting library materials, Bouchot emphasized the importance of works from the West and works written in indigenous languages. Bouchot argued that library collections should emphasize collections in the following order of importance: almanacs, ancient indigenous works (such as books on customs, beliefs, poetry, and legends), children's works, popular works on science, agriculture, and industry, and, lastly, modern literature.[30] This prioritized both didactic, instructional, and practical materials as well as literary and popular works. Bouchot's hybrid private-state plan built upon the existing infrastructure of the Society of Indochinese Studies and the existing Saigon Cochinchina Library rather than proposing a completely new top-down system of publishing and libraries. Recognizing constraints in transportation and environmental challenges to the conservation of reading matter, Bouchot concluded his statement with a demand to maintain hygiene and prevent the spread of infectious diseases throughout the Indochina libraries:

> It must not be forgotten, however, that in a country where epidemics are not rare and tuberculosis is particularly severe, books are the most terrible vehicles of microbes. Neither Java nor America seems to have to worry about this. However, this problem must worry us particularly here, not only for the provincial libraries but also for the library of the capital. It would be advisable to provide for a simple, effective method of periodic disinfection that does not deteriorate the works. On this point the committee notes its incompetence; this task is automatically done in the German and Scandinavian libraries.

This last commentary shows the international scope of Indochinese library development, which looked toward European, American, and other colonial models to implement library organization and maintenance. Furthermore, Bouchot's commentary points to the issue of "dangerous circulation" as both content and disease, and thus called for the urgent control of print. In other words, the content of books as well as their hygienic state needed to be carefully monitored.

On November 28, 1929, Governor of Cochinchina Krautheimer reviewed the two studies by Saint-Marty and Bouchot and submitted them to the governor general of Indochina and the Department of Political Affairs.[31] Krautheimer preferred the popular libraries model proposed by the Society of Indochinese Studies over Saint-Marty's model, which was considered "too administrative." He argued that a "flexible organization outside the administration as much as possible will give better results." On July 12, 1930, Governor General Pasquier approved the Petrus Ky Commission to operate as the publishing office and to select and suggest reading matter for publication, translation, and distribution throughout Cochinchina.[32] Pasquier also approved of the project to create regional and circulating libraries under the management of the Directorate of Archives and Libraries of Indochina.

PAUL BOUDET'S PROPOSED AGENCY FOR BOOK DISTRIBUTION AND THE BIBLIOBUS

Inspired by the Balai Pustaka in the late 1920s, Pierre Pasquier officially enlisted the director of the Directorate of Archives and Libraries of Indochina, Paul Boudet, to research public libraries and circulating libraries around the world. Since the founding of the Directorate in 1917, Boudet had envisioned an expansive network of provincial libraries throughout Indochina. On February 28, 1929, Boudet wrote to the American Library Association office in Paris and requested documents to study the American circulating book vehicle or book shipment service in order to develop a similar project in Tonkin.[33] Boudet was particularly interested in the practical, cost-efficient methods used in the distribution of books by automobile. From this began an extensive exchange of letters between Boudet and libraries all around the world. Boudet received extensive replies and research resources from the American Library Association (ALA) in Paris, the central ALA office in Chicago, and the California State Library in Sacramento. American libraries shipped hundreds of recent pamphlets, legal documents, book catalogs, and newspapers for Boudet to study the organization of circulating libraries and book vehicles in America.[34] The research materials included documentation on school libraries and public libraries in Oakland, Cleveland, Toledo, and Detroit and research pamphlets on library development such as "The County Library Comes Home to the People," "How to Start a Public Library," "Books Wanted: Rural People Interested in County Library Plan," and "The Rural School with and without County Library Service." These resources explored topics such as the curatorial responsibility of librarians, the importance of literacy, and access to "useful" technological knowledge.

On March 6, 1929, Boudet submitted his study on circulating libraries to Pierre Pasquier and the director general of public instruction in Indochina. In the comprehensive study titled "Report on the Creation of Provincial Libraries and a Central Organ for the Distribution of Books," Boudet drew from his extensive research on American, European, and Dutch East Indies libraries and put forward a project to develop a central service for the distribution of books in provinces, which would be managed through the Directorate.[35] Boudet reported that even by 1929, almost no provincial libraries existed. Boudet envisioned a future where at least one French-Vietnamese library existed in each provincial capital; however, that would require long-term commitment of state funding and the development of a cadre of indigenous librarians.

Meanwhile, Boudet proposed an intermediary organization that could help the development of provincial libraries: a central agency for the distribution of books in the provinces. In his March 6, 1929, report, Boudet outlined the framework for the central agency, which would function almost like a circulating mobile library:

> In the first stage of provincial libraries organization, there must be a very flexible organization that allows for the maximum use of the books and benefits the greatest number of inhabitants of the provinces but with minimal cost and personnel. To obtain this result I have the honor to propose to you the creation of a central book distribution agency in the provinces, a sort of mobile library with frequent and easy turnover, which would supplement the collections of the local administration or a teacher.

Boudet referenced the success of the Dutch East Indies' popular literature system, in which a central organization published, collected, sold, and distributed books to the twenty-five thousand designated libraries called the Jardins des lettres (Gardens of Literature). Boudet praised and most likely exaggerated the extent of the Dutch East Indies popular library system: "Each [library] has a collection of three to four hundred books and provides book-lending services to indigenous [readers] for 215 days [out of the year]. In 1924, 210,000 readers from all classes of society borrowed 1,600,000 books." Boudet also praised American library efforts "to bring the book closer to the reader" through systems of circulating libraries based out of the central county library. He detailed the system of American bookmobiles, admiring the county library of Santa Barbara, California, which reportedly had three branches, had eighty-three stations (for circulating libraries) in 1922, and recorded 330,122 book loans.

From these comparative library models, Boudet proposed his circulating library project—to be implemented first in Tonkin, and then later expanded throughout Indochina. The project consisted of two parts: first, the lending of French and *quốc ngữ* books in the provinces, and second, the distribution to the provinces of popular books and pamphlets published by indigenous writers and under official control. Boudet envisioned an elaborate network of book exchange between provinces enabled by book vehicles and operated by librarians, secretaries, and drivers.[36] Boudet proposed that the Indochina general budget contribute to the costs of this project, which totaled approximately ten thousand piastres. Recognizing the high cost of the project, Boudet emphasized the importance of provincial libraries and a book distributor for both the European and indigenous population. Boudet explained,

> How can these expenses be justified? For the European population, this cost, which might appear high at first glance, is in fact very small considering the important needs that it meets. It can be plainly justified by the fact that it can permit the organization of book loans to the Europeans dispersed throughout the provinces. In fact, according to the last official directory in 1928, the European population in Tonkin consisted of 2,807 inhabitants in Hanoi and 3,719 inhabitants in the twenty-three provinces and four military territories. . . . In the provinces, many civil servants and

> settlers, deprived of leisurely distractions, living by themselves, or during the long Tonkinese winters, aspire to educate themselves and develop their intellectual culture. However, they are denied this due to the lack of libraries and the impossibility of purchasing all the essential books. . . . One can affirm without a doubt that the success of the circulating libraries will be even greater than that of the now heavily frequented lending section of the Central Library [in Hanoi].

According to Boudet, a circulating libraries system could provide the European population a productive and educational leisure activity.

Boudet argued that the project could greatly benefit the indigenous population as well. Boudet first explained that the circulating library could help promote the Vietnamese book and publishing industries, since "Vietnamese are avid readers and the success of sales of certain collections published by Vietnamese printers are expected. He then argued that the circulating library project could serve as cultural propaganda to combat the spread of politically "dangerous" reading matter among Vietnamese readers. Boudet enlisted an argument similar to that in Vayrac's proposal for cultural propaganda: that the availability of "politically safe" texts should be increased through state-sponsored distribution, libraries, and publishing in hopes that these texts would flood the Vietnamese print market and compete with the popularity of tendentious reading matter among Vietnamese urban youth.

Wishing to garner support for his project, Boudet submitted his report to Governor General Pasquier, the resident superior of Tonkin, and the director of public instruction. Boudet emphasized the undeniable benefit of this libraries project for all colonial society, indigenous and European, and how it would serve as a vital extension of the French colonial administration:

> Such an organization, whose importance one cannot deny, is an indispensable complement to the libraries of large [city] centers: We should not deny the inhabitants of the provinces, French or indigenous, the benefits of organized reading any longer. From the indigenous point of view, these libraries would develop in parallel to the literary or scientific popularization collections; [from the point of view] of the governor general and the local administration, which is eagerly interested, [these libraries] would become an effective instrument.[37]

Boudet's statements to the colonial administration point to his political commitment to instrumentalize libraries as vehicles for colonial cultural propaganda. Boudet's technical visions for libraries development were also political; his work advanced a Western notion of cultural propaganda and the importance of building good reading and good reading habits, perpetuating a vision of libraries as unquestionably good.

Throughout the 1930s, the governor general and local administration continued to discuss, revise, and implement aspects of the comprehensive project to develop popular libraries and an office of indigenous publishing throughout Indochina.

Implementation was fragmented, and actual literary production and distribution were often left to the decisions of private commercial interests and local officials. An entirely centralized top-down system of popular libraries and indigenous publishing never materialized throughout Indochina. Christiane Pasquel Rageau and Claudine Salmon argue that there was a delay in colonial implementation of the popularizing office and libraries due to the economic crisis, political insurrections such as the Yên Bái mutiny (1930) and the Nghệ Tĩnh soviets uprisings (1930–31), and the subsequent period of violent repression under Pierre Pasquier.[38] Between 1929 and 1933, the colonial government tightened censorship and suppressed a wide range of political texts deemed "dangerous," subversive, communist, or anti-French. During Governor General Eugène Robin's interim governorship between 1930 and 1931, an ineffective top-down mechanism for book distribution was organized. A Vietnamese journalist remarked that "GGI Robin had an idea to set up an organization to propagate Western thought, translating books and sending them to villages, yet often these just ended up abandoned and molding in houses where villages did not even know about the books or where to find them."[39] Pasquier suddenly died in a plane crash on January 15, 1934, ending a period of conservative cultural policy. Under the Popular Front government in France from 1936 to 1938, a period of brief colonial liberalism emerged in French Indochina that removed the requirement that Vietnamese publishers submit their materials to censors prior to publishing. Rather than top-down centralized implementation of book distribution and circulating libraries, Paul Boudet experimented with circulating libraries in Cochinchina and Tonkin throughout the 1930s and 1940s.

INDOCHINA EXPERIMENTS WITHIN THE GLOBAL CIRCULATING LIBRARIES MOVEMENT

Paul Boudet was formally trained as an archivist-paleographer at the École des Chartes in Paris, with an emphasis on scholarly national history and the preservation of historical documents. He was also deeply informed by global public library movements that were spearheaded by England and the United States in the nineteenth century and were slowly gaining traction in France in the twentieth century.[40] As head of the Indochina Directorate and the Central Library in Hanoi, Boudet experimented with different models of libraries, combining the moralizing impulse of public libraries from global initiatives with the French civilizing mission in colonial Indochina. From the 1920s to 1930s, Boudet continued to research and plan circulating mobile libraries that could share reading materials from the Cochinchina Library in Saigon and the Central Library in Hanoi with the provinces. Along with studying library models in the Dutch East Indies and the United States, in 1930 Boudet also wrote to the Metropolitan Library in Beijing, China, and the Mohun Dutt State Library in Baroda, India, to request information on their circulating libraries program.[41] This points to how library development

FIGURE 27. The new bibliobus at the International Colonial Exposition in Vincennes, France, 1931. Each side of the bibliobus could be propped open to reveal eighteen shelves, providing space for approximately 120 books to be shown on each side, and 240 spots for books in total. *Source*: Henri Vendel, "Bibliothèques pour tous en France," in *Arts et métiers graphiques, Special Issue: Les arts et les techniques graphiques* 59 (August 15, 1937).

followed a transnational multidirectional process, not always stemming from metropole to colony.

Not until 1931 did a bibliobus project for the metropole begin to take hold and capture the attention of French metropolitan newspapers. A prototype bibliobus vehicle debuted at the well-attended and widely publicized six-month International Colonial Exposition in Vincennes, France, in 1931. The bibliobus display was part of an exhibition led by the Association des bibliothécaires français (ABF, or Association of French Librarians) inaugurated on July 9, 1931, and was focused on the organization of reading in France and the colonies. This prototype bibliobus was spearheaded by the French libraries intellectual Henri Lemaître, secretary-general of the ABF, who worked together with the automobile manufacturer Renault to construct and showcase the first French bibliobus vehicle.[42] Lemaître was inspired by the circulating libraries of the American, English and Dutch colonies. According to Lemaître, the bibliobus model offered an innovative approach for extending reading matter across locations that were difficult to access, making the system ideal for the French countryside as well as French expatriates in the colonies. Henri Lemaître was committed to reimagining the meaning of French libraries and the French public reader. Earlier that year, in April, he also organized an international conference on public reading in French Algeria, addressing comparative public reading practices and those of French colonial settler populations.[43]

Parisian newspapers reported extensively on the popular bibliobus display at the exposition and commented on the importance of creating circulating libraries within France to cultivate a widespread French reading public.[44] In the 1931 *L'écho de Paris* article, the author lamented the lack of lending libraries in the French countryside. He remarked that other countries such as Russia, the United States, Germany, and England and their colonies had prioritized the development of lending libraries and circulating libraries. After many delays, the bibliobus project in France finally began to circulate officially in limited capacity in September 1933, departing from Soissons in northern France.[45] To inaugurate the bibliobus, the mayor of Soissons invited Henri Lemaître to give a public talk in which he expounded upon the benefits of this circulating library and called for other towns to follow the example of Soissons.

The development of public libraries and book vehicles proceeded much more slowly in France compared to that it England, the United States, and the Dutch East Indies. The bibliobus in Indochina was more frequently organized, highly publicized, and widely utilized by a range of provincial readers throughout the 1930s and 1940s. On one hand, the difference could be attributed to a variety of administrative and fiscal challenges in the metropole to support the development of public libraries and the bibliobus project.[46] On the other hand, the comparative successful implementation of the bibliobus project in Indochina points to the leadership of Paul Boudet in carrying out the elaborate logistical labor of book transportation and tactical methods to gain political support from colonial official to instrumentalize the colonial libraries for French cultural propaganda.[47] What was the on-the-ground use and public reception of the circulating libraries throughout Cochinchina? I uncover how the book vehicle project enmeshed Cochinchinese provincial readers within a global circulation of French translated classics and bestsellers as well as the burgeoning Vietnamese *quốc ngữ* urban publishing sphere.

DISTRIBUTING CULTURAL PROPAGANDA FROM CENTER TO PERIPHERY

On the afternoon of Saturday, February 22, 1936, Edouard Marquis from the Cochinchina Press Office and Saint-Marty, the curator of the Cochinchina Library, brought the inaugural bibliobus to downtown Saigon and stationed it in front of the municipal theater. In a public launch of the bibliobus project, the circulating library began to lend books to anyone present who was interested. The event was highly publicized and reported in the French- and Vietnamese-language press and described as a positive governmental effort to spread French influence through French literature.[48] Another report described the project as an ingenious idea to create a "rolling library" to extend libraries into the countryside beyond Hanoi and

Saigon. An article published in the Vietnamese French-language journal *L'Annam Nouveau* described this effort as part of a well-understood project of social governance and one of the fundamental tasks of the colonial authorities: "Education is a stabilizing element of the first order. Our kings understood this, the French government understood this."[49]

An extensive account of the public inauguration of the first bibliobus was written by a Vietnamese journalist with the initials L.T.N., who published an account of his experience in the French-language periodical *La Tribune Indochinoise*; he also possibly wrote the *quốc ngữ* version of the article that was published the following week in *Hà Thành Ngọ Báo*.[50] The article emphasized how the bibliobus initiative would distribute works from the Saigon library (which had been paid for by taxpayer money from Cochinchina residents) that in the past had only benefited those who resided in Saigon. The article praised Saigon governor Pierre Pagès for his efforts in committing to the "moral improvement of the indigenous masses" and seeking to understand "our moral and material aspirations" through improving schools and creating the circulating library. The article commented on how the bibliobus would extend the benefit of the library into the countryside, bringing books to the provinces for Vietnamese intellectuals, civil servants, merchants, industrialists, teachers, and students to cultivate their learning and prevent their minds from "rusting." The article praised the simplicity of using the bibliobus: "A few Europeans came to register first, followed by young Annamites. No daunting formalities. Do you want to borrow a book? You do not have to consult the catalog. The secretary who accompanies the bookmobile records your name. And that's all. You can keep the books for fifteen days." A suggestion box was included at the back of the bibliobus so that readers could submit suggestions and complaints. The article's author noted that he had suggested to Saigon Library director Saint-Marty and Cochinchina press officer Marquis that *quốc ngữ* materials should be added alongside the French materials. Saint-Marty publicly responded and requested Vietnamese publishers and journalists recommend "good-quality" Vietnamese-language books. Echoing these efforts, the article encouraged "friends of the belles lettres" to join in the task of guiding the addition of *quốc ngữ* literature to the bibliobus project. This article gives a sense of Vietnamese perceptions of the circulating libraries project, albeit filtered through permissible discourse of the colonial press. Furthermore, the article pointed to the efforts of promoting the diffusion of *quốc ngữ* literature as a collective effort and called upon contributions from publishers and intellectuals across Vietnam.

The year 1936 marked a new stage of French colonial cultural propaganda, with the Directorate of Archives and Libraries and the bibliobus as crowning achievements. At a public event commemorating the two-year anniversary of the death of former governor general Pierre Pasquier, Boudet delivered a speech professing the success of libraries development specifically as it supported the work of French cultural propaganda.[51] The event welcomed Governor General René Robin and took place in front of the Hanoi Central Library, renamed the Pierre Pasquier Library in 1935. Boudet situated the work of libraries within the wider colonial project of *mise en valeur* (development, modernization, and exploitation), such as the building of cities and schools. Boudet characterized the significant infrastructural transformations wrought by colonialism: "Times have changed, gardens have replaced ponds, brick houses [replaced] straw huts, and Western science [replaced] traditional culture. But the descendants of the [exam] candidates of the past bring the same enthusiasm to learn according to the new disciplines." Boudet praised the library as a symbol of the success of Franco-Vietnamese collaboration policy, bringing modern Western education and culture to the new generation of scholarly Vietnamese youth. He specifically highlighted the advancement of Vietnamese students through Western higher education, including the achievements of Ngô Đình Nhu, the first Vietnamese graduate from the École des Chartes in 1936.

In his speech Boudet called for the elaborate extension of library initiatives into the provinces as a fundamental instrument of French cultural propaganda and extending French civilization. He mentioned the current success of the bibliobus in Cochinchina, with Tonkin not too far behind. "To fully realize the program of a truly modern library, it will be necessary to widen its reach, to create annexes in the suburban districts, and to make the book penetrate to the depths of the provinces. Thanks to circulating libraries that countries like the United States have thoroughly developed, the book is no longer an inert and cold thing but an instrument of living culture that can go to find its reader." Boudet concluded his speech by reasserting the mission of the Directorate in the work of the civilizing mission and the Franco-Vietnamese collaboration: "Through developing centers of selfless culture [libraries] that serve as an indispensable complement and auxiliary to schools in this country—a country that has always been passionate about study—we are participating in the civilizing work of France. We are sure that the people of Annam are aware of what we bring to them in terms of free culture and intellectual progress, and they will be able to recognize and appreciate the efforts of our country [France] to enable them to rise little by little to the level of the great nations of the West."[52] As an instrument of cultural propaganda, the bibliobus project expanded the Directorate's political and cultural missions.

Shortly following public announcements of the bibliobus system in January 1937, an experimental "*bibliothèque et pharmacie roulante*" (library and mobile pharmacy) circulated throughout Tonkin, lending books and providing a limited number of medicines free of charge. Equipped with over four hundred works in *quốc ngữ* and French, the library moved between central markets within a radius of thirty kilometers.[53] The "rolling library and pharmacy" continued to circulate through April 1937, and its success was publicized on the pages of the periodical *France-Indochine*.[54] The article described how the library was mounted on a horse-drawn carriage and organized by a librarian by the name of Monsieur Léon Ronflant. The library contained French and Vietnamese reading matter divided into four categories: common knowledge; science, literature, and travel; novels; and the periodicals *Cậu Ấm* (Young Fellow Am or Mandarin's Son, the first youth periodical founded by Thái Phỉ), *Khoa Học* (Science), and *Tứ Dân Văn Uyển* (The four social classes literary magazine, a state-sponsored monthly literary review).[55] It reported that the rolling library and pharmacy circulated through the districts and towns of Lạng Giang, Yên Dũng, Việt Yên, and Yên Thế, stopping at populous markets to distribute free medicines to 4,397 patients and lending books free of charge to 265 readers. This experimental circulating library points to the interwoven work of social welfare and healthy leisure. The interwoven distribution of books with pharmaceuticals was not an uncommon practice within the broader book market in Indochina. For example, Vietnamese publishing houses also printed advertisements, pamphlets, and postcards and sold other nonbook items such as stationery, furniture, and pharmaceuticals, such as the successful merchant François Võ Văn Vân, who ran a publishing house in Bến Tre province.[56]

Besides these early bibliobus attempts in Tonkin, most of the circulating libraries were organized out of the Cochinchina Library in Saigon and circulated around the southern provinces between 1936 and 1942. Press coverage of the first bibliobus circulating around Cochinchina provinces in 1936 was celebratory, with calls from government officials and newspapers to extend and expand its services.[57] Directorate reports emphasized the intentional curation of specific works circulating in the book vehicles, "judiciously selected to avoid letting mediocre works or those of questionable morality take the place of more interesting or more useful books."[58] The bibliobus was also presented as a network-building initiative, connecting public readers to the Directorate of Archives and Libraries and unifying the book collections from different organizations such as reading circles, associations, and the provincial administration offices.[59] Framed as an important unified administrative effort, the bibliobus would bring state services to the wider population of young students, curious intellectuals, and government officials who resided outside the cities and in the provinces and ultimately "transform the intellectual life of our provinces." The success of the bibliobus created a precedent for a new model of state services that were localized and flexible; for example, other journalists called for other "circulating services" such as a circulating infirmary based out of each province.[60]

Excitement about the potential of the bibliobus permeated the French- and Vietnamese-language press, yet, over time, press coverage was not without criticisms. Featured prominently on the first page of *La Tribune Indochinoise* in 1937, an article evaluated the operations and limitations of the bibliobus system, noting the extensive cost of the endeavor.[61] The author, who went by "T.D.," calculated the costs of fuel, the wages of the librarian-secretary, automobile maintenance, equipment, and book upkeep, which amounted to an exorbitant 5,016 piastres a year to maintain the service. The author also claimed that when the bibliobus was stationed at a location, three and half hours (or less if there were delays of the bibliobus arrival) were too little time for readers to return and check out new books. The author noted that the

FIGURE 28. Bibliobus circulating library parked in Saigon, at the Garnier Plaza and in front of the Continental Palace on rue Catinat, ca. 1936–1940. *Source*: Tổng Thư viện, Trung tâm lưu trữ quốc gia 2, Ho Chi Minh City, Vietnam, folder 2.

librarian-secretaries were physically burdened, "visibly showing their repugnance for these tiring tours," and would prefer to stay at the Saigon Cochinchina Library, hence the constant rotation of new staff accompanying the circulating library. The author suggested to the governor of Cochinchina extending and supporting the existing network of Cochinchina reading rooms scattered through organizations such as Franco-Vietnamese circles with reading rooms, popular libraries, and branches of the Society of Mutual Education. Although limited and in poor condition, these spaces could be "refreshed" with new library books or works discarded from the Saigon Cochinchina Library. The writer suggested a system of interprovincial exchange of books using the postal and telegraph system to exchange books twice a month among interested circles or libraries.

SOUTHERN PROVINCIAL READING CULTURE AND DEMANDS FOR *QUỐC NGỮ*

Given the success of the first bibliobus, which served over ten thousand readers, a second bibliobus was added on December 6, 1937, bringing 1,685 works on a different route to the Cochinchina provinces of Bạc Liêu, Cà Mau, Rạch Giá, Hà Tiên, Châu Đốc, Tây Ninh, Gò Công, and Bà Rịa–Cap Saint-Jacques. Librarian administrators noted the limitations of the first bibliobus collection, "composed in part by books unintelligible to a majority of the public of the provinces. [The second bibliobus] has replaced them with easy-to-read novels, summaries of travels, and above all novels for youth. The works in *quốc ngữ* have been a big success among the population."[62] Since the beginning of the Cochinchina bibliobus operations, the Vietnamese popular press had called for *quốc ngữ* materials to be added to the primarily French-language materials carried in the vehicles.[63] The desire for police and adventure novels, a popular genre among youth, as well as *quốc ngữ* literature, reflected the literary demands of the growing population of Vietnamese readers in Saigon and the southern provincial regions. The 1939 article reported that the Saigon Cochinchina Library had greatly expanded its services and library use: The reading room had extended its operating hours to ten in the evening, improved its catalog, and welcomed a daily average of 108 readers; the lending section added more youth novels, and the number of registered borrowers increased by 5,000, to a total of 22,908 readers.[64] The report noted that across race and class, readers uniformly demanded police and adventure novels, pointing to the booming practice of leisurely cosmopolitan reading in the late colonial period in Vietnam. With wide popularity and demand, the bibliobus circulating libraries continued rotating reading matter throughout the Cochinchina region between 1936 and 1942. The schedule, route, and updates of the bibliobus would be publicized in the Vietnamese- and French-language press, alerting provincial readers of an upcoming bibliobus tour.[65] A later report summarized the success of the circulating libraries, which brought "French culture to the outer isolated regions of Cochinchina, which served as a healthy leisure activity."[66] The report estimated that circulating libraries brought more than twenty-three thousand books to the provinces of Cochinchina from 1936 to 1946.

Who were these provincial readers, and what did they read? Extensive borrowing records from the circulating library showcase a range of French and Vietnamese borrowers throughout Cochinchina, such as government officials, teachers, students, secretaries, military officers, and private industry workers. In 1942, more than twenty-two provinces as far away as Châu Đốc, Sóc Trăng, and Hà Tiên participated in the circulating library project based out of the Saigon Cochinchina Library. Readers checked out over five hundred materials from the circulating library and shipped them back to Saigon Library or to the provincial capital within the lending period of two weeks. Most of the books borrowed were French popular novels such as those on romance, the police, and espionage by Delly (*Gilles des Crosbres, Des plaintes dans la nuit, Le secret du Kou-kou-nor*) and French translations of popular world literature, like the works of Agatha Christie (*La mort dans les nuages*) and Pearl S. Buck (*Les fils de Wang-Lung*).[67] Readers also checked out French-language historical works on Napoleon, Caesar, and war, books on science and geography, and popular literature such as Marie-Catherine d'Aulnoy's prose fairy tale *La chatte blanche*.

The August 1942 list of books borrowed and returned from the port province of Rạch Giá in the Mekong Delta region (now Kiên Giang province) recorded eighty books borrowed by thirty-one borrowers for the month—of whom two were French men, one was a Vietnamese woman, and the remaining twenty-eight were Vietnamese men. Of the works borrowed, many were French-language works of popular detective fiction, sentimental fiction, and adventure novels, including *Le roi du Kidji* by Delly and *Le Capitaine Fracasse* by Théophile Gautier, first published in 1863 and set in seventeenth-century France. Nonfiction accounts of war and travel also circulated among provincial readers, such as Émile Henry Auguste Vedel's maritime literature on the First World War, *Nos marins à la guerre*, the novella war memoir *Les silences du Colonel Bramble* by André Maurois, and *La Chine en folie*, an investigative reportage on China by Albert Londres. Borrowers from Rạch Giá had also checked out translated global bestsellers, including Tolstoy's *Anna Karenina* and Aldous Huxley's *Ends and Means.*

Through these circulating libraries, readers in the distant provinces accessed not only popular literature and translations in French but also engaged in the booming sphere of Vietnamese *quốc ngữ* literature published in the late colonial period.[68] For example, reader Nguyễn Văn An from Rạch Giá borrowed five *quốc ngữ* works in August 1942:

Lúc còn hoạn nạn tới hồi đoàn viên (Overcoming life's tribulations and difficulties)
Con nhà giầu (Child from a rich household)
Lời thề trước miếu (Oaths at the temple)
Tỉnh mộng (Awakening)
Tại Tôi (Because of me)[69]

The last four works were popular fiction by southern Vietnamese writer Hồ Biểu Chánh, a prolific novelist and translator. Hồ Biểu Chánh (1884–1958) pioneered the southern style of literature, writing over one hundred pieces of poetry, short stories, novels, research, and literary criticism. He also wrote many adaptations, including *Chúa Tàu Kim Qui* (The ship master of Kim Quy Island), which parallels the plotline of confinement and escape in Alexandre Dumas's *The Count of Monte Cristo*. Through the circulating libraries, new experimental forms of *quốc ngữ* literature, primarily produced in the urban centers of Hanoi and Saigon, achieved extensive geographic reach, expanding the Vietnamese reading public to include provincial readers. Hồ Biểu Chánh's literature might have resonated with provincial readers because of their focus on stories of village life, in which his primary characters were farmers, merchants, lower-level government officials, adventurers, and intellectuals. Many of his works focused on navigating morals in the dramas of social life among peasants, paralleling some of the similar themes in Pearl S. Buck's novel *The Good Earth*, published 1931, and its popular French 1932 translation *La terre chinoise*, which circulated widely in the Hanoi and Saigon libraries and beyond. Buck, born into an American missionary family in China, wrote prolifically on rural China, including the best-selling work *The Good Earth*, which won the Pulitzer Prize (1932), the Langlois Prize of the Académie française (1933), and the Nobel Prize (1938). *The Good Earth* depicted everyday family life, gender relations, and the subtle cultural and political tensions between revolution, imperialism, and nationalism in rural China.

From the same province of Rạch Giá, reader Trang Văn Phụng borrowed Vũ Trọng Phụng's popular *Kỹ nghệ lấy Tây* (The industry of marrying Europeans) and *Hán từ luân lý* (Chinese morality). Reader Nguyễn Văn Chính borrowed *Chính trị nước Pháp* (French politics). Many of these works were translations from Chinese and French or were new *quốc ngữ* publications from Vietnamese authors covering topics from morality to contemporary social commentary, politics, and history. Throughout the 1930s and 1940s, the burgeoning body of vernacular Vietnamese literature circulated through the bibliobus network, bringing a new corpus of literature and knowledge to the provinces written in the popular *quốc ngữ* script, which could be understood by the masses. For example, the first historical and archaeological work on the Champa empire and its peoples in *quốc ngữ, Chiêm Thành Lược Khảo* (A summary study of Champa), circulated in the 1942 book vehicle to Bến Tre.[70] First published in 1936, this work was authored by Huỳnh Thị Bảo Hoà (1896–1982), considered a leading modern intellectual advancing the status of women. Written by one of the first female Vietnamese novelists, Huỳnh Thị Bảo Hoà's *Tây phương mỹ nhơn* (The western beauty) was first published in Saigon in 1927.[71]

In this same list of works borrowed and returned from Bến Tre were *quốc ngữ* translations of popular Chinese *wuxia xiaoshuo*, or cloak-and-dagger stories, such as *Song Quang Bửu Kiếm* (The treasured swords of Song Quang Cave, *Shuangguang baojian*, 雙光寶劍), which wove together extensive plotlines of adventure, magic, and martial arts.[72] Other popular Chinese works that circulated throughout the libraries include the historical warring novel *Tam Quốc Chí Diễn Nghĩa* (Romance of the three kingdoms, *Sanguo zhi yanyi*, 三國志 演義), Chinese monk Xuangzang's account of his journey to India, *Truyện Tây Du* (Journey to the West, *Xiyouji*, 西遊), and the dramatic work by playwright Wang Shifu, *Tây sương ký* (Romance of the western wing, 西廂記).

Archival documents record recurring issues with reader accountability and the frequency of overdue, lost, and stolen works. If books were overdue, the librarian secretary demanded readers immediately return the books lest they face the expensive consequences: replace the book with two other books (of equal value to the lost book) or pay a fine of twice the value of the book within one month of the due date.[73] Léon Saint-Marty, the head curator from the Cochinchina Library, actively tried to track down the books by working with the local government and police to find the readers and their home addresses.[74] On November 28, 1942, Saint-Marty submitted the list of readers who worked for administrative offices in hopes that their department employers would demand fines from the overdue borrowers. The list included a diverse number of readers, such as teachers, police officers, medical assistants, copyists, secretaries, and mechanics.[75] However, many of these attempts were futile. By December 17, 1942, the head official named Arrivets updated Saint-Marty that all of these workers were in fact lower-level employees who had moved on from their positions and were thus unreachable. Arrivets strongly suggested the French model of guarantees and deposits to be applied to the circulating libraries before permitting readers to borrow books. The circulating libraries operated in a decentralized manner with limited staff and unofficial regulations. Saint-Marty sought to track down readers who failed to return books, though their only consequence was losing borrowing privileges. Since the circulating libraries did not rotate regularly throughout the provinces, some readers avoided the hassle and costs of mailing their borrowed books back to Saigon Cochinchina Library. Throughout the late colonial period, the *quốc ngữ* newspaper *Sài Gòn* often encouraged readers to return borrowed library books.[76] These public requests showcase the popular use of the bibliobus and the value of reading to provincial readers. While the colonial state initially envisioned a circulating libraries project for cultural propaganda, the actual circulating libraries of the 1930s and 1940s created an uneven yet substantial network of literary exchange in the provinces, circulating contemporary Vietnamese literature and cultivating local and global reading culture in the provinces.

WORLD WAR II AND VICHY CULTURAL PROPAGANDA

During the 1920s to 1930s, under the French Third Republic, the colonial state enacted cultural propaganda through subtle strategies of using circulating libraries to spread "safe" reading matter in attempts to counter anticolonial sentiment. Projects to modernize schools, sponsor publications, and expand the use of *quốc ngữ* were expressed through the language of republicanism, public education, literacy, and colonial benevolence, a hybrid of colonial policies of the civilizing mission (*mission civilisatrice*), Franco-Vietnamese collaboration, and modernization and exploitation (*mise en valeur*). In contrast, World War II and the Vichy state ushered in more authoritarian, direct, and interventionist forms of cultural propaganda through libraries. With the military defeat of France in World War II, on June 22, 1940, Marshal Philippe Pétain commanded the signing of the Franco-German armistice, which dissolved the French Third Republic and created the authoritarian Vichy regime in southern France and the French colonial empire. Admiral Jean Decoux served as the governor general of Indochina from July 1940 to March 9, 1945. Around the same time, Japanese troops continued to move into Southeast Asia, occupying Indochina but leaving most administrative procedures and bureaucracy in the hands of the French Vichy colonial government. This political arrangement continued until 1944, until the collapse of Vichy France, followed by a Japanese-led *coup de force* on March 9, 1945, which officially toppled the French colonial government in Indochina.

In the context of war and authoritarianism, the fascist Vichy administration pursued a much more aggressive policy of direct cultural propaganda in the domains of censorship, publishing, distribution, and libraries. The Vichy administration issued new decrees on publishing and reinforced previously lax rules regarding the submission of all publications to the censor offices.[77] In June 1941, the Service of Information, Propaganda, and the Press (IPP) was created with a central Hanoi office and local offices throughout Indochina. Directed by Navy Commandant Marcel Robbe, the IPP managed the production, control, censorship, and distribution of information throughout Indochina during the Vichy period.[78] Although created during the Vichy period in 1941, the IPP carried on the legacy of conservative information politics and surveillance from the late colonial period.[79] Explicit censorship suppressed any political, cultural, or social critique of Japan or France or any multiperspective discussion of contemporary wartime events, revealing a fragile state authority fearful of dissent. Furthermore, the censorship rules show state anxieties over Vietnamese nationalism, Indochinese patriotism, and pan-Asian solidarity that ultimately threatened to overthrow Vichy colonial power.

Robbe's instructions reinforced Decoux's campaign to spread throughout Vichy Indochina the National Revolution—a conservative anti-Semitic, antiforeign, and anticommunist Vichy political and ideological program. Decoux and the IPP sought to instrumentalize Indochina libraries to spread the National Revolution through circulating reading matter on the topic.[80] Decoux requested an inventory of all the names of French works sent to Indochina since Vichy rule and of the books available in all public and private libraries in Indochina. Decoux noted that many of the books sent to Indochina on the topic of the National Revolution had only a limited number of copies and thus should be republished. Shortly afterward, a department in Vichy France sent over a hundred volumes to Indochina on the National Revolution, economics, biographies of Roger Secretain, Pierre Maurice, and Jack Sanger, and Léo-Paul Desrosiers's novel *Les opiniâtres* (*roman de conquête canadienne*) (1941).[81] A government official additionally vetted the shipment of books and stated that he "removed a large number of books because they mention our defeat in a heartbreaking and degrading narrative; because they are too subjective, confined to an unbearable individualism; because they are marred by political considerations, thus they deserved to be left in the storage; or they were too novel-like and did not bring any element to moral, social, or economic improvement."[82]

In 1942 Commandant Robbe of the IPP conducted extensive studies of the existing Indochina publishing, libraries, and distribution systems. Robbe examined the following documents from 1935 to 1938: reports on the creation of provincial libraries, Boudet's studies on the American bibliobus, official statements from the Dutch East Indies Balai Pustaka project, and other reports from the Directorate of Archives and Libraries of Indochina. Drawing inspiration from 1930s cultural propaganda projects, Robbe called for the expansion of an even wider network of public libraries at the provincial and communal levels for the purpose of distributing official IPP publications. Writing to the heads of local IPP branches in Tonkin, Annam, and Cochinchina, as well as the heads of local services in Cambodge and Laos, Robbe declared that these new libraries should be furnished with the following:

> All works made by the offices of publication and the books vetted by the Office of Censorship of indigenous publications. In addition to the propaganda pamphlets, these libraries can receive a modest collection of French-Vietnamese books carefully selected by qualified personnel. It would be appropriate on this subject, for Tonkin in particular, to solicit the advice of the Service of Archives and Libraries, notably in which it concerns the commissioning of a mobile library attached to a radio-cinema-bus currently in development. I draw your attention again to this matter, which seems to have been somewhat forgotten.[83]

In addition to using the library and bibliobus systems as a distribution network for IPP propaganda, the Vichy administration also recognized the politicizing potential of libraries to inspire a dangerous "spirit of critique." On March 30, 1942, Captain Pericaud, a military official in Saigon, wrote to the director of the Saigon Censorship Office requesting the removal of certain politically sensitive material from the municipal, lending, and circulating libraries.[84] He stated that a certain number of works present a "true danger" and instigate animosity between Vietnamese and French. For example, Jean Marquet's book *Le jaune et le blanc* (The yellow race and the white race) had been read frequently by Vietnamese who added copious anti-French annotations to the margins. The government official argued that certain controversial books such as *Le jaune et le blanc* invite anti-French sentiment by Vietnamese readers. While some other tendentious books, such as *Linette* by Marcelle de Laguardille, were removed, the curator of the Cochinchina Library, Saint-Marty, pushed back against Pericaud's complaint about Marquet's work. Saint-Marty justified the literary value of Marquet's critiques and explained that "graffiti" inscriptions such as the marginalia in library books had in fact been a common practice since the early ages of humanity and did not reflect a contemporary display of political dissidence.[85]

Beyond top-down state policy, Vietnamese public discourse engaged in the intertwined moralized discussion of good reading defined against bad reading. Just as "good reading" had a flexible construct among state officials, librarian administrators and public intellectuals discussed the notion of "bad reading" as ranging from works of moral depravity to tendentious texts. In an urgent essay titled "Muốn chữa nạn thanh niên truỵ lạc, hãy đốt hết những sách khiêu dâm" (In order to cure our debauched youth, we must burn all lewd books), journalist Phạm Mạnh Phan condemned the dangerous spread of lewd, romantic, pornographic books and called for their outright destruction by fire.[86] Published in an early issue of the Hanoi-based literary review magazine *Tri Tân* on August 1, 1941, this article reflected the political context of Vichy state suppression and its extremist cultural project of moralized reading. The author referenced Nazi book burning as a model for what needed to be done to remove the dangerous spread of pornographic books among Vietnamese youth. The urgent tone of the essay points to the rising threat of an uncontrollable force of "Vietnamese youth," an issue of moralized public concern about generational change and the political potential of reading matter.

PURGING THE HANOI LIBRARY READING CULTURE

On August 6, 1942, Decoux wrote to Boudet with the proposal "Purge of the Libraries."[87] Seeking to purge the Hanoi Library of dangerous "bad reading," Decoux explicitly forbade in the libraries the "reading of violent assessments of the French in Indochina that inspired a spirit of critique." Decoux emphasized that the suppression of certain works must also be kept confidential and hidden from readers. Decoux suggested a series of excuses librarians could use, such as pretending that certain books were currently checked out to other readers or were under repair to prevent reader access to politically sensitive reading matter.

Characterizing the task as a "serious and delicate question," on October 2, 1942, Boudet responded to Decoux's demand for widespread suppression of dangerous texts with a thorough study on existing techniques and the possible consequences of a complete purge of the libraries.[88] Boudet categorized two types of libraries existing in Indochina by 1942: (1) working libraries such as the central libraries in Hanoi, Saigon, and Phnom Penh, open to Indochinese and French, and (2) lending libraries "with the purpose to give the public a pure distraction or to popularize literary and scientific works." Boudet reported that working libraries granted the most freedom of access to readers, except for access to some daily newspapers and works in Hanoi, which "are hidden from the eyes of the readers, [works] that we do not want readers to see or read indiscriminately." Boudet proposed to Decoux that the following types of works should be added to the "restricted" category:

1. All the works that are clearly hostile in any way to French colonialism in Indochina or in other colonies;
2. All the works that are excessively immoral. Obviously the criteria of morality are difficult to define. For example, the classics such as *Phèdre, Candide*, or the works of Zola are defined by their literary flourish and passionate depiction of manners and thus cannot be restricted and hidden.[89]

Boudet's list of restricted reading matter appeared to superficially appease Decoux's strict demands for a purge of the public libraries. The first type of works restricted included overt anti-French works, but the second category regarding morality suggested a more nuanced approach. The Vichy regime promoted ideals of tradition, family, and nationalism, often relying upon morality as a tool to convey militaristic paternalism and patriotic community.[90] Boudet seemed to signal to Vichy moral pragmatism, suggesting the restriction of works that went beyond "a moral point of view." For example, Boudet added Charles Baudelaire's *Fleurs du mal* and Gustave Flaubert's *Madame Bovary* to the list of restricted works given that they were overtly sexual, yet Boudet pushed back against an absolute judgment of literature as immoral or excessive. He argued that a "morality criterion is difficult to define" and censor, for example in complex literary classics such as Jean Racine's dramatic tragedy *Phèdre (et Hippolyte)*, Voltaire's *Candide*, and the works of Émile Zola. Furthermore, Boudet concluded that it would be impossible to restrict all political, philosophical, and literary subjects without removing all the essential collections of the libraries.

In his thorough response to Decoux, Boudet classified the types of readers in the libraries as students, autodidacts, officials, and businessmen. Of this group, Boudet continued to critique the Vietnamese students, described as "the worst clientele, the least careful with books, the least disciplined without exception."[91] He described Vietnamese nonstudent readers as "autodidacts . . . who show an ardor against frivolous distractions" and asserted that the library should more closely control the circulation of books to this group of self-motivated readers. Boudet proposed expanding the list of restricted works, removing directly hostile works from the lending section and raising the minimum age of admission to the library from sixteen to eighteen years. Boudet concluded with a plea to allow him to carefully undertake this "delicate" work rather than rely upon a single individual whose "personal initiatives and mood indicates if a particular book is harmful." Boudet reminded Decoux that the task of purging all "criticism" was impossible unless the administration wanted to destroy all libraries: "There is very little [reading matter] that does not have a little malicious criticism; thus the only measure capable of satisfying the worried spirit [of these criticisms] would be the destruction by fire all the libraries, such as in the case of the burning of the Alexandria [library]." Boudet carefully negotiated with Decoux on authoritarian censorship of the Hanoi library reading collection, balancing between top-down policies and carrying out everyday functions of library communication of books to readers.

In addition to politics, economic factors might have influenced the removal of certain books from the collection. In 1943, 113 books from the Central Library were put up for auction.[92] The list of books did in fact include some of the "controversial" volumes discussed in the previous year, such as Baudelaire's *Les fleurs du mal* and Voltaire's *Candide*. However, the editions placed on auction were also luxury watercolor editions, which sold for a higher value. Other books on the list for auction included illustrated, color, or art-bound editions of popular works such as dictionaries and encyclopedias, *Le roman de Tristan et Iseut* (the twelfth-century romance of Tristan and Iseult), *La guirlande d'aphrodite* (the colorfully illustrated *Aphrodite's Garland*), and *Biblia Sacra* (a cloth-bound edition of the Latin holy Bible). By auctioning off some of its most valuable books, the Central Library could offset some of the wartime strain on the library budget for personnel, maintenance, and collections.

Beyond top-down attempts to censor the Hanoi Central Library, everyday reader practices point to continued self-directed reading about "sensitive" Vichy topics as well as leisure reading of novels from the popular lending section. From 1943 to 1944, overall use of the reading room significantly decreased, with 32 percent fewer visits, 30 percent fewer book consultations, and 48 percent fewer periodical consultations. In contrast, for the lending section the total number of new cards registered increased by 38 percent and the total books borrowed increased by 14 percent. This amounts to thirty-five checkouts of books per reader, an especially high number compared to American library users in 1943, who averaged only sixteen book checkouts per year.[93] The Hanoi Central Library served as an important resource for reading matter, offsetting the cost of individual purchases of newspapers and books in the context of rising wartime costs of living. The consumption of lending section books also points to a vibrant culture of leisure reading: Vietnamese and French readers highly preferred the work of Alexandre Dumas in the lending section novels collection. The astonishing proportion of Vietnamese consumption of Dumas is considered even more sizable when compared to the other authors that Vietnamese borrowed. Out of an average of 366 checkouts per month by Vietnamese, 165 checkouts were of Dumas, in comparison with 38 checkouts of Bordereaux, 37 of Delly, and 35 of Balzac. According to statistics from the lending section recorded June 1940 to May 1941, checkouts of works by Dumas comprised 42 percent of total checkouts by Vietnamese readers and 22 percent by French.[94] Vietnamese readers checked out Dumas almost as much as French ones (Vietnamese 165; French 199).

By 1944, the most popular authors in the lending section of the Central Library had shifted. The top five authors preferred by French readers included Pearl S. Buck, Maxence Van der Meersch (Vandermeersch), Henri Ardel, Alexandre Dumas, and Georges Simenon.[95] In comparison, the top five authors preferred by Vietnamese readers included André Gide, Dumas, Buck, Georges Duhamel, and Rudyard Kipling. The authors most read in the lending section reflect popular and award-winning world literature at the time, such as Buck's *The Good Earth*, Kipling's *The Jungle Book*, Ardel's women's literature, and Simenon's detective novels. Popular authors in the lending section include Gide, the pro-Dreyfus, antifascist thinker who wrote prolifically and broadly.[96] Even in the context of the authoritarian Vichy administration, readers were able to access the works of André Gide, who covered sensitive topics such as sexuality, morality, and communism. The popularity and

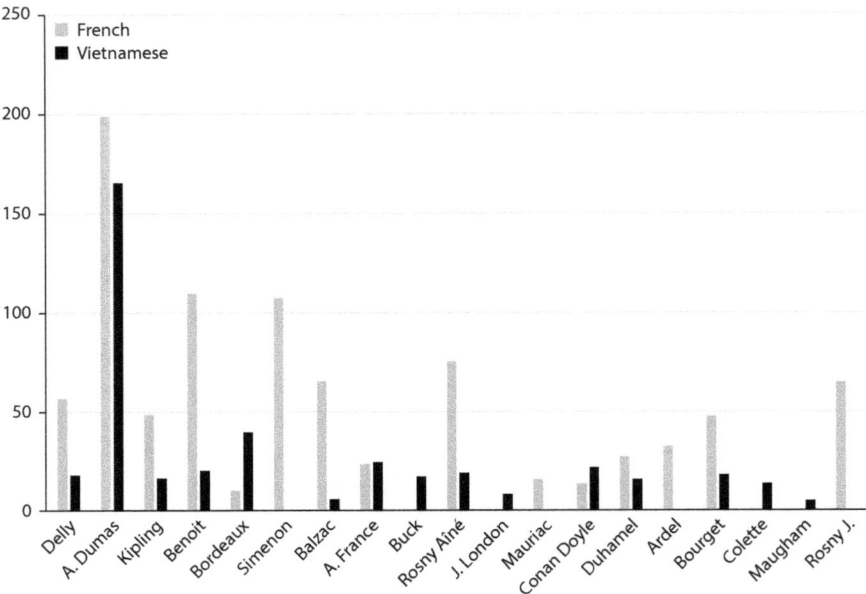

FIGURE 29. Comparison of French and Vietnamese average monthly checkouts from the novels collection in the lending section of the Hanoi Central Library from June 1940 to May 1941. French readers preferred authors like Alexandre Dumas, Pierre Benoit, Georges Simenon, Honoré de Balzac, and J.-H. Rosny Aîné, with Dumas being a favorite. Vietnamese readers also enjoyed Dumas but showed distinct interest in international authors such as Jack London, Arthur Conan Doyle, and Pearl S. Buck. While French readers leaned toward European classics, Vietnamese readers favored adventure and globally popular writers. *Source*: Direction des archives et des bibliothèques, Trung tâm lưu trữ quốc gia 1, Hanoi, Vietnam, folder 2215.

the on-the-ground circulation of politically controversial books in the lending section suggests the limitations of a completely authoritarian control of reading.

CONCLUSION

This chapter has examined the state project of cultural propaganda through library circulation from the 1920s to 1940s. It considered the geographic reach and limitations of French colonial influence through the construction of circulating library systems that extended colonial power beyond the administrative centers of Hanoi and Saigon into the provinces. Drawing from the Dutch East Indies Balai Pustaka publishing, libraries, and distribution network, Pierre Pasquier attempted to construct a top-down central bureau to distribute reading and create popular libraries throughout Indochina. Colonial officials such as Émile Vayrac emphasized publishing and libraries as crucial tools of cultural propaganda for combatting rising urban radicalism, anticolonial revolutionary ideologies, and millenarian influence in the 1920s and 1930s, yet the implementation of a centralized office was diffuse. Cultural propaganda took a more indirect form in the late colonial period, carried out through Paul Boudet's globally inspired experiments in bibliobus book vehicles that circulated materials from the Saigon Cochinchina Library lending section to the provinces. While Paul Boudet was driven by the logistical, technical, and intellectual movements of public libraries and international library sciences, his projects were implicated within the politics of French colonial cultural propaganda of spreading French civilization and benevolent modernization. During World War II, the Vichy French colonial state attempted to enact a more authoritarian and direct mode of information control in publishing, libraries, and propaganda. While driven by a different political discourse of anti-opposition, the Vichy state initiatives were also aspirational infrastructures of cultural propaganda. State attempts to purge the library met with opposition from Paul Boudet, and on the everyday level library readers found ways to access politically sensitive materials in the lending section of the Hanoi Central Library.

While this chapter examined top-down strategies of cultural propaganda, it also highlighted the ways in which provincial readers in the Mekong Delta engaged with circulating libraries to consume a wide range of reading matter—from French-language popular literature and translations of global bestsellers to a growing sphere of Vietnamese vernacular literature. Although limited as a procolonial state strategy, the circulating libraries contributed to the cultivation of provincial multilingual reading culture and the popularity of vernacular reading among Vietnamese. This sphere of Vietnamese *quốc ngữ* literature encapsulated new contemporary literature, genre forms spanning fiction and nonfiction, and French, English, and Chinese translated works and adaptations. As the next chapter shows, top-down state library initiatives were both ignored and redefined by Vietnamese readers, who envisioned alternative types of public libraries for the people.

4

To Read

Bình Dân Thư Viện *and* *Vietnamese Language Nationalism*

Even though a child is ignorant, they must still read poetry and literature [the classics]. (Tử tôn tuy ngu, Thi, Thư bất khả bất độc).

—AN APHORISM AMONG CONFUCIAN EXAMINATION LAUREATES, QUOTED BY HOA BẰNG. THE CITY OUTSKIRTS AND THE COUNTRYSIDE NEED "READING SOCIETIES", *TRI TÂN, 1942*[1]

The level of Vietnam's culture, whether superb or deficient, is dependent upon quốc ngữ. . . . Thus it is the obligation of each person in the country to serve and improve the language since it connects to the rate of progress of our motherland.

—PROPOSAL FOR A *QUỐC NGỮ* NATIONAL LIBRARY SYSTEM BY FORMER COCHINCHINA LIBRARY PERSONNEL LÝ VĨNH KHUÔNG (KHUÔNG VIỆT) *TRI TÂN, 1942*[2]

In 1942 the journalist and scholar of literature and history Hoa Bằng (1902–77) published the article "Các vùng ngoại ô và thôn quê cần có những 'duyệt thư, báo xã'" (The city outskirts and the countryside need "reading societies") in the *quốc ngữ* Hanoi-based weekly periodical *Tri Tân*. Quoting popular aphorisms, Hoa Bằng drew heavily from Confucian values of scholarship to argue for the inherent value of literature and reading and called for the creation of more libraries. Specifically, he proposed the cultivation of reading as "good leisure" and building libraries as an antidote to the spread of "bad leisure," such as gambling, alcohol, and nightclubs.[3] Building upon the metaphor of "reading as eating" and the "cultivation of a reading taste," Hoa Bằng depicted books as desirable food objects with attractive scents and providing spiritual nourishment. He noted how urban readers already had a certain "addiction" to this type of literary consumption and encouraged the spread of reading tastes more evenly throughout society to rural readers. According to the author, existing libraries were concentrated in urban centers and propagated French and Western literature, and thus they failed to pay attention to the rising number of books and newspapers in *quốc ngữ*. The author specifically critiqued the Hanoi Central Library for serving only a limited minority of urban readers literate in French and therefore "fail[ing] to provide a universal" service to all. Hoa Bằng called for the development of alternative reading spaces of *quốc ngữ*-language material located in the rural outskirts to serve countryside Vietnamese-language reading communities. Suggesting to repurpose village temples and provincial shrines, the author argued that rural reading spaces honor the ancestral sages. He concluded his essay with a statement that a *quốc ngữ* libraries system across Vietnam would ultimately benefit the *dân chúng* (public).[4] Hoa Bằng's call to action was part of a broader cultural and political movement from the 1920s to 1940s for the widespread development of *quốc ngữ* reading spaces, characterized as *bình dân thư viện* (libraries for the common people, or "public libraries").

This chapter argues that the movement to create public libraries was an intertwined intellectual, political, and social project of Vietnamese language nationalism. Proposals to form Vietnamese-language public libraries encapsulated larger debates by journalists and community leaders on the meanings of Vietnamese collective identity, social welfare, and nationhood, intrinsically questioning who was the public and whom public institutions should serve. This chapter centers the "public library" as an intellectually and politically debated concept, where "*bình dân thư viện*" could be translated in multiple shifting ways to characterize the shifting meanings of publicity. Public library initiatives questioned the various political meanings of "*bình dân*," the commoner, the people, or accessible to the general public. I show how "public" could mean access to a wide range of people, including women, provincial readers, and youth; social welfare for the commoner and disenfranchised; or collective national identity through shared vernacular language and literary heritage. Experiments in creating public libraries ranged from shared reading resources in membership associations to more ambitious reading rooms that were welcome to all regardless of race, gender, age, or profession. As a public space for cultural exchange, self-erudition, and intellectual discourse in a shared language, Vietnamese public libraries functioned as bottom-up experiments in forming imagined communities of readers and public citizens.

The public libraries movement of the 1920s to 1940s coincided with widespread social and cultural transformations wrought by the intensity of urbanization, a short period of colonial liberalization (1936–38), the expansion of education, and the popularization of the vernacular Vietnamese written script, *quốc ngữ*. The publishing boom of *quốc ngữ* literature, adaptations, translations, and periodicals was spearheaded by a diverse generation of bilingual urbanites and cosmopolitan-informed Vietnamese intellectuals who navigated the political constraints and economic realities of colonial publishing. In Hanoi the Tự Lực Văn Đoàn (Self-Reliant Literary Group, comprised of Nhất Linh, Khái Hưng, Hoàng Đạo, Thạch Lam, Xuân Diệu, Thế Lữ, and Tú Mỡ) and in Saigon the Four Greats of the Newspaper

Village (Phan Khôi, Đào Trinh Nhất, Diệp Văn Kỳ, and Bùi Thế Mỹ) experimented across form and genre, advanced language reform, and worked between publishing markets, civic action, and political change.[5] Their intellectual labors produced a new body of *quốc ngữ* literature and print culture in the language of the masses. Working within state-sponsored publishing, cultural intermediaries such as Nguyễn Văn Vĩnh (1882–1936) and Phạm Quỳnh (1892–1945) produced extensive *quốc ngữ*–translated literature from French, transliterations of earlier *nôm* works such as the nineteenth-century *Tale of Kiều* (*Kim Văn Kiều*), and cultural commentary on Vietnamese culture and literary canon.[6] Between 1926 and 1930, publishers founded over four hundred *quốc ngữ* periodicals.[7] Several scholars have traced the intertwined histories of developing a literary canon in *quốc ngữ* and a Vietnamese national identity. Martina Nguyen uncovers the development of a "cosmopolitan nationalism" through the prolific publications of the Self-Reliant Literary Group, which spanned prose and poetry, periodicals and books, genre fictions, literary criticism, children's literature, social commentary, and translations.[8] John Phan describes the role of modern vernacular Vietnamese as a "rival nationalism" to Vietnamese collective identity grounded in Literary Sinitic and Vietnamese Confucian traditions.[9] Shawn McHale draws attention to the range of public discourse by examining spheres of Confucian, Buddhist, and communist print culture, and Philippe Peycam locates a public sphere of political discourse in Saigon's oppositional journalism. Beyond Vietnam studies, Benedict Anderson argues that "print capitalism"—the rise of mass printed newspapers and novels and the proliferation of vernacular languages—provided the social technology for individuals to think and relate to one another.[10] Su Lin Lewis describes how the press and associations allowed for "the articulation of individual and collective identities within a shared public space, and provided a venue for modern ideas of citizenship, society, and individualism to be discussed."[11] During the late colonial period in Vietnam, literary figures, political thinkers, and social commentators published across genres and media forms, producing a Vietnamese vernacular public sphere of cultural hybridity, cosmopolitan sensibilities, and modernist media. Through a shared language of Vietnamese *quốc ngữ*, networks of intellectuals and publishers advanced an alternative world of letters to Literary Sinitic and Francophone Western canon, a vernacular public sphere of interest-based associations and literary groups formed around public spaces of reading for intellectual exchange and community programming. Drawing from a cultural history of reading and libraries, this chapter examines how the social, political, and cultural movement to create public spaces of reading, *bình dân thư viện*, in the late colonial period gave shape to a Vietnamese language nationalism.

The previous three chapters focused on public reading culture experiments in colonial Francophone institutions of the Hanoi and Saigon state libraries, where Vietnamese readers confronted and experimented with colonial citizenship, state critique, and bureaucratic practices. Hanoi and Saigon urban readers immersed themselves in a self-directed practice of cosmopolitan scholarly reading, accessing wide-ranging reading matter, primarily of French-language texts, afforded through comparatively well-funded institutions. While the Hanoi Central Library developed a sizeable *quốc ngữ* collection through legal deposits of newly published literature, the Cochinchina Library primarily carried French-language materials, with a limited number of *quốc ngữ* publications circulating in the bibliobus vehicles across the Cochinchina provinces. An internal library report in Saigon commented on the dismal state of the Cochinchina Library facilities and lack of language diversity in 1934: "The *quốc ngữ* collection is nonexistent. The Library of Saigon has often forgotten that *quốc ngữ* is the living language."[12] The report also noted a sizable group of Chinese readers and the aspiration to create a Chinese-language section next to the French and future Vietnamese collection.

In contrast to the first half of this book, this chapter examines a bottom-up public libraries movement beyond the urban French language–dominated and state-funded colonial institutions in Hanoi and Saigon. This public library movement addressed the geographic needs of developing libraries in areas with limited opportunity for formal education: the countryside and provinces as well as the central protectorate region of Annam. The public library movement drew upon the central colonial library institutions as a model, but it also evolved to supplement their limitations and to offer alternative public functions. These popular reading spaces brought together the local and global, where multilingual communities of readers came together to access cosmopolitan ideas and modern sensibilities through the burgeoning range of *quốc ngữ*–printed reading matter, including contemporary news periodicals, translated global literature, short stories, multigenre novels, and histories. This chapter addresses the plurality and contentious history of the colonial public, driven by language, social, and political projects of organizing collections of reading matter.

Vietnamese language nationalism encompassed the aesthetic as well as the political, and debates on the individualist art of reading were connected to political projects of publicity, self-strengthening, and modernity. Vietnamese debates on the value of libraries and reading explored the contradictions of tradition and modernity, self and collective, and enlightened knowledge for the few versus universal literacy for all. Vietnamese actively debated the significance of books as cultural practices of urban life, as vehicles for moralization, and as aesthetic objects to be admired. In addition to facilitating solitary reading, public libraries brought together the literate and semiliterate to engage in oral reading and the shared experience of occupying common public space. Through tracing the evolution of Vietnamese vernacular reading practices and the public library movement, this chapter uncovers the social lives and textuality of books as technologies of sociopolitical community, in the words of Leah Price, where books function as "both trophies and as tools, . . . their use engages bodies as well as minds, and . . . printed matter connects readers not just with authors but with other owners and handlers."[13] Proposals to develop libraries in Hue aspired to create intellectual community as well as to preserve Vietnamese cultural heritage. Building collections of books was fundamental to the gathering of like-minded individuals and the sharing of resources, as shown in the case of mutual aid libraries and reading rooms in Cochinchina. This chapter concludes with Lý Vĩnh Khuông, who worked for two decades in the colonial state Cochinchina Library and through his experiences was driven to propose an alternative system of *quốc ngữ* libraries throughout Vietnam in the 1940s.

BOOKISH LEISURE: MODERN INQUIRY AND COSMOPOLITAN CIVILIZATION

Throughout the 1920s to 1940s, a flurry of reflexive discussions on "what people read" and "how to read" emerged in vernacular newspapers. In these vehement discussions writers argued that cultivating proper reading practices was intertwined with advancing civilization and collective identity. In March 1924 someone using the pen name "N.Đ." wrote elegantly of the practice of reading as an incomparable leisure activity of individual and social transformation.[14] The author first situated the emerging leisure activity of reading in the context of other types of vulgar activities, such as drinking, gambling, and listening to the *ả đào* music of beautiful women. The article argued that these latter activities are harmful, fleeting, with a temporary "good taste" that could easily slide into an addiction that would bring out the dangerous flavors of "spicy, bitter, salty," an addiction that would "waste your time, corrupt your mind, and [cause you to] lose yourself, your common sense, and good judgment." As an alternative, the author proposed that people join in the "noble and beneficial" pastime of reading books, where the act of reading inspires new ideas and thrilling experiences. The author emphasized the incomparable wisdom in books and their potential to educate:

> A book is a product of the East and West, passing on the lessons of the ancient world. The miracles of the creator are also recorded in books. The scenes of nature from all around the world are displayed in books. Holding a book in your hands is not too different from being face-to-face with the Confucian sages, teaching you morals of gold and jade, culture of silks and satins, teaching and refining your character. There is truly nothing comparable [to books].

The author waxed lyrical about the joy of reading both socially and solitarily, writing, "Imagine this: On a beautiful moonlit day with a pleasant breeze, a few close friends gather together, discussing a few lines from literature, and together they relish in more and more joyfulness; or alone in the evening hours, under the light a book becomes our friend and any sadness we carry dissipates." Describing himself as an "ignorant and slow learner," the author recounted the transformative experience of reading, which inspired him to feel profound emotions from narratives and experience the endless beautiful seas and landscapes of the world. "Oh the melodious practice of reading! Oh the joyfulness of reading! There is an old saying: 'If you read all the books of the world, you will know everything about the world.'" According to this article, reading books harnessed ideas from faraway societies for the expansion of one's mindset and the noble transformation of one's moral character. This article celebrated the beauty of reading as a scholarly encounter with Confucian wisdom.

A few months later another article appeared to respond to the universal celebration of reading and urgently called for a shift in reading practices. "How do we read in a beneficial way?" an author using the pen name "B.T." asked on the pages of the same publication, *Đông Pháp Thời Báo*, in July 1924.[15] *Đông Pháp Thời Báo: Le Courrier Indochinois* (Indochina Times) was a Saigon-based newspaper from 1923 to 1928 directed by the journalist-intellectual Diệp Văn Kỳ (1862–1929), who was an active leader in the Saigon publishing and cultural community, such as the Hội Khuyến Học (Association for Promoting Education). The author of the second article proposed a distinctly "modern" practice of reading that was characterized by nuanced inquiry, discernment of the past, and practical application to the present. The article opened with a critique of existing cultures of reading grounded in Confucian axioms and the blind repetition of words without critical reflection. Quoting a popular Confucian saying, "Dân khả sử do chi, bất khả sữ tri chi" (You can tell a person to follow your path, but you cannot expect them to understand the underlying reason), the author explained that people often misinterpret this saying, using it as an example of the danger of misunderstanding what one reads. The author explained how literate people read books without paying attention, fail to put into practice what they learn, or attempt to apply outmoded lessons. The author then called for a shift in reading practices toward critical discernment:

> To read, one needs to know when to respect and when to scorn, which phrases are masterful and which are formalities, which parts are good [and] we should follow, which parts are bad [and] we should abandon and avoid. [We need to] learn in a way that is beneficial to us as well as develops a benefit for the public of society, to learn not just to memorize this phrase or that word, hoping to have the occasion to recite; to learn [in a way] that is not just meekly following along.

The author stated that critical discernment can help readers learn from the past and apply lessons to the present. The author called readers to pay delicate attention to each paragraph and phrase as well as the context of the book, and to study the subtle mysteries of books rather than "speaking nonsense and taking the words of the sages and claiming the words as theirs." While the traditional practice of Confucian scholarly reading invited critical mindfulness through the act of copying, recitation, and response, this article called for an outright challenge of textual authority.[16] The article proposed a drastic shift in mentalities on bookish knowledge; readers were responsible for questioning the words of sages and scholars and recognizing that these books could in fact have mistakes or lessons only suitable for a specific time and place. This article intersected with broader modernist-inflected arguments that caricatured the modern against the traditional, calling for a rupture from past modes of scholarly learning rooted in Confucian memorization and honoring the sages. Furthermore, critiques of Literary Sinitic reading stood in for a wider sociopolitical animosity against remnants of the Confucian classical education system that was used to train Vietnamese civil servants in the French colonial period.

A tone of survivalist urgency and self-critique permeated these discussions, in which journalists called for a strengthening of the self and collective in the context of French civilizational dominance. These discussions posited a new type of an individualist reading habit focused on a range of affective experiences and intellectual cultivation, from leisurely pleasures and profound wisdom to social lessons and critical discernment. Reading was presented as a tool for social transformation, raising Vietnamese civilization out of antiquated practices and social vices into a world of modern civilization. In an essay published in February 1928, Đoan Phố argued that reading had a humanitarian potential to bring people out of backwardness.[17] "Reading offers a benefit for all peoples, regardless of their race and where they are in the world . . . especially now as we collectively study and research methods to avoid disease, to live long, to find ways for people to become civilized and escape backwardness." Reading can unlock wisdom that could spread in multitudes, like "one flower becomes ten, ten become a hundred, a hundred become a thousand, [and] then everyone in the country will practice good deeds; in other words, reading books brings a multitude of infinite benefits." Echoing other discussions such as that by B.T., the author called for the development of a discerning (*suy xét*) scholarly reader, one who has a "mind of research and inquiry," to study the prosperous advancements of other societies and to uncover the shortcomings of Vietnamese society. This cosmopolitan and comparative consciousness of the world would bring wisdom and awareness on how to best develop Vietnamese society. The author argued that books could widen mindsets, provide self-clarity, and offer knowledge on what to mimic and what to avoid. He emphasized the cultivation of scholarly inquiry to "study the root cause" (*truy tầm canh nguyên*) of social problems such as poverty, addiction, and brothels. Repeating the necessity of cultivating a discerning reader who is meticulous, critical, and dedicated, the author concluded that if a population develops a good method of reading, "their country will certainly become civilized." This article outlined how to be a modern scholarly reader and the potential for civilizational transformation. Reading has a humanitarian potential, to bring good wisdom and social transformation to those still living in "backwardness" and vice. While abstract on the details of social ills and what type of literature was transformative, this series of public commentary shows how reading was a conduit for self-strengthening and civilizational progress. The articles also point to how the advancement of civilization was not just an externally imposed, top-down French colonial import, but rather part of the intellectual public discourse of Vietnamese engagements with modernity and nationalism.

These discussions situated the practice of reading among other types of modern technologies, likening reading to popular education, world travel, and access to practical knowledge. In a 1929 commentary on audiobook disks, the author reflected upon the global phenomenon of reading and reading technologies. In a commentary titled "Xem sách mà không phải đọc. Lợi cho ai? Hại cho ai?" (Reading books but not actually "reading" them. Whom does this benefit? Whom does this harm?), published in the Hanoi-based daily *Hà Thành Ngọ Báo*, an author reflected upon global reading practices; the author remarked on the emergence of a new technology in the United States, audiobook disks.[18] The author first discussed the prosperity of America and the value placed upon time and convenience in America, which then motivated technological innovation, including the audiobook. It described the audiobook as a technology to save time and provide a novel listening experience. Reflecting on modernity and technological transformation, the author remarked, "We are now living in a time of machine technology." The author then wondered how Vietnamese reading practices might align with this new technology, positing that Vietnamese people would gladly welcome the audiobook disk given the prevalence of Vietnamese oral and social customs of reading and collective listening:

> I myself often like to listen to stories rather than reading them, or [for others] it's because they are lazy or illiterate. For this reason, in the evenings we can often see a lot of houses where folks gather in a room around one man or woman who reads a book, a story for all to listen. If this new technology [of audiobooks] has stories in our language, then certainly a lot of people will like it.

This article positioned Vietnamese oral reading practices among global reading practices and new technologies of communication, reflecting the late colonial discourse on the practices and products of modernity such as beauty products, radio, and medicines that filled the pages of the Vietnamese press and its advertisements.[19] This analysis of the audiobook is more than a fleeting commentary about a peculiar novel technology. It points to a cosmopolitan sensibility about reading as a global, changing techno-cultural practice of changing media forms and social articulations. Although the article is overall positive in tone, the author concludes with some hesitations about the possible risks of this new technology, specifically that listening to audiobooks would still require a lot of time, and that listeners might not remember what they heard as much as what they read with their eyes.

AESTHETIC TECHNIQUES OF READING AND COLLECTING

Vietnamese intellectuals and journalists actively debated reading as an aesthetic technique and book collecting as a modern cultural practice throughout the late colonial period. Commentaries, reader guides, and trilingual translations and glossaries of *quốc ngữ*, French, and Literary Sinitic appeared in the Vietnamese popular press, functioning as paratextual accompaniments facilitating reading as a learned technique among a wider public.[20] Periodicals designed literary sections introducing Vietnamese and translated literature in a range of genres and forms, from serialized novels and literary criticism to humorous anecdotes and poetry. The literary section of the newspaper *Đông Pháp Thời Báo: Le Courrier Indochinois* in 1928 included a list of popular Sino-Vietnamese and French-language sayings, presenting reading culture as part of a universal truism under the title "Eastern and Western Wisdom." Each Sino-Vietnamese (borrowed and adapted Vietnamese language from Literary Sinitic morphemes) and French quotation was accompanied by a detailed vernacular *quốc ngữ* explanation for the everyday contemporary Vietnamese reader to understand. The first quotation was a Sino-Vietnamese saying by Cheng Hao 程顥 (Trình Hạo) (1032–85), a Northern Song dynasty Chinese philosopher, stating, "Ngoại vật chi vị, cửu tắc khả yếm; độc thơ chi vị đủ cữu đủ thâm." The vernacular explanation declared that "One can get bored of the taste of everything over time, except for the pleasure derived from reading books; the longer you taste books the more flavorful they become" (in *quốc ngữ*, "Vật gì cũng thế, hễ nếm lâu thì chán; duy có sách vỡ hễ càng nếm thì càng thấy mặn-mà"). Following was another Sino-Vietnamese saying by Huang Tingjian 黄庭堅 (Huỳnh Đình Kiên) (1045–1105), a Northern Song dynasty poet and calligrapher, "Sĩ đại phu tam nhựt bất độc thư, tắc nghĩa lý bất giao ư hung trung." The quotation was explained in vernacular *quốc ngữ* as meaning "A scholar who does not read a book for three days will find that moral and rational principles in one's body [stomach] become disorganized" ("Kẻ sĩ đại phu không đọc sách trong ba ngày thì trong bụng nghĩa lý không thấy nhóm lại"). The last quotation was by the French philosopher Montesquieu (1689–1755), who proclaimed "Je n'ai jamais eu de chagrin qu'une heure de lecture n'ait dissipé." A Vietnamese translation was given as "I have never known any distress that an hour's reading did not cure" ("Tôi thườ nay chưa từng có cái sấu gì mà một giờ xem sách không giải đi được").[21] Readers of the literary section could glance upon these quotations and engage in a multilingual reading of Sino-Vietnamese, French, and vernacular Vietnamese. The reader might self-identify with and reflect upon these explanations of reading culture, which presented reading as a scholarly life philosophy, providing everyday meaning and nourishment in times of difficulty.

With a self-conscious awareness and personal investment in the development of the Vietnamese print industry, writers and publishers defined a relationship to readers as intellectual guides facilitating new practices around book culture, from how to read and cherish books to how to purchase books and assemble personal libraries. Writers relied upon the purchasing power of readers and sought to shape reader consumption and their literary tastes. In the 1930s, the series Tủ Sách Gia Đình (Family Library) appeared on the pages of the Hanoi-based *Phong Hoá* magazine, which circulated to Saigon, Hue, and Haiphong. The series called for readers to partake in the modernizing practice of book collecting and to transform the Vietnamese print industry through their demands for higher-quality literary content and production.[22] This series was written by Nhị Linh—the pen name of Trần Khánh Giư (1896–1947), more commonly known as Khái Hưng, who was one of the most influential modern novelists and short story writers from the literary group Tự Lực Văn Đoàn (Self-Reliant Literary Group). The series Family Library called readers to curate a collection of reading matter for the household as a distinctly modern practice of conspicuous consumption.

In the first article, published on August 10, 1934, Khái Hưng argued that "*chơi sách*"—literally, "book play," or the practice of reading and collecting books—was a distinct rupture from previous Vietnamese forms of book collecting.[23] He argued that in the past, book collection served only a functional purpose for scholars to prepare for civil service examinations. Furthermore, past scholars relied upon memorization of texts rather than building a large collection of reference books. Khái Hưng claimed that previous family libraries might only contain essential Literary Sinitic Confucian works such as the Four Books and Five Classics, chronicles, and possibly ancient literature or a few Literary Sinitic novels. Drawing comparisons with Westerners who "lived in this modern moment and needed a wider knowledge base," Khái Hưng called for Vietnamese to follow Western practices of building a household book collection.

> [Westerners] cannot just rely upon a few limited books. They need a library of over one hundred, or even one thousand, books. Even though they know there is a library where they could consult materials to understand everything they want, it is still ridiculous to have to journey long distances such as over one hundred kilometers to go to the library and find answers to their questions! Thus Western households all have a family book collection of varying sizes depending on their financial means.

Not only did Khái Hưng call for Vietnamese to develop a family library, but he also argued that Vietnamese readers must demand higher-quality production of Vietnamese-language books. Khái Hưng criticized the dismal state of Vietnamese *quốc ngữ* publishing as pitifully underdeveloped in both print quality and content:

> Among our young people, there are lots of people who also like to "*chơi sách*." However, most of their books are Western books. What about *quốc ngữ* books? There are no books to collect! Should we display in our glass bookshelves the paper-thin books with only a few pages, sold for only three sous to a *hào*? . . . These books are amateurish projects, [and] the printing itself is blurry, unclear, with uneven lines.

Khái Hưng claimed that the demand for novels by readers resulted in an absence of writers and publishers of works on history, geography, science, and philosophy. Drawing a direct connection between reader tastes and production quality, Khái Hưng believed that readers could advance and refine the print industry through their consumer demands for better-quality books and a wider range of topics.

> If we had the knowledge to select books that are interesting and beautiful, then publishers would then appeal to our demands and would thus produce better-quality books. Thus, in order to encourage artists, distributors, and publishers, we ourselves must develop an interest in book collecting. We must follow the Westerners and create a beautiful and interesting library collection in our home.

In the following issue on August 18, 1934, Khái Hưng further explicated his argument on the relationship between consumer demand, development of the print industry, and social change: "I go so far as to say . . . that if the citizens know how to spend and consume in the economy, the industries in this country will develop. . . . Printing artistic and beautiful books have a greater benefit—not just for a certain individual, but also for the possibility of future growth of the country."[24] In other words, Khái Hưng believed that both publishers and readers had a social responsibility to contribute to the advancement of the Vietnamese publishing industry and, by extension, Vietnamese intellectual culture. As a prolific writer and member of the Tự Lực Văn Đoàn, whose publishing house, Đời Nay, published much of Khái Hưng's work, Khái Hưng was also personally invested in the overall development of the Vietnamese print industry. If Khái Hưng could convince readers to invest in purchasing higher-quality print matter, readers might also support his group's publications and creation of luxury editions.

Khái Hưng insisted that the perception of "artistic and intellectual value" in books was just as important as the actual contents of books.

> By printing beautiful books, we can create a movement and practice of book collecting in the same way as those who like to collect antiques. For example, a book collector who sees a valuable book (valuable in regards to appearance) will immediately feel compelled to purchase the book and display it in their own glass bookshelf, even if the individual does not even want to read the book, even if the book is about philosophy or morality (since generally these topics require a bit more thinking and contemplation).

Khái Hưng believed that collecting beautiful books would then result in social and intellectual improvement because "sooner or later collectors would read the book."

Through his Family Library series, Khái Hưng advanced an interconnected three-part argument: First, Vietnamese readers must develop a practice of book collecting and creating household libraries; second, the current Vietnamese print quality must be improved in both form and content; third, consumer tastes and demands for better-quality books would lead to change in the print industry as well as the sociocultural development of the country. He advanced a powerful line of argumentation: There was a direct connection between consumerism and modernity, material products, cultural practices, and sociocultural change. As Martina Nguyen has argued, Khái Hưng and the Self-Reliant Literary Group advanced an intertwined political, cultural, and economic project of a "cosmopolitan nationalism" "to guide the actions and decisions of the burgeoning nation, a method for inculcating the habits of citizenship."[25] Individual practices guided by consumer tastes could ultimately inform the public sphere of cultural production and political identity.

Writers engaged in a deep self-reflexive discussion about the cultivation of reading culture as an aesthetic, social, and cultural movement among Vietnamese readers. In his extensive 1935 article in *Hà Thành Ngọ Báo*, Lan Khai declared that men of letters (writers and poets, or *văn nhân thi sĩ*) are part of the brilliant talented class that can bring "glory to our race."[26] In comparison, the reader was part of a "refined worldly class" whose role was to encourage the development of the literary class. This declaration emphasized the intertwined relationship between writer and reader and the responsibility of the enlightened elite to cultivate a broader public. Lan Khai's self-declaration as part of a "lettered" literary cohort points to a masculine elite intellectualism that characterized much of the discourse of late colonial print culture and literary development. Lan Khai is the pseudonym of Nguyễn Đình Khải (1906–45), who wrote several genres of novels such as historical novels (*tiểu thuyết lịch sử*) and psychosocial novels (*tiểu thuyết tâm lý xã hội*) and expanded his work into literary criticism, translation, and poetry.[27] Lan Khai later earned the nickname "*nhà văn đường rừng*" (writer of the jungle road), due to his well-known adventure travel story set in the northern uplands, *Truyện Đường Rừng*, published in 1940.

Furthermore, Lan Khai conceptualized Vietnamese arts and literature as existing within global cosmopolitanism. The author saw himself as part of the literary class, leading an important social movement to elevate Vietnamese literature to a world stage of "great literature." Lan Khai pushed the boundaries of Vietnamese literary genres by writing poetry, translations, novels, and criticism, and he sought to position Vietnamese literature and reading as part of a global humanistic aesthetics. In his elegant article "Đọc sách là một nghệ thuật" (Reading books is an art), Lan Khai likened reading to art and called for an intimate reflection on what it means to read.[28] With an air of romantic rumination, he described reading as a partaking of life's beauty and sorrows. Opening the article with a beautiful scene of an elder soothing a crying baby with a melodious "*ạ ơi ơi*," the author compared this comforting act to art, "a sacred power that consoles and comforts all of humanity in their suffering." He situated the act of reading and the savoring of literature as a humanistic art among the fields of painting, architecture, music, and dance. He professed the transformative experiences of reading:

> I read, I recite beautiful poetry, interesting essays for what purpose? The purpose is to discover new sensations and strange ideas, to experience in my imagination the strange sceneries and faraway places outside the melancholic tiny, tight frame of my everyday life. In summary, I read in order to find the delights of beauty.

Likening a reader to an artist, Lan Khai detailed how a complete surrender of self to art makes space to "savor art in a refined way . . . giving all their soul [to art] with an utterance of the simple words: 'It's so beautiful.'" Arguing for the artful consumption of literature, Lan Khai remarked, "Works of literature must spark from my heart a desire to savor a certain purity [of life]; I can only truly find this beauty in books."

The second half of his article shifted from a focus on the consumption of literature to the craft of artistic production of literature by writers and poets. Lan Khai proclaimed that we readers should only give our soulful attention to skillful authors who write "splendid sceneries, beautiful words, smooth rhymes." He critiqued authors who write unnecessarily complicated, bizarre stories that occupy readers' minds, and he specifically condemned the enticing yet superficial plotlines of popular adventure, romance, and action stories. To counter "superficial" popular literature, Lan Khai called for writers and poets to "courageously bring into the world great works of literature and poetry . . . refined spectacular words about philosophy and society." He concluded with the adamant assertion that the production of great literature can bring forward Vietnamese literature to stand among the "fresh, radiant, progressive" prose and verse of other countries. Lan Khai directly connected the act of reading in an intertwined practice of individual and collective evolution. Bookish leisure was not simply a mild fleeting entertainment for individuals; to read and produce literature was an artful cultivation of worldliness and a refined mind. Reading elevated the collective to think critically, to discern between superficial enticements and great beauty, and to move closer to a humanistic truth.

READING AS MORALIZATION OF WOMEN, YOUTH, AND THE COUNTRYSIDE

Often the cultivation of bookish leisure and aesthetic techniques of reading were framed against a moralized critique of uncurbed social ills and naive reading tastes. The moralized concern was directed toward an amorphous group of those in need of guidance, specifically women, youth, and rural villagers. In their paternalistic representations, urban—and primarily male—intellectuals constructed caricatures of these demographics as naive, subject to politically "dangerous" ideas, and easily addicted to the temptations of modern life. Many male writers took multiple pseudonyms, sometimes taking on female names to publicly comment on changing gender norms and female behaviors. In the popular commentary section of *Hà Thành Ngọ Báo* on February 13, 1930, an author with the female name of Phạm Thị Lan Khanh argued that female readers loved to read harmful novels and lacked the intellectual capacity to discern between good and bad books. Calling for more parental guidance for female readers, Lan Khanh mentioned in detail another article supposedly written by two women named Hồng-vân and Phạm thị-Thoa on the topic of the harmfulness of novels.[29] In this extensive essay the writers explained the benefits and dangers of reading for women. They claimed that reading good novels has the potential "to broaden one's intelligence in order to follow the road of civilization, bringing happiness to the family and the country." Yet the article also reported that many women were dedicating their time to reading the recent popular wave of sensationalist and morally depraved literature. The authors expressed concern about female readers pouring their hearts and minds into reading novels and incessantly gossiping about fictional romantic storylines.

The authors argued that women readers had not yet evolved into discerning scholars with a "pair of eyes" who could judge the quality of good and bad literature.[30] This framework assumed that literature can be simplistically judged as good or bad, morally uplifting or socially depraved. Female readers were caricatured as naive children without perceptive eyes to discern the lies of an author who was "clever enough to be able to find the spirit of people a certain weakness to prey upon" in order to sell their books. This representation posited a gendered hierarchy of masculine-directed intellectualism, in which women without the wisdom of a scholar or parent fall victim to the clever tricks of a (most likely male) author. According to the article, female readers were hypnotized by popular novels that focus on love, a facetious concept pulling female readers into an entranced, self-pitying state of existence: "[By] reading a lot of novels but not reading with discretion, the brains of women are filled with images of crumbling society [from the stories]. It doesn't take long until the women become accustomed to this, and their personality also changes to mimic these [stories], and no medicine can save them."[31] The authors referenced a French saying to critique the dangers of women mindlessly mimicking dangerous ideas and fictional characters, "Qui se ressemble, s'assemble" (Those who resemble each other assemble together), and included a Vietnamese translation, "Đồng thanh tương ứng, đồng khi tương cầu." The article concluded with the final concern that women's mental and emotional states are fragile, warning that it was better for women to "be immersed in the noble lives of heroes from historical novels" than to "be in the company of fictional characters who end up committing suicide."

The specific commentary about the dangers of suicide reflected broader popular commentary in Vietnamese newspapers on the negative cultural changes wrought by modernity and urbanization upon women and youth. An evolving cultural commentary argued that the introduction of literary topics such as romance and self-determination led to rebellion against constructed traditional gender innocence and familial roles. Discussions of female suicide emerged prominently on the pages of Vietnamese popular press as well as in literature, reflecting wider simplistic critiques on the dangers of "modernity" to gender norms.[32] Overall, this commentary on women's reading coincided with broader social discourse on the change in women's roles in society, characterized as debates over the "Woman's Question" in the 1920s and 1930s.[33] Embedded within these debates were caricatures of the "new woman" and "modern girl" (*gái tân thời, gái mới*), represented as individualistic, leisure driven, and urban. Vietnamese women were cast as symbols of tradition and modernity, reflecting what Hue-Tam Ho Tai describes as a cultural anchor against the changes of colonial society and a platform to discuss "abstract issues of morality, social structure, independence, collaboration, empowerment, liberty, and equality."[34] Furthermore, the debates about women's roles reflected changing demographic shifts of the reading public to include women writers and readers, participating as public intellectuals and urban consumers. Christina Firpo problematizes the framing of the "modern girl" as only understood as carefree urban elite consumerists, and examines modern girls to also include rural migrants who were forced to participate in exploitative labor industries.[35]

In addition to the moralization of the female population, creating spaces to cultivate reading practices and to disseminate reading matter was of critical importance for youth and the rural Vietnamese population. On the first page of the newspaper *Trung Hoà Nhật Báo* on July 18, 1925, an article called for the building of joint initiatives of libraries and community centers in all villages, including those in the countryside.[36] Discussing community gathering spaces and libraries, the author pointed to how libraries offered a space for productive socializing and the cultivation of good habits. "With a bit of leisure time before sleeping, our brothers and sisters who already have the habit of socializing can come stop by the library and together they can discuss books, research literature, and practice how to read newspapers." The author argued that the cultivation of good socializing habits could happen slowly through exposure to reading; those who are literate had a responsibility to come to the library, read out loud for others, and slowly teach the illiterate how to read books and newspapers. The author also argued that this movement to teach reading practices could displace the popular social practice of "folks coming together to gossip and talk nonsense." The author emphasized that the practice of reading was undeniably valuable and good for all citizens and thus should be cultivated in the countryside. Specifically, the author pointed to how libraries could teach youth the good habits of reading books and newspapers instead of bad habits such as gambling, partying, and drinking. He also highlighted the shared responsibility of villagers to maintain the library as a shared community space, a "gathering space for everyone in the village for anyone who wants to learn anything that they want." The author extensively discussed the spatial organization of the library and community space, calling for a flexible space that could be repurposed for community events but still offer a quiet and formal space of chairs, tables, and bookshelves for readers. This article is significant because it called for a widespread movement to develop public libraries for all citizens, young and old, male and female, urban and villagers, arguing that a joint community center and library were universal resources for the development of good leisure habits.

In another article published in April 1932 in the Hanoi periodical *Báo Đông Pháp*, the author Tùng Phong specifically called for the development of a "*bình dân thư viện*," a community public library for the common people to combat social ills.[37] *Báo Đông Pháp* was a Hanoi-based publication operating from approximately 1925 to 1932 and was seen as the Hanoi equivalent to the Saigon-based *Đông Pháp Thời Báo: Le Courrier Indochinois*. In this call for a community public library, reading was promoted as a healthy leisure activity, an alternative to the spread of dangerous addictions such as gambling, alcohol, and drugs:

> When it comes to the benefits of the library, it is incomparable. A village with a library offers a villager a place to read books or borrow books to read at home after their work. Reading makes people avoid sadness and evil; people from the countryside who read books will be happy with the ancient wisdom and will not dream about alcohol, gambling, and drug addiction. If they are not trapped in those terrible material things, they will not commit crimes against the law and will have a spirit of honest work. [With the development of libraries and its accompanying social benefits,] the number of prisoners in prisons will be reduced, hospitals will reduce the number of patients, and rural areas will reduce the number of nomadic idlers; libraries cast a powerful spell to calm the spirits; no one can deny this truth.

The creation of public libraries and the spread of reading was interconnected with the duties of creating morally righteous and productive citizens. The author argued that "a public library is a very valuable resource; all civilized countries have these libraries," and explained that in the Dutch East Indies most villages have a public library.

In addition to this moral argument, Tùng Phong also emphasized the governmental responsibility to cultivate reading culture and popular education through establishing public libraries. The author argued that a good government, like a good family, must be committed to the two tasks of "*nuôi*" and "*dậy*." *Nuôi* is usually connected to child-rearing and familial caretaking, while *dậy* is associated with moralization and teaching. The author described *nuôi* as referring to infrastructural developments such as building roads, dikes, and markets, while *dậy* involved setting up schools, organizing lectures, and building libraries. The author also briefly mentioned that existing public library efforts had been obstructed by corrupt local mandarinate officials who claimed that libraries would negatively brainwash the people. The article concluded with a call to the government first to prioritize building libraries in schools to provide educational materials to poor students and then to expand to build *bình dân thư viện*. The author referenced the efforts of the province Hưng-Yên, which drew from public funds to set up libraries in schools to distribute books to poor students.[38] This article is significant because it connects library development to the fundamental government responsibility to its citizens to provide popular education and social services.

THE BẢO ĐẠI LIBRARY: SERVING THE IMPERIALIST NATION OR THE HUE PUBLIC

Advocates of public libraries questioned the two-pronged meaning of "public," first, as accessible to the underserved population, and, second, as a representation of a public, collective national identity. These two roles of serving the public as a form of social welfare and as a symbolic representation of a collective people were intertwined and at times at odds with one another. The history of library development in the central Vietnamese region points to these tensions between the social function and political symbol of building libraries. Compared to Hanoi and Saigon, the imperial capital of Hue lacked sustained library development from the Directorate of Archives and Libraries of Indochina. An administrative archives-library organized within the regional colonial government (the residence superior) provided a limited number of administrative reference materials in Hue beginning in 1921. Instead, library development in the imperial capital of Hue was shaped by the specific governance structure and cultural intellectual milieu of the central Vietnamese region. For much of the colonial period, the protectorate region of Annam employed a dual system of rule, with nominal authority under the imperial Annamese government (Chính Phủ Nam Triều, Gouvernement Imperial de l'Annam), led by the Nguyễn emperor and with French colonial authority under the resident superior of Annam. The central region maintained a lower-level mandarinate administration, and Hue functioned as the symbolic capital of the Nguyễn dynasty's monarchical authority.[39] Both governor generals Albert Sarraut and Pierre Pasquier sponsored the political and cultural cultivation of monarchical figurehead Bảo Đại as a collaborationist colonial monarch. Christopher Goscha argues that Albert Sarraut designed this first "Bảo Đại solution" in an attempt to control anticolonial movements by relying upon the royal family to exercise influence over the Vietnamese population.[40] Bảo Đại was crowned as emperor in 1926, yet many nationalist royalists, such as Phan Bội Châu, supported Prince Cường Để (1882–1951) as the legitimate heir, and the prince lived in exile in Japan, Siam, and China while garnering support while abroad to reclaim the throne.

On June 26, 1933, a former library institution in the Imperial Academy (Quốc Tử Giám) was renamed the Bảo Đại Library as part of an extensive reorganizing of "national" collections pertaining to Vietnamese precolonial dynastic records as well as contemporary materials. The library was moved to the building behind the Hue imperial palace complex (Di Luân Đường), and after a year of reorganization it was officially opened on August 5, 1934.[41] The political and intellectual debates about the role of the Bảo Đại Library brought together conflicting visions about national collective identity, the public, and cultural heritage. Shortly after the library's opening, the Imperial Ministry of Education sent out a circular to the provinces in the central region and published a copy in newspapers asking for donations of books to the newly reorganized library.[42] This circular outlined imperial administrative efforts and invited the public of the central region to build up national heritage through the library. Emperor Bảo Đại (who served from 1926 to 1945) had envisioned the Bảo Đại Library as part of an effort to "build up national characteristics" through preserving historic national heritage. The circular emphasized that many textual compilations by civil mandarins from previous dynasties were scattered among the common people and asserted the role of the library as a repository for gathering these scattered precious books. The circular communicated to the central region provinces that all scholars and their descendants who had valuable books, such as poetry, literature, stories, autobiography, history, genealogy, novels, and dramas—whether in *chữ hán*, *nôm*, or *quốc ngữ* (that they themselves wrote or purchased)—should submit the books to the Bảo Đại Library in order to compile a "common treasure" (*bửu vật chung*). Donations would be publicly honored with commemorative placards with the names of donors, or, if people did not want to donate a book, they could lend it to the library for it to be copied (and their contributions would also be publicly honored). This call for donations and copying reflects an East Asian practice of libraries as shared collections of valuable texts, tying together donors and readers through the task of preservation and compilation. The circular concluded that "everyone would understand this mission of preserving national education is a matter of common interest" and would be eager to help. It described the mission of the Bảo Đại Library as a place to "store the masterpiece relics of the country." This circular positioned the library as an important royalist national institution to preserve Vietnamese heritage and history and called all individuals to contribute to the task of building a national collection. The practice of donating texts and earning public merit shows how building libraries was a communal task that formed social networks and regional ties.[43] Notably, the Bảo Đại Library represents an attempt to craft an imperial Vietnamese nationalistic identity, continuing the efforts of the precolonial Nguyễn dynasty to weave a timeless united Vietnamese identity with an "ancient" imperial capital in Hue.

The Bảo Đại Library was an imperial Vietnamese national institution organized within a French colonial context, leading to contradictions in its mission and influence. It is unclear how private citizens supported these state-building efforts to preserve Vietnamese heritage institutions under an imperial mantle. Rather, throughout the Vietnamese popular press individuals demanded libraries such as the Bảo Đại Library to serve the Hue reading public. The periodical *Tiểu Long* announced that the long-awaited Bảo Đại Library would soon be opened in Hue and argued for the creation of a second library in Hue.[44] Although smaller in size compared to the "great libraries of Tonkin and Cochinchina," this new library would realize the "dream for the intellectual population of Hue" and satisfy the vibrant intellectual life of writers, thinkers, and important figures in Hue.[45] The author remarked on the limited libraries for those who did not work in the government administration, citing the existence of only one small library created by the Society of Mutual Education. The newspaper article argued that a library is important for intellectual life, "forming thinkers, writers—in other words, great men—because it is there that one comes to draw on centuries of knowledge of humanity." The author called for the generosity of wealthy benefactors as well as dedication from the government administration to create a second library to "raise the intellectual level of the capital and to give it a new luster" and ultimately to contribute to "the development of this country."

Yet it seems that when the Bảo Đại Library finally opened, it failed to be a great public library for the intellectual population of Hue. In a detailed May 1936 article titled "Một vài điều phải sửa đổi ở thư viện Bảo Đại" (A few things that must be changed at the Bảo Đại Library), Trần Danh complained that the library lacked Vietnamese-language materials and had limited operating hours. He described the library as a tiny reading room with a limited collection of seven hundred books and twenty periodicals, primarily in the French language.[46] In addition to the periodicals *Trang Án* and *Trung Bắc Tân Văn*, the author demanded the addition of *quốc ngữ* reading materials, noting that they were widely available and valuable. In terms of operations, Trần Danh demanded extending the operating hours to 7:30 to 11:30 a.m. and 2:30 to 8 p.m., as well as the addition of electric fans to keep away the mosquitos. The author also called attention to issues that interfered with a reader's experience: "The other annoying aspect for readers of this library is that it is very noisy. Firstly, because the library is next to someone's residence, and the noise from the residence carries into the library, [and] . . . secondly, even though in the library there are rules enforcing silence, all the readers come to the library and obey these rules, but the workers of the library are the ones who do not follow the rules."[47] He concluded with a demand that the library permit women to come to read and honor its commitment to be a reading room for all. Although it is uncertain if women were expressly forbidden to come to the library, the author's attention to women's reading is significant because it points to the widening conversation around women as important participants in intellectual culture and the public reading sphere. Noting that women readers were a "fresh opinion and contemporary idea," the author addressed women's ability to read at the Bảo Đại Library as part of the mission of a public library truly open for all.

Some efforts to improve the Bảo Đại Library began to take place, with the library closing for repairs and the installation of ceiling fans in May 1936. Yet, according to a passionate letter signed by "poor students" and addressed to the high officials of the Ministry of National Education, the library had been closed for far too long. Noting the delays on the repairs, the letter argued that the closed library was depriving poor students of a valuable place for study. According to the letter, the library had barely any relevant books, yet poor students still appreciated the space to study and "widen their knowledge."[48] In their summary of the library, the students called attention to the language limitations of the collection:

> The library just recently opened, that is, where candidates can come to the Di Luận Đường reading room and read a handful of old newspapers and a few old magazines from a few years, while the books are in Literary Sinitic and nobody can read them. Regardless of this, we are all so happy for a space to patronize where we can broaden our knowledge, but then the library moved to another building and thus our happiness lasted only two months.

The letter also called for the library to purchase more works, specifically contemporary newspapers with discussions of literature or modern politics rather than historic periodicals. Even with its limitations, the Bảo Đại Library offered a central public space for self-directed learning and exposure to periodicals, particularly for poorer students with limited access to reading material. The letter also points to a transition in language and literacy, with readers demanding modern knowledge and contemporary literature, particularly in *quốc ngữ* rather than Sinitic. The library served as a governmental and symbolic space, as seen in the recruitment of officials held at the library on March 5, 1940.[49] On April 3, 1942, a highly publicized exhibition of historic archives and manuscripts was held at the library and around the Hue citadel, organized by a joint effort of the Directorate of Archives and Libraries and the Service of Information, Propaganda, and the Press, with collaboration from the Association des Amis du Vieux Hue and the Khải Định Museum. During the opening ceremony the day prior, Emperor Bảo Đại inaugurated the exhibition, which was attended by French colonial officials and Vietnamese government ministers. Paul Boudet and Ngô Đình Nhu showcased imperial archives collections, maps, and documents produced by Catholic missionaries.[50] In terms of everyday function as a public library, the development of the Bảo Đại Library collections continued at a slow pace, with the establishment of an inventory for the newspapers and reviews in French and *quốc ngữ* organized only in March 1944.

Top-down library, archives, and documentation efforts did not progress in Hue until the 1940s. In September 1942, the director of the Directorate of Archives and Libraries of Indochina, Paul Boudet, commissioned his assistant director, Ngô Đình Nhu, to centralize, catalog, and reorganize both the imperial Annamese and French colonial administrative archives and libraries in Hue. Throughout the 1930s and 1940s, Nhu had already been involved in important documentation initiatives in the Hue region. For example, since February 1942 Nhu had worked with the mandarin official Trần Văn Lý to catalog and conserve the precious precolonial *châu bản* (royal records) that were maintained through the Quốc Tử Giám.[51] By November 1, 1943, Nhu had established an official public library, a Hue institutional equivalent to the existing Hanoi, Saigon, and Phnom Penh libraries within the Directorate of Archives and Libraries. In the same year the imperial Annamese institutions the Quốc Sử Quán, Tàng Thư Lâu, Nội Các, Cơ Mật Viện, and Bảo Đại Library, as well as the archives of the cabinet, ministries, and agencies in the capital and its provinces, merged into the Cơ Quan Lưu Trữ và Thư Viện Của Chính Phủ Nam Triều (Service des archives et bibliothèques du gouvernement impérial).[52] This service was informally referred to as "les archives et les bibliothèques du gouvernement annamite" and was seen as an imperial-national effort to centralize Vietnamese documentation.[53]

SOCIAL WELFARE THROUGH HUE ASSOCIATIONS AND BÌNH DÂN THƯ VIỆN

Given the limitations of top-down efforts to develop libraries in Hue, associations also served an important role as a space for the intellectual community and for accessing reading matter. On April 9, 1935, Tiêu Diêu Tử published extensively on the development of a specific dedicated literary and arts association in the imperial capital to bring together intellectuals, artists, and writers in Hue.[54] The author noted that the literary arm of the association could have a small library to encourage the spread of literature and to provide reading matter to the students in Hue. Tiêu Diêu Tử emphasized the need for this association library, arguing that the Bảo Đại Library was only helpful for those taking administrative mandarin examinations and that accessing the library required a higher primary education degree.

According to the first meeting to organize what came to be known as the Hội Văn Chương Mỹ Thuật và Thể Thao (Association of Literature, Arts, and Sports), the attendees envisioned the association to be a "gathering place for writers to exchange ideas" and a place to cultivate art activities, exhibitions, and the promulgation of sports.[55] One of the first principles according to the association statutes was to organize a shared collection of reading matter and a shared space for reading, socializing, and events.[56] The rise of multifaceted cultural associations such as the literature, arts, and sports association in Hue points to a growing interest in bottom-up forms of community, intellectual cultivation, and cultural exchange to serve specific needs, leisure interests, and language preferences that were neglected by state efforts related to public education and libraries. The rise of associations in Hue intersected with an expanding publishing industry and readership in the Annam region. While the publishing industry in Annam was small compared to that in Tonkin and Cochinchina, at least fifteen printing and publishing houses existed throughout Hue, Qui Nhơn, and Vinh, producing local and global news, research, and reading matter.[57] As part of top-down state projects to develop popular libraries in Annam (discussed in the previous chapter), the resident superior of Annam studied the existing publishing industry in Annam between 1929 and 1930.[58] This study noted the high demand for *quốc ngữ* literature among male and female readers, particularly children's literature, Vietnamese novels, and translations of popular French and Chinese novels, plays, and poetry. The study revealed an interesting spatial disaggregation of *quốc ngữ* book demands across cities and villages: an estimated two thousand copies in the cities, or two hundred in Thanh Hoá, three hundred in Vĩnh, five hundred in Hue, one thousand in Tourane (Đà Nẵng), Faifoo (Hội An), Quy Nhơn, and Nha Trang), and eight thousand copies in villages.

In addition to calling for an association to cultivate reading culture, the same author, Tiêu Diêu Tử, wrote explicitly about creating a public library space ten days later. On behalf of the biweekly periodical *Tràng An*, Tiêu Diêu Tử published an extensive article calling for the establishment of a *bình dân thư viện*, a common people's public library, in Hue.[59] The article demanded the creation of a truly public library as a social service for the poor inhabitants of Hue. The article contrasted the proposed public library with the efforts of associations in Hue, such as the Hội Văn Chương Mỹ Thuật và Thể Thao (Association of Literature, Arts, and Sports), mentioned in his previous article. The author noted that only those who paid to be part of the association could derive benefit; the article called instead for a different type of public service for those without financial means.

Tiêu Diêu Tử argued that libraries were important services for the poor, the underemployed, and undereducated youth: "Compared to Hanoi and Saigon, Hue citizens are not as rich, and the city does not have as many schools for the teenagers thirsty for knowledge." He noted Hue's large population of students without formal education or jobs and compared them to the idle population in Hanoi and Saigon, who have the potential to "kill time by spending episodes reading books at the library, which is both entertaining and useful. In Hue they do not have money to buy books and ultimately become degenerate outcasts of society."

The author argued for the importance of libraries to cultivate youth, who, left to their own actions, would "become astray and unruly, abandoned by society and a pity for their families." He declared that a public library could provide a resource for self-directed education and extend formal classroom learning to the curious:

> [It can benefit] those students who want to expand beyond the assigned knowledge of the schools. There is nothing comparable to being able to occasionally come to the library to peruse books and copy down notes. And there are other people who want to learn to read, who have no other purpose except to read in order to know. There are so many talented writers in Europe who were forced to leave school too early, then through self-study in libraries they became successful people and known all over the world. In our country, Vietnam, there are also many self-taught people who hold important positions in politics and literature.

The author described the current state of Hue libraries and intellectual culture as a transitional period between Confucian letters and Western learning:

> Fifty years ago, in the time when Confucian education was still prevalent, Hue used to be known as a literary city. Confucian education is now almost all gone. Among a hundred young people it is difficult to find one or two people who know the basics of

> Confucian learning. We do not have to say it, but everyone knows that today's teenagers are interested in Western studies, seeing the beauty of Western learning; they are born with a love for Western studies, leaning toward the West.

Tiêu Diêu Tử critiqued the limitations of the current library institutions, beneficial only to an outmoded and superficial Confucian administrative class. He declared that the Imperial Academy only carried books for the entrance exam for the administration, while the Bảo Đại Library only offered useful books for retired mandarins. These critiques of Confucian learning point to the growing demand for a different, modern world of letters grounded in *quốc ngữ*, translated global literature, and Western learning.

Tiêu Diêu Tử declared, "There is no public library. But if the two governments [French and Annamese] are thinking about saving society, then they should think about setting up this library because it serves the task of social welfare, saving unemployed intellectuals, saving poor students, saving those who are dedicated to learning." The author emphasized the importance of libraries for social welfare with his final argument: To address the plight of the poor, one creates a poorhouse; to address the struggles of unemployed intellectuals, one must create a library for them. Tiêu Diêu Tử remarked, "The sight of unemployed intellectuals faltering in front of this and that administrative building, or abandoned in gambling dens: How tragic is this? Why not think about setting up a library to accommodate them?" Tiêu Diêu Tử reported on the deficit of library and education opportunities in Hue compared to Hanoi and Saigon, emphasizing the dire need to at least establish one public library institution to support the growing population of the disenfranchised, whom he characterized as the unemployed, undereducated youth, and the poor.

Tiêu Diêu Tử's April 1935 proposal to create truly accessible library dragged through 1936 with limited success. Other newspapers continued to emphasize the dire need for this public library and criticized the limitations of the Bảo Đại Library and library developments in Hue. In another article published February 1936, "Bao giờ Huế có một thư viện như thế" (When will Hue have a library like that?), the author compared the Hanoi and Hue libraries.[60] The author reported on the recent visit from the governor general of Indochina, René Robin, to the recently expanded Hanoi Central Library and noted the success of the Hanoi library among students and scholars. In contrast, the author observed that Hue only had the insufficient Bảo Đại Library and declared that in "many ways, Hue does not even have a library." The author also wrote that in the past the *Tràng An* periodical had called for a people's library (*bình dân thư viện*), an initiative that "struck a chord with many readers and intellectuals as timely and important, yet this library only existed in our dreams. Why? Because there is no money." The author called upon the Annamese imperial government to take upon the duty to buy some books and build the library: "It is an important issue that affects the evolution of our citizens, and we should not take it lightly." The author directly criticized the management of the Annamese imperial government, which failed to portion out its funds to support the development of this important social cultural institution in order to support a large group of disenfranchised intellectuals and youth.

A few weeks later, another article in the same journal claimed that Hue would soon have a public library. The author reported that the Ministry of Education would create a public library in Hue, and the author expressed their hope that this library would be worthy of its name and serve the public.[61] Yet it is uncertain if the Ministry of Education actually carried out this plan. Instead, archival documents point to the efforts of Hue associations taking up the initiative to fund and organize a *bình dân thư viện*. According to a letter from the resident superior of Annam to the Directorate of Archives and Libraries in Hanoi on April 9, 1936, the president of the Ligue des Amis de l'Annam (League of Friends of Annam) was in the process of creating a new library in Hue for Vietnamese youth, elites, and French residents in Hue.[62] The letter requested that the Directorate in Hanoi send over documentation about library functions, reading room regulations, and information about borrowing procedures to serve as a model for the new Hue library. On May 1, 1936, the Hanoi Directorate responded with a copy of the reading room and borrowing section rules. The Directorate also applauded the work of the League of Friends of Annam, encouraging them to find sustainable resources to enrich the collections and to hire competent personnel. This exchange demonstrates the important role of cultural and scholarly associations in the development of civic and public institutions such as libraries. Library development was not simply a top-down project stemming from the governor general or decisions from the Directorate of Archives and Libraries. Instead, community libraries emerged also through independent networks of associations that then later sought technical or budgetary assistance from the government and official channels.

ALTERNATIVE READING SPACES AND ASSOCIATIONS

The *bình dân thư viện* initiatives in Hue were embedded within a landscape of formal and informal professional associations, mutual self-help societies, and reading circles organized around specific needs and communities throughout Vietnam. Especially prevalent throughout Cochinchina were a vibrant civil society of associations, businesses, and printing houses developed around special interests ranging from language and literacy to sports and travel. Motivated by shared interests such as professional development or literacy, many groups dedicated their efforts to building a library of information and resources. In this way, the library was a tool of continuing education, individual empowerment, and collective improvement. Philippe Peycam describes these associations as "collective, horizontal structures, organized around criteria of belonging (geographical, professional, educational), which individuals willingly joined and participated in on equal terms."[63] Peycam argues that the proliferation of associations and print journalism promoted the "newspaper village" (*làng báo chí*), an organizing network of journalists, distributors, donors, thinkers, and printers expanding beyond traditional marks of allegiance and cohesion to family, village, or location.[64]

For example, in 1906 the Bibliothèque amicale de Baclieu (Bạc Liệu Friendly Library) in the Mekong Delta was established as a mutual aid society with a library to "improve our knowledge of the French language and to study amicably and collaboratively the means to improve our fate."[65] The Association of Primary Teachers was organized in 1931 to provide support for provincial teachers and emphasized the importance of creating a library for "the purpose of improving the moral and intellectual culture of the members through reading books and newspapers."[66] On November 25, 1937, the self-help association Workers of the Book of Tonkin (Travailleurs du livre du Tonkin, or Bắc kỳ Ấn công Ái hữu hội) declared its founding goals:

> 1) To develop the artistic tastes and intellectual capacity of its members, through opening reading rooms, building libraries, and creating classes for professional development. Regarding instruction, the association follows the current law, regarding private education in Indochina, and 2) To help as much as possible the members of the association when their family are victims of misfortune.[67]

These self-help associations created a mutual aid system of shared resources, from professional knowledge and educational resources to a collective fund to support its members in times of economic need. The Indochinese Circle, founded in September 1937, had over 150 French, Vietnamese, and Chinese members. Its goals included the creation of a meeting space for its members that facilitated mutual understanding, cooperation, and moral and intellectual improvement through lectures, publications, and study circles; helping youth influenced by Western culture with resources to continue to learn and develop in Indochina; and bringing together other mutual associations and social assistance groups to cooperate in the Maison de la Mutualité (Mutuality House), to be built on the corner of Taberd and Verdun Streets in Saigon-Cholon. On November 4, 1939, the leaders of the Indochinese Circle and the Mutuality House requested a grant of six thousand piastres to assist in the collaboration of self-help associations throughout Cochinchina. These associations included a diverse range of mutual aid groups of teachers, engineers, civil services, unions, and regional groups throughout Cochinchina.[68]

Mutual self-help societies gathered financial and educational resources and promoted certain "healthy" forms of educational leisure and social life in the provinces. For example, in 1925 the Cần Thơ Library Circle was established as part of the Cần Thơ Club with the mission to "learn through conversation, reading of newspapers and books, and various games as well as all the other leisurely elements." The Cần Thơ Club's library would open every day from 8 to 11 in the morning and 3 to 6 in the afternoon. Members of the association were permitted to consult newspapers, periodicals, and reference materials on site and to borrow six volumes for not more than fifteen days. In another example, in Hà Tiên in the Western Mekong Delta, a reading circle formed in 1931 with the "aim to constitute a meeting of people of good company desiring to see, learn, and enjoy together as much by conversation as by reading; furthermore, to bring people together through various games and leisure activities (festivals, dinners, parties, etc. . . .). The locals enjoy and call [this group] by the name Hà Tiên Circle, [which offers] a source of leisure granted to the community free by the provincial administration."[69] Colonial law forbade these reading circles from engaging in political, religious, or gambling activity.[70]

The movement to create shared educational resources and public libraries directly intersected with the movement to spread literacy in *quốc ngữ* spearheaded by associations, journalists, and political organizations in the 1930s and 1940s. One such organization for spreading literacy was the active Hội Truyền Bá Quốc Ngữ (Association for the Diffusion of Quốc Ngữ), founded in 1938 and led by Nguyễn Văn Tố. Several of the leaders of Hội Truyền Bá Quốc Ngữ included communist leaders such as the military strategist and intellectual Võ Nguyên Giáp and Trường Chinh, who became the future general secretary of the Indochinese Communist Party in 1940.[71] The expansion of Vietnamese literacy intersected with communist social welfare and public education campaigns in the late 1930s and 1940s.[72] Vietnamese communists envisioned the interwoven role of nationalism and cultural development, specifically focusing on the popularization and development of *quốc ngữ* in the "Đề cương về văn hoá Việt Nam" (Outline of Vietnamese culture), produced in 1943.[73] Carrying out nationalist-driven language instruction, the Hội Truyền Bá Quốc Ngữ between 1938 and 1945 provided *quốc ngữ* language instruction to an estimated fifty-one thousand people throughout Tonkin; the association also had sister branches in Cochinchina and Annam.

In the Annam region, literacy and library initiatives were tied directly to a civilizational cultivation of youth. In the article "Việc khai-dân-tri rât cân của nước ta. Lớp học phổ-thông và thư-viện học-sinh" (The task of developing the minds of the people of our country is very necessary), published in *Trang Án* on September 12, 1939, the author Bắc Hà commended recent efforts by the Association for the Diffusion of Quốc Ngữ, yet he also pushed for more intentional guidance on curricula and libraries within literacy education.[74] He specifically called for the development of a popular general education course covering the fundamentals of geography, natural sciences, history, civics, and mathematics—fields that are "universal" and that "peoples in every country should know," which could empower citizens with the "knowledge on how to defend themselves and not be taken advantage of." The proposal that a universal course would provide Vietnamese the intellectual tools to protect themselves in a global arena reflects a social Darwinistic framing of civilizational competition. The author argued that without proper guidance on reading matter, students would end up falling victim to "extremist newspapers, false books, [and] incestuous ideas that ultimately harm their minds." Likening teaching literacy to "guiding a drunken person who falls from one side to another," the author warned of the potential dangers of misguided literate students. As other authors suggested, Bắc Hà argued that literacy development must be intentionally designed to "properly" guide the naive young generation. Drawing his attention to urban youth, the author argued that elders should dedicate their attention to creating libraries for the younger generation. In his conclusion the author supported the efforts of the Association for the Diffusion of Quốc Ngữ in the central region and called upon the members of the association in Annam to find good teachers and dedicate their efforts to organizing libraries.

Associations provided a space to develop new modes of community around shared politics, moral values, and visions for social reform and public services. Su Lin Lewis describes this vibrant civil society of associations as not simply protonationalism but as cosmopolitan urban civic culture and new modes of citizenship. Van Nguyen-Marshall describes mutual aid groups and associational life as a fundamental part of creating a Vietnamese civil society in Saigon in the colonial and postcolonial periods.[75] The Vietnamese associations produced dynamic, diverse "publics" that defined larger social needs and engaged with other civic organizations, public services, and unofficial channels to provide resources and accomplish specific missions. These associations focused on diverse goals such as technical trade, education, research, and community fundraising. The creation of shared educational and knowledge resources was central to the mission and success of these self-help associations. Many associations and self-help groups formed their own libraries and reading rooms to provide access to valuable, domain-specific knowledge to inform and supplement the formal schooling of the association members.

A PUBLIC SPHERE IN A PUBLIC LIBRARY: THE FEMALE LABOR OF KNOWLEDGE DIFFUSION

In the 1930s in Saigon, a remarkable popular reading room was established that functioned as a people's public library, a *bình dân thư viện*, that was accessible to all rather than only through a membership association. Notably, the reading room was driven by the labor and leadership of Vietnamese women. On April 13, 1933, the Saigon-Cholon administrative office approved Madame Nguyễn Thị Trang's request to open up a public reading room in the cul-de-sac of 29 rue d'Arras, between boulevard Gallieni and rue du General Leman in Saigon.[76] According to her extensive background check at the time of her application, Trang was a twenty-three-year-old woman who had studied to be a midwife at the Maternité de Cholon in the delivery ward of Tran-Ngoc-Sanh. The application stated that the

FIGURE 30. Image from Nguyễn Thị Trang's request for book donations for the Saigon public reading room, 1933. *Source*: "Phòng đọc Sách' đường Arras," *Phụ Nữ Tân Văn*, June 22, 1933, no. 205, 3–4.

proposed reading room would include works concerning agriculture and would not include any works or brochures forbidden by the government. Over the course of the reading room's operations, the space functioned as more than a simple collection of agricultural texts. The reading room operated as a popular urban social space and a community platform for individuals to come together with the shared commitment of self-empowerment through reading a wide range of contemporary periodicals and materials donated from the Saigon community. A few weeks before the opening of the reading room in 1933, Nguyễn Thị Trang requested that the readers of the popular Saigon-based magazine *Phụ Nữ Tân Văn* donate Vietnamese-, French-, Chinese-, and English-language books to the reading room.[77] The article, published in the section of *Phụ Nữ Tân Văn* titled "Cuộc đời với ý tôi" (Life as I mean it), included an image of a female Vietnamese reader in front of a library bookshelf.

The Saigon reading room officially opened on July 1, 1933, in a large and well-ventilated space and invited "anyone wishing to spend their time in a pleasant and useful way." In several of the articles announcing the reading room, writers

NĂM THỨ NĂM-196 GIÁ 0$15 20 AVRIL 1933

Phụ-nữ Tân-văn

XUẤT BẢN NGÀY THỨ NĂM

Phấn son tô điểm sơn-hà
Làm cho rõ mặt đàn-bà nước Nam

TÒA-BÁO

(RÉDACTION ADMINISTRATION)

Nº 48, Rue Vannier, Nº 48

SAIGON

FIGURE 31. Front cover of *Phụ Nữ Tân Văn*, 1933. An image of a reader was the emblematic logo of the popular Saigon-based periodical. Pictured here is a version of the magazine cover depicting reading as a collective act, in which three Vietnamese women (symbolizing the three regions of Vietnam) read the pages of the periodical together. The cover shows the motto of the magazine, "*Phấn son tô điểm sơn hà / Làm cho rõ mặt đàn bà nước Nam*," which translates to "Women and their beauty adorn and enrich the country of Vietnam." *Source*: *Phụ Nữ Tân Văn*, April 20, 1933.

commended the efforts of the young woman Nguyễn Thị Trang and noted that the reading room was "a feminine intellectual work worthy of encouragement" and that Trang served as a "role model for women."[78] *Hà Thành Ngọ Báo* published more extensively on the motivations and mission of the reading room on August 6, 1933: This library was simple since it did not establish itself as part of an association and did not collect fees. Instead, the founder "used her own resources to work for the common good" and "invited all young women and men who were eager to learn."[79] The article outlined the three guiding principles and mission of the reading room: "First, arrange a meeting place suitable for studying and reading to help each other spiritually and intellectually; second, select books and newspapers to provide readers with valuable documents; third, select books specifically for scholars who want to study *phổ thông* (*culture générale*), an effort that is welcomed by most of the people in Saigon."

Throughout its operations, the reading room experimented with different modes of fundraising, including publishing and selling *quốc ngữ* pamphlets, organizing a Vietnamese comedy troupe and theatrical performances, and asking for donations from French and Vietnamese readers.[80] On May 20, at the opera house Thành-Xương, there was a fundraising event where the activities included "Ping-Pong, yo-yo, musical acts, [and] a *cải lương* (Vietnamese opera) performance by the musical troupe Nghĩa hiệp, who performed the act *Gương Trong Nữ Giới* (A role model for women) to raise money for the reading room. Nguyễn Thị Trang could not be present, so Mademoiselle Bích Ngọc read the mission statement of the forthcoming reading room.[81] The event raised thirty-five piastres, which was then used to construct tables and chairs. The reading room brought together the community through soliciting book donations, financial contributions, and creative fundraising social events.

The reading room efforts were publicly documented, especially in the daily periodical *Hà Thành Ngọ Báo*. The literary figure Ngô Bích San wrote an extensive account of his experience in the reading room and the distinguished efforts of its primary reading room librarian, Phương Hoa.[82] Ngô Bích San details his and another journalist's experience visiting the reading room to report on the library and its operations. From the street level a large sign reading "Salle de lecture" directed the reader to the reading room; when one approached the doorway, a poster in Vietnamese announced "Phòng đọc sách. Ra vào thong thả, khỏi trả tiền. Sáng từ 8 giờ đến 11 giờ rưỡi, chiều từ 3 giờ đến 6 giờ" (Reading room: Come and go unhurriedly as you please, no need to pay money. Morning from eight to eleven thirty, afternoon from three to six). According to the narrative, the two visitors discovered that the founder Trang was often not at the library but instead left the duty of managing the library to Phương Hoa, a female librarian-secretary. The journalist reported that during their visit the reading room quickly filled up with ten readers. Phương Hoa explained the mission of the library: "We wanted to create a *bình dân thư viện* [public library]—a building for men and women that did not discriminate based on class, where people can come for intellectual exchange and opinionated discourse."[83] The reading room was significant as a widely publicized female endeavor and female-inclusive space that extended the benefits of "intellectual and cultural nourishment" to the broader public of both male and female readers.

In her interview Phương Hoa shared the financial challenges and extensive labor required to carry out the mission of the library and called on the Saigon community for assistance. As the only official worker of the library, Phương Hoa carried out the ambitious task of building the library collections through donations from Vietnamese benefactors, publishers, journalists, and the general community. Phương Hoa reported that through donations the library accumulated around four hundred books and the following newspapers: *L'Impartial, La Presse Indochinoise, L'Alliance Franco-Annamite, Nhà Nam, Lục Tỉnh Tân Văn, Phụ Nữ Tân Văn, Dzân Báo, Cùng Bạn*, and *Tiếng Dân*. Đào Duy Anh donated a set of his dictionary *Hán Việt Tự Điện*, and other journalists had donated *L'Annam Nouveau, Trung Bắc, Phong Hoá, Văn Học Tạp Chí*, and *Ngọ Báo*. Phương Hoa reported on her extensive letter writing to Vietnamese directors of newspapers and even writing to foreign publishers to ask them to donate works.[84] Built through community donations, the library collections reflected the burgeoning Vietnamese publishing sphere as well as a cosmopolitan network of donated texts. Phương Hoa's next projects were the following: organizing the books by category, developing a lending section for students without money to borrow schoolbooks, and rebinding and reinforcing the books and adding labels with "*phòng đọc sách*" (reading room) and the name of the book donor.

This account reflects an overt gendered representation of women's labor. In the interview the journalist Ngô Bích San pressed Phương Hoa on her family affairs in light of how much labor the reading room involved. Phương Hoa's response was, "I no longer have a desire for a family. I spend all my time, money, and energy on the reading room. This dedicated work is still my dream. I have slowly begun to see this dream come to fruition, and it is encouraging to me that I have begun to realize my goals." Ngô Bích San concluded the exposé of the reading room with a poetic glance over his shoulders, his eyes falling upon the rows of books neatly assembled on the shelves, which symbolized "the hard work of a woman." This account focused on documenting the personality traits of Phương Hoa, including her exceptional dedication to the library and her work ethic, which implied her lack of a family life. Instead of a showing a photograph of the reading room, the column was accompanied by a portrait of the librarian, pointing to the exceptionalism of the librarian-secretary in the efforts to develop the reading room.

The public library reading room showcased the increasingly visible roles of women in shaping the public sphere in 1930s Saigon, where intellectual spaces were dominated by men. The reading room reflected the elaborate labor of two women, Nguyễn Thị Trang and Phương Hoa, who contributed to shaping the public sphere by bringing together reading matter and community members. Phương Hoa also reported on the relative success of the library since its opening, noting that between July and August of 1933, 109 readers had visited, including many women readers and some Western readers. The reading room appeared not to be dedicated to women readers only, yet the library was intentionally inviting to both women and men. The extensive publicity surrounding the mission and the female leadership of the reading room was situated amidst a rising public discourse around "women's issues" in the Vietnamese public press, which included comments on a range of gender topics, such as the global women's political movement to changing Vietnamese definitions of femininity in the context of urbanization and modernity.[85] Newspapers represented Nguyễn Thị Trang and Phương Hoa as notable women worthy of emulation, thus situating them within a global landscape of progressive modern women.[86] For example, a 1936 issue of the popular magazine *Ngày Nay* (These days) published a brief biography of a female librarian in America.[87] An author using the pen name "Eve" wrote that "modern progressive women in America are increasingly occupying higher social positions. For example, Miss Isabel du Bois from the United States Navy has just been appointed the director of libraries. . . . Isn't she a woman who has made a name for the fairer sex?"

By the end of 1933 and the beginning of 1934 after a few months of highly publicized successful operations, Nguyễn Thị Trang and Phương Hoa's reading room seemed to confront several economic obstacles as well as restrictions imposed by the local government. Not listing a specific reason other than government permissions, the press noted that the reading room was forced to close and then relocate to 44 rue de Reims, where it shared a building with an advertising office and reopened on November 17, 1933.[88] A few months after the reopening of the reading room at the new location, a public incident called attention to the educational mission and financial needs of the library. On the night of January 20, 1934, the municipal theater organized a fundraising event to help the victims of the natural disasters in Bình Phú and to support Nguyễn Thị Trang's new reading room. At 8:30 p.m. the director of the fundraiser, Đinh Công Thống, read a letter from Phương Hoa, secretary-general of the reading room on rue de Reims, on the issue of "the *quốc ngữ* problem." But after reading the letter, Thống continued to express his own frustration with the lack of financial support from the local Vietnamese press for the reading room. Thong argued that newspapers must also be invested in building up libraries. He declared that libraries and newspapers belonged to the same mission of "knowledge diffusion," which he described as "the spread and increase of essential knowledge to masses" through the production and circulation of print. Thống proceeded to target the newspaper *Saigon*, inciting a public argument with the *Saigon* journalist and intellectual Trần Văn Giàu, who was present in the audience, ultimately leading to police intervention.[89] This event and Thống's public critique reveal the how the public library functioned as a community platform bringing together organizers, intellectuals, journalists, and benefactors to shape the mission of knowledge diffusion. Public fundraising events and leisure social activities point to the landscape of urban Vietnamese intellectual life. Nguyễn Thị Trang and Phương Hoa's financial and book donation appeals to community members, writers, publishing houses, and foreign publishers illustrates the networked intellectual community contributing to efforts to build libraries and a public sphere. Furthermore, as shown in the 1934 community fundraising event, the Nguyễn Thị Trang reading room efforts symbolized broader sociopolitical efforts to create a Vietnamese *quốc ngữ* public sphere as a project of Vietnamese language nationalism within the context of French colonialism.

POLITICAL SURVEILLANCE OF VIETNAMESE PUBLIC LIBRARIES

Besides navigating the economic costs of operating a library, Vietnamese reading room organizers were required to navigate a colonial bureaucracy that necessitated an official application and surveillance by the colonial *sûreté* (secret police). These public library spaces of communal erudition and cultural nationalism did not go unnoticed by French colonial officials, who recognized the necessity of controlling the circulation of reading matter. If approved to open, libraries and reading rooms had to meet the following regulations: "1) The reading room must close by 9 p.m., 2) The list of French and Vietnamese periodicals available in the reading room must be displayed in a well-marked place, and 3) The reading room is prohibited from meetings of more than twenty people, political or religious discussions, and gambling."[90] These strict regulations demonstrate the colonial government's fears of political or religious organizing and behavior as well as the distribution of censored texts. For example, on April 10, 1932, the publisher and merchant Hồ Văn Sao requested to open a reading salon on 51 rue du Colonel Grimaud, Saigon, called a *bình dân thơ viện* (another spelling for public library). The police report noted that Hồ Văn Sao had been operating a printing house in Sadec since 1921 and had a "notable reputation as a serious merchant."[91] The resident superior in Indochina office approved the request but required that the indigenous public library be relocated to a different area on account of the fact that rue du Colonel Grimaud was the site of many political demonstrations and police crackdowns. The colonial government feared that the opening of a *bình dân thơ viện* at that location could heighten the concentration of intellectuals and readers and thus lead to more politically "dangerous" activity.

Requests to open a library required the submission of a list of book and periodicals to the official censor for prior approval. For example, on November 17, 1931, schoolteacher Phạm Văn Chiêu of Gò Vấp, Gia Định, requested to open a small library for young students and civil servants in the village of Hanh Thông, open Monday to Friday 5 to 9 p.m., Saturday 3 to 10 p.m., Thursday and Sunday 7 to 11 a.m. and 3 to 10 p.m. Chiêu submitted a list of books to the provincial chief.

The book list included "French classics" by authors such as Diderot, Descartes, Fénelon, and Voltaire, as well as the popular "Vietnamese classics" *Kim Vân Kiều* and *Lục Vân Tiên*. The list also included works by Vietnamese poet Nguyễn Công Trứ, twentieth-century cultural commentator Phạm Quỳnh, and novelist Hoàng Ngọc Phách, who was known for his modernist novel *Tố Tâm*, published in 1925.[92] The request traveled upward to the governor of Cochinchina and the resident superior in the Indochina office, and on November 28, 1931, Phạm Văn Chiêu's request was approved on the condition that he submit his books to the censor, post the book list in the reading room, and never permit the total number of readers in the library to exceed twenty. In this way, the content, purpose, and physical location of libraries were heavily monitored by the colonial government and police to prevent political organizing.

Furthermore, the Vietnamese petitioners themselves were subject to extensive investigation involving the office of indigenous political affairs and the local police. On June 18, 1932, An Ngọc Phụng requested permission from the governor of Cochinchina to open a small library of classical works and popular novels in Gia Định province on Hầm Sỏi Street, where "currently there does not exist a library for European and indigenous civil servants to have a spiritual distraction." Phụng continued to explain how the library could introduce French-language works and "civilize the intellectual culture of the poor Vietnamese youth." He attached a three-page list of works to be included in the library. However, on August 10, 1932, the resident superior in Indochina notified the administrative chief of the province of Gia Định that An Ngọc Phụng's request could not be approved. The results of the local chief of police investigation on Phụng's political background revealed a longer history of local police surveillance due to his production of subversive books. From the detailed police report the following personal information was uncovered: An Ngọc Phụng (who also went by the pseudonym Phùng) originated from the province of Phủ Thọ (Tonkin). Phụng finished his studies at the École normale de Hanoi and worked as a journalist for the popular periodical *Phụ Nữ Tân Văn*. Phụng translated the 1924 book on Mahatma Gandhi by French novelist and essayist Romain Rolland. Phụng's translation, titled *Lòng Bác Ái, Lịch sử ông thánh Gandhi*, was banned by the French authorities on November 1929. He also wrote another subversive work titled *Mười Năm Tù Quốc sự—Les 10 ans de prison d'un condamné politique* (Ten years in the national prison as a political convict).[93]

The report revealed that even without government approval, Phụng had already created a small book collection for youth to study free of cost; the library was financed through a fee service for loans of books to the affluent. Additionally, the police report brought attention to the dangerous contents of Phụng's library list; four of the works had been officially banned by the Cochinchina government, and other brochures were labeled as "tendentious" (meaning politically opinionated and controversial according to the colonial administration) by the Office of Translations. The list included banned works such as the 1927 volume of collected works on Phan Châu Trinh (*Gương Chí Sĩ Phan Tây Hồ Lịch Sử Toàn Biên*), controversial works on topics such as Vietnamese self-governance (Phan Bội Châu's *Nam Quốc Dân Tự Trị*), women's issues, the Trưng sisters, and colonialism, and biographies of Chinese political leaders such as Kuomintang nationalist Feng Yuxiang 馮玉祥 (Phùng Ngọc Tường) and political activist and journalist Liang Qichao 梁啓超 (Lương Khải Siêu) (*Tiểu Sử và Tập Diễn* Văn Lương Khải Siêu). This handful of examples points to only a small subset of Vietnamese library initiatives that left documentary traces through encounters with the state bureaucracy; other organizers found ways to evade the state surveillance regime of background checks, approvals, and the submission of materials to censors.[94]

A CASTLE OF NATIONAL CULTURE THROUGH A *QUỐC NGỮ* LIBRARIES SYSTEM

The intertwined project of Vietnamese language nationalism was an organizing principle for the literary magazine *Tri Tân*, whose founding issue announced,

> Reviewing the old! Knowing the new! [from the saying "ôn cũ biết mới or ôn cố tri tân] Aiming for that goal, *Tri Tân* walks its own cultural path. With research glasses, *Tri Tân* reads through each page of history; with honest and optimistic eyes, *Tri Tân* looks wide at the horizon of knowledge. Shoulder to shoulder carrying bricks and lime carts, *Tri Tân* stood in the ranks of engineers, building the cultural castle of Nam Việt.[95]

Throughout the publication's history from 1941 to 1945, topics focused on reviewing literary heritage and carving out a Vietnamese national and cultural identity. The opening quotations in this chapter by Hoa Bằng and Khuông Việt demonstrate the significance of creating libraries as a nationalist project of mass education and cultural heritage.

"The level of Vietnam's culture, whether superb or deficient, is dependent upon *quốc ngữ* . . . thus it is the obligation of each person in the country to serve and improve the language since it connects to the rate of progress of our motherland."[96] With this opening declaration linking together the work of language and national progress, Khuông Việt emphatically proposed a *quốc ngữ* library system, referred to as the "*quốc học viện*" (national academy) and the "*thơ-viện Việt-nam*" (library of Vietnam). Khuông Việt published this four-page essay, "Thử thảo một chương-trình lập thơ-viện Việt-nam" (An attempt to draft a project to establish a library of Vietnam), in the popular Hanoi-based periodical *Tri Tân* in 1942.[97] Khuông Việt was the pen name of Saigon-based intellectual Lý Vĩnh Khuông (1912–78), who wrote for the weekly Hanoi newspapers *Tri Tân* and *Thanh Nghị* as well as the weekly Saigon magazines *Nam Kỳ* and *Đại Việt*; he also actively participated in associations for the diffusion of *quốc ngữ*. Notably, he had worked in the colonial state Cochinchina Library in Saigon for two decades as a librarian-archivist

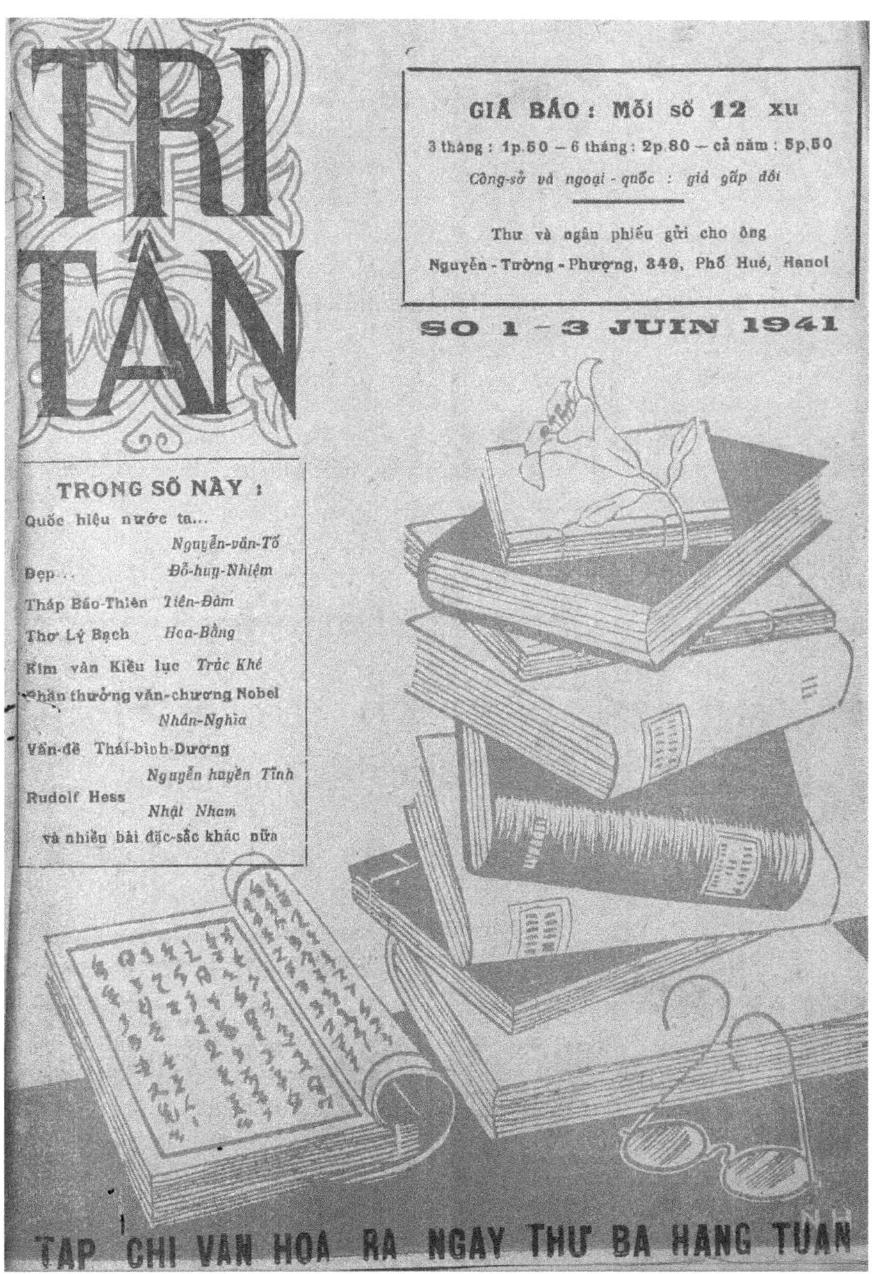

FIGURE 32. Front cover of the first issue of *Tri Tân,* which depicts symbolic research glasses, a recurring motif of the publication, as well as several types of Western and Eastern books, including a thread-bound book with characters. *Source*: *Tri Tân,* June 3, 1941, no. 1.

and completed the training course in Hanoi in 1931. During the colonial period, Khuông Việt was known for his travelogues and research on Vietnamese literature and history which drew from reference works in the Cochinchina Library.[98] During his time at the Cochinchina Library he was exposed to a wide-ranging collection of books, translations, and periodicals in the French language. Khuông Việt's experiences in the state library—researching Indochina's history, reading periodicals, cosmopolitan literature and comparative histories, and witnessing the inner workings and language limitations of the French-language Saigon library—shaped his vision of Vietnamese language nationalism advanced through *quốc ngữ* libraries.

In his 1942 article, Khuông Việt critiqued existing libraries in Indochina, stating that the private libraries of associations permitted access only to its members. He noted that the Hanoi Central Library collection had developed a sizable collection of *quốc ngữ* materials due to legal deposits of newly published literature, yet he criticized the Hanoi Central Library for making it difficult to enter and access its *quốc ngữ* collection. Khuông Việt proposed an ambitious *quốc ngữ* library network modeled on the colonial Directorate library system, with central libraries first in Hanoi, Saigon, and Hue, and later developments of provincial libraries and a book vehicle circulating books to provinces and villages. Khuông Việt advanced a concept of Vietnamese nationhood intrinsically tied to the development of *quốc ngữ* libraries. He detailed two primary goals of a *quốc ngữ* library:

> [first] to help the poor and uneducated be able to have the opportunity to access our country's knowledge through books and newspapers . . . [and second] to conserve the valuable books that serve as clear witnesses to the evolution of the academic thinking of our people, of our country. [This project] teaches us to end our self-centered mindset, and we together can work to build a great fortress for Vietnamese culture.[99]

Khuông Việt's project is significant because it points to how the creation of a public library was, at its foundation, a collective endeavor tied to a Vietnamese national community and the responsibility of compatriots to cultivate, protect, and share that identity. This vision of a national library system was ultimately grounded in Vietnamese language, cultural heritage, and history. A year prior he had written extensively about the importance of reading and knowing Vietnamese history, declaring that "history is also a source of vitality for the national spirit."[100] Some of the discourse of "national culture" and "national history" could have been shaped by the political context of the Vichy regime in Indochina (1940–45), which promoted a conservative paternalistic militarism, traditional morality, and ethnic nationalism. Two decades of direct work experience in the Cochinchina Library had exposed Lý Vĩnh Khuông to the limitations of French colonial institutions and colonial rule more broadly; it had failed to provide public access and substantive social change for the majority Vietnamese population. Over the course of the late colonial period, his political activities became more explicit as he joined the socialist association in Saigon, the Section française de l'Internationale ouvrière (SFIO), and later departed for France as a newspaper correspondent. According to internal library reports, Lý Vĩnh Khuông left his job at the library before 1945 and with his departure took six hundred piastres, the keys to the library safe, dossiers on European government officials, and a manuscript by Anatole France. He burned his personnel file documenting his work in the Cochinchina Library, along with the personnel files of many other Vietnamese workers in Saigon.[101]

CONCLUSION

This chapter traced the movement to develop public libraries, or *bình dân thư viện*, as community spaces of vernacular reading, social welfare, and self-strengthening. Reading was a conduit to civilization, bringing Vietnamese out of "backwardness" toward modern mentalities and cultural practices. Reading was not just an aesthetic, solitary leisure practice but a tool of popular moralization. Libraries and reading culture offered "good" productive leisure practices of self-directed learning as alternatives to the social ills of idleness, gambling, drinking, and gossip. The reassertion of reading as moralization targeted youth, women, and rural inhabitants, reflecting a social concern about restoring a sense of traditionalism and order in a time of tremendous economic, cultural, and political transformation in the late colonial period. The acts of reading and collecting books were interwoven into broader debates on "modernity," an elusive conceptual framework of civilizational comparison and cultural evolution.

Reading was also a social practice of collective organizing as seen through the development of *bình dân thư viện*, public libraries for popular education, literacy, and community welfare. In the case of *bình dân thư viện* initiatives in Hue, the library was a platform for social welfare for a range of the population, from the erudite scholar to the curious everyday man who wanted exposure to new ideas; from the dedicated student seeking supplementary education to the economically disenfranchised. A public sphere of Vietnamese journalists, public intellectuals, and community organizers proposed libraries and literacy as fundamental to the self-strengthening of the Vietnamese culture and collective. Community *bình dân thư viện* such as Nguyễn Thị Trang and Phương Hoa's reading room provided hybrid multilingual spaces of reading matter, connecting individuals to local and global ideas. Building libraries connected directly to the cultural-political project of advancing *quốc ngữ* and language nationalism among the Vietnamese public sphere of intellectuals, publishers, community members, and scholar-journalists such as librarian Lý Vĩnh Khuông. The public library movement and Vietnamese language nationalism of the 1930s and 1940s would lay the foundation for political visions of Vietnamese nationhood and a postcolonial national library in the next decades.

5

To Reassemble

The Decolonization of Libraries

It was the fall of 1945 in Hanoi. The celebratory flags of the independence declaration of the Democratic Republic of Vietnam (DRV) on September 2 remained, yet the crowds had dispersed and the new government had begun their work.[1] Outside the Hanoi Central Library, the sign reading "Bibliothèque de Pierre Pasquier" had been replaced with one reading "Quốc gia Thư viện" (National Library). Inside the building, library administrators continued to issue reading cards, process book returns and requests from readers, and log daily operations. All government offices, including the new Ministry of National Education (Bộ Quốc gia Giáo dục), under which the Hanoi Central Library was now organized, were required to standardize their administrative language and paperwork, switching from French to *quốc ngữ* Vietnamese.[2] The Hanoi archives and library submitted a list of specialized technical words in French with Vietnamese translations and simple explanations of administrative operations. Although colloquially these spaces were already referred to by their Vietnamese names, the *salle de lecture* (reading room) was now officially the *phòng đọc sách*, and the *section de prêt* (lending section) was now the *phòng mượn sách*. Indochina-wide policies bearing the colonial title "Indochine" were now transitioned to a national designation; the Indochina legal deposit regime, *régie du dépôt légal de l'Indochine*, was now the *Sở lưu chiểu văn hoá phẩm toàn quốc* (Department of nationwide deposit of cultural products). The translation of the colonial Hanoi library into a national Vietnamese library was the first symbolic action to rupture its institutional lineage and organization from its French colonial past.

It was the fall of 1945 in Saigon, and the city was still reeling from the chaos and violence that took place after the radio broadcast of the independence declaration from Hanoi. Throughout September and October, Allied forces arrived in southern Vietnam to disarm the Japanese, attacked the fledgling DRV administrative base in Saigon, and assisted French troops in retaking the former colony of Cochinchina. In June 1946, a few months after the departure of the Allied forces, the French High Commissioner and a handful of Vietnamese politicians established the Provisional Government of the Republic of Cochinchina, a semiautonomous state in southern Vietnam that was separate from the northern-based DRV. The High Commission signaled Vietnamese semiautonomy by transferring the Saigon Cochinchina Library to the provisional Vietnamese government on June 28, 1946. The library appears to be one of the first institutions to be transferred and thus served as an important symbol of the eventual transition of all colonial institutions in former Cochinchina into a different postcolonial configuration. The library was placed within the Service of Education for Southern Vietnam and renamed the National Library of Southern Vietnam (Thơ Viện Quốc Gia Nam Việt). Even with the renaming, Vietnamese librarians and readers often referred to the library by its various names, including the old colonial name, Cochinchina Library (Bibliothèque de Cochinchine or Thơ Viện Nam Kỳ), colloquial names such as the Saigon Library (Thơ Viện Saigon), and the administrative name the Library of the Southern Region (Thư Viện Nam Phần) or the Library of Southern Vietnam (Thư Viện Nam Phần Việt Nam).

Between 1945 and 1946, two distinctly postcolonial Vietnamese national libraries were publicly pronounced, one in Hanoi and one in Saigon. These two libraries were the preeminent institutions of public reading culture and literary collections from the French colonial period, operating since 1865 for Saigon and 1919 for Hanoi. The two buildings were symbolic monuments and functional instruments of French colonialism, defined through top-down colonial state building initiatives of *mise en valeur* (development, exploitation), the civilizing mission, and Franco-Vietnamese collaboration policy. Together with the colonial archives and legal deposit, the libraries were part of an elaborate colonial information order, with the Directorate of Archives and Libraries of Indochina as its centralizing body since 1917. The libraries, archives, and directorate developed extensive documentary procedures, trained countless personnel, and shaped the administrative, cultural, and intellectual landscape of twentieth-century Vietnam. Furthermore, with some of the largest collections of reading matter in Asia, the Hanoi and Saigon libraries functioned as an invaluable resource for government officials and urban readers throughout the colonial and into the postcolonial years.

With the regime transitions at the end of World War II toward postcolonial Vietnamese states, political authorities and library administrators of both institutions confronted the infrastructure and conceptual underpinnings of the colonial information order. Yet before the DRV could implement its visions of a national library, France launched a series of military battles against the DRV to recolonize the region, pushing out the DRV administration from Hanoi and establishing Saigon as the center for political recolonization. Throughout the First Indochina War (1946–54), both the Hanoi and Saigon libraries operated as semicolonial, protonational institutions, navigating the changing political designations of administrative autonomy within the context of violent military conflict between France and the Việt Minh. For the next decade, southern Vietnam emerged as the locus of successive attempts to create an autonomous Vietnamese government with Saigon as the national capital. The shifting status, leadership, and priorities of the old Cochinchina Library now turned National Library mirrored the tentative and halting character of decolonization in the southern third of the country.

This chapter traces the logistical and symbolic processes of the decolonization of the Hanoi and Saigon libraries, from colonial infrastructures to national institutions, from 1945 to 1955. I showcase the symbolic ruptures of regime changes and the wartime impact upon the library institutions and their missions. I demonstrate how the struggle for political sovereignty over Indochina during the First Indochina War was a struggle over cultural patrimony in the Hanoi and Saigon Libraries, institutions that navigated a semicolonial administrative structure of changing Vietnamese autonomy. Challenging the notion of an abrupt rupture from colonial to postcolonial, this chapter centers the library institution within debates on French recolonization and a semicolonial French-Vietnamese "associated state." Furthermore, I point to the continued influence of colonial knowledge and nostalgia that shaped the postcolonial developments and cultural significance of the library. I argue that the decolonization of the libraries was an active process of reassemblage, an act of reexamining the colonial infrastructures of information, and translating and making sense of them for a postcolonial future. In her first film *Reassemblage* (1982), Trinh T. Minh-ha collages the everyday sights and sounds of Senegal in a reflexive critique of the ethnographic tool of cinema and linear narrative. In speaking about institutions ranging from the state to religious networks to the family, Shawn McHale poses the question, "How in war do institutions shatter, and then get reassembled out of the fragments left behind?"[3] In this chapter, I show how Vietnamese librarians carried out everyday reassemblage, logistically grafting upon existing colonial infrastructure and operations with new translations, evaluations, and proposals for change. In tracing the infrastructural and operational reassemblage of the national libraries, I unearth a nuanced cultural history of Vietnamese postcolonial nationhood within the context of competing Vietnamese states and French recolonization.

Recent scholarship on the First Indochina War draws attention to an internal perspective on the warring nascent Vietnamese northern and southern postcolonial states, their geographically uneven "archipelagic" and "bricolage" of power bases across the ethnically diverse northwest and Mekong Delta, and the role of violence, civilian mobilization, and state making.[4] Yet existing historiography fails to adequately examine the infrastructural and cultural processes of decolonization in Vietnam. The limited literature on the national library in Saigon provides narrow histories of the libraries in Vietnam as either apolitical storehouses of colonial literature or as weapons of French and American intellectual hegemony. Similarly, the Hanoi national library history also receives oversimplification as a nationalist anticolonial institution, eliding its long colonial history and its significance as a space of public reading culture and colonial documentation. This chapter revises existing twentieth-century Vietnamese historiography by focusing across the time frame of 1945 and 1954 and showcases continuities and gradual transformations of the libraries across the political regime changes. Furthermore, this chapter interrogates the relationship between decolonization and nation building through examining Hanoi and Saigon together, as former institutions of a colonial information order. In the postcolonial period, both institutions reexamined the legacies and significance of their literary collections and physical space within a Vietnamese national context. While postcolonial political ideologies emphasized a rupture from colonial forms of knowledge and institutional histories, I show that both library institutions were deeply shaped by the material infrastructural legacies of a robust colonial information order of technical procedures and extensive colonial-era collections. Furthermore, the decolonization of libraries and evolving role of the national institutions were informed by the social transformations wrought by political upheaval, militarization, violence, and war.

This chapter brings to the forefront the histories of these two national institutions as cultural and political symbols and the operational logistics through periods of decolonial reassemblage. The chapter begins with the early postcolonial graft of the Hanoi Central Library within the context of the Communist Democratic Republic of Vietnam government from 1945 to 1946 and the recolonization of the Hanoi library during the First Indochina War. The second half of the chapter focuses on the rearticulation of the Saigon Cochinchina Library as a "national capital" and center of Vietnamese cultural heritage throughout the First Indochina War. The signing of the Geneva Accords at the end of the First Indochina War in 1954 divided Vietnam into the communist-led Democratic Republic of Vietnam and the anticommunist republicanism-driven Republic of Vietnam. The chapter concludes by examining the division of the Hanoi collections, their movement to Saigon, and debates regarding the documentary patrimony of former French colonial Indochina. This approach of tracing the colonial inheritances and confrontations of both institutions allows for a novel reexamination of decolonization as a tension between postcolonial rupture and operational grafts.

PART 1: HANOI, 1945–1954

DRV Early State Building, 1945–1946

The decolonization of the libraries and archives officially began with the Japanese coup in March 1945, which removed the French colonial Vichy administration. With support from the Japanese, Emperor Bảo Đại declared Vietnam's independence and Trần Trọng Kim was named the prime minister. The Japanese administrator S. Kudo served as the first non-French director of the archives and libraries, from March to August 1945. Kudo requested the immediate replacement of all French high-level administrators with Vietnamese personnel. At the beginning of Kudo's directorship, the following French personnel held positions in the Directorate: Paul Boudet (advisor, age fifty-seven, male, Hanoi), Rémi Bourgeois (curator of the archives, age forty-eight, male, Saigon), Simone de Saint-Exupéry (deputy archivist-librarian, age forty-seven, female, Hanoi), Simon Bản Nguyễn (building manager, age fifty-two, male, Hanoi), and Léa Faugère (contracted archivist-librarian, age twenty-four, female, Hanoi).[5] On June 1, 1945, Kudo signed a new decree to promote several Vietnamese librarian-archivists to administrative positions at the Directorate in Hanoi: Ngô Đình Nhu, the curator of the archives and libraries of Annam, became deputy director of archives and libraries; Trần Văn Kha, senior archivist-librarian, was now head of the library section of the Hanoi Central Library, and Lê Hữu Cúc, senior secretary, took on the role as head of the archives section.[6] Kudo requested that the former directors and head curators Paul Boudet, Rémi Bourgeois, and Simone de Saint-Exupéry maintain their role as advisors to the Japanese director. Kudo noted that Ngô Đình Nhu was "qualified with the necessary credentials and also knowledge of the great traditional culture" in order to help Kudo reorganize the entire libraries and archives service.[7] Citing a reduced budget and the necessity of installing Vietnamese management for "the future of the Kingdom of Viet Nam," Director Kudo signed into agreement the personnel changes on June 20, 1945, symbolically marking the beginning of the end of official French colonial management of the Directorate of Archives and Libraries.[8]

Before Japanese administrative changes in Hanoi were fully implemented, the dropping of the atomic bomb, Japanese capitulation, and the end of World War II ushered in a power vacuum throughout Indochina. On August 19, 1945, the Việt Minh seized power in Hanoi and continued to gain command throughout Annam and Cochinchina for the rest of the month and through what would later become known as the August Revolution. Earlier in 1941 the Indochinese Communist Party had expanded its strategy from proletarian internationalism to national liberation and developed a broadly defined nationalist front, the Vietnamese Independence League, known as the Việt Minh. Throughout the Japanese-Vichy rule in Indochina, the Việt Minh developed bases of support in remote areas of northern Vietnam. Led by the charismatic and internationally connected Hồ Chí Minh and the military leader Võ Nguyên Giáp, the Việt Minh recruited a wide range of popular support for the cause of independence from French colonialism from peasants, women, ethnic minorities, workers, and village leaders. The Việt Minh also gained support from desperate and angry population impacted by the Vichy French and Japanese economic policy and a devastating famine in Tonkin and Annam from October 1944 to May 1945. The August Revolution of 1945 culminated with the official handover of power from Emperor Bảo Đại and Prime Minister Trần Trọng

Kim to the provisional government led by President Hồ Chí Minh. On September 2, 1945, Hồ declared independence from France and formed the Democratic Republic of Vietnam (DRV), which was based in Hanoi.

The task of building a new functioning DRV state was difficult, particularly in the context of internal and external pressures.[9] From September 1945 to December 1946, the early DRV state attempted to build fundamental state operations by relying upon existing colonial institutions, or what Christopher Goscha describes as a "colonial graft."[10] David Marr traces the transformation of personnel and infrastructure of the DRV administration, describing the initial stages in which "the 'wiring' of the colonial state had largely survived, to be used by new masters."[11] Many of the public infrastructures, schools, public services, radio stations, presses, and offices remained initially the same in structure, while the new government initiated a wave of state-building initiatives. The DRV reworked the former governor general of Indochina bureaucracy and personnel into the DRV government structure and regional committees that sought to exert authority of over all three Vietnamese regions. Emphasizing how state building was intertwined with both revolution and war, David Marr argues that the DRV's "aspirations to transform society, end exploitation, develop the economy, and create a new culture had to defer to protection of the new political orders against enemies both foreign and domestic."[12] Within the first three weeks of the DRV administration, at least forty-one decrees were created and distributed, announced on the pages of the former Indochina government bulletin, the *Journal official de l'Indochine*, which had been renamed the *Công Báo Dân Quốc Báo* (Administrative record of Vietnam). The early DRV needed to build an infrastructure for state function and mass mobilization, and some of the earliest decrees focused on citizenship, identification, census, taxation, and the recruitment of soldiers.

Through the process of symbolic and literal translation, government institutions such as the library redefined its services, overall mission, and political role in the new postcolonial Vietnamese context. On September 8, 1945, Võ Nguyên Giáp, chairman of the provisional government (Chủ tịch chính phủ lâm thời), issued Decree Number 13, which absorbed the French colonial Directorate of Archives and Libraries and the Department of Public Instruction (L'instruction publique), all museums, public libraries (excluding libraries of public departments), institutes, and the École française d'Extrême-Orient into the Bộ Quốc gia Giáo dục (Ministry of National Education). The new state positioned the library as well as other cultural heritage institutes within the administrative framework of national education. As part of the decolonization of buildings, official French names were also changed under a nationalistic convention. For example, the Pierre Pasquier Library in Hanoi was henceforth named the National Library (Quốc gia Thư viện), the Louis Finot Museum in Hanoi was renamed the National Museum Institute (Quốc gia Bảo tàng viện), and the Blanchard de la Brosse Museum in Saigon was renamed the Gia Định Museum Institute (Gia Định Bảo tàng viện). The DRV attempted to exert authority over all regions of Vietnam, including Cochinchina, hence the renaming of Saigon institutions. Many of the Vietnamese personnel who worked in the colonial Directorate of Archives and Libraries continued their positions or were promoted into temporary managerial positions. In Decree Number 21, signed on September 8, 1945, Ngô Đình Nhu was designated as the director of the Nha Lưu trữ công văn và Thư Viện toàn quốc (Department of Archive Records and Nationwide Library).[13] However, it seems that Nhu often left for Hue to work at the Institute of Culture and Hue archives between 1945 and 1946, leaving some of the work as director to Phạm Đình Giệm and Trần Văn Kha, who, like Nhu, had worked in the Directorate for several decades.[14] In addition to these renaming decrees, many of the other early decrees focused on national education and supporting initiatives focused on eradicating illiteracy, abolishing French, and instituting Vietnamese as the language of instruction at every education level, including at university.[15]

Evaluating the Library and Visions for a National Library for the People

The early DRV government produced an abundant number of charts and statistics, such as those evaluating the roles, responsibilities, and changes in state institutions such as the libraries and archives. These studies also evaluated long-term inequality and inefficiency in the libraries under the French colonial regime and the impact of governmental transition. In an extensive survey titled "Statement from the March 9th Coup d'État to the End of 1945," signed February 9, 1946, the Department of Archive Records and Nationwide Library (Nhà lưu trứ công văn và thư viện toàn quốc) compared the National Library in 1944 and 1945.[16] As shown in table 1, the number of readers, books read, and books purchased in both the reading and lending sections dropped significantly over the course of a year in 1945. However, for the reading room, there was a small increase in the number of books added to the collection and legal deposit in 1945.

The director of the Department of Archive Records and Nationwide Library concluded that there were four specific reasons for the decrease in numbers between 1944 and 1945: (1) Many schools had closed or transferred out of Hanoi, (2) the library was no longer open during the evenings, (3) the number of foreign readers had decreased to nearly zero, and (4) many of the books were needed by government agencies for research. In addition to these reasons, the historical context of the war economy and governmental transition might have contributed to the overall decrease in library use. The Japanese war economy depleted Indochina food and supply lines and pulled the local economy into near collapse. Together with poor rice harvests and a famine in 1944–45, Tonkin experienced widespread starvation and social discontent. A study of economic transformation from 1925 to 1944 reported that the cost of living for a working-class Vietnamese individual

TABLE 1 Comparative statistics for the Hanoi National Library between 1944 and 1945
Collected by the Service of Archive Records and Nationwide Library in 1946

	1944	1945	Difference
Reading Room			
Number of readers	43,958	20,263	−23,695
Number of books read	46,239	20,900	−25,339
Number of books added to the collections	2,389	2,632	+243
Books purchased	1,973	1,915	−58
Legal deposit	450	893	+443
Lending Section			
Number of borrowers	48,075	19,741	−28,334
Number of books loaned	96,278	39,582	−56,696
Number of books added to the collections	1,702	1,458	−244

SOURCE: Direction des Archives et des Bibliothèques, Trung tâm lưu trữ quốc gia 1, Hanoi, Vietnam, folder 1537.

rose 430 percent in Saigon and 1,040 percent in Hanoi.[17] The challenges of securing food and work during wartime and the closure of several schools correlated to an overall decrease in reading room (on-site reading) activity. With the drastic political, economic, and military transformations in 1945, libraries also underwent challenges in operations. The archives reflect the shortages of paper, as demonstrated by the reuse of the back sides of old reports and the use of locally produced, more cheaply produced paper and ink.[18] Furthermore, the political upheaval also raised certain threats to the Hanoi library collection. On September 15, 1945, the acting director of the National Library noted that the buildings on 48 Nguyễn Trãi Street (previously 48 boulevard Rollandes) should be designated for the librarian-archivists to reside in order to "protect the materials night and day and to prevent [the materials] from theft and fire."[19] Even with the many operational constraints, the National Library in Hanoi only halted its operations for a few days and continued its services between 1944 and 1946.

The report also included another section titled "Proposed Work," which outlined an ambitious postcolonial vision for a National Library that served the public.[20] Depending upon the improvement of the state budget, the proposed work included the following: new equipment for the National Library book storerooms; the expansion of operating hours of the reading room and lending section from 8 a.m. to 5 p.m. to 8 a.m. to 8 p.m. (as well as the improvement of lighting in the rooms); a "*xe sách*" (book vehicle) project to bring books to a larger number of readers in the provincial areas so they could benefit from the "light of literature"; the building of additional bookshelves; and the development of neighborhood libraries (*thư viện khu phố*), which would "provide popular and valuable books to those outside the geographic reach of the national library and the city of Hanoi." Furthermore, the proposal called for a "public library" (*bình dân thư viện*), described as a functional library and community of readers. Once or twice each week, a committee would designate a place and organize an event for the lending and returning of books. People could leisurely come to this area and freely consult books, described as a method where "books find readers" (*sách tìm người đọc*).[21] The proposal for mobile book vehicles seems to be modeled on Paul Boudet's colonial project of the bibliobus and distributing "good reading" to the people. However, the proposals for neighborhood and public libraries distinctly stand out from previous top-down centralized library initiatives from the colonial period. Instead, the public libraries initiatives proposed here carried out the nationalistic and popular literacy impulses from the 1930s public libraries (*bình dân thư viện*) movement as examined in the previous chapter. The *bình dân thư viện* project focused on frequently providing popular reading to the countryside provinces and developing a community practice of reading. This postcolonial approach of "books find readers" through public library efforts was a direct contrast to colonial-era library approaches of "readers find books" (*người đọc tìm sách*), which relied upon readers' individual initiative to search for books. This new library strategy focused on public access and community reading points to early transformations of the French colonial library mission into a national library for the people.

Attempts to resume full library functions and carry out proposed work encountered operational scarcity such as limited personnel, budget, and equipment to carry out library services such as collections development, borrowing, and preservation. A second survey titled "Statement from August 1945 to September 1946" and signed by Interim Director Trần Văn Kha recorded other challenges in everyday library preservation, such as an alarming insect infestation that was rapidly spreading throughout the library, destroying many bookshelves and books.[22] Compared to the colonial period, the reading room witnessed a dramatic decrease in consultation numbers, from 96,997 book consultations in 1941 to only 33,914 in 1946.[23] This extreme decrease in book consultations to a third of its prewar number reflects the impact upon library use by the demands of everyday life in times of social upheaval due to famine, scarcity, economic inflation, and conflict during World War II, as well as the recent political transfer of authority. Compared to the French colonial period, the proportion of genres consulted in the reading room in 1945–46 differs significantly. In the French colonial period literature was often the most popular type of work consulted—for example, it accounted for 30 percent in 1925 and 47 percent in 1941. In comparison, 1946 shows a more even distribution of popular genres such as literature (17 percent), Indochina (15 percent), current affairs (15 percent), and periodicals (14 percent).

This new distribution of preferred topics could be due to changed demographics, with fewer students and French readers. Furthermore, urban intellectuals might have preferred to access their reading matter from other sources, such as *quốc ngữ*–language periodicals and books, smaller association reading rooms, and personal libraries that were created with the growth of the late colonial Vietnamese

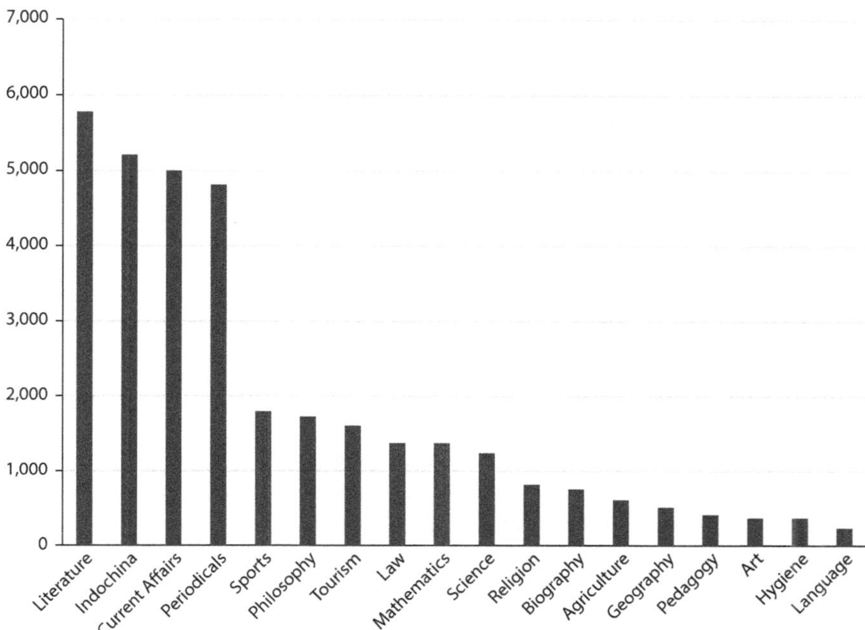

FIGURE 33. Books consulted in the Hanoi Central Library reading room, August 1945–1946. The popular categories of Indochina, current affairs, and periodicals focus on local politics and events. This shift toward local needs suggests the use of the Central Library for reference and administrative needs rather than primarily for leisure and study, as in the colonial period. *Source*: Direction des archives et des bibliothèques, Trung tâm lưu trữ quốc gia 1, Hanoi, Vietnam, folder 2211.

publishing industry and bookshops. In his 1946 report, interim library director Trần Văn Kha declared the importance of the library for economic development and the functioning of the state: "The reading room is not only a place for readers to research but also an opportunity to consult necessary documents to build the industrial sector. The reading room offers 1,832 important books for government offices, unions, and professionals to consult."[24]

In the immediate aftermath of World War II, the Hanoi National Library confronted operational challenges due to a constant lack of supplies, personnel, funding, and equipment that would allow them to maintain the library, opening hours, and services. On December 7, 1945, the Ministry of National Education University Division requested the library extend its operating hours to 7 p.m. so that government officials, workers, and university students could come to the library after their work or classes. However, library director Ngô Đình Nhu stated that in order to extend the operating hours, the Department of Archive Records and Nationwide Library needed at least seven more temporary personnel (two secretaries and five orderlies).[25] At the time, the Department of Archive Records and Nationwide

Library employed thirty-three full-time workers. Nhu added that other positions, such as night guards, gardeners, and bookbinders, had a high turnover rate and requested that the department be able to replace these employees without prior approval from the Ministry of National Education.

In addition to having issues with reliable personnel, the library also lacked enough light for the reading room and storage rooms, especially during the darker months. On December 19, 1945, Nhu requested fifty light bulbs for all the lamps missing light bulbs and a monthly supply of twelve light bulbs for replacements. Nhu requested that future payments be paid for by government check because the library could no longer access its previous budget.[26] Nhu noted the dire lack of light bulbs: Since August, the library had only been able to purchase three light bulbs in cash. Postwar scarcity of supplies did not just impact the library. On January 17, 1946, the municipal administration reported that they also could not procure light bulbs for their office. Instead, they suggested that the library purchase directly from the light bulb factories. This case reveals the everyday challenges of personnel and supplies that prevented the operations of the libraries and other administrative offices in the new state in 1945–46.

Government Reference Reading and Documentation Training

In addition to being an inherited institution from the colonial period, the National Library held an important role for the new DRV state by actively providing reference materials for Vietnamese government officials to inform state-building efforts. In 1946 an anonymous DRV government official submitted a request to the National Library to assemble an official catalog of library books on the topic of politics.[27] The library curated a list featuring political works in the library collection ranging from nation building, patriotism, and political philosophy to histories of revolution and colonialism. For example, the list included the following works: *Political Handbook of the World, 1940*, by Walter H. Mallory, which was a reference volume on world events, governments, political parties, and press policies in countries around the world; *Inventaires I: La Crise sociale et les idéologies nationales*, by Raymond Aron, Célestin Bouglé, Étienne Dennery, Georges Friedmann, Élie Halévy, and Robert Marjolin, a study led by the Center of Documentation at the Paris L'École normale supérieure on the problem of the middle class in French society during the Third Republic; and *L'Homme et l'état totalitaire*, by Richard Nikolaus von Coudenhove-Kalergi, who was an Austrian-Japanese political philosopher and advocate of pan-European integration and human liberties and was opposed to antisemitism, Nazism, and the political models of Bolshevism, totalitarianism, and dictatorship. Other Indochina-specific studies included the political and administrative study *L'Indo-Chine française: Étude politique, économique et administrative sur la Cochinchine, le Cambodge, l'Annam et le Tonkin*, by Jean-Louis de Lanessan, and a study on administrative operations in colonial Indochina with particular attention to taxation policies, *L'Indochine, erreurs et dangers: Un programme*, by Fernand Bernard.[28] This book list reveals the reading and research interests of Vietnamese government departments and the important role of the extensive Hanoi library collections as a valuable source of reference matter during this period of postcolonial state building.

Government officials borrowed copious amounts of reading matter from the Hanoi National Library, often without adhering to library regulations. On October 9, 1945, the director of the Ministry of National Education wrote to the Department of Higher Education requesting that government officials return checked-out library books and also requesting the implementation of a stricter and standardized accounting system for book loans.[29] The director argued that many books were lost during the French period and requested a recataloging of all library books while also calling for the end of special borrowing privileges to government offices. On October 12, 1945, interim director Phạm Đình Giệm from the National Library responded that in this time of "building the nation," governmental offices needed to rely on the library materials, which made it impossible to adhere to a comprehensive recataloging of the collections.[30] However, Giệm reassured the director that each individual lender took care of their borrowed library books. Attached to this statement was a list of books borrowed by government offices from the National Library, signed by Phạm Đình Giệm. The list included such departments as internal affairs, propaganda, education, and foreign affairs.

While interim director Giệm followed a flexible policy of allowing readers to borrow books freely to "build the nation," the library director Ngô Đình Nhu attempted to impose a stauncher standardization of official library procedures. On November 28, 1945, Nhu wrote to the Ministry of National Education reporting that several government officials were exploiting their library privileges by borrowing too many books and for too long.[31] Nhu called for an end to the unfair use of library materials by government officials and argued that "exploiting library privileges negatively impacts the task of preserving library materials, which are valuable to all the citizens of the country." Nhu also attached a list of all the books borrowed by various departments and the dates the books were checked out. For example, the Vietnam Women's Union (Phụ nữ cứu quốc) borrowed fifteen Vietnamese-language books on November 6, 1945, such as *Women and Literature* (*Phụ nữ và văn học*), *The Trưng Sisters* (*Hai Bà Trưng*), *Eastern Women* (Đàn bà Đông Phương), and *Laboring and Suffering Sisters* (*Chị em lao khổ*). The association Cultural Transformation for National Salvation (Văn Hoá Cứu Quốc) borrowed an astonishing 250 books between September and October 1945, such as the periodicals *Phụ Nữ Tấn Văn* and *The Times* (*Báo Thời Thế*), political books such as *Drum Call for Independence* (*Hồi trống tự do*), *Socialism Against Fascism* (*Xã hội chủ nghĩa chống phát-xít*), and *Proletarian Organizing* (*Tổ chức vô sản*). The Ministry of Foreign Affairs borrowed one hundred books in 1945, including thirty-five issues of the *New York Times* from 1941 and several books on contemporary history, Japan, international law, and China. This list of books reveals how associations and departments used the National Library in Hanoi extensively to consult a diverse range of material such as global news, comparative studies, and history in the first few months after the declaration of Vietnam's independence. Furthermore, many of the readers consulted *quốc ngữ* books and periodicals available in the library pertaining to political history in the context of political transition.

In response to Nhu's request, the director of the Ministry of National Education sent out a statement to all the ministries mandating that government officials pay close attention to the following:

1. Careful adherence to the library regulations regarding borrowing library books. For books only necessary for reference, send someone to consult the books on site. Only borrow necessary books to read at home.
2. Return books in accordance with their due dates before borrowing new books.
3. Carefully maintain the books to prevent damage and loss.[32]

The director concluded with the statement that "these rules above must be adhered to in order to preserve and protect the library materials because these documents are very rare."[33] These exchanges show the significance of the National Library reading matter to government offices for building a postcolonial state and society. The discourse regarding library procedures centered on standardization, accounting, and reader responsibility in order to maintain fair and collective use of libraries. It seems that after this internal exchange, the longtime librarian administrator and first Vietnamese Chartist Ngô Đình Nhu stepped away from his work as library director, transitioning full time into political affairs.[34]

Government officials considered the library reading matter as both valuable and essential for state building. In 1946 the new government encouraged officials to consult library and archival materials in order to understand and standardize department functions and communications. On May 21, 1946, the Office of the Administrative Committee of the North (Uỷ ban hành chính bắc bộ, văn phòng) proposed to all the directors of government departments that they participate in a new centralized "administrative training class" (*lớp huấn luyện hành chính*) that would "instruct and guide all new officials in local administration (province and district) the organizational methods of each governmental office as well as the customary legal protocol."[35] The first class would have up to fifty participants. This statement to all governmental departments emphasized the necessity of firsthand consultation of their department archives and printed matter in order to standardize communications between various departments. In subsequent letters on May 29, 1946, the Office of the Administrative Committee of the North requested seventy reader and borrowing cards for government officials to visit the Hanoi national archives and libraries in order to conduct research on their departments' administrative procedures and documentation practices.[36] In the early months of the new DRV administration, the Hanoi Central Library carried on its role as provider of valuable reference materials and training the administration in documentation tasks.

The First Indochina War and Recolonization of the Hanoi Central Library

Under the leadership of General Charles de Gaulle, France attempted to retake all of Indochina and rule Indochina as a colonial federation. However, retaking Indochina was not simply a battle between unified fronts of French and Vietnamese. The French Fourth Republic (1946–58) struggled to recover from World War II and develop its domestic economy, centralize its divisive ministries, and retain control over its overseas colonies. Throughout Vietnam, contending groups carved out overlapping bases of authority with different visions of a postcolonial state. Fighting for political power and popular support were northern communists and nationalists, southern republican nationalists, Việt Minh scattered throughout the country, and, in the south, the Cao Đài, Hoà Hảo, Bình Xuyên, and factions carrying out a civil war between Vietnamese and Khmer.[37] On August 17, 1945, the French Fourth Republic replaced the governor general system in colonial Indochina with the Haut commissariat de France pour l'Indochine (High Commission of France for Indochina) and named Vice Admiral Georges Thierry d'Argenlieu as high commissioner of Indochina. On September 23, 1945, France launched a *coup de force* pushing the DRV forces out of Saigon and retook power south of the sixteenth parallel in Vietnam. Saigon served as the headquarters for rebuilding an Indochina federation with semi-independent local monarchy states under French control. The High Commission was further divided into general territorial organizations—the Commission for Cochinchina and South Annam, the Commission of the Republic for North Indochina (which included Tonkin, the highlands, and Annam down to the sixteenth parallel), the Commission for Laos, and the Commission for Cambodge. In Cambodia, French troops overthrew Son Ngoc Thanh's nationalist government, restored King Norodom Sihanouk, and declared Cambodia an *état libre* (free state) of the Indochina federation. In Laos, the French pushed out the Lao Issara (Free Lao) government and placed Sisavang Vong as the monarch. Cochinchina was managed under a provisional government (Gouvernement provisoire du sud-Vietnam, or Chính phủ lâm thời) under Vietnamese president Nguyễn Văn Thinh, who was followed by Lê Văn Hoạch and Nguyễn Văn Xuân. The French-initiated Provisional Government of the Republic of Cochinchina in Saigon countered the competing administrative project of the DRV to unify all Vietnamese territories (including Cochinchina) under its government administration based in Hanoi.

On December 19, 1946, full-scale war between France and Hồ Chí Minh's DRV began, which became known as the First Indochina War. The first battles began as urban conflicts in Hanoi, which resulted in pushing the DRV government and its infrastructure of communication and personnel out of the city and into the countryside.[38] In the Việt Bắc northern and northwestern mountainous regions of Tonkin, the DRV established a new administrative and military base of command. The French retook Hanoi by February 1947 and installed the Commission of the Republic for North Indochina. Two states—Hồ Chí Minh's DRV government and Georges Thierry d'Argenlieu's High Commission based out of Saigon—competed for power and legitimacy. On March 8, 1949, the former emperor Bảo Đại and French president Vincent Auriol signed the Élysée Accords, which formally recognized Vietnam's limited independence from France and created the Associated State of Vietnam based in Saigon. Bảo Đại was designated as a monarch head of state and gained the temporary support of the Third Force, noncommunist nationalists throughout the three Vietnamese regions. Negotiations to form the Associated State of Laos (July) and Cambodia (November) followed in the same year, signaling the end of the attempt to create an Indochina Federation under the French. However, the associated states were not granted authority over the most important aspects of independent states—the military, diplomacy, and finance—and remained under the power of the High Commission of Indochina under the high commissioner Léon Pignon.[39] It soon became clear that the associated states still functioned as colonial tools to maintain French power, and Bảo Đại and the nationalists distanced themselves from the project. During the First Indochina War, the two warring states functioned as piecemeal "archipelago states" with uneven bases of administrative control, a "bricolage" of fragmented institutions, insufficient military forces, and shifting loyalties among the inhabitants.[40] Comprising troops from French Africa and locally recruited militias in southern Vietnam, the French military Expeditionary Corps forces could not maintain control over the entirety of Vietnam. French and southern Vietnamese held power bases primarily in Saigon, southern cities, and Hanoi. Similarly, the authority of the DRV reached unevenly throughout Vietnam, with power bases concentrated in the rural and ethnically diverse regions of the northwestern highlands and central Vietnam.[41] With widespread violence and coercive tactics for recruiting loyalty to the French colonial federation or Việt Minh nationalist cause, many Vietnamese villagers fled to the cities seeking refuge. Saigon-Cholon grew from 500,000 in 1939 to 1.7 million in 1954, transforming Saigon-Cholon into an expansive urban landscape with limited infrastructure that would allow it receive such a large population of migrants.[42]

During the DRV administration in Hanoi from 1945 to 1946, Saigon was symbolically designated as the headquarters of the former colonial Indochina directorate and managed the legal deposit of "Indochina," a colonial geopolitical construct that grappled with political identities as a colonial federation or semicolonial associated states within French attempts to maintain power from 1946 to 1954.[43] On July 25, 1947, the Directorate of Archives and Libraries of Indochina from the French colonial period was officially renamed the Service of Archives and Library of the High Commission (Nha lưu trữ công văn vă thư viện Cao Uỷ or Service des archives et des bibliothèques du haut-commissariat de France pour l'Indochine), with Saigon as the headquarters rather than Hanoi. The renaming and reorganization of the French colonial Directorate of Archives and Libraries reveal piecemeal attempts by the French High Commission to retain its colonial institutions and to consolidate Saigon as its administrative base for the reconquest of Indochina.

After the French reconquest of Hanoi, the Quốc gia Thư viện National Library in Hanoi managed by the DRV (1945–46) switched its name back to the Pierre Pasquier Library under the direction of the Commission of the Republic for North Indochina. Paul Boudet was reinstated as "federal" director of the Service of Archives and Library of the High Commission of Indochina and director of the Pierre Pasquier Library in Hanoi. In December 1947, at a time of French reassertion of colonial authority, Paul Boudet commended the colonial-era accomplishments of the Directorate of Archives and Libraries of Indochina since its founding.[44] Boudet praised the central archives in Hanoi as incomparable to those in any other French overseas territory; the archives contained over four hundred thousand dossiers, and its storage facility "guaranteed the security and conservation of the documents for at least thirty years against deterioration due to environment (humidity, cholera, rain, typhoons), as well as insects and termites." Boudet added that the archives were furnished with wooden furniture and could respond to requests for administrative documents unlike any other overseas territory archive. He also applauded the development of the Hanoi Pierre Pasquier Library, which he described as an "indispensable organ for the intellectual life of the country," with over 150,000 volumes and important French, Indochinese, and foreign periodicals and welcoming three hundred to six hundred readers a day, two-thirds of whom were Indochinese. Furthermore, from 1930 to 1945 the colonial-era directorate trained over two hundred Indochinese government officials to work as secretaries, archivists, and librarians to serve in various government bureaus. Boudet pointed to the significance of the library, directorate, and archives not only for technical documentation, but also for their ability to facilitate the intellectual life of the local population. Boudet celebrated the Directorate of Archives and Libraries and by extension validated the continued French administrative control of Indochina. On an operational level, Boudet expressed admiration for the continued services of the library and archives even during the administrative transition from French to Vietnamese, and then back to French, save for the removal by the DRV government of two collections that had not been recovered.[45] Boudet remarked again with amazement how Indochinese librarians and secretaries welcomed the French administrators and resumed the library services from the colonial period.

In July 1948 Paul Boudet suddenly became sick, and he was repatriated back to France on August 4, 1948. He passed away shortly afterward on November 11, 1948.[46] His official personnel dossier summarized his work during World War II and the immediate aftermath: "During and despite the Japanese occupation, Boudet endeavored to maintain intellectual relations with the outside world, to ensure, on several occasions, secret links between north and south Indochina during the same period. In spite of the difficult circumstances, thanks to his leadership with Indochinese staff, he was able to save almost the entire precious collections of the Archives and Libraries of Indochina in Hanoi."[47] Simone de Saint-Exupéry delivered a public eulogy at the Society of Indochinese Studies meeting on December 12, 1948, honoring Boudet's admirable life's work.[48] In the political context of semi-colonialism, Saint-Exupéry described Boudet as a dedicated, meticulous cultivator, building a stable vision of colonial documentation and "carrying it out against all odds." Saint-Exupéry spoke directly to his systematic application of a comprehensive archival system unified with the metropolitan archives and implemented throughout Saigon, Hue, Phnom Penh, and government offices. Saint-Exupéry distinguished Boudet from other paleographer-archivists in his commitment to make accessible to "researchers ever more the possibilities of documentation" through his production of bibliographies, bulletins of legal deposits, archival manuals, and collection guides.[49] She concluded with a quote from her renowned literary brother, Antoine de Saint-Exupéry, from *Citadelle*, published posthumously in 1948—"How would great architects be born from a work without grandeur?"—and she described Boudet's great accomplishments and legacy as a source of inspiration in the midst of "a world turned upside down, [where] everything or almost everything has to be done or redone."[50] Ferréol de Ferry, another archivist-paleographer graduate of the École des Chartes who had previously worked at the archives of the Ministry of the Colonies in Paris, became the next director of the Pierre Pasquier Library in Hanoi, serving in this role until March 1953.[51] Edmonde Castagnol (deputy director of the Archives and Libraries for Tonkin and North Annam) succeeded Paul Boudet as director of the entire Service of Archives and Libraries, whose headquarters had been moved to Saigon in 1947.

Vietnamese personnel confronted more challenges and were interrogated to prove their loyalty to the French High Commission regime in Hanoi. For example, former colonial librarian-archivist Trần Văn Kha worked for decades in the Central Library reading room and lending section, legal deposit, periodicals section, and bookbinding department, and he led several training courses for archivist-librarians and secretaries in the 1930s. Kha worked continuously from 1925 throughout the regime changes from French to Japanese to the DRV communists. During the period of DRV control in Hanoi from 1945 to 1946, Kha had served as the interim director of the Department of Archive Records and Nationwide Library. On January 2, 1947, former director Trần Văn Kha requested that the commissioner of the Republic for North Indochina reinstate him as archivist-librarian of the Pierre Pasquier Library.[52] Kha explained to the French commissioner that he continued to work at the library during the DRV government not for political reasons, but to support his family and to protect the library collections. Kha argued that he was forced to work under the DRV government in order to "have enough to live and support my large family, comprised of a wife and seven young children; to avoid being arrested or sent to labor camps by the Việt Minh Party; and to safeguard the cultural wealth (books and archives documents) as much as possible, since I am the most senior and most experienced official in the archives and libraries department." Kha followed up with a proclamation that he had not belonged to any political association since the Japanese coup on March 9, 1945.

Even with his lifetime of contributions to the Directorate and appeals, Kha still had to petition for his reinstatement to the Pierre Pasquier Library in Hanoi for another three years. By October 1950 the personnel office in Saigon had written a statement that praised Kha's extensive library experience and confirmed his "safe" political background. The personnel office in Saigon advocated for his reappointment to the archives and libraries service in Hanoi. The statement also reassessed Kha's long history with the Directorate of Archives and Libraries in Indochina. Kha had joined the administration in January 1925, and by 1950 he had dedicated twenty-six years to the service. The statement commended Kha's work: "Given the various complex, diverse tasks [of the library and archives service] and increasing workload . . . Monsieur Kha has always shown a general culture of superior work, of intelligence, and of cheerful initiative. In addition to his technical knowledge developed through his quarter of a century of work in the service, Kha has proved himself in the field of general administration as a first-rate collaborator and indispensable to the smooth operations of the service." The report noted that Kha had kept himself away from recent political movements and dedicated himself to "safeguard[ing] the rich collections of the libraries and the recovery of the archives of the government general, the resident superior of Tonkin, and the former Department of Finance."

Colonial Nostalgia for a Franco-Vietnamese Library

Throughout the First Indochina War, library administrators struggled to determine the role and function of the Hanoi Central Library in the aftermath of political transitions from the DRV to a contradictory semicolonial "Indochinese federation," hearkening back to a colonial Franco-Vietnamese framework. During the DRV administration and management of the Hanoi Central Library from 1945 to 1946, a former colonial library administrator sought to rekindle the grandeur of the French civilizing mission carried out through the Hanoi library, a monument of Franco-Vietnamese collaboration.[53] The unnamed author expressed a deep nostalgia for the golden years of intellectualism, culture, and education cultivated through French colonial archives and libraries development in Hanoi, Saigon, Hue, and Phnom Penh. The author remarked that the colonial Central Library reflected a complete transformation of the site from the tropical landscape of the bygone days, "frozen in the cold and empty speculation of a traditional culture," into a modern space characterized by a "vast, clear" reading room where "young people flock, eager to get acquainted with the sciences of the West."[54] The statement claimed that members of the vibrant colonial-era community of intellectuals were made equal by the democratizing space of the library: Seated side by side were "professors, senior civil servants, and general officials next to simple students," and "French and Indochinese mixed like brothers."[55] This statement conveyed a desperate nostalgia for the French colonial period in a time of political uncertainty for the French Fourth Republic's control in Indochina.

From 1946 to 1954 the colonial Directorate of Archives and Libraries underwent significant organizational and symbolic changes in the context of the postcolonial transfer of state authorities and war. The Hanoi library was renamed the Pierre Pasquier Library (1946), the Cultural Library (1950), and the General Library (1953), reflecting the extensive debates about the function and administration of the Hanoi French-Vietnamese library during the First Indochina War. Nevertheless, in practice Vietnamese readers continued to refer to the library, located on the newly renamed 31 Tràng Thi (Examination Grounds) Street, as Trung Ương Thư Viện (Central Library). A Vietnamese language newspaper published a reader's opinion piece on the current happenings in the Hanoi library in 1952.[56] This article provides a glimpse of the continued social significance and intellectual prestige of the Hanoi reading room space for the reading public. The author reiterated the spatial significance of the ancient and scholarly city of Hanoi, and specifically the site of the library, where the "incense of the Thập Đạo [the central pavilion of examination candidates] of the previous era casts a dignified and respectful aura." The author argued that the current library reading room (where the Thập Đạo used to be) maintains a "majestic didactic tone." The author proclaimed that "every little movement, every chuckle that accidentally slips out in the reading room," was an insult to the intellectual sanctity of this space. The author contrasted visitors who had a sense of scholarly self-respect with disrespectful "cavaliers" who used the library as a cool resort, resting under the ceiling fans while daydreaming. The author concluded with a public request that the library director impose stricter regulations so that readers would not hamper the reading experience of others. This article mirrored the debates regarding the proper use of public space and a Confucian lettered past from the late colonial period.

In an internal report on March 26, 1952, administrators summarized the current state of the library, which was still often referred to as the Pierre Pasquier Library. "In spite of the current events, the reductions in budget for personnel and equipment, and the considerable decline in French inhabitants in Hanoi (who used to constitute a great proportion of the readers), the success of the library has not ceased to increase among the public, the majority of whom are currently Vietnamese."[57] In December 1951, 3,328 readers visited the library and consulted 5,686 books.[58] The author of the report, most likely a French librarian at the Pierre Pasquier Library, commented that very few French military personnel visited the library. He added that the library stood like an "incomparable center of French culture in a Vietnamese milieu," where Vietnamese readers consulted books and periodicals in French, using a French catalog and library science system.

On July 31, 1953, the interim director Simone de Saint-Exupéry published the official bylaws for the Bibliothèque générale de Hanoi (Tổng Thư Viện Hà Nội) in both French and Vietnamese.[59] The official bylaws stated that the library permitted "a) Asians or Europeans eighteen years and older who have sufficient instruction, and b) students from Hanoi University and students in their final year of French and Vietnamese high schools." Furthermore, readers were required to respect the following rules: "Readers must observe absolute silence. They are forbidden to smoke. . . . The reader must deposit their entry card to the overseer's desk when they enter the library. . . . Before leaving the reader must return the books and periodicals taken from the shelves and return works borrowed back to the orderly. Afterward, their entry card is returned." These reading room regulations were based on colonial rules of proper reader behavior. The regulations also cited consequences for violations of these rules and damages to books: Readers would be subjected to fines or prison according to colonial-era penal code articles 254, 255, and 257.

Library personal created extensive charts to document the changing racial demographics of readers and preferences for the lending section between 1938 and 1953. While the reading room had a decrease in number of books requested (84,395 in 1938 and 56,379 in 1953), in 1953 the lending section remained relatively well utilized by a larger number of readers, averaging 163 reader visits and 324 works checked out daily.[60] In 1938 the number of registered borrowers in the lending section was 2,561 (45 percent European, 55 percent Vietnamese and Asian), and in 1953 the number more than doubled to 5,598 (43 percent European, 57 percent Vietnamese and Asian). With attention to language diversity, the 1953 report also broke down the reading room collection of 155,092 volumes by language—17,0mj88 Vietnamese, 135,156 French, 2,016 English, 432 German, and 400 other—and it included a note that the collection included dictionaries in Russian, Chinese, Japanese, Malay, Siamese, Latin, and other languages.

A 1954 meeting of the board of directors of the General Library and a delegation of Vietnamese library administrators and government officials sheds light on the operations of the library during the First Indochina War. At this meeting the attendees reflected on the state of the Hanoi library, observing its slow development and the limited number of readers to the reading room compared to before 1945.[61] In 1953 the General Library recorded 6,540 registered readers and 165 daily readers, and noted that this low number was due to the mobilization of many of its student readers for the army. Of special note was the development of a children's library section, which was opened in 1952 in a corner of the lending section. By 1953 the children's library had two benches and four armchairs, providing seating for nineteen readers. On average the children's library received 44 visitors daily, who borrowed books to take home or read on site. The report noted that the "beautiful illustrated works are made available to the little readers, who treat the books with great care."[62] In 1953 the children's library subscribed to five illustrated newspapers and comics in French: *Coeurs vaillants, Coq hardi, La semaine de Suzette, Spirou*, and *Tintin*.[63] The meeting participants noted that the children's library "had been received favorably by the young public." The director also asked members of the Vietnamese delegation to create another Vietnamese-language newspaper for children, particularly to carry out a favorable program of "propaganda of children's periodicals in the Vietnamese language."[64] The director noted that the only other current newspaper was *Tuổi Thơ*, which was provided by the services of the army and was intended only for families of combatants.

Book Diplomacy: Hanoi and an International Network of Books

During the First Indochina War, the Hanoi library operated as an important node within a Cold War network of international cultural diplomacy, or what I call "book diplomacy"—book exchanges between libraries, governmental bodies, and private organizations across France, French-backed Saigon, the United States, Britain, Asia, and South America.[65] Beginning as early as 1949, the United States Book Exchange (USBE) embedded the Hanoi library within a network of international exchanges and donations of political and scientific books.[66] The USBE also mediated the transfer of books from the Carnegie Endowment for International Peace, a Washington, DC–based international affairs think tank focused on international cooperation and reducing global conflict. Through this international cooperation the following historical political affairs works were sent to the Hanoi library: "The Hague Court Reports," works from the Institut de droit international (an independent institution focused on international law); the addresses and state papers of Elihu Root, who served as secretary of war, secretary of state, and U.S. senator at the turn of the twentieth century; Hugh Ritchie's study of navigation certificates and distribution system to neutral countries during the British naval blockade during the First World War, *The "Navicert" System During the War*.[67] Throughout the 1950s and 1960s the United Nations Educational, Scientific and Cultural Organization (UNESCO) played a major role in promoting public and rural libraries in the developing world, championing an Anglo-American vision of postwar modernization and global peace.[68] On November 21, 1951, UNESCO collaborated with the British National Book Exchange to provide the Hanoi library with English-language works from the social sciences collection, such as speeches and writings by Franklin D. Roosevelt and human rights and global manifestos by H. G. Wells.[69] These international book exchanges were particularly important given the fiscal impact of war on carrying out everyday library services such as book purchases. Between January and March 1952, Ferréol de Ferry, the director of the Hanoi library, requested of the office of the High Commission in Saigon foreign currency to purchase foodstuffs, equipment, newspapers, and foreign reviews (subscriptions to *Europa, Orbis*, and *Minerva* and American magazines such as *The Far Eastern Quarterly, Publishers Weekly*, and *The United States Quarterly Books Review*) in order to continue operating various government departments.[70]

According to this exchange, UNESCO provided book vouchers through the Ministry of National Education for libraries to purchase foreign books. Additionally, university presses had offered aid by simplifying the process for the northern Vietnam archives and libraries to subscribe to international research periodicals such as *Pacific Affairs, Ricerca Scientifica, Artibus Asiae*, the *German National Bibliography*, and the *Canadian Journal of Biology*.

Throughout the First Indochina War, the Hanoi library maintained active book exchanges with the United States Information Service (USIS) offices in Hanoi and Saigon, an early American cultural and intellectual hegemony project connected to United States Foreign Service and stationed in American embassies and consulates around the world.[71] The mission of USIS offices was to disseminate abroad information about American society, politics, and cultural life (with undercurrents of disseminating ideological commitments to freedom, democracy, and anticommunism) through book distribution, radio, programming, and news.[72] Topics and titles selected for book distribution were broad and open to on-the-ground interpretation by USIS administrators. On December 5, 1952, the USIS office located in Hanoi (also called the Hanoi American Library, or Phòng Đọc Sách Mỹ) sent a shipment of twenty-seven books, including *Crops in Peace and War* by the U.S. Government Printing Office, *The US and World Relations* by Lilian T. Mowrer, and *Tự do hay là chết* (*Freedom or Death*) by Oksana Kasenkina.[73] Another shipment in 1953 included thirty-eight books that addressed a wide range of topics, including the light-hearted book *The First Book of Cats*, written by the popular author of rural life Gladys Taber; the reference construction book *Building for Small Public Libraries* by architect Ernest I. Miller; an examination of the United States convict leasing system, *A New Slavery*, by social activist and cofounder of the American Civil Liberties Union, Roger N. Baldwin; and four brochures and five maps of Southeast Asia.[74] In 1954 the donated books from the USIS offices in Hanoi and Saigon included books that aligned with American Cold War ideologies of global order, from histories of capitalism and the United Nations to journalistic reports of communist "brainwashing" and studies of the American government system.[75] In 1954 the Saigon USIS office also donated to the Hanoi library bibliographic updates and books on library development, such as *Books in Print, 1952, Reading in Modern Education, The Children's Book on How to Use Books & Libraries*, and *The American School and University*.[76]

Many of the books donated by the United States Information Service were overstocked English-language reading matter as well as a reflection of the political and social interests during this period, including history and political science, U.S. world relations, Asian geography, and Cold War politics. Hanoi librarians were aware of the information imperialism persisting in the collections and cataloging system, with a librarian noting in 1952 that the American information services had recognized the French dominance of the library and thus was "flooding us with their publications."[77] On August 13, 1953, the director of the Hanoi library wrote to the USIS to report a politically subversive book in the last shipment of books donated to the library.[78] The Hanoi library director expressed deep concern that two passages in *The Voice of Asia* by James A. Michener "very much favor communism and its leader Hồ Chí Minh . . . and the author is very far away from the position adopted by the United States vis-à-vis the Indochinese problem. I do not think it is useful to spread literature that claims it is documentary but in reality is inspired by superficial and fanciful and haphazard declarations." The Hanoi library director's concern about the circulation of contentious reading matter suggests fears of communist influence in the context of war and a weak governmental authority in Hanoi. As shown in this exchange, top-down structures of intellectual hegemony such as through USIS book distribution in practice functioned with more nuance and debate.

In 1954 the director of the Service of Archives and Libraries Edmonde Castagnol, who was based in Saigon, wrote to the director of the Hanoi library emphasizing the importance of the legal deposit as a method of maintaining a reciprocal relationship between the regional governments and libraries in Hanoi, Saigon, and central Vietnam in the midst of war and the handover of governmental institutions to Vietnamese authorities.[79] Castagnol requested that other regions "send works published in those regions not only to enrich the collections of the Central Library [in Hanoi], but also to give to the reading public in North Vietnam a collection reflecting the evolution of thought and the art of writing in Vietnam after World War II."[80] As shown in these international book exchanges, donations, and requests for legal deposits, the Hanoi library functioned as an important part of American-dominated Cold War cultural propaganda efforts to exert intellectual hegemony within the Pacific region.

PART 2: SAIGON, 1949–1955

The Decolonization of Language in Cochinchina Library Collections

The decolonization of the Cochinchina Library was a gradual and contradictory process reflecting the confrontations between French semicolonial efforts and Vietnamese nationalization in southern Vietnam. With the official administrative handover to the Provisional Government of the Republic of Cochinchina, the Cochinchina Library was renamed the National Library of Southern Vietnam (Thơ Viện Quốc Gia Nam Việt) and carried out official national library operations based out of Saigon: acquisitions, legal deposit, reading room, and lending section. Subsequent negotiations between the French High Commission and Vietnamese politicians resulted in the establishment of the Provisional Central Government of Vietnam in 1948. This government incorporated all three regions of the country, including the short-lived Republic of Cochinchina. In 1949, after another round of negotiations, the Provisional Central Government reconstituted as the nominally independent State of Vietnam (SVN). The SVN was an associated state along with Laos and Cambodia and part of the Indochinese Federation. The federation belonged to a larger French recolonization apparatus called the French Union, which included other French colonies such as Tunisia and Morocco. Reflecting these larger changes, the decolonization of the National Library occurred gradually through three interlocking processes: the designation of the institution as the premier library of an ascending national capital of Saigon, the management of the library by the first Vietnamese director, and the expansion of the library's Asian-language materials.

In February 1948 Đoàn Quan Tấn was appointed as the first Vietnamese director of the National Library following the death of French director Rémi Bourgeois in September 1947. Tấn was active in cultural affairs and Saigon scholarly life. In 1940 he had been the chairman of the Hội Khuyến Học (Association for Promoting Education), a mutual aid society focused on education, the improvement of Vietnamese language, and the study of literature, fine arts, and national history. From 1950 to 1952 Tấn was the chairman of the France-Vietnam People's Academy Association and the Indochina Archaeology Association; from 1953 he served as the assistant chairman of the French Literary Alliance Association. In an interview with Radio Saigon in May 1949, Đoàn Quan Tấn highlighted the mission of the National Library as a national and public institution.[81] Tấn reported that the State of Vietnam proposed the development of an ambitious new national library building on boulevard Norodom (later Thống Nhất Street, today Lê Duẩn Street) to address the overcrowded facilities inherited from the French colonial government.[82] Đoàn Quan Tấn argued that the building project would "equip Saigon—the capital of South Vietnam and a university city—with a museum-library worthy of it."[83] The new buildings would serve as the symbolic library of a national capital and a grand integration of the colonial and postcolonial library collections. The vision for the construction of an expansive museum-library had its origins in the 1940s, as seen in the early sketches for an Indochinese museum-library in Saigon that combined exoticized motifs of the orient (Sinitic characters, statues, and a bas-relief of the Khmer seven-headed Nāga) together with porticos, narrow columns, and stairways characteristic of geometric art deco architecture. By 1949 the building project had expanded into a multifaceted vision for a cultural center with an archives repository, a two-part library with a central room for study and reference and a lending section especially intended for youth, and a historical museum of Indochina.[84] According to Tấn, the proposed museum would be the most important part of the cultural center, devoted to the work of France in the Far East. That the museum should focus on the cultural preservation of France and Indochina rather than Vietnam made it clear that decolonization was still incomplete and called attention to the ambiguity of the SVN as a national government within the French Union.

Confronted with fiscal constraints and shifting governmental regimes, these visions for a French-Indochinese museum-library building remained as draft

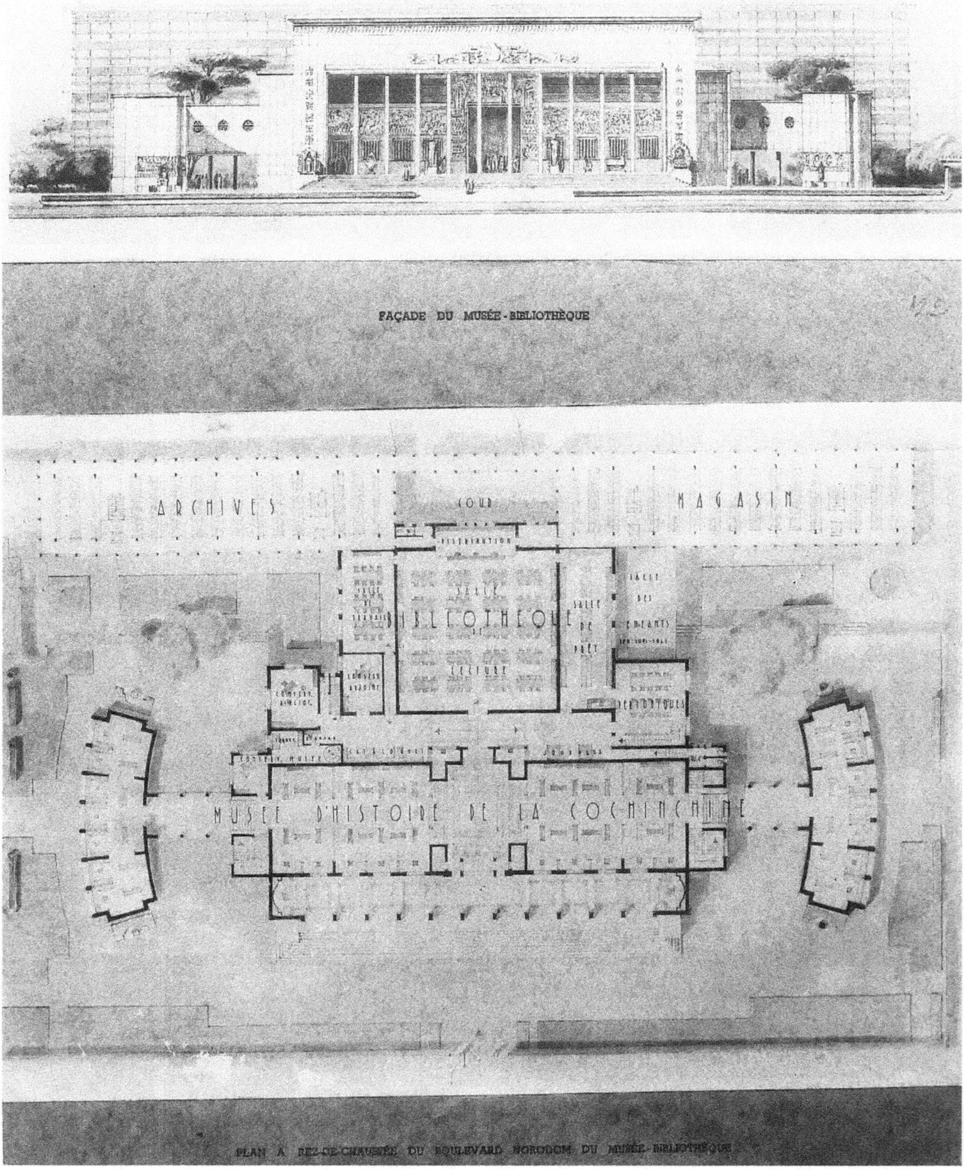

FIGURE 34. Draft plans depicting "Front of the Museum-Library" and "Map of the Ground Floor of the Museum-Library at Norodom Boulevard," 1940. The map of the expansive grounds includes multiple buildings and joint institutions including the library (with separate sections for a reading room, working room, lending section, children's reading room, and periodicals section), the Museum of History of Cochinchina, and the archives and storage depot in the back building. *Source*: Tổng Thư viện, Trung tâm lưu trữ quốc gia 2, Ho Chi Minh City, Vietnam, folder 1.

FIGURE 35. Draft plans depicting a close-up view of the imagined portico entry to the museum-library, 1940. Note the envisioned clientele of the library as both Western and Asian in dress and appearance. *Source*: Tổng Thư viện, Trung tâm lưu trữ quốc gia 2, Ho Chi Minh City, Vietnam, folder 1.

proposals, and the construction of a new national library building did not begin until after 1954. In practice, the National Library continued to operate out of the former colonial building at 34 Gia Long Street (formerly 34 rue de La Grandière). The National Library director Tấn commented on the popularity of the reading room, which was open all day Monday to Saturday and on Sunday mornings and was "heavily frequented by the Saigonese public, such as high school and university students."[85] The room served an average of eighty readers daily, approximately half of whom were Westerners. Tấn was also proud of the collections and explained that his staff were acquiring new library materials to better serve Vietnamese readers and to encourage greater understanding between Vietnamese and French readers. By 1949 the library held fifty-seven thousand volumes on the humanities, arts, philosophy, religion, and geography, and the most popular works among readers were texts about history, the sciences, and law. Since most works were in French, library administrators sought to add more Vietnamese translations of French popular science and technology books. Library administrators also encouraged the translation of Vietnamese works into French and recognized translation as an act of political exchange so "that the effort of mutual understanding was not one-sided." For Đoàn Quan Tấn and other library administrators, it was not enough that the library itself had come under the purview of a Vietnamese government; they believed that even the collection had to undergo a process of decolonization of language to encourage parity between Vietnamese and French library users. The Saigon Library held an important role in the development of education in postcolonial Vietnam, making available an expansive collection of French textbooks that served as valuable curricular and supplementary education materials for Saigon's population of students, teachers, professionals, and the self-educated public. The library translation efforts intersected with wider curricular development efforts led by Saigon teachers and intellectuals to translate and create disciplinary specific, technical Vietnamese-language vocabulary in the 1950s and 1960s.[86]

The National Library at 34 Gia Long Street inherited the collections from the old Cochinchina Library, including Indochinese and French historical periodicals such as the *Revue Indochinoise*, *Bulletin de l'École française d'Extrême-Orient*, and *Bulletin des amis du vieux Hue*. However, this initial collection lacked popular Vietnamese-language periodicals such as *Nam Phong*, *Tri Tân*, and *Đông Dương Tạp Chí*, published in Hanoi during the colonial period, or the serials were incomplete. Between 1949 and 1954 Tấn prioritized the building of the collections in two ways: the completion of missing Vietnamese-language serials and the creation of a comprehensive collection of Vietnamese, Chinese, and English works. Tấn justified the importance of building the Vietnamese collections by noting that Vietnamese had been designated as the official language of archives and governmental operations in the southern regional government. Furthermore, other initiatives focused on diversifying the French-dominated library collections with a wider range of foreign and vernacular languages, including a community effort to develop a Chinese-language collection. In 1951 the Chinese collection emerged from the collaborative efforts of the Chamber of Commerce of Cholon Overseas Chinese, led by the director Viên Thâu Thạch and chairman Phủ Lâm Anh. A committee of ethnic Chinese-Vietnamese scholars, journalists, and bookstore owners personally donated books from their private libraries and ventured to Hong Kong to purchase books. Through these private donations, the Chinese-language section of the National Library contained 3,563 chronicles, historical encyclopedias, and valuable works on Buddhist philosophy and education.[87] The English-language collection grew out of book donations from international offices such as the American and British information services, UNESCO, and the German, British, Dutch, and Indian consulates.[88]

The National Library in Saigon slowly increased and diversified its collections through purchases, gifts, and mandatory legal deposit of copies of new publications. By 1954 the collection had increased by 15,000 works, bringing the total to 79,081 books (6 percent in Vietnamese, 5 percent in Chinese, and 88 percent in French).[89] The National Library also continued to add to its popular periodicals collection a comparatively large number of Vietnamese-language periodicals as well as developing collections of English- and Chinese-language materials.[90] The slow transformation of language in the National Library paralleled wider transformations in southern society, namely the growth of the Vietnamese-language publishing sphere and an increase in student activism, which called for education reform of *trường Tây* (French-modeled schools) and the use of the Vietnamese language as the instructional language in higher education.[91]

Whereas a substantial number of Saigon library users in the late 1940s had been French, the readers shifted to majority Vietnamese in the early 1950s. During the same period the number of total readers steadily increased. In 1953 the monthly average of readers was 1,630, of whom almost 95 percent were Vietnamese. In 1954 the monthly average increased to 2,056 readers, of whom 97 percent were Vietnamese.[92] During this period the reading room at 34 Gia Long Street offered only forty-four seats, constraining the capacity for reader consultation. Students comprised the majority of Vietnamese readers and enjoyed growing clout due to their numbers. In 1954, university students formally requested the administration to shift the opening hours to later in the evening in order to accommodate readers who were busy during the day with school or work. Library administrators honored the students' request and extended opening hours, from nine in the morning until nine at night Monday through Saturday. Since the reading room usually received few readers during lunchtime, it now closed for a three-hour break at noon.[93] These adjustments to library hours point to the influence of readers in shaping library operations. By 1955 the total number of annual visits to the reading room was 31,997, averaging 110 readers per day who consulted a vast library collection numbering 80,396 works.[94]

Ever since the French colonial period, the lending section (and the well-visited children's corner [Thư viện cho Mượn và phòng Đọc thiếu nhi]) was more popular than the reading room. In March 1944 the Cochinchina Library lending section on rue Catinat (today Đồng Khởi Street), which consisted primarily of novels and popular works (literature, history, travel, and science), was moved temporarily to the city hall for safekeeping and temporarily closed in 1945 during the August Revolution and subsequent transfer of authority.[95] In 1951 the lending section collection of about ten thousand works temporarily moved to the Indochinese Circle professional association building on 14 Thủ Tướng Thinh (formerly 14 rue de Verdun and Lê Văn Duyệt, and today Cách Mạng Tháng Tám) in order to accommodate more visitors. From January to May 1954, the lending section welcomed 10,500 readers, 7,500 of them Vietnamese and 3,000 French or foreigners.[96] Fourteen percent of the readers were students who read textbooks on site or borrowed works to take home.

Envisioning a National Library within French Colonial Library Benchmarks

On June 26, 1954, Phan Vô Kỵ, the director of the Service of Archives and Library of Southern Vietnam, summarized library services from the time of French handover in 1946 to the time of writing.[97] Kỵ noted that the National Library of Southern Vietnam continued to carry out its essential services despite a severe deficit in personnel and budget. Three library personnel had been conscripted for the war, and the budget was insufficient for the size of the library and demands from readers. Kỵ argued that the Saigon library must develop into a fully functional modern institution that was worthy of the capital of an independent Vietnam:

> With the complete independence of our motherland and the designation of Saigon as the national capital, the National Library is far too small to provide services for the Saigon population of over two million. The library is too crowded, unable to store books and documents shipped to the library. With only forty-six chairs in the reading room, some readers come to the library but end up leaving due to lack of seating. The estimated annual budget of the library is not enough to purchase books or several copies of certain books in order to let readers check out the books to read at home. The hope is that the National Library will be able to expand and provide the same level of conveniences and services as other large libraries of civilized and modern countries. The National Library must become a space worthy of collecting the spiritual artifacts of a people with four thousand years of civilization.[98]

For Kỵ, the National Library had two primary tasks: the preservation of Vietnamese cultural heritage and providing a public service to the growing population of Saigon. Although he used a vague benchmark of "civilized and modern countries" to evaluate the capabilities of the library, it is significant that he depicted the library as both an everyday institution serving the public and a symbol of nationhood functioning as a repository for Vietnamese civilization. Furthermore, Ky's argument aligns with a broader intellectual and cultural movement led by Vietnamese writers and artists to redefine Saigon as the national literary capital and center of "creative freedom."[99]

In the nine-page plan entitled "Organization of the National Library" (Tổ chức Thơ Viện Quốc Gia), Lê Ngọc Trụ outlined the importance of library collections and methodic organization.[100] A self-taught linguist, Lê Ngọc Trụ (1909–79) worked in the National Library in Saigon from 1948 to 1961 as deputy secretary and then as director of the collections department from 1961 to 1964. Like other library administrators, Trụ was an intellectual in his own right outside of his work for the library. Trụ independently studied Vietnamese linguistics, published in the newspapers *Đông Dương* (1939–41), *Đọc* (1939), *Nghệ Thuật* (1941), and *Bút Mới* (1941), and was an active member of the Southern Association for Promotion of Education (Hội Khuyến Học Nam Kỳ). In 1954 Trụ became the director of the Institute of History, and he later worked as a linguistics professor at the University of Arts and University of Pedagogy in Saigon. Lê Ngọc Trụ declared that the National Library must not be merely a "storage space of books" but must be systematically organized for ease of reader access, research, and use.[101] "Books and newspapers are the foundation of the library," Trụ proclaimed. "We cannot call our library a proper institute with such a large number of books in the library organized without a rational order; with the increasing number of print media published each day, we cannot blindly purchase texts for the library without selective intention." Trụ believed that the first stage of library organization required reassessing the collections (*thâu thập sách báo*), while the later stages included organization (*sắp đặt*) and the preservation of materials (*gìn giữ sách báo*).

Lê Ngọc Trụ described in fine-grained detail the national library collections, focusing especially on accumulating books "of value." Trụ measured the value of books based on the scope and depth of their content, their rarity, and their publication date. Since the budget for book acquisitions and storage space were both limited, Trụ explained that the library director must be deliberate in book acquisitions. Trụ requested that the director first prioritize books of foundational knowledge (*căn bản*), which included encyclopedias, dictionaries, bibliographies, reference works by the French publisher Larousse, and other classic French works on geography, history, and biography. After establishing this foundational knowledge collection, the library director must follow the contemporary news on popular books to determine future acquisitions. Trụ specified that the measurement of "international cultural acclaim" could be based on the following criteria: book prizes, such as the Nobel, Goncourt, Femina, and Ville de Paris; books that were translated into French; new research on society, economics, religion, art, architecture, medicine, and science; and books about Vietnam, the French Union, and Southeast Asia. Trụ advised the library director to read the *National Bibliography of France* each month and to follow the major cultural and literary review magazines in France such as *Revue des deux Mondes, Revue de Paris, Mercure de France, Esprit, Europe, Études*, and *Nouvelles littéraires* in order to guide library purchases. Trụ's statement reveals the meticulous logic of library collections policy and his assessment of "cultural value." He outlined a hierarchy of books based on notions of value deeply rooted in French library sciences (*bibliothéconomie*) and in French literary benchmarks. The reliance on French literary reviews, the French national bibliography, and direct purchases from French booksellers was a legacy of the pervasive French colonial print economy and libraries in Indochina. As a consequence of this colonial carryover, French colonial ideas of cultural value permeated Trụ's standards for library acquisitions and the organization of the National Library in Saigon. Thus, the premier library of southern Vietnam reflected an amalgamation of colonial and postcolonial ideas, simultaneously a legacy of the French past and a concerted effort to build a national future.

Fragmenting Colonial Heritage into National Patrimony

Over the course of the First Indochina War, decolonization entailed the breakup of French Indochina as a single entity, and thus the fragmentation of the institutional repository of the colonial-era information order, the Directorate of Archives and Libraries of Indochina. The former colonial archives, libraries, and legal deposit collections in Hanoi, Saigon, Phnom Penh, Hue, and Vientiane were slowly divided between France, the State of Vietnam, Laos, and Cambodia.[102] The politically complex question of *notre patrimoine* (our patrimony) shaped the fragmentation process: What cultural heritage of a "French Indochina" rightfully belonged to France versus the postcolonial nation-states of Cambodia and Laos and competing Vietnamese authorities in the north and south? Throughout the early decisions to demarcate Indochina patrimony from 1945 to 1950, the governmental discussions were dominated by representatives from the French Fourth Republic, with minimal representation from the Associated State of Vietnam and no representatives from the Associated States of Laos, Cambodia, or the Democratic Republic of Vietnam. Claims of cultural heritage through patrimony intersected with claims of postcolonial modern nationhood and political sovereignty, reverberating throughout the French empire and the metropole.[103]

In the former Indochina region, government officials and library administrators proposed multiple conventions to reorganize the archives and libraries but failed to implement the conventions and later revised the plans in light of changing governmental regimes and the geopolitical realities of war. From June 1950 through February 1953, government officials signed a series of conventions dividing the former colonial directorate materials (libraries, archives, legal deposit) between Cambodia, France, Laos, and the State of Vietnam.[104] On June 15, 1950, head of state Bảo Đại, Prime Minister Trần Văn Hữu (State of Vietnam), and Léon Pignon (High Commissioner of France in Indochina, representing the government of the French Republic) signed the Franco-Vietnamese conventions to divide the archives of the Directorate of Archives and Libraries conserved in the Hanoi and Saigon central depots from the colonial period.[105] Along with statutes on the transfer of archives and libraries, the High Commission of Indochina negotiated the transfer of the authority over museums, schools, and monuments in Cambodia, Laos, and Vietnam and the reorganization of the École française d'Extrême-Orient. The former colonial archives, the library of Cochinchina, and legal deposit of materials on South Vietnam had already been transferred to the government of Vietnam on February 14, 1948.[106] This 1950 convention extended the previous transfer and partitioned the remaining archives in Hanoi and Saigon. Ferréol de Ferry chaired the Franco-Vietnamese conventions as well as the Franco-Cambodian conventions of 1950 to divide the archives and library in Phnom Penh.[107]

Ferréol de Ferry outlined a general concept of *historiques essentiellement françaises* (essential historical French) archives to demarcate documentary heritage belonging to French national heritage and French sovereignty.[108] This concept of patrimony divided the colonial archives between high-level *archives de souveraineté* (archives of sovereignty), which were considered the rightful property of France, and the archives of *territorialité*, archives that facilitated the on-the-ground establishment of the colonial government functions. From this framework, article 7 of the convention outlined the handover of the archives of the imperial government of the Kinh Lược (conserved in the Central Archives) and the local administration of Tonkin, Annam, and Cochinchina to the State of Vietnam. Article 8 followed the transfer of the following collections to French authorities: the archives of the French administration prior to the establishment of the Indochinese Union, the archives of the cabinet and offices of the governor general, the archives of the resident superiors and the Cochinchina governors (specifically the archives of the cabinet, institutions, and French establishments), the French tribunal, the French Civil State and Personnel, the administrative cabinets in the provinces, the residents and resident mayors, and "in general, all archives that carry a political, diplomatic, military, or private characteristic."[109] Along with the partition of the documents of the collections, the convention detailed the transfer of personnel, documentation systems, and furniture to the respective associated states. Between 1951 and 1955, nearly 1,940 boxes, or 120 metric tons, of historic documents were reassembled from Indochina and brought to France by boat.[110] The chief curator of the archives of the Ministère de la France d'outre-mer (Ministry of Overseas France), Carlo Laroche (1907–73), and Marie-Antoinette Ménier (1919–2008) oversaw the transfer.[111] The remaining archives were designated as part of local management, and the associated states would maintain the archives of the administration and local services, the provincial administration, and municipal, communal and local assemblies. Ferréol de Ferry's approach to the decolonization of the Indochina archives would later shape the demarcation of French administrative archives from Madagascar, French Equatorial Africa, and Algeria in the following years.

Separate conventions also signed by Bảo Đại, Trần Văn Hữu, and Léon Pignon on June 15, 1950, detailed the division of the Hanoi Central Library and the legal deposit between France, the State of Vietnam, Laos, and Cambodia.[112] Yet the actual implementation of this division of the Hanoi Central Library was up for debate between 1950 to 1953, involving a wider group of representatives from the Associated States of Laos, Cambodia, and Vietnam, the High Commission of France in Indochina, and the University of Hanoi. Library administrators questioned how to fairly divide up the patrimony of former Indochina and France's commitment to recolonization. An internal 1952 note posed the following questions: "Is it fair and possible that this 'federal' institution [the Hanoi library] be attributed only to Vietnam? Does France have any interest in and means of maintaining some control over this library?"[113] The author suggested financial compensation to Laos and Cambodia if the Hanoi library, which represented former Indochina, were to be divided and transferred only to Vietnamese authority; the author also proposed French financial commitment to the institution if it were to maintain any form of control. In October 1952, draft conventions on the future of the Hanoi library were discussed by Nguyễn Văn Tâm, president of the Council of Ministers of the government of Vietnam (representing the Associated State of Vietnam) and Letourneau, minister of the Associated States (representing the French Republic).[114] The convention outlined the creation of the new Bibliothèque culturelle (Thư Viện Văn Hoá) to replace the Hanoi Central Library. The Cultural Library would "use all the existing furniture and buildings of the former Directorate of Archives and Libraries in Hanoi subject to the provisions of the General Convention, and compensation [would] be granted to the states of Cambodia and Laos." This significant differentiation of Hanoi as a "Cultural Library" points to the official breaking apart of the geopolitical unit of Indochina encompassing all five regions (Cambodia, Laos, and three regions of Vietnam) and Hanoi as Indochina's former capital. From 1952 to 1953, administrators proposed the official division and dissolution of the last remnant of the former Directorate of Archives and Libraries of Indochina, the Service of Archives and Library of the High Commission (Nha Văn khó và Thư viện Cao ủy phụ). The Library of the High Commission, at 32 rue Taberd in Saigon, had served as the headquarters of the Service of Archives and Libraries of the High Commission of Indochina since its creation by Ferréol de Ferry in 1948.[115] Since its founding, this small administrative library had functioned as a figurehead of the High Commission and was attached to the French Cultural Mission Library (Thư viện của Phái bộ văn hoá Pháp) in Saigon.

On July 9, 1953, the Pierre Pasquier Library at 31 Tràng Thi in Hanoi was once again renamed Tổng Thư viện (General Library), designated as a "mixed French-Vietnamese service" jointly managed by the French director Simone de Saint-Exupéry and the Vietnamese director Trần Văn Kha, and transferred to the University of Hanoi.[116] The University of Hanoi had a long history, founded as the University of Indochina (Université indochinoise) in 1906 and reopened in

1917 during Governor General Albert Sarraut's implementation of a colonial policy of Franco-Vietnamese collaboration. A 1949 agreement between France and Bảo Đại's State of Vietnam had transformed the University of Indochina into the University of Hanoi (also called the Université mixte Franco-Vietnamienne), which was then run by a joint French-Vietnamese faculty and had a smaller branch in Saigon. By 1953 the Hanoi General Library collection contained approximately 130,000 works in French, 17,000 in Vietnamese, 2,000 in English, and 400 in German.[117] In addition to attaching the Hanoi General Library to the University of Hanoi, administrators emphasized the continued attachment of the library to the former central archives, stressing the impossibility of dividing the archives collection among four states. Furthermore, the training courses for archivist-librarians had been under the technical management of the director of the General Library, and the archival training had to take place in the Central Archives depot located on the ground floor of a building in the same compound as the General Library.[118] According to the December 1953 statistics, the Central Archives maintained more than two hundred thousand dossiers on the Government General and the General Services, as well as the North Vietnam Archives (local and provincial archives).[119] On January 20, 1954, the board of directors of the General Library of Hanoi met again to discuss the future of the library. The meeting began with the following anecdote: "The president of the board of directors responded with surprise when he realized the importance of the General Library, which exceeded in importance even many libraries in the capitals in France."[120] At this same meeting interim director Simone de Saint-Exupéry, with high recommendation from Ferréol de Ferry, nominated Trần Văn Kha as the sole director of the Hanoi General Library.

The End of the First Indochina War: Division and Transfer of the General Library and Archives to Saigon

In January 1950 the Soviet Union and People's Republic of China began to formally provide military arms, state-building advisors, and financial support to the Democratic Republic of Vietnam. Chinese Communist Party advisors assisted the DRV state in both state building and warfare, providing a Maoist-style model for statecraft and social mobilization strategies (rectification and emulation campaigns, land reform, and peasant recruitment), as well as guerrilla warfare and conventional army tactics. At the same time the United States also began to provide aid to France and the Associated States of Vietnam, Laos, and Cambodia as part of the transnational war against the spread of communism. On May 7, 1954, General Võ Nguyên Gíap led a siege against the French army at Điện Biên Phủ, leading to one of the most symbolic battles in colonial history and one of the most staggering military losses in French history. Negotiations to officially end the war began in Geneva led by France, Great Britain, the Soviet Union, the United States, and the People's Republic of China, with representatives from the Associated States of Vietnam, Laos, and Cambodia and the Democratic Republic of Vietnam. By

July 21, 1954, at the Geneva Conference the DRV and France had signed an armistice and declaration that separated the country at the seventeenth parallel with the pledge of organized elections to reunify the country of Vietnam in two years. Based in Saigon, Ngô Đình Diệm was chosen as prime minister of the State of Vietnam (which later became the Republic of Vietnam [RVN], or Việt Nam Cộng Hoà, on October 26, 1955) with support from the United States. Returning to its headquarters in Hanoi, Hồ Chí Minh's government led the Democratic Republic of Vietnam (DRV), extending communist social and government organization throughout North Vietnam. By October 10, 1954, the General Library in Hanoi was again renamed Thư Viện Trung Ương Hà Nội (Hanoi Central Library) and resumed everyday operations as the new national library. The Hanoi newspaper *Nhân Dân* announced the library's reopening and operating hours on October 19, 1954, which were to be 7:30 to 11 a.m. and 2 p.m. to 5 p.m.[121]

The Geneva Accords of July 20, 1954, which partitioned Vietnam at the end of the war, also marked the formal diplomatic division of the General Library and Central Archives in Hanoi and the transfer of the University of Hanoi to Saigon. Between May 11 and May 26, 1955, soldiers of the State of Vietnam transported boxes of documents, books, and newspapers from the Hanoi General Library, Central Archives, and University of Hanoi to Saigon.[122] The transferred materials included over seventeen thousand books, half of the serials from the colonial period, the archives of the Kinh Lược viceroy located in northern Vietnam (thirty-eight boxes), and thirty-five thousand legal deposit items, which combined to total over seven hundred boxes.[123] Administrators claimed that most of the transferred collections were duplicate copies or from the Indochina legal deposit collected up to June 1954. The Hanoi General Library was first attached to the University of Saigon and then later moved under the secretary of state for the Ministry of National Education.[124] The former University of Hanoi was named Viện Đại học Quốc gia Việt Nam (National University of Vietnam) and later changed to Viện Đại học Sài Gòn (Saigon University).[125] In addition to the movement of materials, sixteen library and archives personnel and university faculty were officially transferred from Hanoi to Saigon. These transferred librarians, archivists, and professors joined the migration of over a million Vietnamese citizens who moved during the three-hundred-day period of open migration, most of whom moved south due to ideological, religious, and personal reasons.[126] Up until he passed away on December 28, 1955, the former director of the Hanoi library, Trần Văn Kha, continued his work in the libraries and archives. In collaboration with Simone de Saint-Exupéry, Kha oversaw the transfer of the Hanoi collections to Saigon from 1954 to 1955.

According to a report from 1955 by the archivist-librarian Nguyễn Hùng Cường, who was transferred to Saigon from the Hanoi General Library, the move signaled the "transformation of the General Library into a completely Vietnamese (library)."[127] For Cường, the physical movement of the Hanoi collections southward suggested the official separation of the General Library from its Hanoi and French colonial lineage and the library's rebirth as a Vietnamese national institution based in Saigon. A French daily newspaper article from 1956 noted that at the time of the relocation to Saigon, the Hanoi library was "considered the largest and most valuable library in Vietnam and judged by other countries as the second greatest in the Far East."[128] Although French and southern Vietnamese commentators remarked on the recentralization and claim of Vietnamese literary heritage through the transfer of the Hanoi collection, the decision to divide and transfer the remaining library and archives materials seemed to be devoid of representation from the administration of the Democratic Republic of Vietnam.

CONCLUSION

The decolonization of the former Directorate of Archives and Libraries of Indochina was not a clearly thought-out plan of nationalization. It was instead a result of wartime fatigue and a continued tentative strategy of the conservation of literary heritage based on changing political regimes and competing authorities. Throughout the First Indochina War, library and archive materials had been slowly fragmented to France and the states of Laos, Cambodia, and Vietnam in a tentative state of semicolonial governance of associated states and joint French-Vietnamese management of institutions. The political decisions regarding the demarcations of literary heritage aligned with French and American political support of the southern Vietnamese regime as the new center and protector of Vietnamese heritage. The removal of Hanoi as the center of Indochina documentation had begun with the French reconquest of Saigon in the fall of 1945 and the designation as the capital as the location of continuing efforts of a service of archives and libraries of former Indochina in 1948. In 1950 the French-Vietnamese convention signed in 1950 between head of state Bảo Đại, Prime Minister Trần Văn Hữu (State of Vietnam), and Léon Pignon (the High Commissioner of France in Indochina, representing the government of the French Republic) determined the division of the colonial archives. These early patrimonial negotiations resulted in the movement to France of the higher-level colonial administrative archives such as those of the cabinet and offices of the governor general, the resident superiors and the Cochinchina governors, the French tribunal, the French civil state and personnel, the administrative cabinets in the provinces, the residents, and the resident mayors. The 1954–55 movement from Hanoi to the Saigon National Library of a sizable portion of the legal deposit, colonial periodicals, and personnel was a haphazard carryover of earlier efforts to fragment colonial Indochina institutions during French attempts to implement a semicolonial federation. The aftermath of these divisions of former Indochina patrimony would impact the organization of national collections in the postcolonial southern and northern Vietnamese states for the next decades. Furthermore, these rushed historic decisions have left long-term legacies upon access to documentary heritage, where the colonial Indochina collections have been divided and integrated into present-day national archives such as the extensive French Archives nationales d'outre mer in Aix-en-Provence, which holds the archives of the French colonial empire.

By 1955 the colonial information order of former Indochina—the libraries, archives, legal deposit, and directorate office—was fragmented and reassembled in the distinct nation-states of the Democratic Republic of Vietnam, Republic of Vietnam, Kingdom of Laos, and Kingdom of Cambodia. The former colonial libraries turned national institutions inherited and made sense of their colonial heritage, grappling with the legacies of the French colonial library: the colonial infrastructure such as buildings and concentration in urban centers; the collections dominated by French-language sources; the library operations based on French library sciences; the limited public use of the libraries that privileged urban Francophone reader elites; and a colonial mission of libraries that functioned as instruments of French modernization and cultural propaganda. Throughout the periods of regime transitions and political conflict from 1945 to 1954, Vietnamese librarians of the Hanoi and Saigon institutions undertook extensive campaigns to reevaluate collections and procedures and to translate terminologies and train personnel. Part of this process was a critical evaluation of the inequity and failures of the colonial library and the envisioning of a Vietnamese national library with a distinctively postcolonial mission. Within the constraints of French recolonization efforts, many of these visions of a postcolonial Vietnamese library took the shape of operational grafting and tentative reassemblage. Yet by 1955 two distinct Vietnamese nation-states, with national capitals in Hanoi and Saigon, were competing for Vietnamese cultural and political authority. In these two national capitals were two national libraries that confronted their colonial legacies and reimagined a postcolonial Vietnamese national library that truly served the Vietnamese nation and public.

Epilogue

This book uncovered the emergence of a colonial public transformed by their direct experiences within and confrontations with the Hanoi Central Library and Saigon Cochinchina Library. Libraries functioned as institutions of hegemony that formalized a body of colonial knowledge on Indochina and a Francophone-dominated Western literary canon through its collections and documentation regime. The Hanoi and Saigon libraries implemented a colonial governmentality through its restrictions on library access and control of reader behaviors. While serving as tools of the French colonial information order, a distinctive public reading culture emerged within the infrastructures of the library. Public reading culture was characterized as urban social life within the public space, self-directed reading of literary collections, and engagements with the state bureaucracy. Public reading culture was an experiment in modern subjecthood and collective political identity through the experience of individualized reading within a colonial state-mediated space. Readers participated in bureaucratic procedures of applying for reader cards and submitting themselves to a contract of shared use of public goods, and through these interactions they engaged with the modern state and participatory citizenship in a tangible everyday fashion. Reading a range of literature, media forms, and local and global news in the colonial library facilitated a distinctly modern cosmopolitan sensibility characterized by self-directed learning and leisure-driven erudition. Given the concentration of library institutions in Hanoi and Saigon, the colonial public was comprised of primarily urban-based French and Vietnamese government officials, Vietnamese students, and French women. Within the colonial period, the library was explicitly a standing contradiction: It purported to be an instrument of intellectual emancipation yet was contained within the structures of French colonial hegemony, Francophone knowledge, and paternalistic social control defined by civilizing discourse and cultural moralization. This book uncovered how the library was a tactical space where Vietnamese readers pursued alternative uses of the library that exceeded its hegemonic intentions of cultural propaganda. Everyday Vietnamese readers reinscribed the urban space as social centers and envisioned political identities of nationhood based on public access, vernacular language, and literary heritage. Others publicly advocated for the reform of state libraries or collectively organized alternative public libraries of *quốc ngữ* literature that served the *bình dân*, expanding the urban reading public to include rural populations, women, and youth. These forms of individual and collective organizing fostered social, language, and nationalist belonging that stretched well past the library's doors.

This epilogue addresses the fundamental transformations and legacies of the colonial information order and public reading culture in the postcolonial nation building of the Democratic Republic of Vietnam (DRV) and Republic of Vietnam (RVN). Focused on the postcolonial national library institutions in Hanoi and Saigon, I point to the ways in which the libraries diverged, driven by different political regimes and social demographics. The signing of the Geneva Accords at the end of the First Indochina War in 1954 divided Vietnam into a communist-led DRV in the north and an anticommunist republicanism-driven RVN in the south. Librarian administrators of the national libraries in Hanoi and Saigon confronted the legacies of the colonial information order in its buildings, operations, collections, and mission. Yet the role of libraries in the postcolonial states took on a distinct form because of a new urgency to define the legitimate postcolonial nation-states of the DRV and the RVN in the context of civil, ideological, and international-based warfare during the Second Indochina War (1956–75) between the Soviet Union– and China-backed DRV and the United States–backed RVN. During these years, in both the northern and southern states, building the national library went hand in hand with building the nation-state, governmental institutions, national culture, and popular legitimacy. The Hanoi and Saigon national libraries functioned as important political and cultural symbols of Vietnamese nationhood as well as spaces for reading, research, and education.

During the first years of Vietnamese postcolonial nation building, the southern Republic of Vietnam library grafted upon existing colonial infrastructure and modernist discourse to integrate the national library as a keystone of building a modern nation-state and democracy in the capital of Saigon. State efforts by the Republic of Vietnam to outline its political vision of republicanism intersected with the practices of public reading culture, characterized as a political-cultural ideology of self-determinism, individualism, and cosmopolitanism.[1] The Saigon RVN library focused on postcolonial republican nation building through the urban landscape of libraries and reading culture. In comparison, the northern Hanoi DRV library adopted Soviet-inspired library models to enact an alternative anticolonial information order focused on the distribution of politically aligned, "rectified" reading matter to the rural masses. Building revolution through mass culture and mass education was of central importance to the Democratic Republic of Vietnam. The library was a key institution for spreading print media and for quantifying socialist transformation. Both the northern and southern states recognized the important role of the library as an instrument of state hegemony, one that could build national legitimacy and distribute cultural propaganda that aligned with the nation-state project of competing Vietnamese state authorities.

SAIGON: REPUBLICAN NATION AND PUBLIC READING CULTURE

In 1955 RVN government officials reignited long-standing plans to build a national library in Saigon with the political vision of building a republican nation. Officials outlined an ambitious proposal to construct the National Library and Cultural Center (Thư Viện Quốc Gia và Trung Tâm Văn Hoá), with a 150-seat reading room, an eight-story storage building large enough for at least three hundred thousand volumes, a cultural center with two lecture rooms, and an auditorium that could hold up to a thousand attendees.[2] Officials used the project to showcase the RVN as the guardian of Vietnamese culture and the legitimate government to preserve and represent Vietnamese culture and history domestically and globally. At the inaugural ceremony for the project on July 3, 1956, President Ngô Đình Diệm declared, "Our country stands as a trailblazer in Southeast Asia—we remember the lessons gifted to us from our ancestors. In addition, our national spirit must evolve in concert with that of the modern peoples of the free world."[3]

President Ngô Đình Diệm proposed to construct the building on the site of the former Saigon Maison Centrale prison (Tù Khám Lớn) at 69 Gia Long Street (now 69 Lý Tự Trọng). At a later bricklaying ceremony that officially marked the beginning of construction in 1968, Mai Thọ Truyền, the secretary of state in charge of cultural affairs, delivered a speech emphasizing the legacy of the colonial prison and the significance of the library for national culture: "Those tiles and stones of the former prison left on the ground bear witness to the noble sacrifices of those fighting for the nation's freedom and its culture. The ghosts of these heroes, if any of them are still haunting this site, certainly would be satisfied with our present enterprise, which aims at protecting and developing our national culture."[4] He continued to describe his dream of the new national library as a "meeting center for Eastern and Western cultures as well as a source of information and communication for mankind." Due to immense wartime difficulties and political instability, the construction of the new building did not officially began until 1968, and the location was not opened until December 23, 1971.

From 1954 to 1971, the national library system existed in a tentative state of frantic operations, struggling to serve the increasing population of Saigon readers.

FIGURE 36. President of the Republic of Vietnam Ngô Đình Diệm inaugurates the Saigon National Library and Cultural Center building project on July 3, 1956, with a bricklaying ceremony. *Source*: Nha Văn khố và Thư viện Quốc gia, Trung tâm lưu trữ quốc gia 2, Ho Chi Minh City, Vietnam, folder 1022, and *Việt Nam Thông Tấn Xã*, no. 1949 (July 3, 1956, afternoon edition), Phủ Tổng Thống Đệ Nhất Cộng Hòa, Trung tâm lưu trữ quốc gia 2, folder 18141.

While the new library building was being constructed at 69 Gia Long Street, the national library system was managed by the Ministry of National Education and comprised three locations scattered throughout Saigon: the reading and consultation library at 34 Gia Long Street, formerly the French colonial Cochinchina Library and since 1949 known as the National Library (Thơ Viện Quốc Gia); the General Library (Thơ viện Tổng Hợp), located at Petrus Ky School, which housed the seven hundred boxes transferred from Hanoi and opened to the public in 1957; and the lending section and children's reading room (Thơ Viện Cho Mượn và

FIGURE 37. Front view of the new Thư Viện Quốc Gia building, at 69 Lý Tự Trọng Street, Saigon, ca. 1971. *Source*: Nha Văn khố và Thư viện Quốc gia, Trung tâm lưu trữ quốc gia 2, Ho Chi Minh City, Vietnam, folder 1022.

FIGURE 38. Rear view of the new Thư Viện Quốc Gia building featuring a fourteen-story storage depot, at 69 Lý Tự Trọng Street, Saigon, ca. 1971. *Source*: Nha Văn khố và Thư viện Quốc gia, Trung tâm lưu trữ quốc gia 2, Ho Chi Minh City, Vietnam, folder 1022.

Phòng Đọc Thiếu Nhi) at 194D Pasteur Street, formerly the colonial-era Cochinchina Library lending section, which reopened on April 1958. The reading room at 34 Gia Long Street inherited the colonial-era collections, building, and operations, yet now it was tasked with serving a rapidly growing population of urban Vietnamese as well as functioning as the national library for South Vietnam. Regular reports make clear that the everyday state of library affairs in the new republic was poor, fragile, and disorganized. Along with other administrative departments in the new government, the Service of Archives and Library of South Vietnam was severely understaffed at all levels—from high-level management to typists and guards—and it urgently organized several courses to train civil servants in documentation work. Everyday infractions such as stolen trash cans and disruptive library patrons demonstrated how the library lacked guards and monitors for the reading room. On March 4, 1957, a library administrator even deplored the poor state of the building, reporting that pieces of the ceiling fell off during reading hours and nearly hit readers.[5]

Vietnamese archivists and librarians remained embedded within a Western-leaning international documentation world, engaging in French professional associations and the French National Bibliography, participating in international conferences and organizations such as UNESCO, and working alongside American initiatives in the RVN such as the Michigan University Vietnam Advisory Group.[6] In an effort to raise the profile of the national library in the international arena, library administrators actively requested books and serials on contemporary politics, science, libraries, and economics from France, new books from America, and other contemporary international works. At the same time, Vietnamese librarian administrators sought to transform and nationalize the library through its collections and services. Librarians such as Phan Vô Kỵ, Nguyễn Gia Phương, and Hoàng Tuấn Anh later founded the Library Association of Vietnam (Hội Thư Viện Việt Nam), which contributed to shaping Vietnamese librarianship as a profession and produced the journal *Library Review* (*Thư Viện Tập San*).[7] Library administrators continued to actively add more Vietnamese works to its predominantly Francophone inherited colonial collections. The National Library also now served as the official legal deposit location for new publications, reflecting a dynamic and shifting landscape of public reading culture in Saigon in the 1950s characterized by Vietnamese, multilingual, and translated works. In 1957, 1,946 Vietnamese-language works and 132 French-language works were deposited into the library.[8] That year there was also a substantial number of legal deposits in other languages as well as bilingual or trilingual works, including works in English (98), Vietnamese-English (80), Vietnamese-French (26), Vietnamese-Chinese (32), English-Chinese (4), and Vietnamese-French-English (2). Periodical legal deposits were mainly in Vietnamese (833), followed by those in French (60), English (39), Vietnamese-English (49), Vietnamese-French (13), and Vietnamese-Chinese (12). In addition to new literary works published in Vietnamese, many of the works

FIGURE 39. Crowd of visitors at an event held at the National Library (Thơ Viện Quốc Gia) at 34 Gia Long Street, Saigon ca. 1956–1971. *Source*: Nha Văn khố và Thư viện Quốc gia, Trung tâm lưu trữ quốc gia 2, Ho Chi Minh City, Vietnam, folder 1022.

in the library were Vietnamese translations from French translations of other language books such as Margaret Mitchell's *Gone with the Wind* or Carlo Lorenzini's Italian-language *Pinocchio*.[9] In 1956, visitors to the reading room could freely peruse the open shelves of reference books, dictionaries, encyclopedia, manuals, and more than fifty journals in French, Vietnamese, and English, or they could submit a request to consult a book from its collection of approximately eighty thousand works.[10]

The limited space in the National Library building at 34 Gia Long Street left it unable to meet the needs of the reading public, and administrators developed policies to restrict access, enforce regulations, and favor certain readers while shutting out others. The growth of the population in Saigon led to increased demand, and the library reported a daily average of two hundred users in the late 1950s, which was double the number of users during the colonial period. Although administrators and foreign readers still relied on the library, university students now made up the majority of users. This shift in clientele reflected the expansion of higher education in the RVN due to the relocation of the University of Hanoi and the most prestigious high schools in Hanoi to Saigon.[11] Students were the most ardent and eager readers, actively using the library to access expensive textbooks and reference matter and to supplement classroom materials with valuable periodicals, novels, and translated texts. Yet the reading room only had forty-eight seats, and Saigon readers competed to secure a spot.

In a letter to the police, the library director Phan Vô Kỵ explained that the problem was especially acute during the summer holiday, when earnest students aggressively fought over the limited seats and crowded out other library users:

> During the summer months, university students clamber in front of the library doors before the morning and noon opening hours. When the library reopens, students rush and flood the central staircase—yelling and pushing each other, necessitating the military police to come to keep them quiet. Because of this commotion, female students hesitate to be part of the scramble and instead retreat home.[12]

In a letter to the Ministry of National Education in 1957, Phan Vô Kỵ proposed a system of daily reading cards to allocate the limited number of seats according to whether one was a student, professor, or official.[13] Kỵ developed this system to restore order to the reading room and as well as to implement greater surveillance of "greedy readers and thieves."[14] The new regulations included a clause that emphasized the communal and public use of the library: "For the benefit of the collective, the library requests that readers protect the books and newspapers by not writing on them, folding the pages, or overextending the binding." Readers were also required to return reference books where they belonged "to convenience and not disadvantage other readers." For the first time, the rules also included a clause that permitted the library to refuse entrance to any reader who "dressed inappropriately or behaved impolitely." Library administrators called for a "complete education" for readers, issuing detailed regulations on reader behavior and the proper care of library materials.[15] These extensive rules defined proper reader comportment within a modern public library, amplifying colonial-era discourse on public decorum and modern subjectivity.[16] The distinction between leisure and serious readers and the decision to prioritize the latter reflected a continual debate over the mission of the libraries in Vietnam to serve as a modern symbol of nationhood and public space of erudition.

In this intertwined period of state building, national legitimacy, and global and civil conflict, the mission of the library in Saigon was brought into question. As in the colonial period, the library held tremendous symbolic value, representing both modern library techniques and state capacity. Administrators of the Saigon National Library situated their institution within international library sciences, seeking to create in urban Saigon a cosmopolitan postcolonial center for modern knowledge. Administrators envisioned a new social, political, and educational mission of the library as both a national and a public institution.[17] In 1956 a library administrator ambitiously declared the National Library to be "a library of information and general culture. With a collection of selectively chosen books and intended for the public, the library has a three-part goal like all public libraries: to inform, to educate, and to entertain."[18] Administrators used republican values to justify the importance of the library to provide educational resources to its diverse reading publics, including Vietnamese students, administrators, foreign researchers, and general readers. The National Library symbolized the vast political idealism of 1950s republicanism in the RVN, characterized by the value of public access and civil society, governmental responsibility to a collective citizenry, and the cultivation of liberal free thinkers through modern cosmopolitan institutions.

HANOI: COMMUNIST INFORMATION ORDER AND QUANTIFYING CULTURE

In stark contrast to the Saigon National Library's urban focus and grafting upon colonial operations and collections, the Hanoi National Library completely redefined its mission as part of mass culture and rural education. With the signing of the 1954 Geneva Accords and the return of the communist government to Hanoi on October 10, the Democratic Republic of Vietnam envisioned the role, functions, and organization of libraries as part of a new anticolonial information order defined by communist ideology and building a socialist society. The library was again renamed, from General Library (Tổng Thư viện) to Hanoi Central Library (Thư viện Trung ương Hà Nội), and in 1958 the library was officially renamed the National Library (Thư Viện Quốc Gia). The new regime confronted the profound infrastructure of the Hanoi library, which was defined by Franco-Vietnamese collaboration and operated as the largest collection of Francophone knowledge and Indochina print culture and as the center of "public reading culture" of cosmopolitan erudition and socialization, especially for Vietnamese youth during the colonial era. Between 1954 and 1958 the Hanoi National Library enacted a campaign of cultural and literary rectification of its library collections.[19] A 1954 to 1957 report summarized the state of the library after the communist takeover of Hanoi: "When our government was able to take over the capital, the Central Library was in a state of disarray: The reading room was closed, a portion of the books and newspapers the enemy had taken away; the remaining number of works were left in chaos and stored slapdash in the middle of the reading room, [and] furniture and things were scattered here and there."[20] Similarly, the archives were also left in a state of disorder, scattered across its four floors. The library report stated that library personnel and cadres quickly restored order, reopening the library and continuing unceasing services to readers. Commending its reader services, the library reported that "a rectification of the organization of services has improved services to readers at the same time as educating them." The report documented that readers increased from 195 to 268 per day, distributing 102,455 books by the end of 1955.

Much of the report was focused on the two staged tasks of the cultural rectification of the Hanoi collections: purging the inherited colonial-era collections and acquiring works that aligned with the cultural policy of the Democratic Republic of Vietnam's political regime. The report recounted the labor of excising colonial knowledge in detail:

> The work of purging the reactionary, backwards, and romantic books and newspapers has been carried out (over nine thousand books have been purged) in order to prevent the spread of reactionary, backwards thinking and the depraved cultural poisons of feudal imperialists who inflict harm upon readers, of whom a large part are young students.

The second task of cultural rectification involved a "vigorous" acquisitions campaign intended to rebuild the library collections. First, the "CP 15 Library," a library of ten thousand works that had been evacuated to the Việt Bắc region, a far northern region that was the base for the DRV during the First Indochina War, was reintegrated into the Hanoi National Library.[21] The report emphasized the efforts of the DRV legal deposit, describing the legal deposit as a fundamental task of "establishing a cultural treasury of our country." The author emphasized that the Geneva divisions stole the entirety of the legal deposit collection, leaving behind only a handful of old, damaged, ripped newspapers in the National Library. As part of reparative efforts to rebuild the documentation on Vietnamese communist history, a retrospective legal deposit was initiated during these early years, and the National Library acquired selected works from the CP 15 Library, from the 1945–46 DRV government, and from the time of the takeover of the capital. The report mentioned that acquiring rare works such as early issues of reviews and the magazines *Sự Thật* (Truth) and *Cứu Quốc* (Saving the Nation) functioned as an important national heritage resource, providing a valuable tool for government offices as well as research materials on "bourgeois" and "enemy" culture.

Through these tasks of rectification and collections development, administrators of the Hanoi National Library created an anticolonial information order embedded within the political and technical world of socialist knowledge. The National Library carried out international book exchanges through DRV embassies in the Soviet Union, the People's Republic of China, and the German Democratic Republic. In 1956, the Soviet National Library and China National Library gifted sixty-thousand works to the National Library in Hanoi, enriching the collections on revolution and Marxism; this year also marked the building of a revolutionary reading room in the library space. In 1957, the National Library embarked on an infrastructural network building project, *thư viện kết nghĩa*, connecting all the libraries in the provinces. Between 1957 and 1960 the National Library developed seven two- to four-month courses to train library workers as part of a longer vision of developing the libraries profession, building libraries in provinces, and creating a networked infrastructure of public libraries. The National Library followed Soviet models of information infrastructure and positioned libraries as part of the project of the global revolution of culture and technology. At the end of 1961 the National Library started to organize subject alphabetic card catalogs and applied a Vietnamized version of the Soviet Union cataloging systems, including the seventeen-class Classification Schedule (Khung 17 lớp), and later applied the Bibliotechno Bibliograficheskaija Klassifikacija (BBK), also called the

Library-Bibliographical Classification Soviet (LBC) framework.[22] The BBK system reflected a Soviet ideological paradigm by organizing print culture into categories in the following schematic order: Marxism-Leninism, sciences, technology, industries, history, economics, state politics, and finally humanistic fields such as culture-science, art, religion-atheism, and philosophy-sciences. This schematic top-down classification of works into natural sciences, applied sciences (technology, agriculture, and medicine) and the social sciences (or the humanities) differed significantly from Paul Boudet's "methodic catalog" system, which claimed to respond to the specific content topics of the Hanoi Central Library collections, as well as coded books based on their size and acquisitions number.[23]

By 1956 the DRV administration had initiated a top-down comprehensive information order of communist culture, moving the National Library from the Ministry of National Education to the newly renamed Ministry of Culture (formerly the Ministry of Propaganda). The Ministry of Culture was responsible for all institutions and activities related to "cultural work"—mass culture, libraries, publishing, museums, exhibitions, art, and cinema—and was subdivided in a way that extended down to the commune (*xã*) level. Kim N. B. Ninh describes this cultural order as a state-controlled creation of civil society within the vision of a socialist system.[24] Official communist policy in the DRV defined culture in materialist terms through cultural products (books, music, film) and institutions (libraries, museums, cultural houses). Culture was also seen as a pragmatic tool for building a new socialist society. The DRV state prioritized the production and circulation of books "of value," such as scientific and technical manuals, language primers, works of Lenin, and socialist realist texts.[25]

In September 1956 the Ministry of Culture published its "Report on the State of Culture," criticizing the "eighty years of colonial state oppression."[26] The report argued that in the past two years, the new DRV state was comparatively more successful in "advancing culture" than the many decades of French colonialism. The report defended this claim by calling out French failures to provide the Vietnamese masses access to cultural resources such as libraries, books, and cinema. It argued that the French colonial authorities only dedicated "1/1000th of its budget for cultural projects" and established a few cultural institutions that served only the urban upper classes. The report stated that "in 1939 only three libraries (Hanoi, Saigon, and Phnom Penh), twenty-two cinemas, and twenty opera houses existed. In the same year, only 1,560,000 books were printed, which averaged to only one book for every fifteen people."[27] In comparison, the report boasted the following statistics on DRV cultural production and distribution: "From January 1955 to September 1956, the Central Publishing Branch [Ngành Xuất Bản Trung Ương] distributed over 8,321,482 books and newspapers . . . averaging one book for every two people. All twenty-nine provinces in the north have a municipal library . . . [and] over one hundred cultural exhibitions were held all over the country, attracting tens of millions of viewers." While these outcries read as communist indictments of colonial oppression, they shed light on two fundamental claims regarding culture and the new communist nation-state. First, the development of "culture" was a measure of state legitimacy and the state's commitment to its citizens. Second, "culture" and social transformation could be quantified through the number of libraries, books, film, and other cultural products (*văn hoá phẩm*).

Libraries continued to serve state hegemonic operations in the postcolonial period, yet with different political and ideological aims. According to the DRV vision of culture, libraries and reading matter could be an instrument for spreading revolutionary thinking and socialist ideas to the people. In principle, these ideas would build a loyal citizenry committed to the ideological and political platform of the Vietnamese Communist Party of the DRV state. By the 1950s most of the rural population had only a basic literacy in the national language, *quốc ngữ*, so DRV strategies involved not only libraries and print culture but also other forms of media (radio, imagery, music) in distributing communist ideology. The communist state combined education, literacy, and ideology as an interwoven cultural project, which paralleled the 1930s projects to extend French colonial propaganda and intellectual hegemony into the countryside. These institutionalized methods of "colonizing the minds" reflect the tactics of authoritarian regimes to expand government legitimacy through culture, education, and language. Newly organized departments such as the Central Book Distributor (Sở Phát Hành Sách Trung Ương) and the Central Vietnamese Printer (Quốc Doanh In Việt Nam) attempted to systematically bring cultural and social transformation to the countryside through the production and distribution of books. The Central Book Distributor brought to the countryside new technical primers on agriculture and hero memoirs for socialist emulation.[28] The materials brought to the countryside emphasized "practical" knowledge and included guides on technology, agriculture, and language. Ideally, the distributor would send to the countryside cadres to introduce new books as well as build libraries in rural towns and villages. In practice, however, these projects were rarely realized, and popular reception of these top-down initiatives are difficult to ascertain without further research using unofficial sources. On November 23, 1959, the party issued Directive 172 CT/TU, emphasizing the importance of "instilling reading practices among cadres and the people, and motivating people to read books for the purpose of improving their level of politics, culture, profession, and technology."[29] By 1960 the Ministry of Culture was praising the widespread success of a "reading movement." The report exclaimed that people had stopped reading novels and newspapers "and instead rush to read argumentative books, science, and works of research, for example, the works of Marx-Lenin, Hồ Chí Minh, and other leaders of the party. . . . There are never enough books shipped from the Central Book Distributor [to meet their needs]."[30] The report portrayed an overwhelmingly positive reception of ideological books by all readers. While most likely an exaggeration, this argumentative framing reveals how the DRV government measured social and ideological transformation. The measurement of state legitimacy was directly correlated with the distribution and reception of communist texts and technological primers. In northern Vietnam top-down policies of library development and book distribution had transformed the colonial library policy of "readers finding their books" to a system where "books [would] find their readers."[31]

THE BIBLIOTACTICS OF THE COLONIAL INFORMATION ORDER AND PUBLIC READING CULTURE

With the end of the Second Indochina War in 1975, the two library institutions transformed once more under the political regime of the Socialist Republic of Vietnam with Hanoi as the designated national capital. The postwar nation and war-torn society underwent prolonged challenges due to the Third Indochina War conflicts, centrally planned economic programs, reeducation camps, and the mass exodus of Vietnamese. Beginning with *đổi mới* (renovation) reforms, the past decades have witnessed substantive changes in Vietnamese economic growth, international engagement, and urbanization. What remains of the two libraries after decades of warfare and rebuilding of society and infrastructure? The former Central Library in Hanoi, the Pierre Pasquier Library and former symbol of Franco-Vietnamese collaboration, now operates as the Thư Viện Quốc Gia on 31 Tràng Thi (Examination Grounds) Street. Recently celebrating its centennial, the National Library stands as a symbol of national prestige and cultural identity for the Socialist Republic of Vietnam. In everyday practice, the reading rooms of the National Library are heavily frequented by university students, researchers, mothers, and their children. The library building has been extensively transformed and expanded with an attached multistory building added behind the former colonial-era building to function as the primary space for wide-ranging reader services, including a main reading room where one can consult requested materials from storage, separate rooms for consulting digitized materials and periodicals, a researcher and businessmen reading room, a social sciences and humanities reading room for contemporary works with open shelving for self-directed selection, and a newly opened children's library.[32] The former colonial-era reading room space now serves as the entryway and central foyer for exhibitions and has an application desk for reader cards and several computers for consulting the library catalog.

In 1971 the National Library in South Vietnam completed the new expansive building on 69 Lý Tự Trọng Street in Saigon (now Ho Chi Minh City), yet it only operated as a national library for a few years, until the end of the Republic of Vietnam regime in 1975. Now the building is known as the Thư Viện Khoa Học Tổng Hợp (General Sciences Library); it contains the legacy of its inherited colonial Cochinchina Library collections and the RVN collections developed from 1955 to

FIGURE 40. Vietnamese readers, many of them youth, in the periodicals section of the newly opened Thư Viện Quốc Gia, at 69 Lý Tự Trọng Street, Saigon, ca. 1971–1975. *Source:* Nha Văn khố và Thư viện Quốc gia, Trung tâm lưu trữ quốc gia 2, Ho Chi Minh City, Vietnam, folder 1022.

1975, which function as the historic collections for the well-utilized researcher's room. This library now operates as a leading research and public library in the southern region of Vietnam. It organizes circulating book vehicles in the countryside and provides technical training for provincial libraries; it also functions as a public gathering space for events like cinema screenings and exhibitions. Its main reading room and designated children's reading room are consistently crowded with Saigon inhabitants.

Just down the street from the General Sciences Library stands the former Cochinchina Library building on 34 Lý Tự Trọng Street. Today it operates as a specialist research library, the Thư Viện Khoa Học Xã Hội (Social Science Library), yet on touring its closed stacks in summer 2023 I found vestiges of the 1950s and 1960s, when it served the Saigon reading public out of its small space. In the now "restricted collection" are American political books like *Viet Cong: The Organization and Techniques of the National Liberation Front of South Vietnam* (1966), written by the public affairs officer for USIS, Douglas Pike; Robert Dahl's study of democracy and representation, *Who Governs?* (1961); global classics in English, like Mary Shelley's *Frankenstein* (1818) and Ray Bradbury's *Fahrenheit 451* (1953);

and popular works like *Gideon's Day* (1955), a police novel by English author John Creasey, known for detective, crime, and science fiction books. The collection also includes books from the French colonial period such as histories of the Far East and maps, French-language works like *Souffrances et bonheur du chrétien* (Sufferings and Happiness of the Christian) by François Mauriac (1931), who was known for his work on Catholicism and morality, and collected volumes of important *quốc ngữ* publications such as the research magazine *Bách Khoa* (Encyclopedia), which operated from 1957 to 1975. Three card catalog cases built during the French colonial period remain in the central foyer of the second floor. One card catalog reflects the BBK classification system that Hanoi mandated be implemented throughout scientific and large libraries in post-1975 unified Vietnam. That system has now been replaced by the Dewey Decimal Classification (DDC) system, adopted in 2006 in the Hanoi National Library, implemented throughout Vietnamese libraries beginning in 2011, and now integrated within the digital catalog system. The collections and organization reflect a palimpsest of political regime transformations, French and American cultural propaganda, and contending Vietnamese states that sought to demarcate and carve out a postcolonial national vision.

Beyond the Hanoi and Saigon libraries as institutions, the practices to document, be in public, circulate, read, and reassemble carry on shaping the evolving questions of Vietnamese cultural identity and literary heritage in the contemporary era of global capitalism, new media, and communication flows. Control of information and suppression of dissent remain core to Vietnamese government surveillance strategies. The reading rooms of both the Hanoi National Library and the Ho Chi Minh City General Sciences Library are some of the most visited and most used public spaces for Vietnamese university students, mothers and their children, and local and international scholarly researchers. Reassemblage takes an operational form for the Hanoi and Ho Chi Minh City libraries, where library administrators seek to create systems of networked libraries across Vietnam and to align with shifting global standards of information, communication, and preservation. Diasporic Vietnamese communities seek to reassemble heritage through official and unofficial museums, archives, and libraries to redefine Vietnameseness across national and political boundaries. The library is more than an institution, an infrastructure of knowledge and hegemony. It is a set of social practices, technical approaches to preservation and communication, and a platform for debate regarding national heritage and the envisioned public of the present and future.

NOTES

INTRODUCTION

1. "Bibliothèques publiques—À la bibliothèque centrale," *L'Annam Nouveau*, November 28, 1935, no. 500, 3.

2. I use the terms *Vietnam* and *Vietnamese* recognizing that these ethnonational terms were popularized in the revolutionary and postcolonial periods. Given the scope of the book crossing colonial-postcolonial divides, I use the anachronistic terminology for the majority ethnic Kinh (Việt) population that form the greater part of the actors in this book. Colonial-era sources might use the term *Annam* to characterize Vietnam or use regional terms such as *tonkinois/e* (Tonkinese), *cochinchinois/e* (Cochinchinese), or *annamite* (Annamese), and I maintain them in the translations for specificity. Colonial sources often use the term *indigène* to categorize a population deemed as "native" to the land, often in comparison to Europeans or French, and I use the English translation "indigenous" to reflect the language and politics of top-down Indochina-wide demographic construction in colonial policy (chapter 1) and state surveillance (chapter 3). In most situations I use other markers of identity, such as reader, student, teacher, or journalist, that might have been used in the vernacular and specify "Vietnamese" when discussing cultural, national, and language identity. My intention is to widen the analytical lens of historical subjects beyond colonizer-colonized and to directly address ethnonationalist nomenclature as a debated process on interwoven issues of colonial citizenship, racialization, migration, indigeneity, and nationhood. See chapter 2.

3. For the transformation of Vietnamese scholarly learning and generational shifts in the intelligentsia, see Hue-Tam Ho Tai, *Radicalism and the Origins of the Vietnamese Revolution* (Cambridge, MA: Harvard University Press, 1992); David G. Marr, *Vietnamese Tradition on Trial, 1920–1945* (Berkeley: University of California Press, 1981); Ben Tran, *Post-Mandarin: Masculinity and Aesthetic Modernity in Colonial Vietnam* (New York: Fordham University Press, 2017).

4. See the comprehensive study of the Cochinchina publishing landscape and the Indochinese collection at the French National Library: Vy Cao, "Histoire de l'imprimerie, du livre et de l'édition vietnamienne en Cochinchine: Traitement et analyse du fonds Indochinois (1890–1945)," PhD diss., Université d'Aix-Marseille, 2025. For studies on religious spheres of publishing in colonial Vietnam, see Shawn McHale, *Print and Power: Confucianism, Communism and Buddhism in the Making of Modern Vietnam* (Honolulu: University of Hawai'i Press, 2004); Charles Keith, *Catholic Vietnam: A Church from Empire to Nation* (Berkeley: University of California Press, 2012).

5. Vy Cao illustrates the vibrant Mekong Delta publishing network and centers the roles of commercial activities, Buddhist temples, and religious institutions in the local book industry. Vy Cao, "Between the Sacred and the Secular: Publishing, Books, and Everyday Life in Colonial Cochinchina," in *Vietnam over the Long Twentieth Century: Becoming Modern, Going Global*, ed. Liam C. Kelley and Gerard Sasges (Singapore: Springer Nature, 2024), 85–100.

6. The second-largest library in Vietnam was the extensive research and reference library of the École française d'Extrême-Orient (EFEO), or the French School of the Far East, in Hanoi. See Cécile Capot, "La bibliothèque et les archives de l'École française d'Extrême-Orient: De la constitution à la crise de la décolonisation (1898–1959)," PhD diss., École doctorale de l'École pratique des hautes études, 2022.

7. For colonial economy and monopolies, see chapters 2 and 3 in Pierre Brocheux and Daniel Hémery, *Indochina: An Ambiguous Colonization, 1858–1954* (Berkeley: University of California Press, 2011), and Gerard Sasges, *Imperial Intoxication: Alcohol and the Making of Colonial Indochina* (Honolulu: University of Hawai'i Press, 2017).

8. After Paris, the most popular municipal French libraries recorded the following number of book consultations (books read on site in the library reading room): Lyon (63,362), Rouen (30,545), and Marseille (25,000). Paul Boudet, *Rapport sur la direction des archives et des bibliothèques (1930–1931)* (Hanoi: Imprimerie d'Extrême-Orient, 1931).

9. Juliane Heyman, "Libraries in Vietnam," in *UNESCO Bulletin for Libraries* 13 (October 1959): 231–32; Report, ca. 1953, Tổng Thư viện (1940–1956) (TTV), Trung tâm lưu trữ quốc gia 2 (TTLTQG2), folder 2.

10. Mary Niles Maack, *Libraries in Senegal: Continuity and Change in an Emerging Nation* (Chicago: American Library Association, 1981), 33. Denis Gazquez emphasizes the importance of the Indochinese collection in the National Library in France, which stands second to the Algerian collection, which by comparison had a longer colonization period and larger European settler colonial population. Denis Gazquez, "Les fonds sur l'Indochine coloniale à la Bibliothèque nationale de France," in *Le Vietnam: Une histoire de transferts culturels*, ed. Hoai Huong Aubert-Nguyen and Michel Espagne (Paris: Demopolis, 2015), 283–90.

11. This examination of the library as social space of cultural practices joins recent historical scholarship on public infrastructures and media technologies in Vietnam. See Lonán Ó Briain, *Voices of Vietnam: A Century of Radio, Red Music, and Revolution* (Oxford: Oxford University Press, 2021); Stéphanie Ponsavady, *Cultural and Literary Representations of the Automobile in French Indochina: A Colonial Roadshow* (Cham, Switzerland: Palgrave Macmillan, 2018); Christina Schwenkel, "Spectacular Infrastructure and Its Breakdown in Socialist Vietnam," *American Ethnologist* 42, no. 3 (2015): 520–34; Christina Schwenkel,

Building Socialism: The Afterlife of East German Architecture in Urban Vietnam (Durham, NC: Duke University Press, 2020).

12. Geoffrey C. Bowker and Susan Leigh Star, *Sorting Things Out: Classification and its Consequences* (Cambridge: MIT Press, 2000). See also Susan Leigh Star, "The Ethnography of Infrastructure," *American Behavioral Scientist* 42, no. 3 (1999): 377–91; Geoffrey C. Bowker, "Information Mythology and Infrastructure," in *Information Acumen: The Understanding and Use of Knowledge in Modern Business*, ed. L. Bud-Frierman (London: Routledge, 1994), 231–47; Shannon Mattern, *A City Is Not a Computer: Other Urban Intelligences* (Princeton, NJ: Princeton University Press, 2021); Eric Klinenberg, *Palaces for the People: How Social Infrastructure Can Help Fight Inequality, Polarization, and the Decline of Civic Life* (New York: Crown, 2018).

13. Deborah Cowen, "Following the Infrastructures of Empire: Notes on Cities, Settler Colonialism, and Method," *Urban Geography* 41, no. 4 (2020): 469–86; Jennifer Hart, *Making an African City: Technopolitics and the Infrastructure of Everyday Life in Colonial Accra* (Bloomington: Indiana University Press, 2024); Ara Wilson, "The Infrastructure of Intimacy," *Signs: Journal Of Women in Culture and Society* 41, no. 2 (2016): 247–80.

14. For debates on French colonial state and civic responsibility, see Van Nguyen-Marshall, *In Search of Moral Authority: The Discourse on Poverty, Poor Relief, and Charity in French Colonial Vietnam* (New York: Peter Lang, 2008).

15. Gary Wilder highlights the intertwined constitution of metropole and colony in the French imperial nation-state, where subject-citizens "confronted the emancipatory and oppressive aspects of both the universalizing and particularizing dimensions of French colonial politics." Gary Wilder, *The French Imperial Nation-State: Negritude and Colonial Humanism Between the Two World Wars* (Chicago: University of Chicago Press, 2005), 5. See Alice Conklin and Martin Thomas for studies of associationist-driven colonial policy rooted in republican idealism, racial hierarchy, and economic modernization. Alice L. Conklin, *A Mission to Civilize: The Republican Idea of Empire in France and West Africa, 1895–1930* (Stanford, CA: Stanford University Press, 1997); Martin Thomas, *The French Empire Between the Wars: Imperialism, Politics and Society* (Manchester: Manchester University Press, 2005).

16. This framing of networked mobility adds to the scholarship on Vietnamese class identities and urbanism. See Haydon Cherry, *Down and Out in Saigon: Stories of the Poor in a Colonial City* (New Haven, CT: Yale University Press, 2019); Erik Harms, *Saigon's Edge: On the Margins of Ho Chi Minh City* (Minneapolis: University of Minnesota Press, 2011); Van Nguyen-Marshall, Lisa Drummond, and Danièle Bélanger, eds., *The Reinvention of Distinction: Modernity and the Middle Class in Urban Vietnam* (Dordrecht: Springer, 2012).

17. For feminist critiques of the public-private divide, see Carole Pateman, "Feminist Critiques of the Public/Private Dichotomy," in *Public and Private in Social Life*, ed. Stanley Benn and Gerald Gaus (London: St. Martin's Press & Croom Helm, 1983), 281–303.

18. For work on unequal public spheres and public space in other contexts, see Mary Elizabeth Berry, "Public Life in Authoritarian Japan," *Daedalus* 127, no. 3 (1998): 133–65; Mary Elizabeth Berry, *Japan in Print: Information and Nation in the Early Modern Period* (Berkeley: University of California Press, 2006); Todd A. Henry, *Assimilating Seoul: Japanese Rule and the Politics of Public Space in Colonial Korea, 1910–1945* (Berkeley: University of California Press, 2016); Jun Uchida, "The Public Sphere in Colonial Life: Residents'

Movements in Korea Under Japanese Rule," *Past & Present* 220, no. 1 (August 1, 2013): 217–48; Jasmine Nadua Trice, *City of Screens: Imagining Audiences in Manila's Alternative Film Culture* (Durham, NC: Duke University Press, 2021); Cheryl Knott, *Not Free, Not for All: Public Libraries in the Age of Jim Crow* (Amherst: University of Massachusetts Press, 2015); Shannon Mattern, "Fugitive Libraries," *Places Journal*, October 2019; Shannon Mattern, "Library as Infrastructure," *Places Journal*, June 2014.

19. Ho Tai, *Radicalism and the Origins of the Vietnamese Revolution*; Marr, *Vietnamese Tradition on Trial.*

20. McHale, *Print and Power*, 60.

21. McHale, *Print and Power*, 11, 36.

22. Philippe Peycam, *The Birth of Vietnamese Political Journalism: Saigon, 1916–1930* (New York: Columbia University Press, 2012).

23. See Martina Thucnhi Nguyen, *On Our Own Strength: The Self-Reliant Literary Group and Cosmopolitan Nationalism in Late Colonial Vietnam* (Honolulu: University of Hawai'i Press, 2020); Duy Lap Nguyen, *The Unimagined Community: Imperialism and Culture in South Vietnam* (Manchester: Manchester University Press, 2019); Van Nguyen-Marshall, *Between War and the State: Civil Society in South Vietnam, 1954–1975* (Ithaca, NY: Cornell University Press, 2023); Kevin D. Pham, *The Architects of Dignity: Vietnamese Visions of Decolonization* (Oxford: Oxford University Press, 2024).

24. Nancy Fraser, "Rethinking the Public Sphere: A Contribution to the Critique of Actually Existing Democracy," *Social Text* 25/26 (1990): 70.

25. Fraser, "Rethinking the Public Sphere," 60. I also draw from Geoff Eley's emphasis on competing publics and the argument that "the public sphere was always constituted by conflict." Geoff Eley, "Nations, Publics, and Political Cultures: Placing Habermas in the Nineteenth Century," in *Habermas and the Public Sphere*, ed. Craig Calhoun (Cambridge, MA: MIT Press, 1993), 306.

26. By placing debates of modern subjectivity and colonial citizenship within a bureaucratic institution, this work examines the *longue durée* intertwined process of modernity and modernization. Dipesh Chakrabarty, *Provincializing Europe: Postcolonial Thought and Historical Difference* (Princeton, NJ: Princeton University Press, 2000); Dipesh Chakrabarty, "The Muddle of Modernity," *American Historical Review* 116, no. 3 (June 1, 2011): 663–75.

27. Edward Said, *Orientalism* (New York: Pantheon Books, 1978); V. Y. Mudimbe, *The Invention of Africa: Gnosis, Philosophy, and the Order of Knowledge* (Bloomington: Indiana University Press, 1988); Gaurav Desai, *Subject to Colonialism: African Self-Fashioning and the Colonial Library* (Durham, NC: Duke University Press, 2001).

28. Homi K. Bhabha, "Cultural Diversity and Cultural Differences," *The Post-Colonial Studies Reader*, 2nd ed., ed. Bill Ashcroft, Gareth Griffiths, and Helen Tiffin (New York: Routledge, 2003), 209.

29. Robert Darnton, "What Is the History of Books?," *Daedalus* 111, no. 3 (July 1, 1982): 65–83; Robert Darnton, "An Early Information Society: News and the Media in Eighteenth-Century Paris," *American Historical Review* 105, no. 1 (February 1, 2000): 1–35.

30. Thomas R. Adams and Nicolas Barker, "A New Model for the Study of the Book," in *A Potencie of Life: Books in Society*, ed. Nicolas Barker (London: The British Library, 1993), 5–44.

31. "It [space] is in a sense actuated by the ensemble of movements deployed within it. Space occurs as the effect produced by the operations that orient it, situate it, temporalize it, and make it function in a polyvalent unity of conflicted programs or contractual proximities. . . . Space is a practiced place." Michel de Certeau, *The Practice of Everyday Life*, trans. Steven Rendall (Berkeley: University of California Press, 2011), 117. Roger Chartier investigates the relationship between material spaces—the "order" of libraries—and the affective experience of reading and interpretation or the "actualization of texts." Roger Chartier, *The Order of Books: Readers, Authors, and Libraries in Europe Between the Fourteenth and Eighteenth Centuries* (Stanford, CA: Stanford University Press, 1994).

32. Michel de Certeau contrasts "tactics" to "strategies," the disciplinary structures and normative behavior of an official site of power.

33. I draw from the history and sociology of work, and specifically the concepts of "mandates" (power to define proper conduct) and "mistakes" (violations, failures), to understand the evolution of professional culture and patron-personnel relations in colonial libraries. Sarah Schneewind, *The Social Drama of Daily Work: A Manual for Historians* (Amsterdam: Amsterdam University Press, 2024).

34. David Scott, "Colonial Governmentality," in *Anthropologies of Modernity: Foucault, Governmentality, and Life Politics*, ed. Jonathan Xavier Inda (Malden, MA: Blackwell Publishing, 2005), 35.

35. Lisa Lowe examines intimacies in colonialism and slavery as laying the groundwork for "the practical conditions for liberal forms of personhood, society, and government." Lisa Lowe, *The Intimacies of Four Continents* (Durham, NC: Duke University Press, 2015), 19; Ann Laura Stoler, *Haunted by Empire: Geographies of Intimacy in North American History* (Durham, NC: Duke University Press, 2006).

36. Hannah Arendt, *The Human Condition*, 2nd ed. (Chicago: University of Chicago Press, 1998); Margaret Canovan, "Politics as Culture: Hannah Arendt and the Public Realm," *History of Political Thought* 6, no. 3 (1985): 617–42. Xavier Marquez compares Arendt's spaces of appearance (horizontal relationships of equality) with Michel Foucault's spaces of surveillance (vertical relationships of inequality). Xavier Marquez, "Spaces of Appearance and Spaces of Surveillance," *Polity* 44, no. 1 (2012): 6–31.

37. I recognize the possibility of inflation of statistics and include them if they consistently reoccur as part of internal and external recordkeeping over time.

38. Ann Laura Stoler, "Colonial Archives and the Arts of Governance," *Archival Science* 2, no. 1 (March 1, 2002): 7; Lowe, *The Intimacies of Four Continents*.

39. Ann Laura Stoler, *Along the Archival Grain: Epistemic Anxieties and Colonial Common Sense* (Princeton, NJ: Princeton University Press, 2009).

40. Adams and Barker, "A New Model for the Study of the Book."

41. For a comparative study of the archives in French West Africa and Indochina within the context of French metropolitan archives, see Fabienne Chamelot, "The Politics of French Colonial Archives," PhD diss., University of Portsmouth, 2022.

42. Agathe Larcher-Goscha, "La voie étroite des réformes coloniales et la 'collaboration franco-annamite' (1917–1928)," *Outre-Mers. Revue d'histoire* 82, no. 309 (1995): 387–420. My study on the library is situated in scholarship on French colonial institutions in Vietnam, which uncover how colonial bureaucracy and state power shaped social life and political community. Peter Zinoman, *The Colonial Bastille: A History of Imprisonment in Vietnam,*

1862–1940 (Berkeley: University of California Press, 2000); Claire E. Edington, *Beyond the Asylum: Mental Illness in French Colonial Vietnam* (Ithaca, NY: Cornell University Press, 2019); Sasges, *Imperial Intoxication*. For Southeast Asia institutions, I build on the following work on the role of institutions and nationhood: Penny Edwards, *Cambodge: The Cultivation of a Nation, 1860–1945* (Honolulu: University of Hawai'i Press, 2007); "Census, Map, Museum," in Benedict R. O'G Anderson, *Imagined Communities Reflections on the Origin and Spread of Nationalism*, rev. ed. (London: Verso, 1991).

43. I embed the colonial information order within a longer history of libraries as information infrastructure shaped by Enlightenment classification and the production of bibliographic documentation systems. Ann M. Blair, *Too Much to Know: Managing Scholarly Information Before the Modern Age* (New Haven, CT: Yale University Press, 2010); Ronald E. Day, *The Modern Invention of Information: Discourse, History, and Power* (Carbondale: Southern Illinois University Press, 2001); Suzanne Briet, *Qu'est-ce que la documentation?* (Paris: Éditions documentaires, industrielles et techniques, 1951); Peter Burke, *Social History of Knowledge: From Gutenberg to Diderot* (Cambridge: Polity, 2000); John Seely Brown and Paul Duguid, *The Social Life of Information*, rev. ed. (Boston: Harvard Business Review Press, 2017); Wayne Bivens-Tatum, *Libraries and the Enlightenment* (Los Angeles: Library Juice Press, 2012); Uday S. Mehta, "Liberal Strategies of Exclusion," in *Tensions of Empire: Colonial Cultures in a Bourgeois World*, ed. Frederick Cooper and Ann Laura Stoler (Berkeley: University of California Press, 1997), 59–86.

44. Alexander Woodside, *Lost Modernities: China, Vietnam, Korea, and the Hazards of World History* (Cambridge, MA: Harvard University Press, 2006).

45. Peter Zinoman, "Provincial Cosmopolitanism: Vũ Trọng Phụng's Foreign Literary Engagements," in *Traveling Nation-Makers: Transnational Flows and Movements in the Making of Modern Southeast* Asia, ed. Caroline S. Hau and Kasian Tejapira (Singapore and Kyoto: NUS Press, 2011), 127–52.

46. Gaetan Benoit, *Eugene Morel: Pioneer of Public Libraries in France* (Duluth, MN: Litwin Books, 2014); Wayne Wiegand, *American Public School Librarianship: A History* (Baltimore, MD: Johns Hopkins University Press, 2021).

47. This chapter contributes to the scholarship on the social life of reading and vernacular print culture in Asia, specifically Justin McDaniel, *Gathering Leaves and Lifting Words: Histories of Buddhist Monastic Education in Laos and Thailand* (Seattle: University of Washington Press, 2008); Chie Ikeya, *Refiguring Women, Colonialism, and Modernity in Burma* (Honolulu: University of Hawai'i Press, 2011); Berry, *Japan in Print*; Joseph McDermott, *A Social History of the Chinese Book: Books and Literati Culture in Late Imperial China* (Hong Kong: Hong Kong University Press, 2006).

48. See the interventions of critical refugee studies to rethink postcolonial conditions that were shaped by competing claims to national authority and overlapping colonial and military projects. I draw from Nguyễn-võ Thu-hương's challenge of narratives of progressive temporalities centered on the nation-state and Ma Vang's examination of archives and state knowledge in movement across periods and terrains of conflict. Nguyễn-võ Thu-hương, *Almost Futures: Sovereignty and Refuge at World's End* (Oakland: University of California Press, 2024); Ma Vang, *History on the Run: Secrecy, Fugitivity, and Hmong Refugee Epistemologies* (Durham, NC: Duke University Press, 2021).

49. See Olga Dror, *Making Two Vietnams: War and Youth Identities, 1965–1975* (Cambridge: Cambridge University Press, 2018); Thaveeporn Vasavakul, "Schools and Politics in

South and North Viet Nam: A Comparative Study of State Apparatus, State Policy, and State Power (1945–1965)," PhD diss., Cornell University, 1994.

1. TO DOCUMENT: BUILDING LIBRARIES AND A COLONIAL INFORMATION ORDER

1. Pierre Pasquier, "Avant-Propos," *Les archives et les bibliothèques de l'Indochine* (Hanoi: Imprimerie d'Extrême-Orient, 1919), 3.

2. For Boudet's biography, see the folder "Dossier Relatif à Paul Boudet," undated, Archives Privées Papiers Boudet (PB), Archives nationales d'outre-mer (ANOM), Aix-en-Provence, folder 86; and André Masson, "Paul Boudet," *Bibliothèque de l'école des Chartes* 107, no. 2 (1948): 335–37.

3. Paul Boudet, *Les archives et les bibliothèques de l'Indochine* (Hanoi: Imprimerie d'Extrême-Orient, 1919).

4. "Arrêtés du 29 Novembre 1917 et 26 Decembre 1918 au sujet de l'organisation du Dépôt Central d'archives et de la Bibliothèque Publique Centrale de Hanoi (1917–1918)," PB, ANOM, folder 48.

5. This book builds on the following scholarship on library developments and the colonial collections: Đào Thị Diến, "Les archives coloniales au Vietnam (1858–1954): Les fonds conservés au dépôt central de Hanoi; les fonds de la résidence supérieure au Tonkin," PhD diss., Université Paris VII Denis Diderot, 2004; Lê Thanh Huyền, "Thư viện Việt Nam thời kỳ pháp thuộc," PhD diss., Trường Đại học văn hoá Hà Nội—Thông tin thư viện, 2014; Nguyễn Ngọc Mô, *Tìm hiểu lịch sử ngành thư viện lưu trữ hồ sơ Việt Nam* (Hanoi: Nhà Xuất Bản Thế Giới, 2002); Bích Hồng Dương, *Lịch sử sự nghiệp thư viện Việt Nam trong tiến trình văn hoá dân tộc* (Hanoi: Vụ Thư Viện, 1999).

6. Pierre Pasquier (1877–1934) served as administrator of the civil services in Indochina and resident superior of Annam (1921). He would later serve as governor general of Indochina from 1926 to 1927 (as temporary replacement) and officially from 1928 to 1934.

7. Pierre Pasquier respectfully commended Boudet's "courage and firm resolution" to organize the documents of Indochina and to preserve French colonial history. He described Boudet's mission to "rescue the tragic state of documents . . . from the hordes of 'African termites' that, like a scourge, ravage everything in its path" through the application of "Western science." Pasquier, "Avant-Propos," 3–5.

8. A 1931–32 report recorded that the Hanoi Central Library total budget was 300,000, with 178,590 francs for personnel and 120,750 francs for material costs such as purchasing books, binding, furniture, card catalogs, printing, correspondence and communications, ventilation, and uniforms for security guards. The Hanoi Central Library had a budget that was comparable those of libraries in France such as the ones in Lyon (staff: 196,915 francs; material: 124,600 francs) and Rouen (staff: 190,800 francs; material: 73,152 francs). Paul Boudet, *Rapport sur la direction des archives et des bibliothèques (1931–1932)* (Hanoi: Imprimerie d'Extrême-Orient, 1933). For a comparative context, the Hanoi Central Library budget was 0.15 percent of the total budget for operating all Cochinchina in 1930 (200 million francs). P. Gastaldy, Exposition Coloniale Internationale Paris, ed., *La Cochinchine* (Saigon: Société des Études Indochinoises, 1931), 36.

9. "Notre Bibliothèque," *L'Opinion*, November 17, 1920. The article references another account of the visit of the governor general of Indochina to the Hanoi Central Library

published on November 6 and 8, 1920, in *Le Courrier d'Haiphong*, Direction des archives et des bibliothèques (DABI), Trung tâm lưu trữ quốc gia 1 (TTLTQG1), Hanoi, folder 4.

10. The *trường thi* was an important space in many urban centers in precolonial Vietnam, serving multiple uses, including as a location for festivals and public rice distributions, as well as the Confucian examinations.

11. The regional examination led to the degree of *tú tài* (licentiate) and *cử nhân* (provincial graduate), and ranked candidates would proceed to the palace examination at the royal court in Hue.

12. For a detailed study of the Vietnamese Confucian examination systems, see Nola Cooke, "Nineteenth-Century Vietnamese Confucianization in Historical Perspective: Evidence from the Palace Examinations (1463–1883)," *Journal of Southeast Asian Studies* 25, no. 2 (1994): 270–312; Ngô Đức Thọ, Nguyễn Thuý Nga, and Nguyễn Hữu Mùi, *Các nhà khoa bảng Việt Nam 1075–1919* (Hà Nội: Nhà xuất bản Văn học, 2006).

13. John K. Whitmore, "Paperwork: The Rise of the New Literati and Ministerial Power and the Effort Toward Legibility in Đại Việt," in *Southeast Asia in the Fifteenth Century*, ed. Geoff Wade (Singapore: NUS Press, 2010), 104–25.

14. This "early modern period" was characterized by an independent Đại Việt kingdom after a period of Chinese domination from first century BCE to the tenth century CE. It includes a period of Chinese Ming occupation in 1407–27, and the Vietnamese conquest of the southern kingdom of Champa in 1471. For a decentered history of Vietnam beyond the ethnic Việt and a teleology of expansion from the northern Red River Delta into the south, see chapter 14 in Christopher Goscha, *Vietnam: A New History* (New York: Basic Books, 2016), 506–46.

15. Alexander Woodside, *Lost Modernities: China, Vietnam, Korea, and the Hazards of World History* (Cambridge, MA: Harvard University Press, 2006).

16. This shared literary culture was based on memorization of Literary Sinitic–language texts and the literary writing style of the eight-legged essay, the prose format for imperial examinations implemented during the Ming and Qing dynasties in China. For a survey of information practices such as libraries, archives, gazetteers, censorship, education, and language in early modern East Asia, see Devin Fitzgerald and Carla Nappi, "Information in Early Modern East Asia," in *Information: A Historical Companion*, ed. Ann Blair, Paul Duguid, Anja-Silvi Goeing, and Anthony Grafton (Princeton, NJ: Princeton University Press, 2021), 60–83.

17. Liam C. Kelley, *Beyond the Bronze Pillars: Envoy Poetry and the Sino-Vietnamese Relationship* (Honolulu: University of Hawai'i Press, 2005).

18. For an extensive linguistic study of sinographic writing in Vietnam, see John D. Phan, *Lost Tongues of the Red River: Annamese Middle Chinese and the Origins of the Vietnamese Language* (Cambridge, MA: Harvard University Press, 2025).

19. Kathlene Baldanza, "Publishing, Book Culture, and Reading Practices in Vietnam: The View from Thắng Nghiêm and Phổ Nhân Temples," *Journal of Vietnamese Studies* 13, no. 3 (August 1, 2018): 25. See also Li Tana, "The Imported Book Trade and Confucian Learning in Seventeenth- and Eighteenth-Century Vietnam," in *New Perspectives on the History and Historiography of Southeast Asia: Continuing Explorations*, ed. Michael Arthur Aung-Thwin and Kenneth R. Hall (New York: Routledge, 2011); Vinh Sinh, "Chinese Characters as the Medium for Transmitting the Vocabulary of Modernization from Japan to Vietnam in the Early Twentieth Century," *Asian Pacific Quarterly* (October 1993): 1–16.

20. Nguyễn Tuấn Cường, "Private Academies and Confucian Education in 18th-Century Vietnam in East Asian Context: The Case of Phúc Giang Academy," in *Confucian Academies in East Asia*, ed. Vladimir Glomb, Eun-Jeung Lee, and Martin Gehlmann (Leiden: Brill, 2020), 3: 89–125.

21. George Dutton, *The Tây Son Uprising: Society and Rebellion in Eighteenth-Century Vietnam* (Honolulu: University of Hawai'i Press, 2006); Alexander Woodside, *Vietnam and the Chinese Model: A Comparative Study of Vietnamese and Chinese Government in the First Half of the Nineteenth Century* (Cambridge, MA: Harvard University Press, 1971).

22. George Dutton, "The Nguyen State and the Book Collecting Project," unpublished manuscript, March 2013.

23. See the role of documentation in mandarinate states such as gazettes in imperial China: Emily Mokros, "Documentary Authority," in *Information: A Historical Companion* (Princeton, NJ: Princeton University Press, 2021), 767; Emily Mokros, *The Peking Gazette in Late Imperial China: State News and Political Authority* (Seattle: University of Washington Press, 2021).

24. *Đại Nam thực lục chính biên, đệ nhất, nhị, tam kỷ*, II, I:21, as cited in Alexander Woodside, *Vietnam and the Chinese Model*, 123.

25. André Masson, *Hanoï pendant la période héroïque, 1873–1888* (Paris: Librairie orientaliste Paul Geuthner, 1929), 52.

26. For an extensive history of the EFEO scholarly collections and the relationship between the EFEO and DABI, see Cécile Capot, chapter 4 in "La bibliothèque et les archives de l'École Française d'Extrême-Orient: De la constitution à la crise de la décolonisation (1898–1959)," PhD diss., École doctorale de l'École pratique des hautes études, 2022. For the history of the EFEO, see Catherine Clémentin-Ojha and Pierre-Yves Manguin, *A Century in Asia: The History of the École Française d'Extrême-Orient, 1898–2006* (Singapore: Editions Didier Millet, 2007); Phương Ngọc Nguyễn, *À l'origine de l'anthropologie au Vietnam: Recherche sur les auteurs de la première moitié du XXe siècle* (Aix-en-Provence: Presses de l'Université de Provence, 2012); Pierre Singaravélou, *L'École Française d'Extrême-Orient ou l'institution des marges: Essai d'histoire sociale et politique de la science coloniale* (Paris: L'Harmattan, 1999).

27. Trần Văn Ky, *Les archives du gouvernement de la Cochinchine: Organisation, méthode de classement* (Hanoi: Imprimerie Tonkinoise, 1915), 9.

28. Trần Văn Ky, *Les archives du gouvernement de la Cochinchine*, 10.

29. An internal library had been in operation since 1862. Throughout its early history, the Cochinchina Library went by many names: Bibliothèque de Saigon (Saigon Library), Bibliothèque de documentation du Gouvernement de la Cochinchine (Library of Documentation of the Cochinchina Government), Bibliothèque de Cochinchine (Library of Cochinchina), and Bibliothèque de la secrétariat du Gouvernement de la Cochinchine (Library of the Secretariat of the Cochinchina Government). "La Bibliothèque nationale du Sud-Vietnam," ca. 1956, Thư viện Quốc gia Nam Việt (1945–1957) (TVQGNV), Trung tâm lưu trữ quốc gia 2 (TTLTQG2), folder 102; "Les Bibliothèques de l'Indochine—II—La Bibliothèque Centrale de Cochinchine—Saigon," ca. 1946, PB, ANOM, folder 53.

30. "Les Bibliothèques de l'Indochine—II—La Bibliothèque Centrale de Cochinchine—Saigon," ca. 1946, PB, ANOM, folder 53.

31. "Les Bibliothèques de l'Indochine—II—La Bibliothèque Centrale de Cochinchine—Saigon," ca. 1946, PB, ANOM, folder 53.

32. Letter from Admiral de la Grandière to the Minister of Colonies, Saigon, October 26, 1866, DABI, TTLTQG1, folder 614.

33. Letter from Admiral de la Grandière to the Minister of Colonies, Saigon, May 9, 1867, DABI, TTLTQG1, folder 614.

34. For a study of Europeans in Indochina, see Marie-Paule Ha, *French Women and the Empire: The Case of Indochina* (Oxford: Oxford University Press, 2014); and Haydon Cherry, chapter 7, "A Prodigal Son," in *Down and Out in Saigon: Stories of the Poor in a Colonial City* (New Haven, CT: Yale University Press, 2019).

35. Christopher Goscha, *Going Indochinese: Contesting Concepts of Space and Place in French Indochina* (Copenhagen: NIAS Books, 2012).

36. Trần Thị Phương Hoa, "Pragmatizing Schools: A History of Vocational Training in Colonial Vietnam," *French Colonial History* 19 (2020): 111–62.

37. David G Marr, *Vietnamese Anticolonialism, 1885–1925* (Berkeley: University of California Press, 1971).

38. In a letter between the director of the Ministry of Interior and the governor of the Ministry of the Navy in 1883, the director of the Ministry of Interior remarked that the only library open to the public in Cochinchina was the Saigon Library. "La bibliothèque nationale du sud-vietnam" (The National Library of South Vietnam), TVQGNV, TTLTQG2, folder 102.

39. Requests to borrow books to read at home, 1903–6, Gouvernement de la Cochinchine (GC), TTLTQG2, folder 11894.

40. Applications requesting borrowing home privileges, 1907–19, GC, TTLTQG2, folder 11886; Reader requests, 1905–17, GC, TTLTQG2, folder 11974.

41. L. Griffa and Bibliothèque du Secrétariat du Gouvernement de la Cochinchine, *Catalogue méthodique des ouvrages, avec table alphabétique des auteurs* (Saigon: Coudurier et Montégout, imprimeurs-éditeurs, 1907), GC, TTLTQG2, folder 11974.

42. Circular Number 36-C from Governor General of Indochina, Albert Sarraut, to the heads of local administration and heads of services, July 6, 1917, DABI, TTLTQG1, folder 38.

43. "Arrêtés du 29 Novembre 1917 et 26 Decembre 1918 au sujet de l'organisation du Dépôt Central d'archives et de la Bibliothèque Publique Centrale de Hanoi (1917–1918)," PB, ANOM, folder 48.

44. Lara Jennifer Moore, *Restoring Order: The Ecole des Chartes and the Organization of Archives and Libraries in France, 1820–1870* (Duluth, MN: Litwin Books, 2008).

45. See Fayet-Scribe Sylvie, *Histoire de la documentation en France: Culture, science et technologie de l'information 1895–1937* (Paris: CNRS Editions, 2000); Mary Niles Maack, "The Lady and the Antelope: Suzanne Briet's Contribution to the French Documentation Movement," *Library Trends*, 52, no. 4 (Spring 2004): 719–47.

46. Masson, "Paul Boudet," 336.

47. Paul Boudet and André Masson, *Iconographie Historique de l'Indochine française. Documents sur l'histoire de l'intervention française en Indochine* (Paris: G. Van Oest, 1931).

48. Moore, *Restoring Order*, 199–202.

49. In addition to the Central Library transforming the space, the chamber of commerce and a police station were installed in the old examination enclosure in 1897 and 1898, and in 1900 a professional school was built in the southern part of the former Confucian examination campgrounds. For a study of colonial architecture, see Caroline Herbelin,

Architectures du Vietnam colonial: Repenser le métissage (Paris: Comité des Travaux Historiques et Scientifiques, 2016); and Gwendolyn Wright, chapter 4, "Indochina: The Folly of Grandeur," in *The Politics of Design in French Colonial Urbanism* (Chicago: University of Chicago Press, 1991).

50. Paul Boudet, *Rapport sur la direction des archives et des bibliothèques (1927–1928)* (Hanoi: Imprimerie d'Extrême-Orient, 1928), 6.

51. Boudet, *Les archives et les bibliothèques de l'Indochine*, 14–15.

52. From 1922 to 1929 the Directorate was attached to the Directorate of Public Education of Indochina, created in 1922.

53. Cécile Capot, "Concurrentes ou complémentaires? Quand l'École française d'Extrême-Orient créa la direction des Archives et des Bibliothèques de l'Indochine," in *Chartistes en Asie: Science historique et patrimoine au lointain (XIXe–XXIe siècle)*, ed. Jacques Berlioz, Cécile Capot, and Olivier Poncet (Paris: École nationale des chartes—École française d'Extrême-Orient, 2021), 137–50.

54. C.H., "Le service des archives et la bibliothèque centrale de Hanoi," *L'éveil économique*, ca. 1919, DABI, TTLTQG1, folder 4.

55. C.H., "Le service des archives et la bibliothèque centrale de Hanoi," *L'éveil économique*, ca. 1919, DABI, TTLTQG1, folder 4.

56. Boudet, *Rapport sur la direction des archives et des bibliothèques (1927–1928)*, 10–11.

57. "Régie du dépôt legal," ca. 1927, Résident Supérieure du Tonkin nouveau fonds (RSTNF), ANOM, folder 4197.

58. Maurice Monguillot, "Rapport sur le fonctionnement du dépôt légal en Indochine," Hanoi, June 22, 1927, RSTNF, ANOM, folder 4197; "Régie du dépôt légal," ca. 1953, DABI, TTLTQG1, folder 2014-02.

59. Boudet, *Les archives et les bibliothèques de l'Indochine*, 19.

60. "Régie du dépôt legal," ca. 1927, RSTNF, ANOM, folder 4197; Monguillot "Rapport sur le fonctionnement du dépôt légal en Indochine."

61. Boudet, *Rapport sur la direction des archives et des bibliothèques (1927–1928)*, 11.

62. Paul Boudet, "Pour mieux connaître l'Indochine: Essai d'une bibliographie," in *Bibliographie de l'Indochine* (Hanoi: Imprimerie d'Extrême-Orient, 1922).

63. Boudet critiqued the ambitions of Cordier's four-tome bibliography of works on Indochina, which he deemed as unusable due to its comprehensiveness. Henri Cordier, *Bibliotheca indosinica. Dictionnaire bibliographique des ouvrages relatifs à la péninsule Indochinoise* (Paris: Imprimerie nationale, E. Leroux, 1912).

64. Boudet, "Pour mieux connaître l'Indochine," 4.

65. Boudet, "Pour mieux connaître l'Indochine," 1.

66. Pasquier, "Avant-Propos."

67. The triennial provincial level examination (*thi hương*) was ended in 1918, and the mandarin examination system was formally abolished by decree on July 14, 1919. See Gouvernement général de l'Indochine, *Rapports au Conseil supérieur* (Hanoi: Imprimerie d'Extrême-Orient, 1919), 44.

68. Ben Tran, *Post-Mandarin: Masculinity and Aesthetic Modernity in Colonial Vietnam* (New York: Fordham University Press, 2017).

69. Agathe Larcher-Goscha, "La voie étroite des réformes coloniales et la 'collaboration franco-annamite' (1917–1928)," *Outre-Mers. Revue d'histoire* 82, no. 309 (1995): 387–420.

70. Martin Thomas, "Albert Sarraut, French Colonial Development, and the Communist Threat, 1919–1930," *Journal of Modern History* 77, no. 4 (2005): 917–55.

71. Martin Thomas, "French Empire Elites and the Politics of Economic Obligation in the Interwar Years," *Historical Journal* 52, no. 4 (2009): 989–1016.

72. Tuân Hoang Van, "L'Université Indochinoise et l'œuvre culturelle de la France au Vietnam," in *Le Vietnam: Une histoire de transferts culturels*, ed. Hoai Huong Aubert-Nguyen and Michel Espagne (Paris: Demopolis, 2015), 151–67. For centralization of education initiatives under Paul Beau and Albert Sarraut, see Trần Thị Phương Hoa, "From Liberally-Organized to Centralized Schools: Education in Tonkin, 1885–1927," *Journal of Vietnamese Studies* 8, no. 3 (2013): 27–70.

73. Nguyễn Khắc Nguyên, *Trung Bắc Tân Văn*, September 24, 1919. See the translated version in "La bibliothèque centrale à Hanoi," PB, ANOM, folder 48.

74. Nguyễn Khắc Nguyên, *Trung Bắc Tân Văn*, September 24, 1919. See the translated version in "La bibliothèque centrale à Hanoi," PB, ANOM, folder 48.

75. Yen N. Vu, "Phạm Quỳnh, Borrowed Language, and the Ambivalences of Colonial Discourse," *Journal of Southeast Asian Studies* 51, no. 1–2 (June 2020): 114–31.

76. Henri Lemaître, "Les bibliothèques en Indochine," *La Dépêche coloniale*, October 23–24, 1927, no. 8941, 1.

77. Henri Lemaître, "Les bibliothèques en Indochine."

78. According to Masson's records the lending section was highly popular, and from August 1, 1925, to June 30, 1926, it recorded fifty-five thousand instances of works that were borrowed and taken home.

79. Lemaître, "Les bibliothèques en Indochine."

80. Isabelle Antonutti, "Lemaître Henri," in *Figures de bibliothécaires* (Villeurbanne: Presses de l'enssib, 2020), 167–70; Nathalie Magne, "Henri Lemaître 1881–1946: De la lecture publique à aa documentation," Master's thesis, Université Panthéon Sorbonne—Paris I, 1995.

81. Henri Lemaître, "Les bibliothèques des colonies," *La Dépêche coloniale*, November 30, 1927, no. 8970, 1.

82. See his articles on the dissemination of French books overseas for the communication of French language, modern literature, and French culture: Henri Lemaître, "Des livres français aux colonies" *Dépêche coloniale*, September 23, 1927, no. 8916, 1; "Des livres pour les colonies," *Dépêche coloniale*, December 13, 1927, no. 8981, 1.

83. Boudet, *Les archives et les bibliothèques de l'Indochine.*

84. Boudet, *Les archives et les bibliothèques de l'Indochine*, 20.

85. Boudet, *Les archives et les bibliothèques de l'Indochine*, 19.

86. "Report on inauguration of the Bibliothèque Pierre Pasquier," ca. 1934, DABI, TTLTQGQ1, folder 598.

87. A. T., "Inauguration de la Bibliothèque Pierre Pasquier," *L'Avenir du Tonkin*, March 1, 1935, no. 11652, 5 (supplement).

88. "Tại thư viện P. Pasquier," *Trung Bắc Tân Văn*, March 2, 1935, no. 5375, 1.

89. "Quan Toàn-quyền đến khánh thành Thư-viện mới đổi tên," *Báo Đông Pháp*, March 2, 1935, no. 2877.

90. A. T., "Inauguration de la Bibliothèque Pierre Pasquier."

91. See Vietnamese political critiques of the Franco-Vietnamese Association in Larcher-Goscha, "La voie étroite des réformes coloniales," 387–420.

92. See specifically the work on documentation sciences by Paul Otlet (1868–1944), who published *Traité de documentation: Le livre sur le livre (1934)*, and Suzanne Briet (1894–1989), who worked for thirty years at the Bibliothèque nationale and transformed the French documentation movement and the field of librarianship. On developments in the library sciences, see W. Boyd Rayward, *The Universe of Information: The Work of Paul Otlet for Documentation and International Organisation* (Moscow: Published for International Federation for Documentation [FID520], 1975); Suzanne Briet, *Qu'est-ce que la documentation?* (Paris: Éditions documentaires, industrielles et techniques, 1951); Michael Buckland, "The Centenary of 'Madame Documentation': Suzanne Briet, 1894–1989," *Journal of the American Society for Information Science* 46, no. 3 (April 1995): 235–37.

93. See the discussion of libraries, bibliographies, and international concepts of *bibliothéconomie* in the popular Saigon periodical *L'Écho Annamite*: Ứng Hoè, "A propos de bibliothèques et de bibliographies," *L'Écho Annamite*, April 17, 1926, no. 556, 1. Ứng Hoè was the pseudonym of Nguyễn Văn Tố (1889–1947), a journalist for the periodicals *Tri Tân* and *Thanh Nghị* who was also involved in the Association for the Diffusion of Quốc Ngữ.

94. Jacques Berlioz, Cécile Capot, and Olivier Poncet, eds., *Chartistes en Asie: Science historique et patrimoine au lointain (XIXe–XXIe siècle)* (Paris: École nationale des Chartes—École française d'Extrême-Orient, 2021).

95. Masson studied at the École des Chartes from 1920 to 1922 and was the assistant curator at the municipal library in Rouen. Masson returned to France in 1934 to work in the French libraries and later served as inspector general of the libraries (1945–70), advancing the mission of public libraries and librarianship in France. Louis Desgraves and Léon de Groër, "André Masson (1900–1986)," *Bibliothèque de l'École des Chartes* 144, no. 2 (1986): 443–45.

96. Pierre Lelièvre recounted several dramatic anecdotes by André Masson while he worked at the Directorate. Pierre Lelièvre, "À propos d'un cinquantenaire pour André Masson," *Bulletin Bibliothèque de France* 39, no. 5 (January 1, 1994): 56–59.

97. Unsigned letter to the library curator, 1922, GC, TTLTQG2, folder 12634.

98. These benchmarks were used by curators to evaluate Vietnamese workers for promotion. Evaluation report, GC, TTLTQG2, folder 12629.

99. Letter from Saint-Marty to the governor of Cochinchina (Office of Personnel), June 14, 1925, GC, TTLTQG2, folder 12634.

100. Letter from Saint-Marty to the governor of Cochinchina.

101. Registry of library works borrowed, ca. 1920–25, GC, TTLTQG2, folder 11930.

102. March to May 1925 reports from Saint-Marty, curator of the Cochinchina Library, to the Director of Archives and Libraries in Hanoi, DABI, TTLTQG1, folder 314.

103. Letter from Saint-Marty to the governor of Cochinchina.

104. Letter from Paul Boudet to the governor general, November 5, 1921, DABI, TTLTQG1, folder 88.

105. Letter from Paul Boudet to the general director of public instruction in Indochina, February 3, 1926, DABI, TTLTQG1, folder 88.

106. Letter from Phúc to Director Paul Boudet, November 17, 1922, DABI, TTLTQG1, folder 27.

107. Letter from Jacques Quesnel to *directeur des bureaux*, December 11, 1922, GC, TTLTQG2, folder 12629. A 1922 letter from Quesnel to the *directeur des bureaux* commended Ruffier's "zealousness, dedication, and competence," which merited an exceptional

bonus for January 1923. Quesnel was later appointed to serve as the colonial-era director of the Cambodia library.

108. Letter from Paul Boudet to the director of public education of Indochina on November 14, 1924, GC, TTLTQG2, folder 12629. Boudet's critique of female labor could be in response to the practice of reserving certain types of jobs for widows and daughters of civil servants and colonists. See Marie-Paule Ha, chapter 6, "Poor, White, Single, and Female in the Colony," in *French Women and the Empire.*

109. Letter from Paul Boudet to the director of public instruction, November 5, 1924, GC, TTLTQG2, folder 12629; Georgette Naudin, "Jean Bouchot (1886–1932)," *Bulletin de l'École française d'Extrême-Orient* 33 (1933): 557–60.

110. Recommendation for appointment of Saint-Exupéry by Paul Boudet, February 23, 1932, TVQGNV, TTLTQG2, folder 128.

111. Proposal of Saint-Exupéry to the French Legion of Honor, January 1, 1951, TVQGNV, TTLTQG2, folder 128. See her personnel dossiers in "Mme de Saint-Exupéry," undated, GC, TTLTQG2, folder 12629.

112. Olivia Pelletier, "'Le chartiste et les colonies': Le modèle archivistique français en Indochine," *La Gazette des archives* 256 (2019): 51–67. For a brief summary of the lives of Paulette Téchiné and Simone de Saint-Exupéry, see Ha, *French Women and the Empire,* 210–11.

113. Meixin Tambay, *Destins d'archivistes. Ngo Dinh Nhu (1910–1963), un archiviste hors du commun*, master's thesis, Université d'Angers, 2014.

114. Charles Keith, *Catholic Vietnam: A Church from Empire to Nation* (Berkeley: University of California Press, 2012), 196.

115. For an extensive intellectual study of Emmanuel Mounier's Marxist critique of capitalism and liberal democracy and of Nhu's political project of personalism and social revolution, see Duy Lap Nguyen, *The Unimagined Community: Imperialism and Culture in South Vietnam* (Manchester: Manchester University Press, 2019); and Phi Vân Nguyen, "The Vietnamization of Personalism: The Role of Missionaries in the Spread of Personalism in Vietnam, 1930–1961," *French Colonial History* 17 (2017): 103–34.

116. "Notice sur M. Ngo Dinh Nhu, archiviste-paléographe, conservateur adjoint de 2eme classe des archives et des bibliothèques," undated, DABI, TTLTQG1, folder 1537.

117. Internal archival reports speak positively of Nhu's technical, linguistic, and bibliographical skill sets. His meticulous scholarly work received some public attention, as seen in the summary of Nhu's opening remarks at the Institut Indochinois pour l'étude de l'homme general assembly in 1940. *L'Écho Annamite,* April 2–3, 1941, no. 207, 4.

118. On Ngô Đình Nhu's politics and later life, see Nu-Anh Tran, *Disunion: Anticommunist Nationalism and the Making of the Republic of Vietnam* (Honolulu: University of Hawai'i Press, 2022); and Edward Miller, *Misalliance: Ngo Dinh Diem, the United States, and the Fate of South Vietnam* (Cambridge, MA: Harvard University Press, 2013).

119. Andrew Hardy, "The Economics of French Rule in Indochina: A Biography of Paul Bernard (1892–1960)," *Modern Asian Studies* 32, no. 4 (October 1, 1998): 807–48.

120. Boudet, *Rapport sur la direction des archives et des bibliothèques (1931–1932),* 3.

121. Direction des Archives et des Bibliothèques, *Arrêtés portant organisation du personnel indigène de la Direction des archives et des bibliothèques et instituant à la direction des archives et des bibliothèques des cours d'application destinés à former des secrétaires-archivistes indigènes* (Hanoi: Imprimerie d'Extrême-Orient, 1930).

122. Training course materials for indigenous personnel, 1928, DABI, TTLTQG1, folder 430; Training course materials for secretaries, archivists, librarians in Hanoi, ca. 1954, DABI, TTLTQG1, folder 2041-09.

123. "Programme des cours d'application pour la formation des secrétaires-archivistes indigènes," in Direction des Archives et des Bibliothèques, *Arrêtés portant organisation du personnel indigène.*

124. Boudet, *Rapport sur la direction des archives et des bibliothèques (1931–1932)*, 3.

125. Letter from Saint-Exupéry (curator of the Government of Cochinchina) to the governor of Saigon (*direction des bureaux*), March 7, 1939, GC, TTLTQG2, folder 30341.

126. Letter from R. Schneyder (*directeur des bureaux du gouvernement*) to the head of the personnel office in Saigon, March 17, 1939, GC, TTLTQG2, folder 30341, March 17, 1939. R. Schneyder (director of the Government Office) denied the request to reorganize the Cochinchina Library, insisting that financial and administrative control remain with the local administration.

127. Report, September 1934, DABI, TTLTQG1 folder 1423-01.

128. Paul Boudet, *Rapport sur la direction des archives et des bibliothèques (1924–1925)* (Hanoi: République Française, 1925), 5.

129. "Le transfert de la section des prêts de la bibliothèque," *L'Écho Annamite*, December 16, 1926, no. 757, 1.

130. Report, September 1934, DABI, TTLTQG1, folder 1423-01.

131. Letter from Paul Boudet to the governor general on November 5, 1921, and letter from Paul Boudet to the general director of public instruction in Indochina on February 3, 1926, DABI, TTLTQG1, folder 88.

132. Report, September 1934, DABI, TTLTQG1, folder 1423-01.

133. The term *boy*, which was derived from the English used to address male domestic servants and slaves, was used in the French colonial context to refer to a male domestic servant. The term *village negrè* could also refer to the 1889 World's Fair exhibit in Paris that created an ethnological exhibit featuring hundreds of peoples from the French colonies performing an orientalist essentialism of colonial populations as "savages" in "human zoos." See Pascal Blanchard, Nicolas Bancel, Gilles Boëtsch, Éric Deroo, and Sandrine Lemaire, eds., *Human Zoos: Science and Spectacle in the Age of Colonial Empires* (Liverpool: Liverpool University Press, 2008).

134. Report on state of service, June 1935, DABI, TTLTQG1, folder 1423-01.

135. Fabienne Chamelot argues that the fragmentation of archival efforts between French metropole and colonies paralleled a distinction between French citizens and colonial subjects. Fabienne Chamelot, "The Politics of French Colonial Archives," PhD diss., University of Portsmouth, 2022, 40.

136. Bourgeois studied at École des Chartes from 1918 to 1923. See André Masson, "Rémy Bourgeois (1897–1947)," *Bibliothèque de l'École des Chartes* 107, no. 2 (1948): 342–43.

137. "Rapport sur le fonctionnement du dépôt légal en Indochine."

138. For notes on the collection of *quốc ngữ* legal deposits in the BNF, see Christiane Rageau, preface to *Catalogue du fonds indochinois. Vol. 1: Livres vietnamiens imprimés en quốc ngữ, 1922–1954* (Paris: Bibliothèque nationale de France, 1979), and *Les ouvrages relatifs au Vietnam dans les collections de la Bibliothèque nationale* (Paris: Bibliothèque nationale de France, 1980).

139. Paul Boudet, *Rapport sur la direction des archives et des bibliothèques (1937–1938)* (Hanoi: Imprimerie Le Van Tan, 1938), 17.

140. Vy Cao, "Between the Sacred and the Secular: Publishing, Books, and Everyday Life in Colonial Cochinchina," in *Vietnam over the Long Twentieth Century: Becoming Modern, Going Global*, ed. Liam C. Kelley and Gerard Sasges (Singapore: Springer Nature, 2024), 92.

141. Cao, "Between the Sacred and the Secular," 91.

142. See the folder titled "Inspection des Archives et des bibliothèques de l'Indochine 1921–1928," DABI, TTLTQG1, folder 1242.

143. Paul Boudet, *Rapport sur la direction des archives et des bibliothèques (1928–1929)* (Hanoi: Imprimerie d'Extrême-Orient, 1929), 15.

144. Đào Thị Diến, "Ngô Đình Nhu—Nhà lưu trữ Việt Nam thời kỳ 1938–1946," *Tạp chí Nghiên cứu và Phát triển*, no. 6–7 (2013): 238–43.

145. Helen Jarvis, "The National Library of Cambodia: Surviving for Seventy Years," *Libraries & Culture* 30, no. 4 (October 1, 1995): 391–408.

146. Lending section borrowing log, 1924–37, Résidence Supérieure du Cambodge (RSC), National Archives of Cambodia, Phnom Penh (NAC), folder 17367.

147. Penny Edwards "Making a Religion of the Nation and Its Language: The French Protectorate (1863–1954) and the Dhammakay," in *History, Buddhism, and New Religious Movements in Cambodia* (Honolulu: University of Hawai'i Press, 2004), 63–84.

148. Penny Edwards, *Cambodge: The Cultivation of a Nation 1860–1945* (Honolulu: University of Hawai'i Press, 2007).

149. Letters between the directorate of public instruction in Vientiane and Hanoi, 1922, DABI, TTLTQG1, folder 328.

150. Archives de l'EFEO, "Rapport de Chao Sithammarat [Tiao Citammarat]," Luang Prabang, January 10, 1924, as cited in Gregory Kourilsky, "The Institut Bouddhique in Laos: Ambivalent Dynamics of a Colonial Project," in *Theravada Buddhism in Colonial Contexts*, ed. Thomas Borchert (New York: Routledge, 2018), 163. See also Ordonnance royale March 21, 1918, which placed the Royal Library under the technical control of the EFEO.

2. TO BE IN PUBLIC: INFRASTRUCTURES OF PUBLIC READING CULTURE

1. Thái Phỉ, "Mấy cái tệ lưu hành ở thư viện" (Bad things circulating at the library), *Hà Thành Ngọ Báo*, March 16, 1932, no. 1373, 1.

2. Thái Phỉ, "Mấy cái tệ lưu hành ở thư viện," 1.

3. Thái Phỉ, "Mấy cái tệ lưu hành ở thư viện," 1.

4. Hanoi and Saigon library administrators were aware of and influenced by public discourse about its services. Library administrators excerpted newspaper articles covering public discussion of libraries into a scrapbook used internally for library administrators' reference. See, for example, the following: Folder 442, titled "Articles du journal 'Annam Nouveau' sur le fonctionnement des Bibliothèques en Indochine 1932–1936" (Articles from the newspaper *New Annam* on the function of Libraries in Indochina), and Folder 4, titled "Archivage des articles des journaux dans la Direction des Archives et des Bibliothèques à Hanoi 1918" (Archive of articles from newspapers on the Directorate of Archives and Libraries in Hanoi 1918), Direction des archives et des bibliothèques (DABI), Trung tâm lưu trữ quốc gia 1 (TTLTQG1).

5. The French colonial state prioritized technical training, as seen in the development of vocational schools (industrial, arts, and museum schools), scholarships for technical training in France, and the development of technical reference reading matter in the central libraries. Trần Thị Phương Hoa, "Pragmatizing Schools: A History of Vocational Training in Colonial Vietnam," *French Colonial History* 19 (2020): 111–62. For the Indochina University, see Tuân Hoang Van, "L'Université indochinoise et l'œuvre culturelle de La France au Vietnam," in *Le Vietnam: Une histoire de transferts culturels*, ed. Hoai Huong Aubert-Nguyen and Michel Espagne (Paris: Demopolis, 2015), 151–67. This limited number of institutions also drove many Vietnamese to study abroad; see "Cultural Sojourners" in Charles Keith, *Subjects and Sojourners* (Oakland: University of California Press, 2023).

6. Pierre Brocheux and Daniel Hémery, *Indochina: An Ambiguous Colonization, 1858–1954* (Berkeley: University of California Press, 2011), 222.

7. For an overview of the Vietnamese colonial school system and the ways in which class and national conflict manifested within schools, see Gail P. Kelly, "Conflict in the Classroom: A Case Study from Vietnam, 1918–38," *British Journal of Sociology of Education* 8, no. 2 (January 1, 1987): 191–212; Gail P. Kelly, "Colonial Schools in Vietnam: Policy and Practice" and "Teachers and the Transmission of State Knowledge: A Case Study of Colonial Vietnam," in *French Colonial Education: Essays on Vietnam and Africa* (New York: AMS Press, 2000), 3–25, 107–31. See also Micheline Lessard, "Tradition for Rebellion: Vietnamese Students and Teachers and Anticolonial Resistance, 1888–1931," PhD diss., Cornell University, 1995.

8. For example, Nguyễn Tuyết Vân was a female student of the P.C.B. who in 1941 had applied for and received a lending card from the Hanoi Central Library. Application for Lending Section Library Card for Pierre Pasquier Library, January 4, 1941, DABI, TTLTQG1, folder 2299.

9. Estimates of functional literacy in the 1920s and 1930s range from 5 to 10 percent of the total urban and rural Vietnamese population.

10. Giang-Huong Nguyen, *La Littérature vietnamienne francophone (1913–1986)* (Paris: Classiques Garnier, 2018), 50.

11. Sabine Huynh, *Mécanismes d'intégration des mots d'emprunt français en vietnamien* (Paris: L'Harmattan, 2010), 44.

12. For a comparative study of early colonial society, see Milton Osborne, *The French Presence in Cochinchina and Cambodia: Rule and Response (1859–1905)* (Ithaca, NY: Cornell University Press, 1969); Gregor Muller, *Colonial Cambodia's "Bad Frenchmen": The Rise of French Rule and the Life of Thomas Caraman, 1840–87* (London: Routledge, 2006).

13. Philippe Peycam, *The Birth of Vietnamese Political Journalism: Saigon 1916–1930* (New York: Columbia University Press, 2012), 27–28.

14. Letter from the Cochinchina Secretariat Library to the lieutenant governor of Cochinchina, May 7, 1902, Gouvernement de la Cochinchine (GC), Trung tâm lưu trữ quốc gia 2 (TTLTQG2), Ho Chi Minh City, folder 11974.

15. For studies of Asian populations such as ethnic Chinese, Khmer, Lao, Malay, Indian, and Tamil, migrations, and legal rights in colonial Indochina, see Natasha Pairaudeau, "Indians as French Citizens in Colonial Indochina, 1858–1940," PhD diss., University of London, School of Oriental and African Studies, 2009; Anh Sy Huy Le, "From Subjects to Subversives: Chinese Migrants and the Evolution of the French Colonial Surveillance Regime in Sài Gòn-Chợ Lớn, 1874–1930," *Asian Ethnicity* 24, no. 4 (October 2, 2023): 544–70.

16. "Règlement intérieur pour la Bibliothèque," 1902, GC, TTLTQG2, folder 11974.

17. Throughout the 1930s, the average daily wages were approximately 0.3 piastre for north Vietnam and 0.6 piastre for the Saigon-Cholon region. Women's salaries were often 20 to 30 percent lower than those of men. This calculation is based on Le Manh Hung's analysis of *Annuaire Statistique de l'Indochine* 1941–1942, 209, in Le Manh Hung, *The Impact of World War II on the Economy of Vietnam 1939–45* (Singapore: Eastern Universities Press, 2004), 80.

18. "Règlement intérieur pour la Bibliothèque," May 7, 1902, GC, TTLTQG2, folder 11974.

19. Cochinchina Library borrowing rules for nongovernmental employees, 1905, GC, TTLTQG2, folder 11894.

20. "Règlement intérieur," April 22, 1922, signed by Boudet, DABI, TTLTQG1, folder 3; "Manuel d'apprentissage du classement des bibliothèques," ca. 1935, chapter 7, "Communication of Books to the Readers," DABI, TTLTQG1, folder 1276. The manual emphasized that the last three categories required authorization prior to using the reading room through an application for a reader card with supporting identification documents and two photographs.

21. For a study of *métis* in Indochina, racial categorization, and legal identity, see Christina Elizabeth Firpo, *The Uprooted: Race, Children, and Imperialism in French Indochina, 1890–1980* (Honolulu: University of Hawai'i Press, 2016), and Emmanuelle Saada, *Empire's Children: Race, Filiation, and Citizenship in the French Colonies* (Chicago: University of Chicago Press, 2012). For concepts of Indochina citizenship, particularly of Vietnamese in Laos and Cambodia, see Christopher E. Goscha, "Widening the Colonial Encounter: Asian Connections Inside French Indochina During the Interwar Period," *Modern Asian Studies* 43, no. 5 (September 2009): 1189–228.

22. Hue-Tam Ho Tai, "The Politics of Compromise: The Constitutionalist Party and the Electoral Reforms of 1922 in French Cochinchina," *Modern Asian Studies* 18, no. 3 (January 1, 1984): 382.

23. Christopher Goscha notes that in 1921, Cochinchina had about sixty-five thousand foreign Asians, or Sino-Vietnamese *minh hương*, a classification of ethnic Chinese who married Vietnamese during the Nguyen dynasty. See Christopher Goscha, *Vietnam: A New History* (New York: Basic Books, 2016), 211, and Christopher Goscha, chapter 4 in *Going Indochinese: Contesting Concepts of Space and Place in French Indochina* (Copenhagen: NIAS Press, 2012).

24. "Règlement général de la Bibliothèque centrale de Cambodge," December 15, 1924, signed by Resident Superior of Cambodge, Baudoin, Résidence supérieure du Cambodge (RSC), National Archives of Cambodia, Phnom Penh (NAC), folder 37488.

25. Request from the Lycée de Hanoi, 1922, DABI, TTLTQG1, folder 234.

26. Letter number 504 from LAN at Tonkinese Fraternity to Paul Boudet, May 24, 1933, DABI, TTLTQG1, folder 2313.

27. "À la bibliothèque centrale," *L'Annam Nouveau*, December 15, 1935, no. 505, 2. This series of articles titled "At the Central Library" was published from 1935 to 1936 in the section of the newspaper accounting for news around Hanoi on a range of topics such as scholarships, teachers, the lottery, and the Ligue des droits de l'homme (League of Rights of Man). The series was often unsigned, but there was a high probability that the section was written by the directors of the journal, Nguyễn Văn Vĩnh and Phạm Huy Lục.

28. Cochinchina Library borrowing rules for nongovernmental employees, 1905, GC, TTLTQG2, folder 11894.

29. Direction des archives et des bibliothèques de l'Indochine, *Guide du lecteur à la Bibliothèque centrale de l'Indochine* (Hanoi: Imprimerie Le Van Tan, 1933).

30. Direction des archives et des bibliothèques de l'Indochine, *Guide du lecteur à la Bibliothèque centrale de l'Indochine.*

31. Direction des archives et des bibliothèques de l'Indochine, *Guide du lecteur à la Bibliothèque centrale de l'Indochine.*

32. Direction des archives et des bibliothèques de l'Indochine, *Guide du lecteur à la Bibliothèque centrale de l'Indochine.*

33. Notice no. 1620, April 13, 1921, signed by Paul Boudet, DABI, TTLTQG1, folder 3.

34. Letter from Phạm Thế Ban to the Director of the Central Library, May 15, 1923, DABI, TTLTQG1, folder 302.

35. Letters from Đoàn Thanh Chước to Director of the Library and Nguyễn Khắc Nguyên and Tham Liễn, October 22, 1922, DABI, TTLTQG1, folder 484.

36. Appeals from Nguyễn Xuân Tạo, Nguyễn Đồng Thăng, Nguyễn Văn Điểm, and official library responses, 1922, DABI, TTLTQG1, folder 303.

37. "Règlement intérieur pour la Bibliothèque," 1902, GC, TTLTQG2, folder 11974.

38. Report from Monsieur Exiga to Lieutenant Governor of the Second Bureau, ca. 1907, GC, TTLTQG2, folder 11974.

39. Proposal for the Cochinchinese Government Local Service for 1926 binding from the Curator of Archives and Libraries, Saigon, August 12, 1925, GC, TTLTQG2, folder 12028. This list ranked the priorities of reading matter for binding in the following order: (1) all newspapers softbound, hardbound, and repaired; (2) in-quarto large books, illustrations, official newspapers; (3) in-octo official bulletins and magazines; (4) small books with illustrations; (5) in-12 and in-6 novels, reference books; (6) miscellaneous repairs; (7) biographies. Luxury and limited-edition works were also bound and added to the special collections.

40. Folder of lost or stolen books, ca. 1907–19, GC, TTLTQG2, folder 11886.

41. Inventory of lost books from the lending section of the Hanoi Central Library, ca. 1923, DABI, TTLTQG1, folder 331.

42. Paul Boudet, *Rapport sur la direction des archives et des bibliothèques (1931–1932)* (Hanoi: Imprimerie d'Extrême-Orient, 1933), 9.

43. Boudet, *Rapport sur la direction des archives et des bibliothèques (1931–1932)*, 9–10.

44. For detailed demography analysis, see Marie-Paule Ha, *French Women and the Empire: The Case of Indochina* (Oxford: Oxford University Press, 2014), 122–25. For city populations, see Eugène Teston and Maurice Percheron, *Indochine moderne: Encyclopédie administrative, touristique, artistique, et économique* (Paris: Librairie de France), 454, 537, 543.

45. "Fréquentation de la bibliothèque centrale de Hanoi," 1920–41, DABI, TTLTQG1, folder 1627.

46. Ha, *French Women and the Empire*, 123.

47. "Statistiques du nombre des lecteurs indigènes et européens fréquentés à la Bibliothèque centrale de Hanoi, 1920–1941," DABI, TTLTQG1, folder 1631.

48. "Fréquentation de la bibliothèque centrale de Hanoi," 1920–41, DABI, TTLTQG1, folder 1627.

49. "Bibliothèques publiques—À la bibliothèque centrale," *L'Annam Nouveau*, November 28, 1935, no. 500, 3.

50. "Bibliothèques publiques—À la bibliothèque centrale."

51. Thái Phỉ, "Mấy cái tệ lưu hành ở thư viện," 1.

52. In 1930 Thái Phỉ published the comedic play "Học làm sang" (Le Richard Mandarin) on Vietnamese social customs, which was performed in the Hanoi opera house. It was a comedic adaptation inspired by Molière's "Le Bourgeois gentilhomme" (The Prodigious Snob). The periodical *Cậu Ấm* was founded at the end of 1930, later changed into *Cậu Ấm Cô Chiêu* on February 21, 1935, and continued until November 1937. In 1941 Thái Phỉ published a nationalistic call for educational reform (in the context of Vichy France), *Một nền giáo dục Việt Nam mới* (A new Vietnamese education), and he was later imprisoned in 1942 for anticolonial activity.

53. Peter Zinoman, "Introduction to Vũ Trọng Phụng's *Dumb Luck* and the Nature of Vietnamese Modernism," in Vũ Trọng Phụng, *Dumb Luck: A Novel*, trans. Nguyễn Nguyệt Cầm and Peter Zinoman (Ann Arbor: University of Michigan Press, 2002), 1–30.

54. Gregory Lockhart and Monique Lockhart, trans., "Broken Journey: Nhất Linh's 'Going to France,'" *East Asian History* 8 (1994): 111.

55. Phạm Quỳnh, "Pháp-du hành trình nhật ký" (Journey to France diary, Saturday, May 13, 1922, in the Terminus Hotel, Lyon), *Nam Phong* 68 (February 1923): 101.

56. Lockhart and Lockhart, trans., "Broken Journey: Nhất Linh's 'Going to France,'" 111.

57. Paul Boudet, *Rapport sur la direction des archives et des bibliothèques (1927–1928)* (Hanoi: Imprimerie d'Extrême-Orient, 1928), 11.

58. Paul Boudet, *Rapport sur la direction des archives et des bibliothèques (1928–1929)* (Hanoi: Imprimerie d'Extrême-Orient, 1929), 12.

59. "Du 1er juin 1935 au 31 mai 1936—Bibliothèque Pierre Pasquier," DABI, TTLTQG1, folder 1421.

60. "Bibliothèque P. Pasquier," *L'Annam Nouveau*, January 5, 1936, no. 511, 2.

61. "Bibliothèque P. Pasquier," 2. Other internal records note that the seats increased from sixty to eighty-four.

62. "A qui ces places sont réservées à la bibliothèque centrale?," *L'Annam Nouveau*, January 30, 1936, no. 517, 3.

63. Statistics on Vietnamese reader cards by profession, 1937–1941, DABI, TTLTQG1, folder 1629.

64. Hy Tống, "La crise des salles de lecture à Hanoi," *L'Annam Nouveau*, December 11, 1932, DABI, TTLTQG1, folder 442.

65. Hy Tống, "La crise des salles de lecture à Hanoi."

66. "L'amélioration de la Bibliothèque," *France Indochine*, July 19, 1931, no. 3515.

67. Thế Chương, "À la bibliothèque" (At the library), *L'Annam Nouveau*, January 2, 1936, no. 510, 2. Several other articles complained about the lack of bicycle storage for readers, such as "À la bibliothèque centrale," *L'Annam Nouveau*, January 23, 1936, no. 516.

68. Statistics from June 1940 to May 1941 on books and periodicals consumed by genre, DABI, TTLTQG1, folder 1629.

69. "Manuel d'apprentissage du classement des Bibliothèques," ca. 1935, Chapter 8, "Section de Prêt" and "La Bibliothèque Centrale de Hanoi," DABI, TTLTQG1, folder 1276.

70. "Manuel d'apprentissage du classement des Bibliothèques."

71. "Statistiques des lecteurs," DABI, TTLTQG1, folder 1627. A handwritten note explains the process of approximating daily reader numbers by dividing the loan records by two.

72. "Du 1er juin 1935 au 31 mai 1936—Bibliothèque Pierre Pasquier," DABI, TTLTQG1, folder 1421.

73. Report, 1935–36, DABI, TTLTQG1, folder 1421.

74. For gender breakdown over time and by region, see Ha, *French Women and the Empire*, 125–32.

75. May 1939 statistics of registered lending section cards, DABI, TTLTQG1, folder 2211. An increasing number of new Vietnamese readers registered to borrow materials from the lending section. During the one-year period from May 1938 to May 1939, 1,054 new cards were created, 427 French and 627 Vietnamese (this number does not count renewed cards). Many of these cards were for students of law and medicine.

76. Walter H. Kaiser, "Statistical Trends of Large Public Libraries, 1900–1946," *The Library Quarterly: Information, Community, Policy* 18, no. 4 (1948): 278. Kaiser draws these statistics from public libraries in cities with populations over 200,000 in the United States.

77. Report on reader statistics 1938–39, DABI, TTLTQG1, folder 2211.

78. Report on reader statistics 1938–39.

79. Report on reader statistics 1938–39.

80. See, for example, Lê Hữu Thọ's excitement when he sees in person Marseille and Château d'If, where the main protagonist of *The Count of Monte Cristo* was jailed. Lê Hữ Thọ, *Itinéraire d'un petit mandarin* (Paris: L'Harmattan, 1977), 28, as described in Keith, *Subjects and Sojourners*, 58.

81. Peter Zinoman, "Reading Revolutionary Prison Memoirs," in *The Country of Memory: Remaking the Past in Late Socialist Vietnam*, ed. Hue-Tam Ho Tai (Berkeley: University of California Press, 2001), 21–45.

82. See, for example, literary mention of translated versions of *La patronne* and *Le crime au père Boniface* by Guy de Maupassant circulating in Vietnamese reading circles. Vũ Trọng Phụng, *Dumb Luck: A Novel*, trans. Nguyễn Nguyệt Cầm and Peter Zinoman (Ann Arbor: University of Michigan Press, 2002), 175.

83. Elizabeth B. Fitzpatrick, "The Public Library as Instrument of Colonialism: The Case of the Netherlands East Indies," *Libraries & the Cultural Record* 43, no. 3 (2008): 283.

84. Many Chinese translations of global literature were retranslations of Japanese translations of Western works. Teruo Tarumoto, trans. D. E. Pollard, "A Statistical Survey of Translated Fiction 1940–1920," in *Translation and Creation: Readings of Western Literature in Early Modern China, 1840–1918*, ed. David E. Pollard (Amsterdam: John Benjamins Publishing, 1998).

85. Report by Léon Saint-Marty submitted to Governor Georges Maspero, February 15, 1920, DABI, TTLTQG1, folder 314.

86. "La bibliothèque coloniale," *La Tribune Indigène*, April 1, 1920, no. 279, 2.

87. "La bibliothèque colonial."

88. "La bibliothèque colonial." This population accounting might only encompass the Saigon urban center.

89. Report from Saint-Marty to the Director of the Archives and Libraries in Hanoi, July 23, 1921, DABI, TTLTQG1, folder 314.

90. "À la bibliothèque," *La Tribune Indigène*, April 29, 1920, no. 289, 3.

91. Léon Saint-Marty, "Rapport relatif au fonctionnement des Archives et de la Bibliothèque depuis 1919 à ce jour," July 10, 1920, DABI, TTLTQG1, folder 314. In July 1920

Saint-Marty reported that the reading room of the Saigon Library contained approximately seven thousand works.

92. Report from Saint-Marty to the Director of Archives and Libraries in Hanoi, July 23, 1921, DABI, TTLTQG1, folder 314.

93. "Note sur le fonctionnement du service des archives et bibliothèques de la Cochinchine pendant le mois d'Avril 1924," May 2, 1924, DABI, TTLTQG1, folder 314.

94. Léon Saint-Marty, "Rapport relatif au fonctionnement des Archives et de la Bibliothèque depuis 1919 à ce jour," July 10, 1920, DABI, TTLTQG1, folder 314.

95. Report from Saint-Marty to the Director of the Archives and Libraries in Hanoi, July 23, 1921.

96. Report on the Function of the Archives and Library 1923–24 by Jacques Quesnel, May 28, 1924, DABI, TTLTQG1, folder 314.

97. Boudet, *Rapport sur la direction des archives et des bibliothèques (1927–1928)*, 14.

98. "Registre de Prêts des ouvrages de la Bibliothèque années 1920–1925," GC, TTLTQG2, folder 11930. Sometimes in the borrowing log the name was marked "private" but the borrower's address was provided.

99. The first recorded loan was on April 7, 1920, by M. Maspero, who borrowed *Oeuvres de Jeaneau (Cambodge)* and returned the work six weeks later, on May 17, 1920. The last loan recorded in this registry was by D. Bureau, who borrowed *J.O.R.T. Du mois decembre 1923* on June 2, 1925, and returned the work a day later, on June 3.

100. Compiled statistics, 1923–41, GC, TTLTQG2, folder 1626.

101. Compiled statistics, 1923–41.

102. Paul Boudet, *Rapport sur la direction des archives et des bibliothèques (1935–1936)* (Hanoi: Imprimerie G. Taupin & Cie, 1937), 10.

103. Archives et bibliothèques du gouvernement de la Cochinchine, *Guide du Lecteur à la Bibliothèque du Gouvernement de la Cochinchine* (Saigon: Imprimerie C. Ardin, 1939).

104. "T.I.," "Le cas bouchot," *La Tribune Indochinoise*, July 27, 1928, no. 292. This case was also documented in the official library archives together with the dossier of Jean Bouchot, GC, TTLTQG2, folder 12629. At this time Bouchot worked at the Musée Blanchard de la Brosse and the Saigon Cochinchina Library. The Museum Blanchard de la Brosse was built in 1928 and opened in 1929 as the central colonial museum of Saigon and managed by the EFEO. The museum became the national Museum of Vietnam in 1956 and is today the Ho Chi Minh City branch of the Vietnam History Museum.

105. "T.I.," "Le cas bouchot."

106. Peycam, *The Birth of Vietnamese Political Journalism*.

107. See Philippe Peycam, "In Search of a Political Role," in *The Birth of Vietnamese Political Journalism*; Hue-Tam Ho Tai, "The Politics of Compromise: The Constitutionalist Party and the Electoral Reforms of 1922 in French Cochinchina," *Modern Asian Studies* 18, no. 3 (January 1, 1984): 371–91.

108. R. B. Smith, "Bui Quang Chiêu and the Constitutionalist Party in French Cochinchina, 1917–30," *Modern Asian Studies* 3, no. 2 (January 1, 1969): 131–50.

109. Nguyễn Phan Long, "Relisez l'histoire de France, Monsieur Bouchot!," *L'Écho Annamite*, July 18, 1928, no. 223, 1. See other commentary on the case, "Lý-Sự Giữa Sa-Mạc," *Đông Pháp Thời Báo: Le Courrier Indochinois*, August 2, 1928, no. 751, 1.

110. "Des arguments aux injures," *La Volonté Indochinoise*, August 9, 1928, no. 747, 1.

111. E. A., "Pourquoi 'L'Écho Annamite' ne se trouve-t-il pas à la bibliothèque du gouvernement?," *L'Écho Annamite*, October 20, 1926, no. 711, 1.

112. M. N., "La bibliothèque de Saigon," *L'Écho Annamite*, September 27, 1928, no. 1284, 1.

113. "La bibliothèque de Saigon ne donne plus que deux volumes par famille," *La Dépêche Indochine*, December 7, 1934, no. 2019, 2.

114. "À propos de livres prêtés au public," *La Dépêche Indochine*, December 12, 1934, no. 2023, 3.

115. Bourgeois, *Rapport sur la direction des archives et des bibliothèques (1938–1939)*, 13.

116. "À la bibliothèque," *L'Écho Annamite*, April 3–4, 1942, no. 440, 4.

117. From 1920, young French readers who were less than fourteen years old and were registered borrowers from the children's section were also permitted to read periodicals from the periodical section. À la bibliothèque," *La Tribune Indigène*, April 29, 1920, no. 289, 3.

118. For the relationship between colonial civility, youth, and women, see Ha, *French Women and the Empire*; Marie-Paule Ha, "'La Femme française aux colonies': Promoting Colonial Female Emigration at the Turn of the Century," *French Colonial History* 6, no. 1 (2005): 205–24; Ann Stoler, "Sexual Affronts and Racial Frontiers: European Identities and the Cultural Politics of Exclusion in Colonial Southeast Asia," *Comparative Studies in Society and History* 34, no. 3 (July 1, 1992): 514–51; Firpo, *The Uprooted*; David M. Pomfret, *Youth and Empire: Trans-Colonial Childhoods in British and French Asia* (Stanford, CA: Stanford University Press, 2015).

3. TO CIRCULATE: LIBRARIES AS VEHICLES OF CULTURAL PROPAGANDA

1. Paul Boudet, *Rapport sur la direction des archives et des bibliothèques (1931–1932)* (Hanoi: Imprimerie d'Extrême-Orient, 1933), 10.

2. Statement of accident by Lỗ Công Lạc and Trần Văn Trà, September 1, 1937, Gouvernement de la Cochinchine (GC), Trung Tâm Lưu Trữ Quốc Gia 2 (TTLTQG2), Ho Chi Minh City, folder 29904. For an extensive study of automobiles, the social navigation of road spaces, and the logistical responsibilities of Vietnamese drivers in colonial Indochina, see "Sharing the Road: Road Users," in Stéphanie Ponsavady, *Cultural and Literary Representations of the Automobile in French Indochina: A Colonial Roadshow* (Cham, Switzerland: Palgrave Macmillan, 2018), 99–138.

3. Letter from Simone de Saint-Exupéry to Governor of Cochinchina, November 17, 1937, Gouvernement de la Cochinchine (GC), Trung tâm lưu trữ quốc gia 2 (TTLTQG2), folder 29904.

4. Schedule of "Bibliothèque circulante de la Cochinchine," ca. November 1937, GC, TTLTQG2, folder 29904.

5. Note from Simone de Saint-Exupéry, November 16, 1937, GC, TTLTQG2, folder 29904.

6. Letter from Simone de Saint-Exupéry to Governor of Cochinchina, November 17, 1937, GC, TTLTQG2, folder 29904.

7. Martin Thomas, "Albert Sarraut, French Colonial Development, and the Communist Threat, 1919–1930," *Journal of Modern History* 77, no. 4 (2005): 917–55.

8. Shawn McHale, *Print and Power: Confucianism, Communism, and Buddhism in the Making of Modern Vietnam* (Honolulu: University of Hawai'i Press, 2004), 51.

9. For censorship and state repression of print, see McHale, *Print and Power*, 48–57.

10. Christopher Goscha, "The Modern Barbarian: Nguyen Van Vinh and the Complexity of Colonial Modernity in Vietnam," *European Journal of East Asian Studies* 1, no. 3 (2004): 99–134; Yen N. Vu, "Phạm Quỳnh, Borrowed Language, and the Ambivalences of Colonial Discourse," *Journal of Southeast Asian Studies* 51, no. 1–2 (June 2020): 114–31; Hue-Tam Ho Tai, "The Politics of Compromise: The Constitutionalist Party and the Electoral Reforms of 1922 in French Cochinchina," *Modern Asian Studies* 18, no. 3 (January 1, 1984): 371–91; Kevin Pham, chapter 5, "Phạm Quỳnh's Cultural Resistance," in *The Architects of Dignity: Vietnamese Visions of Decolonization* (Oxford: Oxford University Press, 2024), 102–30.

11. This research builds upon the following studies of French colonial popular libraries and the Balai Pustaka: Emmanuelle Affidi, "Vulgarisation du savoir et colonisation des esprits par la presse et le livre en Indochine française et dans les Indes néerlandaises (1908–1936)," *Moussons* 13–14 (December 1, 2009): 95–121; Christiane Pasquel Rageau and Claudine Salmon, "Un projet colonial en Indochine inspiré de Balai Pustaka (1928–1930)," *Archipel* 44, no. 1 (1992): 57–74.

12. After Indonesian independence in 1945, Balai Pustaka resumed its activities as a governmental publishing house that primarily produced school textbooks rather than widely read literary works. See debates on the impact of the Balai Pustaka upon literacy, language standardization, and colonial Indonesia reading practices: Elizabeth B. Fitzpatrick, "The Public Library as Instrument of Colonialism: The Case of the Netherlands East Indies," *Libraries & the Cultural Record* 43, no. 3 (2008): 270–85; Andries Teeuw, "The Impact of Balai Pustaka on Modern Indonesian Literature," *Bulletin of the School of Oriental and African Studies* 35, no. 1 (1972): 111–27; Doris Jedamski, "Balai Pustaka: A Colonial Wolf in Sheep's Clothing," *Archipel* 44, no. 1 (1992): 23–46.

13. Pasquier studied the report titled "Volks-Lectuur" by the French consul general in the Dutch East Indies, Albert Bodard, and the report was distributed to the local administration in Tonkin, Annam, Laos, Cambodge, Cochinchina, and the Director of Public Instruction in Indochina on November 26, 1928. Albert Bodard, "Volks-Lectuur," October 23, 1928, Direction des archives et des bibliothèques (DABI), Trung tâm lưu trữ quốc gia 1 (TTLTQG1), folder 451.

14. Émile Vayrac was the former head of the Governmental General Service of Propaganda and the Press. During his time at the Office of Indigenous Publishing, Vayrac received Albert Bodard's study of the Balai Pustaka, which informed his own comprehensive report from 1928–29, "Notes on the Volkslectuur." Émile Vayrac, "Notes on the Volkslectuur," 1927–28, Gouverneur Générale de l'Indochine (GGI), Archives nationales d'outre-mer (ANOM), Aix-en-Provence, folder 47458.

15. Vayrac, "Notes on the Volkslectuur."

16. Émile Vayrac, "Au sujet des efforts faits au Tonkin depuis vingt-cinq ans environ pour fournir de bonnes lectures aux annamites" (On the subject of efforts made in Tonkin for twenty-five years to provide good reading for Vietnamese), February 17, 1937, Résidence supérieure au Tonkin (nouveau fonds) (RSTNF), ANOM, folder 5219.

17. Vayrac, "Notes on the Volkslectuur,"

18. Hue Tam Ho Tai, *Radicalism and the Origins of the Vietnamese Revolution* (Cambridge, MA: Harvard University Press, 1992), 1.

19. David G. Marr, *Vietnamese Tradition on Trial, 1920–1945* (Berkeley: University of California Press, 1981), 31.

20. For the range of political activity and a reframing of the historiography of colonial and postcolonial republicanism, see the introduction to Nu-Anh Tran and Tuong Vu, eds., *Building a Republican Nation in Vietnam, 1920–1963* (Honolulu: University of Hawaiʻi Press, 2023), 1–25. See also R. B. Smith, "Bùi Quang Chiêu and the Constitutionalist Party in French Cochinchina, 1917–30," *Modern Asian Studies* 3, no. 2 (1969): 131–50.

21. Christopher Goscha, *Thailand and the Southeast Asian Networks of the Vietnamese Revolution, 1885–1954* (Richmond: Curzon, 1999); Charles Keith, chapter 7, "Political Sojourners from Peace to War," in *Subjects and Sojourners: A History of Indochinese in France* (Oakland: University of California Press, 2024), 183–215.

22. Pierre Brocheux and Daniel Hémery, "Resistance, Nationalism, and Social Movements, 1900–1939," in *Indochina: An Ambiguous Colonization, 1858–1954* (Berkeley: University of California Press, 2011), 306.

23. Vayrac, "Notes on the Volkslectuur."

24. Vayrac, "Notes on the Volkslectuur."

25. Pierre Pasquier, Circular 346-S on the "Publications and Creation of Libraries for Use by Vietnamese" (De l'édition de publications et de la création de bibliothèques à l'usage des Annamites), June 7, 1929, GGI, ANOM, folder 47458.

26. Letter from Saint-Marty to Governor of Cochinchina, September 25, 1929, GGI, ANOM, folder 47458.

27. Penny Edwards, *Cambodge: The Cultivation of a Nation 1860–1945* (Honolulu: University of Hawaiʻi Press, 2007), 198–201.

28. Letter from Jean Bouchot to Governor General of Indochina Pierre Pasquier, November 14, 1929, GGI, ANOM, folder 47458.

29. Georgette Naudin, "Jean Bouchot (1886–1932)," *Bulletin de l'École française d'Extrême-Orient* 33 (1933): 557–60.

30. Naudin, "Jean Bouchot (1886–1932)."

31. Jean-Félix Krautheimer, Summary and attached Bouchot and Saint-Marty responses submitted to governor general of Indochina, November 28, 1929, GGI, ANOM, folder 47458. Jean-Félix Krautheimer was governor of Cochinchina from 1929 to 1934.

32. "Publications for indigenous usage and popular libraries," from Pierre Pasquier to the Governor of Cochinchina, July 12, 1930, GGI, ANOM, folder 47458.

33. Letter from Paul Boudet to Director Burton Stevenson of the American Library Association Office in Paris, February 28, 1929, DABI, TTLTQG1, folder 451.

34. Response from Burton Stevenson from ALA Paris with included booklet "Harriet Long's County Book Service" to Paul Boudet, April 20, 1929, DABI, TTLTQG1, folder 451; Response from Carl Milam from the ALA executive office in Chicago to Paul Boudet, May 9, 1929, DABI, TTLTQG1, folder 451.

35. Paul Boudet, "Rapport sur la creation de bibliothèques provinciales et d'un organisme central de distribution de livres," March 6, 1929, DABI, TTLTQG1, folder 451.

36. Boudet, "Rapport sur la creation de bibliothèques provinciales et d'un organisme central de distribution de livres."

37. Letter from Paul Boudet to the Rector of the Academy, Director General of Public Education in Indochina, March 6, 1929, GGI, ANOM, folder 47458.

38. Pasquel Rageau and Salmon, "Un projet colonial en Indochine inspiré de Balai Pustaka (1928–1930)."

39. Tùng Phong, "Bình dân thư-viện" (A people's library), *Báo Đông Pháp*, April 17, 1932, no. 1932, 1.

40. Gaetan Benoit argues that a truly free public library only gained acceptance in France after World War II. Gaetan Benoit, *Eugene Morel: Pioneer of Public Libraries in France* (Duluth, MN: Litwin Books, 2014). See also Sylvie Fayet-Scribe, "The Cross-Fertilization of the U.S. Public Library Model and the French Documentation Model (IIB, French Correspondent of FID) through the French Professional Associations between World War I and World War II," in *Historical Studies in Information Science*, ed. Trudi Bellardo Hahn and Michael Keeble Buckland (Medford, NJ: Information Today, 1998), 181–92.

41. Exchange of letters between Paul Boudet and the Metropolitan Library in Beijing, China, and State Library of Baroda, India, May–July 1930, DABI, TTLTQG1, folder 451.

42. At the international Congrès international de la lecture publique in Alger, April 13–18, 1931, discussions regarding comparative libraries in London, Denmark, and the Netherlands and Dutch East Indies were brought up in the context of discussing the meaning of the public reading for France.

43. See Henri Lemaître, *La lecture publique: Mémoires et voeux du Congrès international d'Alger* (Paris: Librairie E. Droz, 1931); Nathalie Magne, "Henri Lemaître 1881–1946: De la lecture publique à la documentation," master's thesis, Université Panthéon Sorbonne—Paris I, 1995; Martine Blanc-Montmayeur, "Le Congrès d'Alger (13–18 Avril 1931): Prémices de la 'lecture Publique'?," *Bibliothèque(s): Revue de l'Association des bibliothécaires français* 28 (June 28, 2006): 32–36.

44. See J. G. Lemoine, "On va voir à l'exposition colonial le premier 'bibliobus,'" *L'écho de Paris*, May 25, 1931, no. 18847, 1; "Bibliobus," *Le Madécasse*, September 12, 1931, no. 1133, 2; "Le premier bibliobus français," *Journal des débats*, July 9, 1931, no. 189, 2. *Le petit journal* discussed the implications of public reading and lending books through the bibliobus in "Nos échos," *Le petit journal*, July 12, 1931, no. 25014, 2, and "Le problème de la 'lecture publique' peut-il être résolu par le prêt et le port des livres au domicile du lecteur?," *Le petit journal*, January 17, 1932, no. 25203, 1–2; Henri Vendel, "Bibliothèques pour tous en France," in *Arts et métiers graphiques, Special Issue: Les arts et les techniques graphiques* 59 (August 15, 1937). Henri Vendel was the curator of the municipal library of Châlons-sur-Marne and vice president of the Association pour le développement de la lecture publique (Association for the Development of Public Reading).

45. "Mise en service du premier 'bibliobus' français," *La Dépêche d'indochine*, October 10, 1933, no. 1661, 4. The article mentioned that a previous circulating library initiative using former military trucks for exchanging books had been organized in the region but had been on pause for several years. Director of the libraries Victorine Verine spearheaded and organized the Soissons circulating library project and the Soissons bibliobus project, which continued to operate until 1940.

46. According to Nathalie Magne, public library developments were slowed down due to unfavorable legislative measures related to modernizing the library, economic crisis, and traditionalists within libraries who opposed these developments. See Magne, "Henri Lemaître 1881–1946," 45.

47. From 1932 to 1935 Boudet corresponded with Henri Lemaître and the Renault organization to inquire about purchasing the vehicle that was on display at the 1931 colonial

exposition to carry out a circulating libraries program in Indochina. Letters between 1932 and 1935 between Paul Boudet, Henri Lemaître, and the Société anonyme des usines Renault Paris, DABI, TTLTQG1, folder 436.

48. A *quốc ngữ* version of this article appeared in a different publication a week later with the title "Việc truyền-bá tư tưởng pháp qua miền đồng ruộng nam-kỳ" (The disseminating of French thinking through the countryside of Cochinchina) and includes a photograph of Governor Pagès and the bibliobus. "Một cái xáng-kiến rất có ích cho việc mới-mang dân-trí của quan Thống-đốc Pagès," *Hà Thành Ngọ Báo*, March 3, 1936, no. 2641, 1.

49. "Bibliothèque roulante," *L'Annam Nouveau*, February 27, 1936, no. 523, 2. This description was published in the section "Chronique de Hanoi et d'ailleurs."

50. L.T.N., "Pour le rayonnement des lettres françaises—Une heureuse initiative de M. Pagès," *La Tribune Indochinoise*, February 24, 1936, no. 1394, 1.

51. "Commémoration de l'anniversaire de la mort du Gouverneur Général Pierre Pasquier—Discours prononcé par M. Boudet directeur des Archives et bibliothèques de l'Indochine," *France Indochine*, January 16, 1936, no. 4863, 7.

52. "Commémoration de l'anniversaire de la mort du Gouverneur Général Pierre Pasquier," 7.

53. Christiane Pasquel Rageau, "Les bibliothèques de l'Indochine française," in *Histoire des bibliothèques françaises*, ed. Martine Poulain (Paris: Promodis, Ed. du Cercle de la librairie, 1988), 113.

54. "Bibliothèque roulante," *France Indochine*, June 15, 1937, no. 5281, 3.

55. *Tứ Dân Văn Uyển* was a *quốc ngữ* monthly review first published in 1935 through the Office of Indigenous Publications, and its name (also referred to as a "Garden of Letters for the Four Classes of Society") was possibly inspired by the Taman Pustaka "Gardens of Reading." Both Nguyễn Văn Vĩnh and Émile Vayrac had been involved in this publication and other state-sponsored literary and translation publications such as *Les lectures tonkinoises* and *La pensée de l'Occident*. See Goscha, "The Modern Barbarian," 99–134, and Affidi, "Vulgarisation du savoir et colonisation des esprits," 95–121.

56. Vy Cao, "Between the Sacred and the Secular: Publishing, Books, and Everyday Life in Colonial Cochinchina," in *Vietnam over the Long Twentieth Century: Becoming Modern, Going Global*, ed. Liam C. Kelley and Gerard Sasges (Singapore: Springer Nature, 2024), 93.

57. "Le Bibliobus," *La Dépêche d'Indochine*, November 13, 1936, no. 2484, 9. For example, four members of the Colonial Council emphasized the success of the bibliobus and called for the extension of its services.

58. Paul Boudet, *Rapport sur la direction des archives et des bibliothèques (1936–1937)* (Hanoi: Imprimerie d'Extrême-Orient, 1937).

59. "Pour favoriser le développement intellectuel dans l'intérieur," *La Tribune Indochinoise*, February 21, 1936, no. 1398, 1.

60. B. Jendet, "Pourquoi ne pas créer une infirmerie ambulante dans chaque province?," *La Tribune Indochinoise*, August 31, 1936, no. 1469, 3.

61. T. D., "A propos des bibliothèques circulantes—Une suggestion," *La Tribune Indochinoise*, November 26, 1937, no. 1645, 1.

62. "Bibliothèque de la Cochinchine," *La Tribune Indochinoise*, February 1, 1939, no. 1816, 2.

63. "Mốt cái thư viện luận chuyển đi khắp xứ Nam-kỳ," *Trung Hoà Nhật Báo* (Tin đông-pháp section), October 31, 1935, no. 1713, 3; "Sẽ có một chiếc xe chở sách đi khắp Nam-kỳ cho dân mượn đọc," *Hà Thành Ngọ Báo*, October 30, 1935, no. 2441, 1.

64. "Bibliothèque de la Cochinchine," 2.

65. For example, *La Tribune Indochinoise, La Dépêche d'Indochine*, and the *quốc ngữ* newspaper *Sài Gòn* publicized the schedule and route of the bibliobus from 1936 to 1941, noting its schedule, repairs, and delays. These extensive articles point to the popularity and importance of the circulation libraries project for provincial readers.

66. "Les Bibliothèques de l'Indochine," unsigned, ca. 1946, Archives Privées Papiers Boudet (PB), ANOM, folder 83.

67. List of works borrowed and returned from the province of Soctrang, April 15, 1942, and List of books and borrowers from Rachgia, May 28, 1942, GC, TTLTQG2, folder 12010.

68. For late colonial Vietnamese publishing and public life in Cochinchina, see McHale, *Print and Power*, 17–35.

69. List of works borrowed and returned from the province of Rachgia, August 17, 1942, GC, TTLTQG2, folder 12010.

70. List of works borrowed and returned from the province of Bentre, April 27, 1942, GC, TTLTQG2, folder 12010. The April 1942 list counts twenty-seven borrowers, five of whom were French and twenty-two of whom were Vietnamese.

71. Nguyễn Phuong Ngọc, "Huỳnh Thị Bảo Hòa (1896–1982): A Woman Who Wrote to Change Vietnamese Society," in *Vietnam Over the Long Twentieth Century*, 37–61; Lại Nguyên Ân, "Một cuốn truyện bị quên lãng," *Tạp chí văn học* 6 (June 2001).

72. This work was first translated by Dương Tấn Long and published in Saigon in 1934. Drawing from Cordier, Boudet, and Bourgeois's printed catalogs, the legal deposit works preserved at the Bibliothèque nationale de France, and the card files of the EFEO, Yan Bao accounts for at least 316 *quốc ngữ* translations of Chinese novels. Yan Bao, "The Influence of Chinese Fiction on Vietnamese Literature," trans. Noel Castelino, in *Literary Migrations: Traditional Chinese Fiction in Asia (17th–20th centuries)*, ed. Claudine Salmon (Singapore: Institute of Southeast Asian Studies, 2013), 163–95.

73. Léon Saint-Marty demands for returns, ca. 1942, GC, TTLTQG2, folder 12010. These recall slips referenced article nine of the Cochinchina Library Regulations of February 1936.

74. Letter from Monsieur Arrivets of local government to the curator of the archives and library in Saigon, November 4, 1942, GC, TTLTQG2, folder 50342.

75. Letter from Léon Saint-Marty to government administrative office, November 28, 1942, GC, TTLTQG2, folder 50342.

76. See, for example, *Sài Gòn*, July 28, 1939, no. 14183, 8, and *Sài Gòn*, April 11, 1942, no. 15033, 2.

77. Confidential statement 80-S/IPP from Jean Decoux to the Heads of General Services, December 5, 1941, DABI, TTLTQG1, folder 2135. In the statement the Vichy governor general of Indochina, Admiral Jean Decoux, issued to the heads of the local administration a list of newspapers and periodicals "to encourage, to not encourage, or to ignore." For example, periodicals not to encourage included *Voix d'empire, La Dépêche d'Indochine, La Tribune Indochinoise, Cahiers de la jeunesse, Écho d'Extrême-Orient, Quotidien d'indochine, Nouvelles*, and *Cơn Chiến*.

78. "Réglementation de l'insertion des communiqués dans la presse," 1941–43, TTLTQG1, DABI, folder 895. Marcel Robbe served as the first head of the IPP, followed by Maurice Michaudel from 1944 to March 1945. Michaudel was a colonial official in Laos and served as chief of the office of the Lao resident superior (1942–44).

79. For example, longtime conservative colonial official Jean Cousseau served as the head of the local Information Office for Propaganda and the Press in Tonkin from April 1943 until the Japanese *coup de force* on March 9, 1945. Cousseau was born in northern Vietnam and graduated from the École nationale des langues orientales vivantes in Paris. A fluent Vietnamese speaker, Jean Cousseau worked with the director of the secret police, Louis Marty, on a colonial intelligence mission to monitor and spy on Vietnamese communists at the Sơn La prison in northwest Tonkin in 1932. For more on Cousseau, see Christopher E. Goscha, *Historical Dictionary of the Indochina War (1945–1954): An International and Interdisciplinary Approach* (Honolulu: University of Hawai'i Press, 2012).

80. Circular Number 144-N/IPP Jean Decoux and the office of the service de l'Information de la propagande et de la Presse, December 27, 1942, DABI, TTLTQG1, folder 2313.

81. Response to GGI and IPP, January 29, 1943, DABI, TTLTQG1, folder 2313.

82. Response to GGI and IPP, January 29, 1943.

83. Letter from Marcel Robbe, director of IPP, February 24, 1942, DABI, TTLTQG1, folder 451.

84. Letter from Captain L. Pericaud to the head of the Office of Censorship in Saigon, March 30, 1942, GC, TTLTQG2, folder 38019.

85. Letter from Saint-Marty to director of the Saigon censor office, August 5, 1942, GC, TTLTQG2, folder 38019.

86. Phạm Mạnh Phan, "Muốn chữa nạn thanh niên truỵ lạc, hãy đốt hết những sách khiêu dâm," *Tri Tân*, August 1, 1941, no. 9, 7–8, 18. Phạm Mạnh Phan (1914–?) was born in Bạch Mai, Hà Đông (today part of Hanoi), and served as the secretary of the editorial office during the entire operations of the weekly periodical *Tri Tân* from 1941 to 1945.

87. Jean Decoux, "Épuration des bibliothèques," August 6, 1942, DABI, TTLTQG1, folder 2135.

88. Confidential letter from Paul Boudet to Jean Decoux, October 2, 1942, DABI, TTLTQG1, folder 2135.

89. Confidential letter from Paul Boudet to Jean Decoux, October 2, 1942.

90. Decoux also advanced a policy of traditionalism in Indochina, rallying behind local unifying forces of hierarchical power such as the mandarins and an imagined traditional lost past prior to French colonialism. Phạm Quỳnh played an important role as Bảo Đại's prime minister to instill this sense of local nationalisms and the mandarin responsibility to cultivate the past. Eric Jennings, *Vichy in the Tropics: Pétain's National Revolution in Madagascar, Guadeloupe, and Indochina, 1940–1944* (Stanford, CA: Stanford University Press, 2001).

91. Confidential letter from Paul Boudet to Jean Decoux, October 2, 1942.

92. Internal report, "Venté aux enchères des livres par la Bibliothèque de l'Indochine," November 19, 1943, DABI, TTLTQG1, folder 1451.

93. Walter Kaiser draws these statistics from public libraries in cities with populations over 200,000 in the United States. Walter H. Kaiser, "Statistical Trends of Large Public Libraries, 1900–1946," *Library Quarterly: Information, Community, Policy* 18, no. 4 (1948): 278.

94. "Rapport sur les activités de la Bibliothèque de 'Pierre Pasquier' section de prêt pendant les Années 1939–1943," DABI, TTLTQG1, folder 2215.

95. "Section de Prêt: Ordre de Préférence," ca. 1944–45, DABI, TTLTQG1, folder 1669.

96. André Gide's work spanned literature and autobiography and included an examination of morality in *L'immoraliste* (*The Immoralist*) (1902), a discussion of homosexuality in

Les faux-monnayeurs (*The Counterfeiters*) (1925), and his personal dabbling in and ultimate criticisms of communism under the Soviet regime in *Retour de l'U.R.S.S.* (*Return from the U.S.S.R.*) (1936). This list of books provides insight into the range of popular publications that might have circulated within the Central Library lending section, or at least within the local Indochinese reading market.

4. TO READ: *BÌNH DÂN THƯ VIỆN* AND VIETNAMESE LANGUAGE NATIONALISM

1. Hoa Bằng, "Các vùng ngoại ô và thôn quê cần có những 'duyệt thư, báo xã,'" *Tri Tân*, March 4, 1942, no. 37, 2–3. Hoa Bằng was the pen name of Hoàng Thúc Trâm. See his history on the transformation of Vietnamese publishing in Hoa Bằng, "Lịch trình nghề ấn loát Việt Nam: Từ lối in mộc bản xưa đến thuật in hoạt bản bây giờ," *Tri Tân*, June 9, 1942, no. 49, 2–4, 21. The original quote most likely came from maxim 15 子孫雖愚經書不可不讀, which translates to "Although children and grandchildren be simpletons, they must read the Classics" from "Maxims for Managing the Home" by the Confucian scholar Zhū Bólú (1617–1688).

2. Khuông Việt, "Thử thảo một chương-trình lập thơ-viện Việt-nam," *Tri Tân*, February 25, 1942, no. 36, 2–4, 23.

3. This comparison of good leisure and bad leisure also reflects underlying late colonial tensions around social vices and the clandestine sex industry. See the social history of Tonkin's bars, nightclubs, singing houses, and clandestine sex industry, Christina Firpo, *Black Market Business: Selling Sex in Northern Vietnam, 1920–1945* (Ithaca, NY: Cornell University Press, 2020).

4. Hoa Bằng proposed that reading societies could be built in the existing temples of literature and shrines in the villages and hamlets. He called for individual districts to "sacrifice" 50 percent of their budget used for festivals to contribute to developing the libraries.

5. Martina Nguyen, "French Colonial State, Vietnamese Civil Society: The League of Light [Đoàn Ánh Sáng] and Housing Reform in Hanoi, 1937–1941," *Journal of Vietnamese Studies* 11, no. 3–4 (2016): 17–57; Jack Sidnell, "The Inconvenience of Tradition: Phan Khôi's Pragmatism and His Proposals for Modernizing Language Reform," *Journal of Vietnamese Studies* 18, no. (2023): 56–97.

6. Christopher Goscha, "The Modern Barbarian: Nguyen Van Vinh and the Complexity of Colonial Modernity in Vietnam," *European Journal of East Asian Studies* 1, no. 3 (2004): 99–134; Yen N. Vu, "Phạm Quỳnh, Borrowed Language, and the Ambivalences of Colonial Discourse," *Journal of Southeast Asian Studies* 51, no. 1–2 (June 2020): 114–31; Yan Bao, "The Influence of Chinese Fiction on Vietnamese Literature," trans. Noel Castelino, in *Literary Migrations: Traditional Chinese Fiction in Asia (17th–20th Centuries)*, ed. Claudine Salmon (Singapore: Institute of Southeast Asian Studies, 2013), 163–95.

7. Alexander Woodside, "The Development of Social Organizations in Vietnamese Cities in the Late Colonial Period," *Pacific Affairs* 44, no. 1 (April 1, 1971): 39–64.

8. Martina Thucnhi Nguyen, *On Our Own Strength: The Self-Reliant Literary Group and Cosmopolitan Nationalism in Late Colonial Vietnam* (Honolulu: University of Hawai'i Press, 2020).

9. John Phan, "Rival Nationalisms and the Rebranding of Language in Early 20th-Century Tonkin," *IIAS: The Newsletter* 79 (Spring 2018): 40–42; John Phan, "The Twentieth-Century Secularization of the Sinograph in Vietnam, and Its Demotion from the Cosmological to the Aesthetic," *Journal of World Literature* 1, no. 2 (January 1, 2016): 275–93.

10. Benedict R. O'G Anderson, *Imagined Communities Reflections on the Origin and Spread of Nationalism*, rev. ed. (London: Verso, 1991).

11. Su Lin Lewis, *Cities in Motion: Urban Life and Cosmopolitanism Southeast Asia, 1920–1940* (Cambridge: Cambridge University Press, 2016), 179.

12. Unpublished report, September 1934, Direction des archives et des bibliothèques (DABI), Trung tâm lưu trữ quốc gia 1 (TTLTQG1), folder 1423-01.

13. Leah Price, *How to Do Things with Books in Victorian Britain* (Princeton, NJ: Princeton University Press, 2012), 18.

14. N.Đ., "Thú dọc sách," *Đông Pháp Thời Báo: Le Courrier Indochinois*, March 26, 1924, no. 124, 1.

15. B.T., "Đọc sách thế nào có ích?," *Đông Pháp Thời Báo: Le Courrier Indochinois*, July 16, 1924, no. 167, 2.

16. For a detailed study of readerly agency in engaging with, reinterpreting, and deviating from classical Sinitic texts in the early modern period, see Fan Wang, "How Late Imperial Chinese Literati Read Their Books: Inscribing, Collating, Excerpting," *Book History* 24, no. 2 (2021): 320–51.

17. Đoan Phố, "Đọc Sách," *Đông Pháp Thời Báo*, February 9, 1928, no. 680, 7.

18. "Xem sách mà không phải đọc. Lợi cho ai? Hại cho ai?," *Hà Thành Ngọ Báo*, September 20, 1929, no. 639, 1.

19. See George Dutton, "Advertising, Modernity, and Consumer Culture in Colonial Vietnam," in *The Reinvention of Distinction: Modernity and the Middle Class in Urban Vietnam*, ed. Van Nguyen-Marshall et al. (Singapore: Springer, 2012), 21–42; Lonán Ó Briain, "Sound, Technology, and Culture in French Indochina," in *Voices of Vietnam: A Century of Radio, Red Music, and Revolution* (Oxford: Oxford University Press, 2021); Erich Dewald, "Taking to the Waves: Vietnamese Society around the Radio in the 1930s," *Modern Asian Studies* 46, no. 1 (2012): 143–65.

20. See the extensive intellectual and linguistic projects of dictionaries, glossaries, and histories by Đào Duy Anh (1904–88). For an example of a reader guide focused on assisting readers to understand a specific text, see Phan Khôi, "Giúp độc giả khi đọc cuốn *Nước Nhựt bổn 30 năm duy tân* của ông Đào-Trinh-Nhất," *Sông Hương*, March 27, 1937, no. 52, 2, 8.

21. "Tư tưởng đông tây," *Đông Pháp Thời Báo: Le Courrier Indochinois*, February 11, 1928, no. 681, 10.

22. Focusing on the cultural practice of book collecting and aesthetics, I build upon Martina Nguyen's extensive analysis of the Family Library and Đời Nay Publishing House publishing practices. Nguyen, *On Our Own Strength*, 32–36.

23. Nhị Linh, "Tủ Sách Gia Đình," *Phong Hoá*, August 10, 1934, no. 110, 1–2.

24. Nhị Linh, "Tủ Sách Gia Đình," *Phong Hoá*, August 18, 1934, no. 111, 1–2.

25. Nguyen, *On Our Own Strength*, 6.

26. Lan Khai, "Đọc sách là một nghệ thuật," *Hà Thành Ngọ Báo*, September 19, 1935, no. 2466, 1.

27. Nguyễn Vỹ, *Văn Thi Sĩ Tiền Chiến* (Hanoi: Nhà xuất bản Văn Học, 2007), 98–100.

28. Lan Khai, "Đọc sách là một nghệ thuật," *Hà Thành Ngọ Báo*, September 19, 1935, no. 2466, 1.

29. Hồng-vân and Phạm thị-Thoa, "Cái hại tiểu-thuyết," *Hà Thành Ngọ Báo*, February 13, 1930, no. 754, 2.

30. Hồng-vân and Phạm thị-Thoa, "Cái hại tiểu-thuyết," 2.

31. Hồng-vân and Phạm thị-Thoa, "Cái hại tiểu-thuyết," 2.

32. See, for example, how the author Vũ Trọng Phụng satirizes female suicide related to the uptake of consumerist Western fads and cultural capital in *Dumb Luck*. For an introduction to this discourse around female suicide and romance literature, see Linh Vu, "Drowned in Romances, Tears, and Rivers: Young Women's Suicide in Early Twentieth-Century Vietnam," *Explorations* 9, no. 1 (Spring 2009): 25–46.

33. Judith Henchy, "Vietnamese New Women and the Fashioning of Modernity," in *France and "Indochina": Cultural Representations*, ed. Katherine Robson and Jennifer Yee (Lanham, MD: Lexington Books, 2005), 121–38; Hue-Tam Ho Tai, chapter 3, "Daughters of Annam," in *Radicalism and the Origins of the Vietnamese Revolution* (Cambridge, MA: Harvard University Press, 1992), 88–113.

34. Ho Tai, *Radicalism and the Origins of the Vietnamese Revolution*, 90.

35. Firpo, *Black Market Business*, 166–67, 175–76.

36. H.L., "Các làng nên có nhà hội đồng và nhà thư viện" (The villages should have a community center and library), *Trung-Hoà Nhật Báo*, July 18, 1925, no. 188, 1. *Trung-Hoà Nhật Báo* operated from 1923 to 1945 under the ownership of G. Lebourdais (who wrote many articles under the pseudonym Đông Bích) and the directorship of Nguyễn Bá Chính.

37. Tùng Phong, "Bình dân thư-viện" (A public library), *Báo Đông Pháp*, April 17, 1932, no. 1932, 1.

38. The author references these efforts and the discussion about creating village libraries in the schools for poor students to borrow textbooks. "Xem qua các tỉnh xứ Bắc kỳ—Hừng yến Thư viện," *Báo Đông Pháp*, April 16, 1932, no. 1931, 2.

39. For an extensive study on the role of the Vietnamese monarchy during the colonial period, see Bruce McFarland Lockhart, *The End of the Vietnamese Monarchy*, Lạc Việt Series no. 15 (New Haven, CT: Council on Southeast Asia Studies, 1993).

40. See Christopher Goscha, *Vietnam: A New History* (New York: Basic Books, 2016), 210–13; Christopher Goscha, "Colonial Monarchy and Decolonisation in the French Empire: Bảo Đại, Norodom Sihanouk and Mohammed V," in *Monarchies and Decolonisation in Asia*, ed. Robert Aldrich and Cindy McCreery (Manchester: Manchester University Press, 2020), 152–74.

41. The Bảo Đại Library was estimated to be in operation between 1923 and 1947, and the chronology of its location, whether within or behind the imperial palace complex, is unclear. Some sources say that the original organization of the library was motivated by the Tân Thơ Viện (Tân Thư Viện) (1909–23) becoming the Khải Định museum, and as a result the Quốc tử Giám (Imperial Academy) needing to organize a new library, moving the books from the former Tân Thơ Viện to the building behind and to the left of the imperial palace complex. This building thus became the Bảo Đại Library. According to Nguyễn Công Trí, many of the materials in the central region libraries were reorganized and moved into the Bảo Đại Library and managed by the Viện Văn Hoá Trung kỳ, established in 1940. "Bộ Giáo-dục đang cho sưu tập sách để vào Bảo-Đại thư-viên," *Đông Pháp*, September 26, 1934, no. 2748, 1–2; Nguyễn Công Trí, "Những thư viện lớn của triều Nguyễn ở kinh đô Huế xưa," *Nghiên cứu và Phát triển*, no. 6–7 (2013): 104–5.

42. The circular was published on September 26, 1934, in the periodical *Đông Pháp*. "Bộ Giáo-dục đang cho sưu tập sách để vào Bảo-Đại thư-viện," *Đông Pháp*, September 26, 1934, no. 2748, 1–2.

43. For a study of book copying and library culture during the late Ming period, described as a "community of learning," see Joseph P. McDermott, *A Social History of the*

Chinese Book: Books and Literati Culture in Late Imperial China (Hong Kong: Hong Kong University Press, 2006).

44. "Faut-il créer une seconde bibliothèque à hue?" (Should a second library be created in Hue?), January 13, 1934, excerpt from an article in the newspaper *Tiểu Long*, DABI, TTLTQG1, Hanoi, folder 585.

45. "Faut-il créer une seconde bibliothèque à hue?"

46. Trần Danh, "Một vài điều phải sửa đổi ở thư viện Bảo Đại" (A few things that must be changed at the Bảo Đại Library), *Tràng An*, May 19, 1936, no. 124, 4.

47. Trần Danh, "Một vài điều phải sửa đổi ở thư viện Bảo Đại."

48. "Bức thư không niêm gởi cho quan Thượng Quốc dân Giáo dục," *Tràng An*, November 3, 1936, no. 170, 1–2.

49. "Một kỳ thi tuyển hai vị thuộc quan ngạch Nam-Triều," *Tuần Lễ*, January 6, 1940, no. 87, 1.

50. "L'exposition de l'Annam d'aturefois," *L'Écho Annamite*, April 3–4, 1942, no. 440, 1.

51. For accounts of Nhu's work in the Directorate, see Diến Đào Thị, "Ngô Đình Nhu—Nhà lưu trữ Việt Nam thời kỳ 1938–1946," *Tạp chí Nghiên cứu và Phát triển* 6–7 (2013): 238–43.

52. Decree on the formation of the Service des Archives et bibliothèques du gouvernement impérial, signed by Bảo Đại, August 11, 1943, Châu Bản Triều Nguyễn (CBTN), TTLTQG1, volume 34, p. 182.

53. In November 1943 a new institution called the Văn Thơ Viện was founded that worked closely and at times in cooperation with the Bảo Đại Library and the Quốc Sử Quán. Report on the activities of the Văn Thơ Viện since its creation, November 1943 to December 1944, DABI, TTLTQG1, folder 2214.

54. Tiêu Diêu Tử, "Cần phải có một Hội Văn-chương Mỹ-thuật và Thể-thao ở Kinh-đô" (There needs to be an Association of Literature, Arts, and Exercise in the capital), *Tráng An*, April 9, 1935, no. 12, 1–2.

55. On May 8, 1935, the group was renamed Mỹ Hoà Hội, and the French name was Cercle artistique, littéraire et sportif annamite. Đỗ Minh Điền, "Mỹ Hòa Hội—Hội Văn Chương, Mỹ Thuật và Thể Thao Đầu Tiên Tại Huế," *Tạp Chí Sông Hương*, April 29, 2021, http://tapchisonghuong.com.vn/tin-tuc/p2/c15/n30089/My-Hoa-hoi-Hoi-Van-chuong-My-thuat-va-The-thao-dau-tien-tai-Hue.html.

56. The group was officially recognized by Graffeuil according to decree no. 1281 on June 17, 1935. See *Statuts du Cercle artistique, littéraire et sportif annamite—Mỹ Hoà hội en Annam* (Hue: Imprimerie Đắc Lập, 1936).

57. Vy Cao lists the names of the publishing houses: A. J. S., Canh Tân, Đắc Lập, Imprimerie de la Mission de Huế, Imprimerie de la Mission de Qui Nhơn, Imprimerie du Mirador (Viễn Đệ), Hương Giang, Phúc Long, Tiếng Dân, Tôn Thất Cảnh, Imprimerie de Qui Nhơn, Châu Tinh, Imprimerie du Nord Annam, Nguyễn Đức Tư, and Vương Đình Châu. Vy Cao, "Between the Sacred and the Secular: Publishing, Books, and Everyday Life in Colonial Cochinchina," in *Vietnam over the Long Twentieth Century: Becoming Modern, Going Global*, ed. Liam C. Kelley and Gerard Sasges (Singapore: Springer Nature, 2024), 91.

58. Note on the bookstores in Annam attached to Report 1129-G, "Note sur les conditions dans lesquelles pourraient être organisées en Annam des bibliothèques populaires," June 2, 1930, DABI, TTLTQG1, folder 451.

59. Tiêu Diêu Tử, "Nên có một bình-dân thư-viện ở Huế" (There should be a public library in Hue), *Tràng An*, April 19, 1935, no. 15, 1.

60. "Bao giờ Huế có một thư viện như thế" (When will Hue have a library like that?), *Tràng An*, February 7, 1936, no. 96, 2.

61. "Huế sắp có bình-dân thư-viện" (Hue will soon have a public library), *Tràng An*, February 25, 1936, no. 100, 2.

62. Letter from the resident superior of Annam to director of the Services des archives et bibliothèques à Hanoi, April 9, 1936, DABI, TTLTQG1, folder 643.

63. Philippe Peycam shows how these structural transformations in Cochinchina resulted in an urban structural dualism between the Saigon-Cholon city and the countryside villages. Philippe Peycam, "From the Social to the Political: 1920s Colonial Saigon as a 'Space of Possibilities' in Vietnamese Consciousness," *Positions* 21, no. 3 (July 1, 2013): 497–546, 526–27.

64. Philippe Peycam, *The Birth of Vietnamese Political Journalism: Saigon, 1916–1930* (New York: Columbia University Press, 2012), 39.

65. Statutes of the Baclieu Friendly Library, 1906, Gouvernement de la Cochinchine (GC), Trung Tâm Lưu Trữ Quốc Gia 2 (TTLTQG2), Ho Chi Minh City, folder 11966.

66. Statutes of the Association of Primary Teachers, January 8, 1941, GC, TTLTQG2, folder 51050.

67. Travailleurs du Livre du Tonkin, *Statuts—Association des "Travailleurs Du Livre" du Tonkin* (Hanoi: Imprimerie Ngo Tu Ha, 1938).

68. Requests for a Mutuality House, GC, TTLTQG2, folder 51050. However, by May 4, 1940, the request for the government subsidy still had not been approved. The list of self-help groups included the Cochinchina Mutual Education Society, the Friendly Association of Former Students of the Chasseloup-Laubat College, the Federation of Cochinchine Unions, and the Association of Annamite Engineers and Technicians.

69. Cần Thơ Library Circle Statutes, 1925, GC, TTLTQG2, folder 51124. Other reading clubs mentioned in the same dossier include the library circle in Sóc Trăng established in 1914, Bà Rịa in 1924, Mỹ Tho in 1925, Thủ Dầu Mộtin 1930, and the French-Vietnamese library circle of Bến Tre established in 1940.

70. Hà Tiên Library Circle Statutes, 1931, GC, TTLTQG2, folder 51124.

71. David Marr, *Vietnamese Tradition on Trial, 1920–1945* (Berkeley: University of California Press, 1981), 179–83.

72. Pierre Brocheux and Daniel Héméry, *Indochina: An Ambiguous Colonization, 1858–1954* (Berkeley: University of California Press, 2011), 345.

73. Hieu Nam Trung Le, "Another Kind of Vietnamization: Language Policies in Higher Education in the Two Vietnams," in *Vietnam over the Long Twentieth Century*, 131.

74. Bắc Hà, "Việc khai-dân-tri rât cân của nước ta. Lớp học phổ-thông và thư-viện học-sinh," *Trang Án*, September 12, 1939, no. 451, 2.

75. Van Nguyen-Marshall, *Between War and the State: Civil Society in South Vietnam, 1954–1975* (Ithaca, NY: Cornell University Press, 2023), 32–36.

76. Summary of Nguyễn Thị Trang's application and police report, April 13, 1933, GC, TTLTQG2, folder 17005.

77. "Phòng đọc Sách' đường Arras," *Phụ Nữ Tân Văn*, June 22, 1933, no. 205, 3–4.

78. "La salle de lecture de la rue d'Arras est ouverte," *La Dépêche d'Indochine*, July 5, 1933, no. 1581, 2. "Phòng xem sách mới lập" (The reading room recently founded), *Phụ Nữ Tân Văn*, June 1, 1933, no. 202, 22.

79. "'Phòng đọc sách' của cô Nguyễn Thị Trang ở đường d'arras" (The reading room of Nguyễn Thị Trang on Arras Street), *Hà Thành Ngọ Báo*, August 6, 1933, no. 1778, 2.

80. "La salle de lecture de la rue d'Arras est ouverte," *La Dépêche d'Indochine*, July 5, 1933, no. 1581, 2.

81. "Phòng xem sách mới lập," 22. This was reported in the section "Tin tức trong nước" (News around the country).

82. In some accounts the librarian-secretary's name is written as Phương Huê. "Nữ Tổng-thư-ký phòng đọc sách đường Arras là cô Ng. thị Phương Huê," *Hà Thành Ngọ Báo*, December 9, 1933, no. 1881, 3.

83. Ngô Bích San, "Phòng đọc sách và cô Phương-Hoa" (The reading room and Mademoiselle Phương Hoa), *Hà Thành Ngọ Báo*, September 13, 1933, no. 1808, 1–2.

84. Phương Hoa mentioned that she had written countless letters to directors of newspapers and periodicals but often didn't receive a response. She also mentioned that many Westerners came to the library, and that they gave her the idea to request books from foreign countries.

85. See the following discussions about women's debates in the Vietnamese popular press: Đặng Thị Vân Chi, "Báo chí tiếng Việt và vấn đề mại dâm dưới thời Pháp thuộc," *Nghiên cứu Gia Đìnhvà Giới* 1 (2008): 34–42; Đặng Thị Vân Chi, *Vấn Đề Phụ Nữ Trên Báo Chí Tiếng Việt Trước Năm 1945* (Hanoi: Nhà Xuất Bản Khoa Học Xã Hội, 2007); Shawn McHale, "Printing and Power: Vietnamese Debates over Women's Place in Society, 1918–1934," in *Essays into Vietnamese Pasts*, Studies on Southeast Asia 19 (Ithaca, NY: Cornell University Press, 1995); David Marr, "The 1920s Women's Rights Debates in Vietnam: Introduction," *Journal of Asian Studies (Pre-1986)* 35, no. 3 (May 1976): 371; Thanh Phùng and Đăng Minh Vũ, "An Educational Regime of Truth for Social Reform in Late Colonial Vietnam: The Journalistic Art of the Possible in *Phụ nữ tân văn*'s 'Travel Stories' and 'Letters for You,'" in *Vietnam Over the Long Twentieth Century*.

86. See Madeleine E. Aitchinson, who studies the historical representation of women as "mirrors" (*tấm gương*) or "lessons" (*bài học*) for communicating new ideals of womanhood. Madeleine Aitchison, "Mirrors and Visions: Nữ Lưu Thơ Quán and the Woman Question in Interwar Vietnam," PhD diss., University of Ottawa, 2023.

87. "Một người đàn bà coi thư-viện," *Ngày Nay*, August 2, 1936, no. 19, 18.

88. "Phòng đọc sách đã mở cửa rồi," *Hà Thành Ngọ Báo*, December 1, 1933, no. 1874, 1.

89. Surveillance report on indigenous public library reading room at 44 Reims Street, January 22, 1934, GC, TTLTQG2, folder 17005.

90. Rules for reading room operations, ca. 1932–35, GC, TTLTQG2, folder 17005.

91. Hồ Văn Sao would later create the prolific Imprimerie du Mékong in 1933 Sa Đéc and also codirected the weekly newspaper *Tân Tiến* from 1935 to 1938.

92. Application by Phạm văn Chiêu to open a reading room, November 17, 1931, GC, TTLTQG2, folder 17005. Phạm Văn Chiêu (1907–91) was born in Long Hoà in Gia Định province. In the 1940s Chiêu led a series of revolutionary activities as part of the Indochinese Communist Party and later as chairman of the Administrative Resistance Committee (1945–51) in the Gia Định provincial bases of resistance against French forces. See his memoir, Phạm Văn Chiêu, *Cuộc kháng chiến chống Pháp của đồng bào Gia Định (1945–1954)* (Ho Chi Minh City: Nhà xuất bản Tổng hợp Thành phố Hồ Chí Minh, 2017).

93. Confidential police response to An Ngọc Phụng's application to open a library in Giadinh, August 10, 1932, GC, TTLTQG2, folder 17005.

94. See David Marr's countless examples of how publishers, editors, and writers evaded and navigated censors throughout the colonial period, *Vietnamese Tradition on Trial, 1920–1925* (Berkeley: University of California Press, 1981).

95. Lại Nguyên Ân, introduction to *Tạp chí Tri tân 1941–1945, truyện và ký: sưu tập tác phẩm*, ed. Lại Nguyên Ân and Nguyễn Hữu Sơn (Hanoi: Nhà xuất bản Hội nhà văn, 2000), 5.

96. Khuông Việt, "Thử thảo một chương-trình lập thơ-viện Việt-nam," 2–4, 23.

97. Khuông Việt, "Thử thảo một chương-trình lập thơ-viện Việt-nam," 2–4, 23.

98. For example, Khuông Việt published a book on the historical figure Tôn Thọ Tường, who was notoriously one of the first to collaborate with the French administration in the 1860s. Most of the works cited in the book's bibliography were from the Cochinchina Library.

99. Khuông Việt, "Thử thảo một chương-trình lập thơ-viện Việt-nam," 2.

100. Khuông Việt, "Nên đọc sử nước nhà," *Tri Tân*, July 18, 1941, no. 7, 2.

101. Reports by Léon Saint-Marty (March 20, 1946) and Rémi Bourgeois (June 12, 1946), Thư viện Quốc gia Nam Việt (1945–1957) (TVQGNV), TTLTQG2, folder 11.

5. TO REASSEMBLE: THE DECOLONIZATION OF LIBRARIES

1. For a detailed account of September 2, 1945, throughout Vietnam, see David G. Marr, *Vietnam 1945: The Quest for Power* (Berkeley: University of California Press, 1995), 520–37.

2. Letter and attached Circular Number 18 from Hoàng Minh Giám, Minister of Bộ Nội Vụ Việt Nam Dân Chủ Cộng Hoà (Ministry of Internal Affairs of the Democratic Republic of Vietnam) to Bộ Quốc Gia Giáo Dục (Ministry of National Education), September 18, 1945, Direction des archives et des bibliothèques (DABI), Trung tâm lưu trữ quốc gia 1 (TTLTQG1), folder 1581.

3. Shawn McHale, *The First Vietnam War: Violence, Sovereignty, and the Fracture of the South* (Cambridge: Cambridge University Press, 2021), 2.

4. Christopher Goscha, *The Road to Dien Bien Phu: A History of the First War for Vietnam* (Princeton, NJ: Princeton University Press, 2022); McHale, *The First Vietnam War*; Brett Reilly, "The Sovereign States of Vietnam, 1945–1955," *Journal of Vietnamese Studies* 11, no. 3–4 (November 1, 2016): 103–39; Christian Lentz, *Contested Territory: Điện Biên Phủ and the Making of Northwest Vietnam* (New Haven, CT: Yale University Press, 2019).

5. Report on European Personnel at the Directorate, signed S. Kudo and Paul Boudet, May 2, 1945, DABI, TTLTQG1, folder 1669. Bourgeois had served as director of the Cochinchina Library following Léon Saint-Marty.

6. Decree, July 14, 1945, DABI, TTLTQG1, folder 1669. Nguyen Van Suoc would replace Lê Hữu Cúc after Suoc returned from leave in six months.

7. Letter from S. Kudo, Director of Archives and Libraries of Indochina, to the GGI (Personnel Department) in Hanoi, May 28, 1945, DABI, TTLTQG1, folder 1669.

8. Đào Diến Thị, "Ngô Đình Nhu—Nhà lưu trữ Việt Nam thời kỳ 1938–1946," *Tạp chí Nghiên cứu và Phát triển*, no. 6–7 (2013): 242.

9. For a meticulous account of early on-the-ground state building by the DRV, see David Marr, *Vietnam: State, War, and Revolution (1945–1946)* (Berkeley: University of California Press, 2013).

10. Christopher Goscha, *Vietnam: A New History* (New York: Basic Books, 2016), 174.

11. Marr, *Vietnam: State, War, and Revolution*, 5.

12. Marr, *Vietnam: State, War, and Revolution*, 8–9.

13. Võ Nguyên Giáp also signed Decree Number 21 on September 8, 1945. Đào Diến Thị, "Ngô Đình Nhu—Nhà lưu trữ Việt Nam thời kỳ 1938–1946," 104–5.

14. Letter from S. Kudo, Director of Archives and Libraries of Indochina, to the GGI (Personnel Department) in Hanoi.

15. Marr, *Vietnam: State, War, and Revolution*, 20; Hieu Nam Trung Le, "Another Kind of Vietnamization: Language Policies in Higher Education in the Two Vietnams," in *Vietnam over the Long Twentieth Century: Becoming Modern, Going Global*, ed. Liam C. Kelley and Gerard Sasges (Singapore: Springer Nature, 2024), 132.

16. Report "Tờ trình từ ngày đảo chính mồng 9 tháng 3 đến hết năm 1945" by Department of Archive Records and Nationwide Library, February 9, 1946, DABI, TTLTQG1, folder 1537.

17. J. Martin, *Revue d'histoire de la Seconde Guerre mondiale* 138 (April 1985): 91, as cited in Pierre Brocheux and Daniel Hémery, *Indochina: An Ambiguous Colonization, 1858–1954* (Berkeley: University of California Press, 2011), 347.

18. Paper shortages had impacted the government administration and documentation procedures since World War II, as seen in Paul Boudet's exhibition (held in the city of Dà Lạt) of locally produced papers in order to supplement the dwindling supply of imported papers. "Quan Toàn quyền khánh thành cuộc tửng bầy giấy và sách," *Trung Hoà Nhật Báo*, August 12, 1943, no. 2871, 1.

19. Letter to the Ministry of Foreign Affairs, September 15, 1945, DABI, TTLTQG1, folder 1669.

20. Report "Tờ trình từ ngày đảo chính mồng 9 tháng 3 đến hết năm 1945."

21. Report "Tờ trình từ ngày đảo chính mồng 9 tháng 3 đến hết năm 1945."

22. Report "Tờ trình từ tháng 8 năm 1945 đến tháng 9 năm 1946" by Interim Director Trần Văn Kha, September 12, 1946, DABI, TTLTQG1, folder 1537.

23. From August 1945 to August 1946 the Central Library recorded the monthly number of consultations of books in the reading room by genre. "Quốc gia thư viện- phòng đọc sách—bản kê khai từ tháng và từ loại," 1946, DABI, TTLTQG1, folder 2211.

24. Report "Tờ trình từ tháng 8 năm 1945 đến tháng 9 năm 1946."

25. Letter number 1835 from Ngô Đình Nhu to the Ministry of National Education, December 15, 1945, DABI, TTLTQG1, folder 1559.

26. Letter number 1843 from Ngô Đình Nhu to the Ministry of Internal Affairs, December 19, 1945, DABI, TTLTQG1, folder 1559.

27. Catalog "Bảng kê khai sách ở QUỐC GIA THƯ VIỆN về chính- trị," ca. 1945–46, DABI, TTLTQG1, folder 1649.

28. Walter H. Mallory, *Political Handbook of the World, 1940* (New York: Harper and Brothers, Council on Foreign Relations, 1940); Raymond Aron et al., *Inventaires I: La Crise sociale et les idéologies nationales* (Paris: F. Alcan, 1936); Richard Nikolaus von Coudenhove-Kalergi, *L'Homme et l'état totalitaire* (Paris: Plon, 1939); Jean-Louis de Lanessan, *L'Indo-Chine française: Étude politique, économique et administrative sur la Cochinchine, le Cambodge, l'Annam et le Tonkin* (Paris: F. Alcan, 1889).

29. Letter from the Director of the Ministry of National Education to the Director of the Department of Higher Education, October 9, 1945, DABI, TTLTQG1, folder 1527.

30. Letter from Phạm Đình Giệm from Nha lưu trữ công văn và thư viện toàn quốc to the Ministry of National Education and attached "*bảng kê các sách cho mượn*" (list of borrowed books), October 12, 1945, DABI, TTLTQG1, folder 1527.

31. Letter from Ngô Đình Nhu from Nha lưu trữ công văn và thư viện toàn quốc to the Ministry of National Education.

32. Letter from Minister of National Education to the ministries of foreign affairs, internal affairs, information and propaganda, national defense, national economy, youth, justice, health, public works and transportation, labor, and finance, undated, DABI, TTLTQG1, folder 1527.

33. Letter from Minister of National Education to the ministries of foreign affairs, internal affairs, information and propaganda, national defense, national economy, youth, justice, health, public works and transportation, labor, and finance.

34. In the 1950s Nhu would lead the Revolutionary Personalist Labor Party (Cần Lao Nhân Vị Cách Mạng Đảng, known as the Cần Lao), and later he served as the security chief and political leader in the government administration of his younger brother, Ngô Đình Diệm, who was the first president of the Republic of Vietnam. See Nu-Anh Tran, *Disunion: Anticommunist Nationalism and the Making of the Republic of Vietnam* (Honolulu: University of Hawai'i Press, 2022), and Edward Miller, *Misalliance: Ngo Dinh Diem, the United States, and the Fate of South Vietnam* (Cambridge, MA: Harvard University Pres, 2013).

35. Letter from Nguyễn Xuân (Uỷ ban hành chính bắc bộ, văn phòng số 2527 VP/T) to several government departments on the topic of the Trường Huấn luyện hành chính (Administrator Training School), May 21, 1946, DABI, TTLTQG1, folder 1553. The departments addressed included the Central Treasury, the National Library, the Northern Land Cadastral Survey, Primary Schools, and Popular Schools.

36. Requests from Uỷ ban hành chính bắc bộ for reader cards, May 1946–June 1946, DABI, TTLTQG1, folder 1553. By June 3, 1946, Trân Văn Kha authorized the library cards and sent another seven, bringing the total up to seventy-seven cards.

37. McHale, *The First Vietnam War.*

38. See Christopher Goscha, chapter 4, "The City At War," and chapter 5, "Wiring War," in *The Road to Dien Bien Phu*, 121–90.

39. Bảo Đại and High Commissioner Léon Pignon signed another set of accords on December 30, 1949, which transferred major educational institutions such as the departments of public instruction, schools, and personnel to the southern government.

40. Goscha, *The Road to Dien Bien Phu*, 22; Reilly, "The Sovereign States of Vietnam, 1945–1955," 103–39.

41. For a study of the geography and ethnic diversity (notably of Tai/Thái, Hmong/Mèo, Khmu/Xá, Dao/Mán, Mường, and Tày/Thổ) of the northwestern Vietnam region within the DRV state-building process, see Lentz, *Contested Territory*. See also the role of violence and ethnicity in the Mekong Delta in McHale, *The First Vietnam War.*

42. Christopher Goscha, *Vietnam: A New History*, 173.

43. Letter from Paul Boudet, federal director of the Archives and Libraries of Indochina, to the high commissioner of France for Indochina, August 27, 1946, Tổng Thư viện (1940–1956) (TTV), Trung tâm lưu trữ quốc gia 2 (TTLTQG2), folder 32.

44. "La Direction des archives et des bibliothèques de l'Indochine," by Paul Boudet, Paris, December 11, 1947, Archives Privées Papiers Boudet (PB), Archives nationales d'outremer (ANOM), folder 48.

45. "La Direction des archives et des bibliothèques de l'Indochine."

46. André Masson, "Paul Boudet," *Bibliothèque de l'École des Chartes* 107, no. 2 (1948): 335–37.

47. Paul Boudet personnel summary, ca. 1945–48, PB, ANOM, folder 86.

48. Simone de Saint-Exupéry, "Paul Boudet," *Bulletin de la Société des études indochinoises* 23, no. 3–4 (1948): 135–38.

49. Saint-Exupéry, "Paul Boudet," 137.

50. Saint-Exupéry, "Paul Boudet," 138.

51. Bruno Delmas, "Ferréol de Ferry (1915–2008)," *Bibliothèque de l'École des Chartes* 166, no. 2 (2008): 669–72.

52. Letter from Trần Văn Kha to the Commissioner of the Republic for North Indochina, January 25, 1947, TTV, TTLTQG2, folder 24.

53. Unnamed author, "Les bibliothèques de l'Indochine," unsigned, ca. 1945–46, PB, ANOM, Aix-en-Provence, folder 83.

54. Unnamed author, "Les bibliothèques de l'Indochine."

55. Unnamed author, "Les bibliothèques de l'Indochine."

56. "Người ta đồn . . . Đó . . . Đây," *Tia Sáng*, March 8, 1952, no. 1175, 4. *Tia Sáng* operated in Hanoi from 1943 to 1954 with a few pauses. In 1952 Ngô Vân was editor in chief and the director was Phạm Trung Phổ.

57. "Note sur la Bibliothèque centrale de l'Indochine (Bibliothèque Pierre Pasquier) à Hanoi," March 26, 1952, Haut Commissariat de France pour l'Indochine (HCI), ANOM, folder 60-205.

58. The administrator reported a slightly higher number for the lending section compared to the reading room: 3,626 readers in the lending section in December 1951. "Note sur la Bibliothèque centrale de l'Indochine (Bibliothèque Pierre Pasquier) à Hanoi."

59. "Bibliothèque générale de Hanoi—Tổng Thư Viện Hà Nội—Règlement Intérieur—Nội Quy," July 31, 1953, DABI, TTLTQG1, folder 2041-05.

60. The lending section recorded 92,508 books loaned in 1938, averaging 36 books per reader per year, and 83,857 books loaned in 1953, averaging 22 books per reader per year. "Comparative table of readers and books between 1938 and 1953," ca. 1953, TTV, TTLTQG2, folder 2.

61. "Projet de procès-verbal du conseil d'administration de la Bibliothèque de Hanoi réunion 20 janvier 1954" and "Rapport sur l'activité de la Bibliothèque générale de Hanoi pendant l'année 1953," DABI, TTLTQG1, folder 2041-08.

62. "Rapport sur l'activité de la Bibliothèque générale de Hanoi pendant l'année 1953."

63. "Rapport sur l'activité de la Bibliothèque générale de Hanoi pendant l'année 1953."

64. "Projet de procès-verbal du conseil d'administration de la Bibliothèque de Hanoi réunion 20 janvier 1954."

65. For a comparative study of Cold War libraries in Francophone Africa, see Mary Niles Maack, "Books and Libraries as Instruments of Cultural Diplomacy in Francophone Africa during the Cold War," *Libraries & the Cultural Record* 36, no. 1 (2001): 58–86.

66. For example, on April 20, 1949, the USBE requested the Hanoi Library establish a library exchange with the Alabama Polytechnic Institute for regular submissions of the *Bibliographie de l'Indochine*. The Polytechnic Institute would be able to provide publications on science, engineering, and library news. Book lists, DABI, TTLTQG1, folder 1771.

67. Elihu Root, *The Military and Colonial Policy of the United States* (Cambridge, MA: Harvard University Press, 1916); Hugh Ritchie, *The "Navicert" System During the War* (Washington, DC: Carnegie Endowment for International Peace, 1938).

68. Amanda Laugesen, "UNESCO and the Globalization of the Public Library Idea, 1948 to 1965," *Library & Information History* 30, no. 1 (February 1, 2014): 1–19.

69. Book lists, DABI, TTLTQG1, folder 1771. Some of the books sent include the following: Franklin D. Roosevelt, *Looking Forward* (London, 1933) and *On Our Way* (London, 1934); H. G. Wells, *Phoenix: A Summary of the Inescapable Conditions of World Reorganization* (London, 1942) and *The Rights of Man, or What Are We Fighting For?* (London, 1940); and Walter Theimer, *The Penguin Political Dictionary* (London, 1940).

70. Letters from the Haut commissariat de France en l'Indochine, affaires économiques, Saigon, January 30, 1952; F. de Ferry, Délégation des archives et des bibliothèques, Hanoi, February 19, 1952, February 21, 1952, and March 12, 1952, "Objet: Besoin en Devisés Étrangères" (Objective: In need of foreign currencies), DABI, TTLTQG1, folder 1214.

71. Many USIS offices had their origins in the collections and work of its predecessor, the Office of War Information, during World War II, which included the radio broadcasting service as well as book collections. A more centralized body, the United States Information Agency was formed in 1953 and incorporated former USIS offices located around the world.

72. See Margaret Jack, chapter 1, "Media History," in *Media Ruins: Cambodian Postwar Media Reconstruction and the Geopolitics of Technology* (Cambridge: MIT Press, 2023); John Henderson, *United States Information Agency* (New York: Prager, 1969); Nicholas Cull, *The Cold War and the United States Information Agency: American Propaganda and Public Diplomacy, 1945–1989* (Cambridge: Cambridge University Press, 2008).

73. Shipment of books from USIS Hanoi to Hanoi Central Library, December 5, 1952, DABI, TTLTQG1, folder 1754. Two addresses are noted for the Hanoi office, 110 Hàng Trống (formerly Jules Ferry) and 36 boulevard Ngô Quyền.

74. Shipment of books from USIS Hanoi to Hanoi Central Library, November 25, 1953, DABI, TTLTQG1, folder 1754.

75. Books shipped to the Hanoi Library in 1954 from the American Information Service included Edward Hunter's *Brainwashing in Red China* and Marshall Edward Dimock's *American Government in Action*, as well as other titles such as *The U.S.A. and Its People and Its Home, Capitalism and America, Man's Right to Knowledge, The Chinese Yearbook 1944–1945*, Bernard Baruch's *Peace Can Be Won, and Everyman's United Nations*. Shipment of books from USIS Saigon to Hanoi Central Library, March 15, April 13, and May 24, 1954, DABI, TTLTQG1, folder 1754.

76. Shipment of books from USIS Saigon to Hanoi Central Library, April 13, 1954, DABI, TTLTQG1, folder 1754. The Saigon branch of the American Information Service was listed as being at 82 rue Paul Blanchy.

77. "Note sur la Bibliothèque centrale de l'Indochine (Bibliothèque Pierre Pasquier) à Hanoi."

78. Letter 544 from the Director of the General Library of Hanoi to the Director of the American Information Service, August 13, 1953, DABI, TTLTQG1, folder 1754.

79. Throughout the First Indochina War, legal deposits and book exchanges were actively sent between Hanoi and Saigon; from 1938 to 1948 the library recorded that books

were sent between Saigon and Hanoi libraries nearly every week. Book list, 1948, DABI, TTLTQG1, folder 1841; list of Indochina legal deposit books, 1951–54, TTV, TTLTQG2, folder 37.

80. Request from Edmonde Castagnol, January 12, 1954, DABI, TTLTQG1, folder 2041-02. This request was titled "Searching for documents" and was sent out from 32 rue Taberd, Saigon, from the Haut commissariat de France en Indochine, Mission culturelle française archives et bibliothèques office.

81. Đoàn Quan Tấn's response to interview questions from *Ngôn Luận* newspaper, March 26, 1955, Thư viện Quốc gia Nam Việt (1945–1957) (TVQGNV), TTLTQG2, Ho Chi Minh City, folder 2.

82. Đoàn Quan Tấn's response to interview questions from Radio Saigon, May 1949, TVQGNV, TTLTQG2, folder 2.

83. Đoàn Quan Tấn's response to interview questions from Radio Saigon.

84. Đoàn Quan Tấn's response to interview questions from Radio Saigon.

85. Đoàn Quan Tấn's response to interview questions from Radio Saigon.

86. Hieu Nam Trung Le, "Another Kind of Vietnamization" 135–36.

87. Đoàn Quan Tấn's response to interview questions from *Ngôn Luận* newspaper, March 26, 1955, TVQGNV, TTLTQG2, folder 2.

88. Lê Ngọc Trụ, "Tổ chức Thơ Viện Quốc Gia," ca. 1954, TVQGNV, TTLTQG2, folder 102.

89. "La Bibliothèque nationale du Sud-Vietnam," ca. 1956, TVQGNV, TTLTQG2, folder 102.

90. Phan Vô Kỵ, "Hoạt động của thơ viên quốc gia từ khi giao lại cho chánh phủ việt nam đến ngày nay," June 26, 1954, TVQGNV, TTLTQG2, folder 102.

91. See Olga Dror, *Making Two Vietnams: War and Youth Identities, 1965–1975* (Cambridge: Cambridge University Press, 2018); Hieu Nam Trung Le, "Another Kind of Vietnamization," 137–38.

92. "Le développement des Bibliothèques au Viet-nam de 1953 à 1957," ca. 1957, TVQGNV, TTLTQG2, folder 102.

93. "La Bibliothèque nationale du Sud-Vietnam," May 1956, TVQGNV, TTLTQG2, folder 102.

94. "La Bibliothèque nationale du Sud-Vietnam."

95. On Wednesday, March 15, 1944, a group of prison laborers from the Maison Centrale were tasked with moving the valuable lending section collections for safekeeping. The Cochinchina Library was forced to temporarily close during the *coup de force* and transfer of authority in 1945. "Demande d'escorte pour surveiller une corvée de 8 prisonniers en vue de déménagement de la Bibliothèque année 1944," TTLTQG2, GC, folder 52630.

96. Report from Phan Vô Kỵ to attaché of French information in South Vietnam, January 23, 1953, TVQGNV, TTLTQG2, folder 102.

97. Phan Vô Kỵ, "Hoạt động của thơ viên quốc gia từ khi giao lại cho chánh phủ việt nam đến ngày nay."

98. Phan Vô Kỵ, "Hoạt động của thơ viên quốc gia từ khi giao lại cho chánh phủ việt nam đến ngày nay."

99. Hoàng Phong Tuấn and Nguyễn Thị Minh, "Striving for the Quintessence: Building a New Identity of National Literature Based on Creative Freedom," in *Building a Republican*

Nation in Vietnam, 1920–1963, ed. Nu-Anh Tran and Tuong Vu (Honolulu: University of Hawai'i Press, 2023), 186–201.

100. Lê Ngọc Trụ, "Tổ chức Thơ Viện Quốc Gia."

101. Lê Ngọc Trụ, "Tổ chức Thơ Viện Quốc Gia."

102. Conventions, 1949–53, DABI, TTLTQG1, Hanoi, folder 2041-05; Conventions and Statutes, 1953, Haut commissariat de France pour l'Indochine (HCI), ANOM, Aix-en-Provence, folder 60-205.

103. For the decolonization of the EFEO collections, see Cécile Capot, "La bibliothèque et les archives de l'École française d'Extrême-Orient: De la constitution à la crise de la décolonisation (1898–1959)," PhD diss., École doctorale de l'École Pratique des Hautes Études, 2022. For a comparison case of patrimony and decolonization, see Andrew Bellisari, "The Art of Decolonization: The Battle for Algeria's French Art, 1962–70," *Journal of Contemporary History* 52, no. 3 (July 1, 2017): 625–45.

104. Nha văn-khố và thư-viện quốc-gia, *Organization and Administration of the Directorate of National Archives and Libraries* (Saigon: Republic of Vietnam, Ministry of National Education, Directorate of National Archives and Libraries, 1964).

105. "Convention relative aux services d'archives relevant en ce qui concerne le Viet-Nam de la Direction des Archives & Bibliothèques," signed June 15, 1950, by Léon Pignon, Bảo Đại, and Trần Văn Hữu, HCI, ANOM, folder 58-200.

106. Ferréol de Ferry, "Les archives en Indochine," *La Gazette des archives* 8, no. 1 (1950): 33–41.

107. In the case of Cambodia, fifteen days after the transfer of Cambodia in 1950, Pach Chhoeun became the head of the library of Phnom Penh, and he later advanced in the Ministry of Information. Pach Chhoeun took over from Madame Renée Duquesnay. During his first year he requested the renaming of the Centrale bibliothèque to the Nationale bibliothèque and proposed to expand the library collections and increase the number of professional archivist-librarian staff.

108. Delmas, "Ferréol de Ferry (1915–2008)," 671.

109. "Convention relative aux services d'archives relevant en ce qui concerne le Viet-Nam de la Direction des Archives & Bibliothèques," 5.opjk

110. Olivia Pelletier breaks down the stages of transfer in detail from 1951 to 1955. The majority of the materials were brought from Hanoi, Saigon, and Phnom Penh, with a small number of materials from Hue and Vientiane. For a detailed study of the division and transfer of the archives, see Olivia Pelletier, "De Paul Boudet à Ferréol de Ferry: Les archives françaises en Indochine (1917–1955)," in *Chartistes en Asie: Science historique et patrimoine au lointain (XIXe–XXIe siècle)*, ed. Jacques Berlioz, Cécile Capot, and Olivier Poncet (Paris: École nationale des chartes—École française d'Extrême-Orient, 2021), 153–70.

111. Carlo Laroche studied at the École des Chartes from 1927 to 1931 and was the director of the Archives of the Ministry of Overseas France from 1943 to 1972. Marie-Antoinette Ménier was a student of the École des Chartes from 1941 to 1945 and succeeded Laroche as head of the overseas section of the archives.

112. "Convention relative aux bibliothèques" and "Convention relative au transfert des services de dépôt légal"

113. "Note sur la bibliothèque centrale de l'Indochine (Bibliothèque Pierre Pasquier) à Hanoi."

114. Conventions "Organisation et fonctionnement de la Bibliothèque générale de Hanoi 1953," ca. 1952, DABI, TTLTQG1, folder 2041-05.

115. "La Bibliothèque générale nationale du viet-nam est la seconde bibliothèque de l'Extrême-Orient," *Mouvement de la Révolution Nationale* 232, April 18, 1956, PB, ANOM, folder 48.

116. "Lịch sử của Thư viện quốc gia Việt-Nam," ca. 1954–57, TVQGNV, TTLTQG2, folder 102; Wynn Wilcox, "Universities and Intellectual Culture in the Republic of Vietnam," in *Toward a Framework for Vietnamese American Studies: History, Community, and Memory*, ed. Linda Ho Peché, Alex-Thai Dinh Vo, and Tuong Vu (Philadelphia: Temple University Press, 2023), 57–75.

117. "Projet de proces-verbal du conseil d'administration de la bibliothèque de hanoi réunion 20 janvier 1954," DABI, TTLTQG1, folder 2041-08.

118. Undated report ca. 1954, DABI, TTLTQG1, folder 2041-02.

119. "Répartition des dossiers conserves aux archives centrales entre les divers fonds (Decembre 1953)," DABI, TTLTQG1, folder 2041-02.

120. "Projet de proces-verbal du conseil d'administration de la bibliothèque de hanoi réunion 20 janvier 1954" and "Rapport sur l'activité de la Bibliothèque générale de Hanoi pendant l'année 1953."

121. *Nhân Dân*, October 21, 1954, no. 242, 4.

122. Tuân Hoang Van, "L'Université indochinoise et l'œuvre culturelle de la France au Vietnam," in *Le Vietnam: Une histoire de transferts culturels*, ed. Hoai Huong Aubert-Nguyen and Michel Espagne (Paris: Demopolis, 2016), 151–67.

123. Information on the transfer of collections is compiled from the following sources: Internal reports and inventory lists, 1954–58, Nha Văn khố và Thư viện Quốc gia (1950–1975) (NVKTVQG), TTLTQG2, folder 11; Internal reports, 1957–58, NVKTVQG, TTLTQG2, folder 12; Catalog signed by Tran Van Kha regarding transfer of documents, books, newspapers belonging to France, the Hanoi Central Library, and the archives of the provinces Phủ Thọ, Sơn Tây, 1953–55, TTV, TTLTQG2, folder 41.

124. Nha văn-khố và thư-viện quốc-gia, *Organization and Administration of the Directorate of National Archives and Libraries* (Saigon: Republic of Vietnam, Ministry of National Education, Directorate of National Archives and Libraries, 1964), 11.

125. Hieu Nam Trung Le, "Another Kind of Vietnamization," 135.

126. Over a million Vietnamese migrated to the south, referred to as the "Bắc 54," "Bắc di Cư," or "northern Migrants" (a large proportion of them Vietnamese Catholic civilians or those who had worked in the French colonial administration), and approximately 120,000 Vietnamese (personnel and military aligned with the DRV) moved from the south to the north.

127. Report by Nguyễn Hùng Cường, January 12, 1955, NVKTVQG, TTLTQG2, folder 11.

128. "La Bibliothèque générale nationale du Viet-Nam est la seconde bibliothèque de l'Extrême-Orient," *Mouvement de la Révolution Nationale* 232 (April 18, 1956), PB, ANOM, folder 48.

EPILOGUE

1. My research on public reading culture in the RVN intersects with the recent attention to the colonial roots of republicanism and its role in shaping southern Vietnamese political life and nationhood. See Nu-Anh Tran and Tuong Vu, eds., *Building a Republican Nation in Vietnam, 1920–1963* (Honolulu: University of Hawai'i Press, 2023).

2. Report, March 18, 1955, Thư viện Quốc gia Nam Việt (1945–57) (TVQGNV), Trung tâm lưu trữ quốc gia 2 (TTLTQG2), folder 2.

3. Ngô Đình Diệm's speech at the inaugural ceremony, published in *Việt Nam Thông Tấn Xã*, no. 1949 (July 3, 1956, afternoon edition), Phủ Tổng Thống Đệ Nhất Cộng Hòa (PTTDICH), TTLTQG2, folder 18141.

4. Speech by Mai Thọ Truyền delivered at the bricklaying ceremony for the National Library, December 28, 1968, Nha Văn khố và Thư viện Quốc gia (1950–1975) (NVKTVQG), TTLTQG2, folder 383. In 1968 the Khám Lớn prison was destroyed, and the Chí Hoa prison, built in March 1953, replaced Khám Lớn as the regional detention facility.

5. Internal reports, 1957, NVKTVQG, TTLTQG2, folder 7.

6. Correspondence and inventory lists, 1957, NVKTVQG, TTLTQG2, folder 7. Many libraries and institutions from all over the world, such as UNESCO, the French National Bibliography, and the Michigan University Vietnam Advisory Group, donated many works to the National Library. See Odile Welfelé, "D'hier à aujourd'hui, les liens entre l'École des Chartes et les Archives nationales du Vietnam," in *Chartistes en Asie: Science historique et patrimoine au lointain (XIXe–XXIe siècle)* (Paris: École nationale des Chartes—École française d'Extrême-Orient, 2021), 204–14.

7. Lâm Vĩnh Thế, "Phát Triển Thư Viện Tại Việt Nam Cộng Hoà Tước Ngày 30-4-1975 (Kỳ 1)," *US Vietnam Research Center*, https://usvietnam.uoregon.edu/phat-trien-thu-vien-tai-viet-nam-cong-hoa-truoc-ngay-30-4-1975-ky-1/; Lâm Vĩnh Thế, "Phát Triển Thư Viện Tại Việt Nam Cộng Hoà Tước Ngày 30-4-1975 (Kỳ 2)," *US Vietnam Research Center*, https://usvietnam.uoregon.edu/phat-trien-thu-vien-tai-viet-nam-cong-hoa-truoc-ngay-30-4-1975-ky-2/; Van Nguyen-Marshall, *Between War and the State: Civil Society in South Vietnam, 1954–1975* (Ithaca, NY: Cornell University Press, 2023).

8. Statistics of legal deposits and purchases of periodicals at 34 Gia Long, 1957, NVKTVQG, TTLTQG2, folder 10.

9. Survey on state of translation in Vietnam, July 17, 1957, NVKTVQG, TTLTQG2, folder 7.

10. "La Bibliothèque nationale du Sud-Vietnam," May 1956, TVQGNV, TTLTQG2, folder 102.

11. "La Bibliothèque nationale du Sud-Vietnam." May 1956.

12. Phan Vô Kỵ to the District 1 Police, Saigon, June 13, 1957, NVKTVQG, TTLTQG2, folder 7. Phan Vô Kỵ replaced Đoàn Quan Tấn as the director of the library in July 1957.

13. Phan Vô Kỵ to Ministry of National Education, June 28, 1957, NVKTVQG, TTLTQG2, folder 7.

14. Phan Vô Kỵ to Ministry of National Education, June 28, 1957.

15. Đoàn Quan Tấn's response to Radio Saigon questionnaire, May 1949, TVQGNV, TTLTQG2, folder 2.

16. Cindy Nguyen, "Reading Rules: The Symbolic and Social Spaces of Reading in the Hà Nội Central Library, 1919–1941," *Journal of Vietnamese Studies* 15, no. 3 (August 2020): 17–18.

17. Cindy Nguyen, "Creating the National Library in Saigon: Colonial Legacies, Fragmented Collections, and Reading Publics, 1946–1958," in *Building a Republican Nation in Vietnam, 1920–1963*, ed. Nu-Anh Tran and Tuong Vu (Honolulu: University of Hawai'i Press, 2023), 164–85.

18. "La Bibliothèque nationale du Sud-Vietnam," May 1956, TVQGNV, TTLTQG2, folder 102.

19. "Báo cáo thành tích của ngành thư viện quốc gia từ ngày Hoà bình lập lại đến cuối 1957," May 16, 1958, Bộ Văn Hoá (BVH), Trung tâm lưu trữ quốc gia 3 (TTLTQG3), Hanoi, folder 49.

20. For accounts of the early DRV, see Uyen Nguyen, "Guerillas in the City: The Administrative Takeover of Hà Nội and DRV State-Making in the Urban Postwar Period (1954–1960)," *Journal of Vietnamese Studies* 17, no. 1 (February 1, 2022): 1–52.

21. The report noted that 16,000 books were inherited from the French collections, thus bringing a total of 24,000 books in the National Library. This accounting of books seems much smaller than the number of books accounted for by the end of the French colonial period, which surpassed 150,000. Another record notes that 20,000 books, revolutionary Vietnamese-language newspapers, and magazines of the CP 15 Library were integrated into the Hanoi Library collection. The inconsistent accounting of the Hanoi Library collections points to ambiguity over how many books were taken to Saigon, purged, lost, stolen, or damaged over the course of the First and Second Indochina Wars.

22. For histories of the Soviet Union classification system, see Edward Sukiasyan, "Description and Analysis of the Library-Bibliographical Classification (BBK/LBC)," *Tools for Knowledge Organisation and the Human Interface. Proceedings of the First International ISKO Conference, Darmstadt, 14–17 August 1990, Part 1, 1991*, 114–21.

23. "Instructions pour le classement des bibliothèques," Direction des Archives et des Bibliothèques (DABI), Trung Tâm Lưu Trữ Quốc Gia 1 (TTLTQG1), Hanoi, folder 444.

24. Kim N. B. Ninh, *A World Transformed: The Politics of Culture in Revolutionary Vietnam, 1945–1965* (Ann Arbor: University of Michigan Press, 2002).

25. For an examination of socialist realism and the Nhân Văn–Giai Phẩm affair during the 1950s, see Peter Zinoman, "Nhân Văn–Giai Phẩm and Vietnamese 'Reform Communism' in the 1950s: A Revisionist Interpretation," *Journal of Cold War Studies* 13, no. 1 (2011): 60–100.

26. "Báo Cáo của Bộ Văn Hoá về Tình Hình Hoạt động của Văn Hoá Của Nước Việt Nam Dân Chủ Cộng Hoà Trong 2 Năm Hòa Bình Tháng 1/1955–9/1956," 1956, BVH, TTLTQG3, folder 6.

27. "Báo Cáo Thống Kê Tình Hình Phân Phối Công Việc Cho Các Nhà in và Tổng Kết Công Tác Phát Hành Của Các Hiệu Sách Nhân Dân Năm 1955 Của Nhà in Quốc Gia Trung ương," May 24, 1956, BVH, TTLTQG3, folder 1994.

28. "Báo Cáo Tổng Kết 3 Năm (1955–1957) Của Sở Phát Hành Sách," BVH, TTLTQG3, folder 36.

29. "Báo cáo tổng kết công tác phát hành sách năm (1965–1968) và phương hướng nhiệm vụ hai năm (1969–1970)," BVH, TTLTQG3, folder 318.

30. "Tập Tài Liệu về Tuyên Truyên, Giới Thiệu Việt Nam ở Nước Ngoài Năm 1960," September 28, 1960," BVH, TTLTQG3, folder 1384.

31. "Báo Cáo Tổng Kết Hội Nghị Thí điểm Nhà Văn Hoá Nông Thôn Toàn Miền Bắc Của Bộ Văn Hoá Năm 1956," October 1956, BVH, TTLTQG3, folder 7.

32. The library continues to be extensively renovated with extended services and spaces in collaboration with other national libraries, international networks, and companies. Through a partnership with Samsung Vina Electronics Company, the Không Gian Chia Sẻ S.hub (S.hub Sharing Space) was launched in 2016, and in 2024 it was upgraded and reopened. The children's space, Thư Viện Văn hoá Thiếu nhi (Children's Cultural Library), was opened in 2017.

BIBLIOGRAPHY

ARCHIVAL SOURCES

Vietnam

Trung tâm lưu trữ quốc gia 1, Hanoi—National Archives Center 1 [TTLTQG1]
- Direction des archives et des bibliothèques de l'Indochine—Directorate of Archives and Libraries of Indochina [DABI]
- Gouvernement général de l'Indochine—General Government of Indochina [GGI]
- Résidence supérieure au Tonkin (ancien fonds)—Resident Superior of Tonkin Former Collection [RSTAF]

Trung tâm lưu trữ quốc gia 2, Ho Chi Minh City—National Archives Center 2 [TTLTQG2]
- Gouvernement de Cochinchine—Phủ thống đốc Nam Kỳ, Cochinchina Government [GC]
- Nha Văn khố và Thư viện Quốc gia (1950–1975)—National Archives and Library [NVKTVQG]
- Phủ Tổng Thống Đệ Nhất Cộng Hòa—Office of the President of the Republic of Vietnam, First Republic [PTTDICH]
- Thư viện Quốc gia Nam Việt (1945–1957)—National Library of Southern Vietnam [TVQGNV]
- Tổng Thư viện (1940–1956)—General Library [TTV]

Trung tâm lưu trữ quốc gia 3, Hanoi—National Archives Center 3 [TTLTQG3]
- Bộ Văn Hoá—Ministry of Culture [BVH]

Cambodia

National Archives of Cambodia, Phnom Penh [NAC]
  Résidence supérieure du Cambodge—Resident Superior of Cambodge [RSC]

France

Archives nationales d'outre-mer, Aix-en-Provence—National Archives of Overseas Territories [ANOM]
  Archives Privées Papiers Boudet 86—Private Archives Boudet Papers [PB]
  Gouvernement général de l'Indochine—Governor General of Indochina [GGI]
  Résidence supérieure au Tonkin (ancien fonds)—Resident Superior of Tonkin Former Collection [RSTAF]
  Résidence supérieure au Tonkin (nouveau fonds)—Resident Superior of Tonkin New Collection [RSTNF]
  Haut Commissariat de France pour l'Indochine—High Commission of France for Indochina [HCI]

PUBLISHED PERIODICALS AND REPORTS

Vietnamese Language

Báo Đông Pháp
Công Báo Dân Quốc Báo
Đông Pháp Thời Báo: Le Courrier Indochinois
Hà Thành Ngọ Báo
Nam Phong
Ngày Nay
Nhân Dân
Phong Hoá
Phụ Nữ Tân Văn
Sài Gòn
Sông Hương
Tia Sáng
Tiểu Long
Tràng An Báo
Tri Tân
Trung Bắc Tân Văn
Trung Hoà Nhật Báo
Tuần Lễ

French Language

L'Annam Nouveau
L'Avenir du Tonkin
Bibliothèque de l'École des Chartes
Bulletin de la Société des études indochinoises
Bulletin de l'École française d'Extrême-Orient
La Dépêche Coloniale
La Dépêche d'indochine
L'Écho Annamite
France Indochine
La Gazette des archives
Journal official de l'Indochine
Rapport sur la direction des archives et des bibliothèques
La Tribune Indigène
La Tribune Indochinoise
La Volonté Indochinoise

SELECTED PUBLISHED SOURCES

Adams, Thomas R., and Nicolas Barker. "A New Model for the Study of the Book." In *A Potencie of Life: Books in Society*, edited by Nicolas Barker, 5–44. London: The British Library, 1993.

Affidi, Emmanuelle. "Vulgarisation du savoir et colonisation des esprits par la presse et le livre en Indochine française et dans les Indes néerlandaises (1908–1936)." *Moussons* 13–14 (December 1, 2009): 95–121.

Aitchison, Madeleine. "Mirrors and Visions: Nữ Lưu Thơ Quán and the Woman Question in Interwar Vietnam." PhD diss., University of Ottawa, 2023.

Anderson, Benedict R. O'G. *Imagined Communities: Reflections on the Origin and Spread of Nationalism*. Rev. ed. London: Verso, 1991.

Baldanza, Kathlene. "Publishing, Book Culture, and Reading Practices in Vietnam: The View from Thắng Nghiêm and Phổ Nhân Temples." *Journal of Vietnamese Studies* 13, no. 3 (August 1, 2018): 9–28.

Bao, Yan. "The Influence of Chinese Fiction on Vietnamese Literature," translated by Noel Castelino. In *Literary Migrations: Traditional Chinese Fiction in Asia (17th–20th Centuries)*, edited by Claudine Salmon, 163–95, Singapore: Institute of Southeast Asian Studies, 2013.

Benoit, Gaetan. *Eugene Morel: Pioneer of Public Libraries in France*. Duluth, MN: Litwin Books, 2014.

Berry, Mary Elizabeth. *Japan in Print: Information and Nation in the Early Modern Period*. Berkeley: University of California Press, 2006.

Berry, Mary Elizabeth. "Public Life in Authoritarian Japan." *Daedalus* 127, no. 3 (1998): 133–65.

Bhabha, Homi K. "Cultural Diversity and Cultural Differences." *The Post-Colonial Studies Reader*, 2nd ed., edited by Bill Ashcroft, Gareth Griffiths, and Helen Tiffin, 155–57. New York: Routledge, 2003.

Bích Hồng Dương. *Lịch sử sữ nghiệp thư viện Việt Nam trong tiến trình văn hoá dân tộc*. Hanoi: Vụ Thư Viện, 1999.

Bivens-Tatum, Wayne. *Libraries and the Enlightenment*. Los Angeles: Library Juice Press, 2012.

Blair, Ann M. *Too Much to Know: Managing Scholarly Information Before the Modern Age*. New Haven, CT: Yale University Press, 2010.

Boudet, Paul. *Bibliographie de l'Indochine*. Hanoi: Imprimerie d'Extrême-orient, 1922.

Boudet, Paul, and André Masson. *Iconographie historique de l'Indochine française: Documents sur l'histoire de l'intervention française en Indochine*. Paris: G. Van Oest, 1931.

Bowker, Geoffrey C., and Susan Leigh Star. *Sorting Things Out: Classification and Its Consequences*. Cambridge, MA: MIT Press, 2000.

Briet, Suzanne, *Qu'est-ce que la documentation?* Paris: Éditions documentaires, industrielles et techniques, 1951.

Brocheux, Pierre, and Daniel Hémery. *Indochina: An Ambiguous Colonization, 1858–1954*. Berkeley: University of California Press, 2011.

Canovan, Margaret. "Politics as Culture: Hannah Arendt and the Public Realm." *History of Political Thought* 6, no. 3 (1985): 617–42.

Cao, Vy. "Between the Sacred and the Secular: Publishing, Books, and Everyday Life in Colonial Cochinchina." In *Vietnam over the Long Twentieth Century: Becoming Modern, Going Global*, edited by Liam C. Kelley and Gerard Sasges, 85–100. Singapore: Springer Nature, 2024.

Cao, Vy. "Histoire de l'imprimerie, du livre et de l'édition vietnamienne en Cochinchine: Traitement et analyse du fonds Indochinois (1890–1945)." PhD diss., Université d'Aix-Marseille, 2025.

Capot, Cécile. "La bibliothèque et les archives de l'École française d'Extrême-Orient: De la constitution à la crise de la décolonisation (1898–1959)." PhD diss., École doctorale de l'École pratique des hautes études, 2022.

Capot, Cécile. "Concurrentes ou complémentaires? Quand l'École française d'Extrême-Orient créa la direction des Archives et des Bibliothèques de l'Indochine." In *Chartistes en Asie: Science historique et patrimoine au lointain (XIXe–XXIe siècle)*, edited by Jacques Berlioz, Cécile Capot, and Olivier Poncet, 137–50. Paris: École nationale des Chartes—École française d'Extrême-Orient, 2021.

Chamelot, Fabienne. "The Politics of French Colonial Archives." PhD diss., University of Portsmouth, 2022.

Chartier, Roger. *The Order of Books: Readers, Authors, and Libraries in Europe Between the Fourteenth and Eighteenth Centuries*. Stanford, CA: Stanford University Press, 1994.

Cherry, Haydon. *Down and Out in Saigon: Stories of the Poor in a Colonial City*. New Haven, CT: Yale University Press, 2019.

Conklin, Alice L. *In the Museum of Man: Race, Anthropology, and Empire in France, 1850–1950*. Ithaca, NY: Cornell University Press, 2013.

Cooper, Frederick. *Citizenship between Empire and Nation: Remaking France and French Africa, 1945–1960*. Princeton, NJ: Princeton University Press, 2014.

Cowen, Deborah. "Following the Infrastructures of Empire: Notes on Cities, Settler Colonialism, and Method." *Urban Geography* 41, no. 4 (2020): 469–86.

Cull, Nicholas. *The Cold War and the United States Information Agency: American Propaganda and Public Diplomacy, 1945–1989*. Cambridge: Cambridge University Press, 2008.

Đặng Thị Vân Chi. *Vấn đề phụ nữ trên báo chí tiếng Việt trước năm 1945*. Hanoi: Nhà Xuất Bản Khoa Học Xã Hội, 2007.

Đào Thị Diến, ed. *Hà Nội qua tài liệu và tư liệu lưu trữ (1873–1954), 2 Volumes. Hà Nội: Trung tâm Lưu trữ quốc gia I, Nhà Xuất Bản Hà Nội, 2010.*

Đào Thị Diến. *Hà Nội thời cận đại: từ nhượng địa đến thành phố (1873–1945). Hà Nội: Nhà Xuất Bản Hà Nội, 2024.*

Đào Thị Diến. "Les archives coloniales au Vietnam (1858–1954): Les fonds conservés au dépôt central de Hanoi; les fonds de la résidence supérieure au Tonkin." PhD diss., Université Paris VII Denis Diderot, 2004.

Đào Thị Diến. "Ngô Đình Nhu—Nhà lưu trữ Việt Nam thời kỳ 1938–1946." *Tạp chí Nghiên cứu và Phát triển* 6–7 (2013): 238–43.

Darnton, Robert. "What Is the History of Books?" *Daedalus* 111, no. 3 (July 1, 1982): 65–83.

Day, Ronald. *The Modern Invention of Information: Discourse, History, and Power*. Carbondale: Southern Illinois University Press, 2001.

de Certeau, Michel. *The Practice of Everyday Life*, translated by Steven Rendall. Berkeley: University of California Press, 2011.

Desai, Gaurav. *Subject to Colonialism: African Self-Fashioning and the Colonial Library*. Durham, NC: Duke University Press, 2001.

Đỗ Đức Hiếu. *Từ điển văn học (Bộ mới)*. Hà Nội: Nhà Xuất Bản Thế Giới, 2004.

Đỗ Quang Hưng, Nguyễn Thành, and Dương Trung Quốc, eds. *Lịch sử báo chí Việt Nam, 1865–1945*. Hà Nội: Nhà Xuất Bản Đại Học Quốc Gia Hà Nội, 2000.

Dror, Olga. *Making Two Vietnams: War and Youth Identities, 1965–1975*. Cambridge: Cambridge University Press, 2018.

Dương Bích Hồng. *Lịch sử sự nghiệp thư viện Việt Nam trong tiến trình văn hoá dân tộc*. Hà Nội: Vụ Thư viện—Bộ văn hoá Thông tin, 1999.

Dutton, George. *The Tây Son Uprising: Society and Rebellion in Eighteenth-Century Vietnam*. Honolulu: University of Hawai'i Press, 2006.

Edington, Claire. *Beyond the Asylum: Mental Illness in French Colonial Vietnam*. Ithaca, NY: Cornell University Press, 2019.

Edwards, Penny. *Cambodge: The Cultivation of a Nation, 1860–1945*. Honolulu: University of Hawai'i Press, 2007.

Firpo, Christina. *Black Market Business: Selling Sex in Northern Vietnam, 1920–1945*. Ithaca, NY: Cornell University Press, 2020.

Firpo, Christina Elizabeth. *The Uprooted: Race, Children, and Imperialism in French Indochina, 1890–1980*. Honolulu: University of Hawai'i Press, 2016.

Fitzgerald, Devin, and Carla Nappi. "Information in Early Modern East Asia." In *Information: A Historical Companion*, edited by Ann Blair, Paul Duguid, Anja-Silvi Goeing, and Anthony Grafton, 60–83. Princeton, NJ: Princeton University Press, 2021.

Fitzpatrick, Elizabeth B. "The Public Library as Instrument of Colonialism: The Case of the Netherlands East Indies." *Libraries & the Cultural Record* 43, no. 3 (2008): 283.

Fraser, Nancy. "Rethinking the Public Sphere: A Contribution to the Critique of Actually Existing Democracy." *Social Text* 25/26 (1990): 56–80.

Gazquez, Denis. "Les fonds sur l'Indochine coloniale à la Bibliothèque nationale de France." In *Le Vietnam: Une histoire de transferts culturels*, edited by Hoai Huong Aubert-Nguyen and Michel Espagne, 283–90. Paris: Demopolis, 2015.

Goscha, Christopher. "Colonial Monarchy and Decolonisation in the French Empire: Bảo Đại, Norodom Sihanouk and Mohammed V." In *Monarchies and Decolonisation in Asia*, edited by Robert Aldrich and Cindy McCreery, 152–74. Manchester: Manchester University Press, 2020.

Goscha, Christopher. *Going Indochinese: Contesting Concepts of Space and Place in French Indochina*. Copenhagen: NIAS Press, 2012.

Goscha, Christopher. "The Modern Barbarian: Nguyen Van Vinh and the Complexity of Colonial Modernity in Vietnam." *European Journal of East Asian Studies* 1, no. 3 (2004): 99–134.

Goscha, Christopher. *The Road to Dien Bien Phu: A History of the First War for Vietnam*. Princeton, NJ: Princeton University Press, 2022.

Goscha, Christopher. *Vietnam: A New History*. New York: Basic Books, 2016.

Ha, Marie-Paule. *French Women and the Empire: The Case of Indochina*. Oxford: Oxford University Press, 2014.

Henchy, Judith. "Vietnamese New Women and the Fashioning of Modernity." In *France and "Indochina": Cultural Representations*, edited by Katherine Robson and Jennifer Yee, 121–38. Lanham, MD: Lexington Books, 2005.

Henry, Todd A. *Assimilating Seoul: Japanese Rule and the Politics of Public Space in Colonial Korea, 1910–1945*. Berkeley: University of California Press, 2016.

Herbelin, Caroline. *Architectures du Vietnam colonial: Repenser le métissage*. Paris: Comité des Travaux Historiques et Scientifiques, 2016.

Ho Tai, Hue-Tam. *Radicalism and the Origins of the Vietnamese Revolution*. Cambridge, MA: Harvard University Press, 1992.

Hoàng Phong Tuấn and Nguyễn Thị Minh. "Striving for the Quintessence: Building a New Identity of National Literature Based on Creative Freedom." In *Building a Republican Nation in Vietnam, 1920–1963*, edited by Nu-Anh Tran and Tuong Vu, 186–201. Honolulu: University of Hawai'i Press, 2023.

Hoang Van, Tuân. "L'Université indochinoise et l'œuvre culturelle de la France au Vietnam." In *Le Vietnam: Une histoire de transferts culturels*, edited by Hoai Huong Aubert-Nguyen and Michel Espagne, 151–67. Paris: Demopolis, 2015.

Huynh, Sabine. *Mécanismes d'intégration des mots d'emprunt français en vietnamien*. Paris: L'Harmattan, 2010.

Ikeya, Chie. *Refiguring Women, Colonialism, and Modernity in Burma*. Honolulu: University of Hawai'i Press, 2011.

Jack, Margaret. *Media Ruins: Cambodian Postwar Media Reconstruction and the Geopolitics of Technology*. Cambridge, MA: MIT Press, 2023.

Jarvis, Helen. "The National Library of Cambodia: Surviving for Seventy Years." *Libraries & Culture* 30, no. 4 (October 1, 1995): 391–408.

Jennings, Eric. *Vichy in the Tropics: Pétain's National Revolution in Madagascar, Guadeloupe, and Indochina, 1940–1944*. Stanford, CA: Stanford University Press, 2000.

Keith, Charles. *Subjects and Sojourners*. Oakland: University of California Press, 2023.

Kelley, Liam C. *Beyond the Bronze Pillars: Envoy Poetry and the Sino-Vietnamese Relationship*. Honolulu: University of Hawai'i Press, 2005.

Lại Nguyên Ân. "Một cuốn truyện bị quên lãng." *Tạp chí văn học* 6 (June 2001).

Lại Nguyên Ân and Nguyễn Hữu Sơ, eds. *Tạp chí Tri tân 1941–1945, truyện và ký: sưu tập tác phẩm*. Hanoi: Nhà xuất bản Hội nhà văn, 2000.

Larcher-Goscha, Agathe. "La voie étroite des réformes coloniales et la 'collaboration franco-annamite' (1917–1928)." *Outre-Mers. Revue d'histoire* 82, no. 309 (1995): 387–420.

Laugesen, Amanda. "UNESCO and the Globalization of the Public Library Idea, 1948 to 1965." *Library & Information History* 30, no. 1 (February 1, 2014): 1–19.

Le, Hieu Nam Trung. "Another Kind of Vietnamization: Language Policies in Higher Education in the Two Vietnams." In *Vietnam over the Long Twentieth Century: Becoming Modern, Going Global*, edited by Liam C. Kelley and Gerard Sasges, 127–43. Singapore: Springer Nature, 2024.

Lê Thanh Huyền. "Thư viện Việt Nam thời kỳ pháp thuộc." PhD diss., Trường Đại học văn hoá Hà Nội—Thông tin thư viện, 2014.

Lebovics, Herman. *True France: The Wars over Cultural Identity, 1900–1945*. Ithaca, NY: Cornell University Press, 1992.

Lelièvre, Pierre. "À propos d'un cinquantenaire pour André Masson." *Bulletin Bibliothèque de France* 39, no. 5 (January 1, 1994): 56–59.

Lemaître, Henri. *La lecture publique: Mémoires et voeux du Congrés international d'Alger*. Paris: Librairie E. Droz, 1931.

Lessard, Micheline. "Tradition for Rebellion: Vietnamese Students and Teachers and Anticolonial Resistance, 1888–1931." PhD diss., Cornell University, 1995.

Lewis, Su Lin. *Cities in Motion: Urban Life and Cosmopolitanism in Southeast Asia, 1920–1940*. Cambridge: Cambridge University Press, 2016.

Lockhart, Bruce McFarland. *The End of the Vietnamese Monarchy*. Lạc Việt Series no. 15. New Haven, CT: Council on Southeast Asia Studies, 1993.

Lockhart, Greg, and Monique Lockhart. "Broken Journey: Nhất Linh's 'Going to France.'" *East Asian History* 8 (December 1994): 73–134.

Lowe, Lisa. *The Intimacies of Four Continents*. Durham, NC: Duke University Press, 2015.

Maack, Mary Niles. "Books and Libraries as Instruments of Cultural Diplomacy in Francophone Africa during the Cold War." *Libraries & the Cultural Record* 36, no. 1 (2001): 58–86.

Maack, Mary Niles. "The Lady and the Antelope: Suzanne Briet's Contribution to the French Documentation Movement." *Library Trends* 52, no. 4 (Spring 2004): 719–47.

Maack, Mary Niles. *Libraries in Senegal: Continuity and Change in an Emerging Nation*. Chicago: American Library Association, 1981.

Magne, Nathalie. "Henri Lemaître 1881–1946: De la lecture publique à la documentation." Master's thesis, Université Panthéon Sorbonne—Paris I, 1995.

Marquez, Xavier. "Spaces of Appearance and Spaces of Surveillance." *Polity* 44, no. 1 (2012): 6–31.

Marr, David G. *Vietnam 1945: The Quest for Power*. Berkeley: University of California Press, 1995.

Marr, David. *Vietnam: State, War, and Revolution (1945–1946)*. Berkeley: University of California Press, 2013.

Marr, David G. *Vietnamese Anticolonialism, 1885–1925*. Berkeley: University of California Press, 1971.

Marr, David G. *Vietnamese Tradition on Trial, 1920–1945*. Berkeley: University of California Press, 1981.

Masson, André. *Hanoï pendant la période héroïque, 1873–1888*. Paris: Librairie orientaliste Paul Geuthner, 1929.

Mattern, Shannon. *A City Is Not a Computer: Other Urban Intelligences*. Princeton, NJ: Princeton University Press, 2021.

Mattern, Shannon. "Library as Infrastructure." *Places Journal*, June 2014.

McDaniel, Justin. *Gathering Leaves and Lifting Words: Histories of Buddhist Monastic Education in Laos and Thailand*. Seattle: University of Washington Press, 2008.

McDermott, Joseph. *A Social History of the Chinese Book: Books and Literati Culture in Late Imperial China*. Hong Kong: Hong Kong University Press, 2006.

McHale, Shawn. *The First Vietnam War: Violence, Sovereignty, and the Fracture of the South*. Cambridge: Cambridge University Press, 2021.

McHale, Shawn. *Print and Power: Confucianism, Communism, and Buddhism in the Making of Modern Vietnam*. Honolulu: University of Hawai'i Press, 2004.

Mehta, Uday S. "Liberal Strategies of Exclusion." In *Tensions of Empire: Colonial Cultures in a Bourgeois World*, edited by Frederick Cooper and Ann Laura Stoler, 59–86. Berkeley: University of California Press, 1997.

Mokros, Emily. *The Peking Gazette in Late Imperial China: State News and Political Authority*. Seattle: University of Washington Press, 2021.

Moore, Lara Jennifer. *Restoring Order: The Ecole des Chartes and the Organization of Archives and Libraries in France, 1820–1870*. Duluth, MN: Litwin Books, 2008.

Nguyen, Cindy. "Creating the National Library in Saigon: Colonial Legacies, Fragmented Collections, and Reading Publics, 1946–1958." In *Building a Republican Nation in Vietnam, 1920–1963*, edited by Nu-Anh Tran and Tuong Vu, 164–85, Honolulu: University of Hawaiʻi Press, 2023.

Nguyen, Cindy. "Reading Rules: The Symbolic and Social Spaces of Reading in the Hà Nội Central Library, 1919–1941." *Journal of Vietnamese Studies* 15, no. 3 (August 2020): 17–18.

Nguyễn Công Trí. "Những thư viện lớn của triều Nguyễn ở kinh đô Huế xưa." *Nghiên cứu và Phát triển* 6–7 (2013): 104–5.

Nguyen, Duy Lap. *The Unimagined Community: Imperialism and Culture in South Vietnam*. Manchester: Manchester University Press, 2019.

Nguyen, Giang-Huong. *La Littérature vietnamienne francophone*. Paris: Classiques Garnier, 2018.

Nguyen, Martina Thucnhi. *On Our Own Strength: The Self-Reliant Literary Group and Cosmopolitan Nationalism in Late Colonial Vietnam*. Honolulu: University of Hawaiʻi Press, 2020.

Nguyễn Ngọc Mô. *Tìm hiểu lịch sử ngành thư viện lưu trữ hồ sơ Việt Nam*. Hanoi: Nhà Xuất Bản Thế Giới, 2002.

Nguyễn, Phương Ngọc. *À l'origine de l'anthropologie au Vietnam: Recherche sur les auteurs de la première moitié du XXe siècle*. Aix-en-Provence: Presses de l'Université de Provence, 2012.

Nguyễn, Phuong Ngọc. "Huỳnh Thị Bảo Hòa (1896–1982): A Woman Who Wrote to Change Vietnamese Society." In *Vietnam Over the Long Twentieth Century: Becoming Modern, Going Global*, edited by Liam C. Kelley and Gerard Sasges, 37–61. Singapore: Springer Nature, 2024.

Nguyễn, Tuấn Cường. "Private Academies and Confucian Education in 18th-Century Vietnam in East Asian Context: The Case of Phúc Giang Academy." In *Confucian Academies in East Asia*, edited by Vladimir Glomb, Eun-Jeung Lee, and Martin Gehlmann, 3: 89–125. Leiden: Brill, 2020.

Nguyen, Uyen. "Guerillas in the City: The Administrative Takeover of Hà Nội and DRV State-Making in the Urban Postwar Period (1954–1960)." *Journal of Vietnamese Studies* 17, no. 1 (February 1, 2022): 1–52.

Nguyen-Marshall, Van. *Between War and the State: Civil Society in South Vietnam, 1954–1975*. Ithaca, NY: Cornell University Press, 2023.

Nguyen-Marshall, Van. *In Search of Moral Authority: The Discourse on Poverty, Poor Relief, and Charity in French Colonial Vietnam*. New York: Peter Lang, 2008.

Nguyễn-võ Thu-hương. *Almost Futures: Sovereignty and Refuge at World's End*. Oakland: University of California Press, 2024.

Ninh, Kim N. B. *A World Transformed: The Politics of Culture in Revolutionary Vietnam, 1945–1965*. Ann Arbor: University of Michigan Press, 2002.

Ó Briain, Lonán. *Voices of Vietnam: A Century of Radio, Red Music, and Revolution*. Oxford: Oxford University Press, 2021.

Pelletier, Olivia. "'Le chartiste et les colonies': Le modèle archivistique français en Indochine." *La Gazette des archives* 256 (2019): 51–67.

Pelletier, Olivia. "De Paul Boudet à Ferréol de Ferry: Les archives françaises en Indochine (1917–1955)." In *Chartistes en Asie: Science historique et patrimoine au lointain (XIXe–XXIe siècle)*, edited by Jacques Berlioz, Cécile Capot, and Olivier Poncet, 153–70. Paris: École nationale des chartes—École française d'Extrême-Orient, 2021.

Peycam, Philippe. *The Birth of Vietnamese Political Journalism: Saigon, 1916–1930*. New York: Columbia University Press, 2012.

Phan, John. "Lacquered Words: The Evolution of Vietnamese Under Sinitic Influences from the 1st Century BCE Through the 17th Century CE." PhD diss., Cornell University, 2013.

Phan, John. *Lost Tongues of the Red River: Annamese Middle Chinese and the Origins of the Vietnamese Language*. Cambridge, MA: Harvard University Press.

Ponsavady, Stéphanie. *Cultural and Literary Representations of the Automobile in French Indochina: A Colonial Roadshow*. Cham, Switzerland: Palgrave Macmillan, 2018.

Price, Leah. *How to Do Things with Books in Victorian Britain*. Princeton, NJ: Princeton University Press, 2012.

Reilly, Brett. "The Sovereign States of Vietnam, 1945–1955." *Journal of Vietnamese Studies* 11, no. 3–4 (November 1, 2016): 103–39.

Saada, Emmanuelle. *Empire's Children: Race, Filiation, and Citizenship in the French Colonies*. Chicago: University of Chicago Press, 2012.

Said, Edward. *Orientalism*. New York: Pantheon Books, 1978.

Salmon, Claudine, and Christiane Pasquel Rageau. "Un projet colonial en Indochine inspiré de Balai Pustaka (1928–1930)." *Archipel* 44, no. 1 (1992): 57–74.

Sasges, Gerard. *Imperial Intoxication: Alcohol and the Making of Colonial Indochina*. Honolulu: University of Hawai'i Press, 2017.

Schneewind, Sarah. *The Social Drama of Daily Work: A Manual for Historians*. Amsterdam: Amsterdam University Press, 2024.

Schwenkel, Christina. *Building Socialism: The Afterlife of East German Architecture in Urban Vietnam*. Durham, NC: Duke University Press, 2020.

Scott, David. "Colonial Governmentality." In *Anthropologies of Modernity: Foucault, Governmentality, and Life Politics*, edited by Jonathan Xavier Inda, 23–49. Malden, MA: Blackwell Publishing, 2005.

Sidnell, Jack. "The Inconvenience of Tradition: Phan Khôi's Pragmatism and His Proposals for Modernizing Language Reform." *Journal of Vietnamese Studies* 18, no. 3 (2023): 56–97.

Singaravélou, Pierre. *L'École française d'Extrême-Orient ou l'institution des marges: Essai d'histoire sociale et politique de la science coloniale*. Paris: L'Harmattan, 1999.

Stoler, Ann Laura. *Along the Archival Grain: Epistemic Anxieties and Colonial Common Sense*. Princeton, NJ: Princeton University Press, 2009.

Stoler, Ann Laura. "Colonial Archives and the Arts of Governance." *Archival Science* 2, no. 1 (March 1, 2002).

Sylvie, Fayet-Scribe. *Histoire de la documentation en France: Culture, science et technologie de l'information 1895–1937*. Paris: CNRS Editions, 2000.

Tambay, Meixin. *Destins d'archivistes. Ngo Dinh Nhu (1910–1963), un archiviste hors du commun*. Master's thesis, Université d'Angers, 2014.

Thiện Mộc Lan. *Phụ nữ tân văn: Phấn son tô điểm sơn hà*. Sài Gòn: Nhà xuất bản Văn hóa Sài Gòn, 2010.

Thomas, Martin. "Albert Sarraut, French Colonial Development, and the Communist Threat, 1919–1930." *Journal of Modern History* 77, no. 4 (2005): 917–55.

Thomas, Martin. *The French Empire Between the Wars: Imperialism, Politics and Society*. Manchester: Manchester University Press, 2005.

Tran, Ben. *Post-Mandarin: Masculinity and Aesthetic Modernity in Colonial Vietnam*. New York: Fordham University Press, 2017.

Trần Thị Phương Hoa. "From Liberally-Organized to Centralized Schools: Education in Tonkin, 1885–1927." *Journal of Vietnamese Studies* 8, no. 3 (2013): 27–70.

Trần Thị Phương Hoa. "Pragmatizing Schools: A History of Vocational Training in Colonial Vietnam." *French Colonial History* 19 (2020): 111–62.

Trần Văn Ky. *Les archives du gouvernement de la Cochinchine: Organisation*, méthode de classement. Hanoi: Imprimerie Tonkinoise, 1915.

Trịnh Văn Thảo. *L'École française en Indochine*. Paris: Karthala, 1995.

Vang, Ma. *History on the Run: Secrecy, Fugitivity, and Hmong Refugee Epistemologies*. Durham, NC: Duke University Press, 2021.

Vasavakul, Thaveeporn. "Schools and Politics in South and North Viet Nam: A Comparative Study of State Apparatus, State Policy, and State Power (1945–1965)." PhD diss., Cornell University, 1994.

Vũ Trọng Phụng. *Dumb Luck*. Translated by Nguyễn Nguyệt Cầm and Peter Zinoman. Ann Arbor: University of Michigan Press, 2002.

Vu, Yen N. "Phạm Quỳnh, Borrowed Language, and the Ambivalences of Colonial Discourse." *Journal of Southeast Asian Studies* 51, no. 1–2 (June 2020): 114–31.

Wang, Fan. "How Late Imperial Chinese Literati Read Their Books: Inscribing, Collating, Excerpting." *Book History* 24, no. 2 (2021): 320–51.

Welfelé, Odile. "D'hier à aujourd'hui, les liens entre l'École des chartes et les Archives nationales du Vietnam." In *Chartistes en Asie: science historique et patrimoine au lointain (XIXe–XXIe siècle)*, edited by Jacques Berlioz, Cécile Capot, and Olivier Poncet, 204–14, Paris: École nationale des chartes—École française d'Extrême-Orient, 2021.

Whitmore, John K. "Paperwork: The Rise of the New Literati and Ministerial Power and the Effort Toward Legibility in Đại Việt." In *Southeast Asia in the Fifteenth Century*, edited by Geoff Wade, 104–25. Singapore: NUS Press, 2010.

Wiegand, Wayne. *American Public School Librarianship: A History*. Baltimore, MD: Johns Hopkins University Press, 2021.

Wilcox, Wynn. "Universities and Intellectual Culture in the Republic of Vietnam." In *Toward a Framework for Vietnamese American Studies: History, Community, and Memory*, edited by Linda Ho Peché, Alex-Thai Dinh Vo, and Tuong Vu, 57–75. Philadelphia: Temple University Press, 2023.

Wilder, Gary. *The French Imperial Nation-State: Negritude & Colonial Humanism Between the Two World Wars*. Chicago: University of Chicago Press, 2005.

Woodside, Alexander. *Lost Modernities: China, Vietnam, Korea, and the Hazards of World History*. Cambridge, MA: Harvard University Press, 2006.

Woodside, Alexander. *Vietnam and the Chinese Model: A Comparative Study of Vietnamese and Chinese Government in the First Half of the Nineteenth Century*. Cambridge, MA: Harvard University Press, 1971.

Wright, Gwendolyn. *The Politics of Design in French Colonial Urbanism*. Chicago: University of Chicago Press, 1991.

Yeager, Jack. *The Vietnamese Novel in French*. Hanover: University Press of New Hampshire, 1987.

Zhang, Mindi. "Cultural Business at the Commercial Press, ca. 1900 to ca. 1940." *Twentieth-Century China* 50, no. 1 (2025): 3–24.

Zinoman, Peter. "Nhân Văn–Giai Phẩm and Vietnamese 'Reform Communism' in the 1950s: A Revisionist Interpretation." *Journal of Cold War Studies* 13, no. 1 (2011): 60–100.

Zinoman, Peter. "Provincial Cosmopolitanism: Vũ Trọng Phụng's Literary Engagements." In *Traveling Nation-Makers: Transnational Flows and Movements in the Making of Modern Southeast Asia*, edited by Caroline Hau and Kasian Tejapira, 126–52. Singapore and Kyoto: Kyoto University Press, 2011.

Zinoman, Peter. "Reading Revolutionary Prison Memoirs." In *The Country of Memory: Remaking the Past in Late Socialist Vietnam*, edited by Hue-Tam Ho Tai, 21–45. Berkeley: University of California Press, 2001.

INDEX

Founded in 1893,
UNIVERSITY OF CALIFORNIA PRESS
publishes bold, progressive books and journals on topics in the arts, humanities, social sciences, and natural sciences—with a focus on social justice issues—that inspire thought and action among readers worldwide.

The UC PRESS FOUNDATION
raises funds to uphold the press's vital role as an independent, nonprofit publisher, and receives philanthropic support from a wide range of individuals and institutions—and from committed readers like you. To learn more, visit ucpress.edu/supportus.

www.ingramcontent.com/pod-product-compliance
Ingram Content Group UK Ltd.
Pitfield, Milton Keynes, MK11 3LW, UK
UKHW011355101225
465928UK00003B/15

9 780520 416222